D0402793

the POWER *of the* HERD

Also by Linda Kohanov

Riding between the Worlds:
Expanding Our Potential through the Way of the Horse

The Tao of Equus: A Woman's Journey of Healing
and Transformation through the Way of the Horse

Way of the Horse: Equine Archetypes for Self-Discovery
— A Book of Exploration and 40 Cards

the POWER
of the HERD

A Nonpredatory Approach
to Social Intelligence, Leadership, and Innovation

LINDA KOHANOV

New World Library
Novato, California

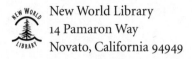
New World Library
14 Pamaron Way
Novato, California 94949

The material in this book is intended for education. It is not meant to take the place of diagnosis and treatment by a qualified medical practitioner or therapist. No expressed or implied guarantee of the effects of the use of the recommendations can be given or liability taken.

Text design by Tona Pearce Myers

Library of Congress Cataloging-in-Publication Data
Kohanov, Linda.
  The power of the herd : a nonpredatory approach to social intelligence, leadership, and innovation / Linda Kohanov.
      p.   cm.
Includes bibliographical references and index.
ISBN 978-1-57731-676-3 (hardcover : alk. paper) — ISBN 978-1-57731-681-7 (ebook)
1. Social intelligence. 2. Leadership. 3. Horses—Psychological aspects. 4. Animals—Therapeutic use. I. Title.
HM1261.K64 2013
152.4—dc23   2012044855

First printing, March 2013
ISBN 978-1-57731-676-3
Printed in Canada on 100% postconsumer-waste recycled paper

New World Library is proud to be a Gold Certified Environmentally Responsible Publisher. Publisher certification awarded by Green Press Initiative. www.greenpressinitiative.org

10 9 8 7 6 5 4 3 2 1

For

Steve Roach,

my husband, anchor, confidant,

and muse

:: **NICHOLLS**

:: Holbrook, Elizabeth Anne

"

3906512316 0630 Transited: August 17, 2020 11:12 AM

CONTENTS

Part III. Horse Sense at Work:
The Twelve "Power of the Herd" Guiding Principles

INTRODUCTION

Throughout history, knights in shining armor often rode spirited, well-trained horses like those featured on the cover of this book. If you're an experienced equestrian, you know that these luminous creatures aren't white; they're gray. And they were, in all likelihood, born black.

Pure white horses are extremely rare. Some experts argue that they don't even exist. All those movie heroes racing around on snow-colored stallions are riding older mounts whose youthful coal-colored coats lightened dramatically over time — as their focus, self-control, and athletic prowess increased through years of careful training.

Dark horses slowly turning gray, then silver, then white are the *perfect* metaphor for developing power — innovative, compassionate, and mentally, emotionally, and socially intelligent power. The more faithfully we work to bring our talents out of the shadows, shining a light on those notoriously elusive areas related to creativity, charisma, and mutually supportive relationships, the more quickly we are bound to excel.

If black horses represent unconscious, unbridled spirit, energy, intuition, and instinct, the process of developing this raw "material," of making it fully conscious, is, truly, the path we must undertake today. We can no longer wait for great leaders to emerge accidentally, as radiant freaks of nature whose inspiring presence nonetheless remains mysterious, untranslatable, unteachable to others. The stakes are much too high.

In my fifty-plus years on this planet, so much has changed. Like millions of other baby boomers, I've seen racial segregation and "traditional," 1950s-style family structures erode and evolve under the influence of civil rights, women's liberation, the sexual revolution, the fall of the communist empire, financial deregulation, economic strife, and the creation of the Internet, among other social and technological upheavals.

Many of these forces combined in 2008, leading to the election of Barack Obama, our first mixed-race U.S. president, a development my conservative southern grandparents couldn't have imagined in their wildest dreams. Yet no matter who runs for this coveted office in the future, this presidential race marked a significant turning point in American history — for other reasons as well.

The Republican ticket would have been equally disturbing to my prim and proper grandma: a conventionally respectable war hero with an outspoken woman vice-presidential running mate — whose daughter was pregnant out of wedlock, no less? In the mid-twentieth century, this self-proclaimed "mama grizzly" would have been completely, unquestionably ostracized by members of her own sex for all kinds of behavior unbecoming a matriarch.

Despite her seemingly militant support of traditional values, Sarah Palin's very presence on that political stage represented a significant innovation for a new kind of family, one in which empowered women might become leaders while also showing compassion and acceptance for the many challenges future generations face upon entering this world. What she was *saying* in her conservative, at times aggressive, speeches hadn't yet caught up to the promise of what she was living. Maverick, indeed!

No wonder so many people are reeling from the sensation of a finely woven antique rug being pulled out from under them. Over the past century, rapid social change has led to more freedom for more people, of course, and plenty of fear and conflict to go with it, challenging the descendants of slaves and masters alike to modify not only their self-image and beliefs but their most cherished, deeply entrenched, primarily unconscious behaviors.

It is the latter that we will investigate in this book and, hopefully, transform: the power plays, traumas, and relational habits we must alter to move forward productively as free, empowered people. Here we stretch beyond "liberal" and "conservative" agendas, looking at behavior patterns that wreak havoc beneath the surface of all cultural, religious, business, political, scientific, and philosophical persuasions.

In part 1, "A Brief History of Power," we'll learn some surprising things about our ancestors as we take a look at *key*, time-tested, yet long-ignored features of innovative leadership. In part 2, "The Necessity of Vision," we will wrestle with issues related to visionaries, including those who became religious figures, in order to understand how we can move beyond crucifying or worshipping creative, inspired thinkers, artists, and social activists — and become innovators and leaders ourselves. Finally, in part 3, "Horse Sense at Work," we'll practice new leadership and social-intelligence skills that build on the expanded view of history, science, and religion explored in the first twelve chapters.

To make this potentially treacherous journey more enjoyable, we'll travel on horseback, riding an animal that has, since the beginning of civilization, helped us negotiate new territory with much more speed and grace than we could possibly manage on our own two legs. But here's the rub: After leaving the main road, we're going to drop the reins and let the horses lead us at times, revealing a socially intelligent, *nonpredatory* approach to leadership, innovation, collaboration, and power. And it is here that some readers will feel another rug slipping out from underneath them.

In recognizing that animals have much to teach us — that they have, as the recent scientific research presented in this book suggests, been tutoring, empowering, healing, and transforming us all along — we will have to let go of the idea that we are the only intelligent species on the planet.

On July 7, 2012, a prominent international group of scientists made this assertion official. Based on decades of physiological and behavioral experiments with multiple species, *The Cambridge Declaration on Consciousness* stated "unequivocally" that "non-human animals have the neuroanatomical, neurochemical, and neurophysiological substrates of consciousness states along with the capacity to exhibit intentional behaviors. Consequently, the weight of evidence indicates that humans are not unique in possessing the neurological substrates that generate consciousness." The document acknowledges that "neural networks aroused during affective states in humans are also critically important for generating emotional behaviors in animals." This includes "all mammals and birds, and many other creatures, including octopuses."

Accepting that other species can think, feel, and make intentional decisions is a game changer for everyone. This does not mean, however, that animals always share our perspectives or priorities. As this book unfolds, you'll discover reasons to be grateful that they often don't, especially in the case of highly social, nonpredatory animals like horses, who offer alternative approaches to power, collaboration, and freedom-through-relationship, lessons they've occasionally taught exceptional leaders throughout history.

Imagine if all of us could, finally, bring these lessons out of the shadows and employ them consciously, creating a form of shared leadership that taps the talents of the entire herd. What might we accomplish if we finally understood how to be powerful, together?

— Linda Kohanov
Amado, Arizona
September 2012

Part I

A BRIEF HISTORY *of* POWER

Chapter One

THE HORSE IN MY CATHEDRAL

Nearly a century after Antoni Gaudí's death, his architectural masterpiece Sagrada Familia is barely half finished, yet millions of people travel from around the world to marvel at Barcelona's controversial cathedral in progress. Several on-site conversions have taken place over the years, fortifying a Vatican-sanctioned movement to grant sainthood to the reclusive artist. Gazing into Sagrada Familia's parabolic arched doorways, soaring towers, and other gravity-defying effects, Japanese architect Kenji Imai had a religious experience, eventually converting to Christianity as he studied the work in depth. And it's no wonder: Gaudí's neomedieval structures and biomorphic forms combine the highest aspirations of humanity with the flowing artistry of nature. Somehow defying logic, convention, and, at times, the laws of physics, this massive stone basilica has a soft, melting appearance, creating the impression that it's slowly being molded into existence by God's own everlasting hand.

For Gaudí, Sagrada Familia (Holy Family) was a mission transcending personal concerns. He worked on it for over four decades, eventually taking up residence on-site and devoting his final years to the project with increasing obsession. "My client is not in a hurry," he once said, responding to the frustration that workers voiced as he made constant changes to the architectural plans.

Gaudí literally lived the concept of *cathedral thinking*. This term describes an emerging philosophy of sorts, one that explores the mind-set involved in tackling any long-term vision. It contrasts sharply with our modern, quick-fix mentality, but socially conscious leaders recognize that significant, sustainable change requires generational effort. And so, an increasing number of innovative thinkers — in business, art, politics, and science — are interested in the 150-year process that built Saint Peter's Basilica in Rome. They're even more fascinated with Germany's Cologne Cathedral, which survived numerous wars, recessions, political movements, and religious reforms during the 632 years of construction before the final stone was set in place.

For cathedral thinkers, Sagrada Familia represents the ultimate, real-time case study of how an ambitious vision persists and evolves over time. Construction started in 1882 and continued uninterrupted after Gaudí's sudden death in 1926 — that is, until communists in the Spanish Civil War set fire to the architect's study ten years later, destroying his primary drawings. The project resumed in 1952 with dedicated and imaginative devotees piecing together surviving notes and models. Since then a succession of at least a half-dozen talented architects have immersed themselves in the project, with the son of one of them introducing computers into the design process in the 1980s.

The opportunity provided by Sagrada Familia is far more valuable than the details of its construction. Here we have the chance to interview workers about the human concerns involved. Historical accounts rarely reveal the emotional, organizational, and interpersonal challenges; the daily failures and frustrations no one really wants to talk about; and the vulnerabilities no one wants to admit to, let alone recount in nauseating detail — unless, that is, the subjects are still alive and can somehow be convinced that their personal foibles are as important as their triumphs in assisting others with ambitious, perhaps divinely inspired goals. People who build neogothic basilicas are the most likely candidates, as they're already psychologically predisposed to support the ongoing education and initiation of future generations.

Whether you're building a church, a business, or a mandate for social change, cathedral thinking presupposes that the vision you initiate *must* be handed over to others, that everyone involved will be laboring on faith at times, that people will share their most innovative ideas and tools, that the plans *will* change, that the blueprints may even be lost, and that the most important part of your job will be to inspire, in every neophyte who joins your team, reverence for a project you will never see completed. This mind-set comes with a host of emotional quagmires, some of which are so existential in nature that they question the very foundations of survival-oriented behavior, challenging us to resist flight-or-fight impulses, urging us to evolve beyond our current obsession with safety, comfort, and predictability, let alone personal gain and recognition. At the same time, multigenerational thinking demands that we use our human resources wisely. We must take care of each other to bring out the best in each other.

In this book — for lack of the funding, connections, and Spanish language skills necessary to travel to Barcelona and talk key members of the Sagrada Familia staff into confessing their deepest, darkest cathedral-building secrets — I will, at times, share a few of the more pertinent, sometimes insightful, sometimes embarrassing details of my own efforts to create something of lasting value.

A brief history: In 1997, Epona Equestrian Services, an equine-facilitated learning program and referral agency, was founded by a group of Tucson-based horse trainers, educators, and counselors. The cathedral we were building had no walls or ceiling, but it did combine humanity's highest aspirations with nature's flowing wisdom as we partnered with horses to teach cooperative, nonpredatory forms of empowerment, emotional fitness, social intelligence, and authentic community building. We named it after the Celtic horse goddess associated with healing and transformation, Epona, who seemed a fitting symbol for an organization that employed horses in the work of human development.

In 2001, when my first book was published, the organization suddenly attracted international attention through the force of a vision that I hadn't realized would move so many people to action. Based on growing demand, we started a multiweek apprenticeship program that qualified talented facilitators to incorporate our principles and techniques into their own programs. Along the way, we found it necessary to distinguish our carefully trained instructors from those in organizations in other states and countries that were also named after the goddess Epona. By 2012, nearly two hundred Eponaquest Instructors were operating on five continents, as Epona Equestrian Services became Eponaquest Worldwide.

The momentum had been building for years. In 2005, for instance, an influx of international students inspired us to establish an equestrian-based retreat and conference center at a historic Arizona ranch. There, a group of adventurous, highly individualistic people put our most ambitious theories to the test, and I was thrust into a leadership role that I struggled to understand and live up to. The daily challenges of running a business based on the concepts of collaboration and authentic community were significant. Our equine-facilitated learning program at Apache Springs Ranch became a living laboratory, complicated by the fact that several of us stayed on-site with clients coming and going seven days a week. Many times, I felt more like a giant lab rat than a researcher or teacher, but the power of what we preached was enhanced by the act of living it, continually working out the kinks along the way.

By 2009, the center had reached a high level of functionality, offering daylong seminars and weeklong residential workshops. Our clients included educators, counselors, clergy, trauma survivors, parents, teens, artists, engineers, and entrepreneurs looking for ways to empower themselves while relating more effectively to others. We also helped returning soldiers and their spouses practice the emotional fitness skills necessary to handle posttraumatic stress and other warrior-reintegration challenges. Even so, the business suffered debilitating financial blows when the economic crisis coincided with a crucial growth stage. By summer, our beautiful ranch had been put up for sale, and we were once again operating as an agency (albeit a more sophisticated, well-connected global one), sending clients to multiple venues.

The dynamics of living and working at Apache Springs accentuated our explorations in leadership, power, creativity, intuition, personal healing, and social transformation. All the while, the horses kept urging clients and staff alike to enjoy the ride — to soar to new heights of inspiration and expanded awareness one moment; to feel the depths of fear, vulnerability, frustration, anger, and sadness the next; to access the wisdom behind our blunders; and then to calmly, reverently go back to grazing.

As nomadic, nonpredatory beings, horses radiate immense trust in the universe. Intelligent and highly adaptable, they embody strength, freedom, spirit, gentleness, beauty, authenticity, loyalty, and grace, fully immersing themselves in the moment and always ready to explore new opportunities and ever wider vistas of experience. Equine "philosophy" values relationship over territory. In their honest, sophisticated interactions, these animals easily navigate the paradox of nourishing individual and group consciousness simultaneously. As we continue to build our cathedrals, launch our space stations, refine our governments, and explore our visions of a peaceful global society, can we, as humans, learn to do the same?

Obsession and Depression

It's no small task to think like God's architect. That's what the director of the Museum of the Barcelona Archdiocese called Gaudí after he was hit by a tram in 1926 and died in a pauper's hospital. Within days people were nominating him for sainthood, and even the most virulently anti-Catholic newspaper had nothing but praise for his artistry and dedication. His alliance with the divine, however, did not exempt him from the complexities and sorrows of earthly existence. One anonymous Internet historian cited Gaudí's unexpected demise as "a graphic illustration of the almost absurd misfortune that filled the life and work of the enigmatic Spanish architect." Sketchy reports on his final years suggest the man was severely depressed. As a number of close friends and relatives passed away, he retreated further and further into his work until nothing was left but his beloved Sagrada Familia.

Though no one knows what the seventy-four-year-old artist was thinking in those final, fateful moments, rumor has it that he absentmindedly stepped into the street to gain a wider perspective of the cathedral, only to be slammed into eternity's embrace by the relentless, impersonal momentum of public transportation. Gaudí's selfless dedication continued to work against him over the five days it took him to actually expire from his injuries. As a public figure who shunned reporters and photographers, Gaudí had seldom been photographed, so the chances of anyone recognizing him on the street were severely limited. What's more, the man cared little for appearance. Dressed like a vagabond, complete with empty pockets, he looked like a homeless man, which no doubt influenced several taxi drivers who refused to take him to the hospital. (They were later fined for negligence.) Two days after he went missing, Gaudí's friends finally found him wasting away in an indigents' ward, but he refused to be moved, reportedly saying, "I belong here among the poor."

Being hit by a tram and dying a pauper's death: that comes close to characterizing how it initially felt to lose my home and my life's savings when a massive downturn in the economy forced the closing of Apache Springs Ranch — although I think I described it to my veterinarian as being "bitch-slapped by the universe" at the end of one particularly demoralizing day. I had just returned to my newly rented home in exile after the most heart-wrenching task of all, laying off the Epona Center staff, only to find Rasa, my soul mate in equine form, suffering a life-threatening bout of colic. With my husband selling off musical equipment to support the move, I had borrowed funds from a few close friends to save my herd and cover the final ranch expenses, as I was determined that no loyal employee or vendor would be left unpaid. Yet my good intentions seemed to go unnoticed as the powers that be demanded yet another, even more heart-wrenching sacrifice. Alternately feeling supremely sorry for myself and downright resentful at my growing list of losses, I was faced with the decision to sell one of my most talented lesson horses to pay for Rasa's trip to the hospital — and endure the very real possibility of her death despite investing in her care.

Rasa carried an unusual burden for a horse. She was the original inspiration behind my equine-facilitated learning practice, the subject of my first two books, and the symbol of a growing international movement. Some people treated Rasa like a celebrity, which was a relief for me and a bit of a curse for her, as they often approached this steady, matter-of-fact mare with more reverence, excitement, and expectation than they had for the organization's human founder. That night, however, I was as guilty as anyone in associating her illness with the ultimate demise of the entire vision. Luckily, I caught myself in the act and began gently, compassionately, separating my flesh-and-blood companion from a calling she had initiated and influenced, one she nonetheless could never be held responsible for completing.

As a horse, Rasa could inspire people. She could shift consciousness, showing us new ways of relating to the world and to each other. But she was incapable of handling the organizational details involved in taking this project to the next level. In fact, the vision had already grown beyond *my* wildest dreams, taking on a life of its own, and I had to concede that I wasn't likely to see its completion, either.

At that moment, though I hadn't yet encountered the term, a strange surge of energy turned my brain inside out and a mind-bending dose of "cathedral thinking" completely changed my perspective.

This sudden shift was not unlike being hit by a tram and blasted into eternity's embrace, where I floated for a moment, or an hour, in a potent yet peaceful clarity, where everything suddenly made sense in the grand scheme of things. And I knew, deep in my bones, that my experience at Apache Springs was a stepping-stone, an advanced-degree program in the challenges of jumpstarting a multigenerational project aimed at balancing the aggressive, needlessly destructive aspects of our culture and offering people the personal and professional tools to create lasting, meaningful change. Like Gaudí, Rasa and I had tapped into a source of inspiration that was not the least bit concerned with human concepts of time. Our client was in no hurry.

My horse survived that day, as did the mission she represented. She lived two more years, doing her best work despite an increasingly debilitating arthritic condition that led to her death at age twenty. With Rasa by my side, I felt energized and inspired, but the human element seemed relentlessly problematic. My horse remained blissfully unaware of the organizational challenges and interpersonal dramas I found so incredibly tedious. Even so, her strong, supportive presence helped me endure the elations and frustrations of blazing a new trail — with groups of people who fully expected me to know the way, no less.

In the beginning, all I had was curiosity, an adventurous spirit, a potent yet incomplete vision, and an ability to write about it. But that was enough to attract others who had an expanded view of human potential. However, while the majority of my students, colleagues, and employees were eager to step into their own power and experiment, some of them wanted me to psychically sense their needs and answer questions they didn't know how to voice. A few came looking for the perfect parent they never had, expecting me to protect them from the same interpersonal challenges I had initially found so shocking and perplexing. Still others resented my success and couldn't wait for me to fail. For years, I rode a roller coaster of inspiration, admiration, confusion, disappointment, pain — and ever deepening insight.

Over time, through much trial and error, my colleagues and I developed some leadership and authentic community-building skills to make the ordeal more manageable, and eventually more enjoyable, for everyone involved. Oddly enough, while I employed the valuable services of an executive coach, read every leadership book I could get my hands on — and learned a lot in the process — the most innovative tools came from working with the horses, from translating their highly adaptable, intensely social, nonpredatory perspective on power into a human context. In becoming more horselike, my students too began to thrive, finding the courage to follow their dreams and honing the skills to manifest them.

As newspaperman Walter Winchell observed, "Leadership is the capacity to translate vision into reality." Working with horses taught me how to move fluidly between practical, earthly existence and that strange, amorphous otherworld where the as-yet-unimagined hovers, waiting, always waiting, for someone with the nerve, endurance, ingenuity, and charisma to coax the formless into form. *This* is how we change the world. By the time Rasa left me in 2011, I had learned to manage the stress, confusion, and significant emotional distress that anyone saddled with a vision is bound to encounter. In fact, if I were to mythologize the trajectory of Rasa's life, I would have to conclude that she hung around, quietly tutoring me, even carrying me at times, until I gained a more sophisticated view of leadership and could be trusted to walk the path without her. In this sense, I was lucky to have a horse to not just hold me up but cheer me up too.

Artists and innovators invariably suffer for their visions, a cliché we've all heard before. But recognition of that classic pattern doesn't lessen the impact of feeling misunderstood, used, hurt, shamed, blamed, degraded, and betrayed along the way. Knowing the sacrifices and intrigue involved, who would sign up to live the life of Mahatma Gandhi, Nelson Mandela, or Martin Luther King Jr., regardless of the colossal shifts they set in motion? In long-term projects, inspiration all too easily gives birth to a rowdy set of twins: obsession and depression. The energy of the first can carry you through any havoc wreaked by the second, it's true. But I know the price this kind of power exacts on a human body. Pushing yourself year after year, stretching the limits of personal health and well-being in service to a demanding vision, is like plugging your living room lamp into a 220-volt industrial socket, day after day, and blaming the lamp for burning out. Without any previous training, innovators must learn to negotiate their own individual human needs within the supercharged agenda of inspiration and calling.

In myriad sanity-saving ways, my horses taught me how to deal with the drama and exhaustion. They exercised the courage, compassion, patience, and equanimity I needed in order to face the next round of challenges. They showed me how a herd could be a source of strength and creativity, not compliance, disempowerment, and suppression. And they exemplified a mind-set capable of navigating change, even tragedy.

Deep Peace

Many people assume that prey animals live in a state of constant fear and hypervigilance. Spend enough time around horses, especially those who haven't been traumatized by abusive handling, and you realize this isn't at all the case. Horses don't stay up all night worrying about lions, and they certainly don't manufacture trouble in order to control the ensuing drama. Secure, well-adjusted horses *collaborate* with fate. Instead of fixating on what *should* or *shouldn't* happen, they sense what is happening and what *wants* to happen. Then they decide whether the developing situation is in their best interest, and they either go with the flow or get out of the way.

Horses don't try to alter the environment, spending much of their time in a relaxed yet heightened state of awareness, ready for anything. As a result, they're masters at assessing the evolving nuances of reality, deftly avoiding that human tendency to distort reality by engaging in wishful thinking or focusing on the worst possible outcome. For leaders, adopting this expanded, nonpredatory perspective creates an advanced capacity for risk management: paying attention to the subtle dynamics of a situation gives people a leg up in evaluating what they can control or change — and what they can't — early enough to grasp an unexpected opportunity or avoid being eaten.

No matter what happens, horses exhibit exceptional emotional agility: They experience each moment openly and authentically, blazing through fear, power, pain, excitement, loss, playfulness, and unmitigated joy. And then they go back to grazing, spending a significant portion of each day milling languidly about in a state of deep peace that arises naturally when you're not afraid of *life*.

Sitting quietly with Rasa, breathing in sync with her mindful acceptance of each and every moment, entrained by the beat of her massive heart, I always felt a sense of calm engulf me, no matter what trials I might otherwise be enduring. This in itself was a daily miracle. Her presence, however, was powerful, not passive. Horses, she taught me early on, actively respond to how people show up each day, highlighting our hidden gifts, our wounds, our vulnerabilities, and our worn-out worldly habits. And yet somehow they manage to be discerning without a hint of judgment, communicating that, at the core, we too are beautiful, powerful, and wise, capable of endless renewal.

Looking through the eyes of my horse Rasa, I came to see human dysfunctions as surface scintillations, dramatic and sometimes irritating to be sure, but certainly not set in stone. Whenever I managed, through grace or sheer stubborn will, to let go of an old pattern and embody a fresh perspective, Rasa would mirror the transformation, welcoming me home to an even deeper understanding of who I really was. And without the slightest hint of ambition, she would continually up the ante, stretching, relentlessly, my own limited ideas about my place in the world, my calling, and my untapped potential, helping me become a more effective human, one capable not only of dreaming big dreams but of riding a vision with a destiny of its own — and encouraging it to outlive me.

The view from eternity, after all, is clear: Pleasures and obstacles come and go, but the call to build something of lasting value cannot be denied. If people are "made in the image of their creator," then human beings are designed to *create*. And those who accept the challenge of creating something truly remarkable, something imbued with a touch of the divine, aren't given mortal excuses, reasonable timelines, and voluminous bank accounts. I can't think of a single visionary who won the lottery to support a brilliant, socially significant idea.

Struggle is a part of innovation, there's no doubt. It helps to know this up front, especially when the initial high of inspiration gives way to the realities of manifestation. But it's also important to realize that we can experience peace on earth, *deep* peace, right here, right now. Horses do it every day. People all too often ignore this crucial, life-sustaining factor, reducing heaven to a deferred reward. Perhaps that's why Gaudí hid out in a pauper's ward after regaining consciousness, waiting for the end rather than fighting against it. Floating in the pure white light of a wider perspective, he was honored; he was inspired. And he was tired. Without a dose of horse wisdom to calm his mind, cheer him up, and carry him through the inevitable stress, his was a religion of turmoil, sacrifice, and strife.

He had no choice but to suffer for his art.

Mass Transit

Anyone who applies logic to visionary leadership is sure to blow a major fuse now and then. There are way too many paradoxes involved, countless pairs of opposites you must juggle artfully, sometimes while in your underwear. Gaudí's skivvies were held together with safety pins. His meals often consisted of lettuce with a bit of milk sprinkled on top. He was a very cranky guy at times. These are the kinds of facts that history books record if you do something significant. And the analysis that follows would be humiliating to a man who refused to have his picture taken. Was Gaudí pious, anorexic, accessing altered states through starvation, or so distracted by the details of creating a massive monument to God that he couldn't be bothered with thoughts of food, clothing, and social niceties? (I suspect the answer is yes to all four options.)

Selfless dedication to a calling results in behavior that appears alternately selfish and eccentric to family and friends. Part of the inevitable crankiness stems from trying to listen to your muse over the din of skeptics who don't believe in what you're doing, while you learn to set appropriate boundaries between yourself and people so enraptured with your vision that you'd never get anything done if you accepted all their dinner invitations. Of course, in Gaudí's case, a good meal now and then would have helped. It's hard to function when you're obsessed, overworked, *and* starving. But even while dining with wealthy clients, the architect rarely strayed from a daily vegetarian regime so strict that most people would consider it a form of fasting.

The willingness to relinquish personal comfort in service to a goal is so common among trailblazers of all kinds, even in corporate settings, that best-selling authors Richard Boyatzis and Annie McKee have a term for it: the "Sacrifice Syndrome." In *Resonant Leadership*, they characterize it as a counterproductive yet hard-to-resist trap that leaders fall into when they "sacrifice too much for too long — and reap too little." Deeply religious, Gaudí also subscribed to the Catholic concept of "mortification of the flesh" at a time when early-twentieth-century painters and composers were romanticizing the idea of suffering for one's art. And while we're at it, let's add the pressures of the visionary state itself. The muses don't give a hoot about keeping your mortal body in optimal working order. When inspiration hits, it's common to forget to eat or sleep for hours, even days, on end. And when inspiration fails, usually near some crucial deadline, a full-blown sleep *disorder* is on the horizon. With all these factors combined, Gaudí was lucky he lived long enough to meet a tragic end at seventy-four, let alone exhibit the endurance and clarity to continually raise funds for the cathedral while managing its construction and perfecting its revolutionary design.

And here's perhaps the most unwieldy paradox of all: new perspectives demand sensitivity, creativity, and time spent alone to take form, while the subsequent manifestation of any significant, long-term vision requires motivating large numbers of people to pursue a common goal. A loner wandering around in that pulsating, open-nerve state may be able to mainline inspiration, but can he deal with the conflict, miscommunication, power plays, judgment, and politics of bringing his finest ideas to fruition? At the opposite end of the spectrum, intensely social people who develop a skin thick enough to let them navigate interpersonal and organizational dramas often lose connection to the very sensitivity that breeds inventive, nuanced thinking.

The solution involves a simple division of labor, you might say, but history has proven otherwise. Shrewd, charismatic managers and entrepreneurs have been known to prey upon brilliant yet socially awkward artists and inventors, whose ideas get diluted in the process. This kind of relationship, at its most benign, becomes codependent as the visionary loses touch with worldly concerns while his business partners neglect to further develop their own creative capacities. And both sides of this human equation are susceptible to the Sacrifice Syndrome as ambitious ideas face innumerable hurdles along the way, demanding visionaries and more practical leaders alike to break through the pressures, prejudices, and habits of the status quo on their way to creating lasting, meaningful change.

Finally, there's the ultimate, arguably supernatural challenge: ensuring that the vision remains healthy after your poor worn-out bones are buried in the ground. Gaudí's cathedral currently faces a threat more insidious than Catholic-hating communists: public transportation. One proposal involves construction of a subway nearby, which architects fear would damage the basilica over time. Another plan would turn the church *into* a train station. Apparently, it wasn't enough to hit Gaudí with a tram. The assault of mass transit continues unabated nearly a century after his death.

These possible compromises to Sagrada Familia's integrity illuminate one crucial aspect of managing individual and group needs over the long term. Not only do leaders have to convince colleagues, investors, and employees to buy into significant ideas, but at some point these innovators must also inspire a much larger public to support the vision as well. Whether in business, politics, art, or religion, initiating significant change is a lot like trying to overhaul an entire railway system while runaway trains continue to speed through it. No matter how defective the current model, people en masse resist the inconvenience and uncertainties of innovation with the hostility you'd expect them to reserve for immediate threats to their survival. Heated debates over public health care in the United States provide a glaring example. The average working man or woman isn't trained or even encouraged to engage in cathedral thinking. And really, why should people be willing to sacrifice their own hard-earned comfort without an injection of the same 220-volt shot of inspiration that got the original innovator going? Acting as both lightning rod and transformer is part of the skill and thrill — and inevitable burnout — visionary leaders must learn to manage if they plan to achieve anything consequential.

Sacrifice and Renewal

As Mother Teresa once inscribed on the wall of her children's home in Calcutta, "If you are successful, you win false friends and true enemies; Succeed anyway.... What you spend years building, someone could destroy overnight; Build anyway." Pull this off, and you hit the PhD level of leadership development. Or maybe we're talking sainthood here. Yet even those of us still working on the necessary prerequisites for great leadership — inspiration, innovation, communication, and emotional and social intelligence — need to understand how to navigate what Boyatzis and McKee call "the Cycle of Sacrifice and Renewal" if we plan to align our God-given talents and hard-won knowledge with long-term goals.

In the old pyramid-building days, slave labor ensured that generations would be conditioned through dominance and demoralization to act as drones for an agenda they were forced to support. This system, active in the United States less than two hundred years ago, "evolved" into the assaults on mind, body, and spirit that factory workers endured regardless of the lip service paid to their status as free men and women. Labor laws and unions protecting workers eventually emerged. Yet once you graduate to a significant leadership position, particularly one with entrepreneurial elements, the rules change. There are no government regulations to protect you. You must suddenly learn to advocate for yourself while also organizing, motivating, and inspiring others. To raise the difficulty level, some people will rave enthusiastically about whatever mission you represent while covertly undermining some aspect of the plan, often unconsciously, sometimes for reasons even they don't understand. As the vision expands and takes on a life of its own, you must constantly modify your original expectations and strategies to align with unforeseeable challenges and opportunities, or you too will compromise the dream. And no one ensures that you receive fair pay for working no more than a reasonable number of hours, either. In the most daring, potentially paradigm-shifting fields, you're likely to spend years compensating others before yourself. All the while, employees will assume you're raking in the bucks, a throwback to the old robber-baron days, when the resentment was truly justified. Mass media reinforces this age-old mistrust, offering far more coverage of CEOs flying in private jets to receive government bailout funds than of innovators who sacrifice time and money while supporting a worthy vision. In the public mind, leaders are, quite simply, guilty until proven innocent. This is why, even though people are conditioned to at least feign respect for anyone in a supervisory role, authentic trust and compassion must be won, sometimes slowly over time, sometimes as dramatically as a warrior running a gauntlet of tribal abuse.

In 1999, Mike Judge, of *Beavis and Butthead* fame, satirized egotistical yet clueless bosses and insipid management practices in the film *Office Space*. A decade later, after running his own increasingly successful media enterprise, he couldn't help but take the opposite position in his film *Extract*. Here Judge explored, with his usual brand of twisted social commentary, what the founder of a company deals with on a daily basis. In a radio interview with *Fresh Air*'s Terry Gross, he revealed the reasons behind this change in perspective:

> I'd worked just dozens and dozens of jobs before I started my animation career. And by that point, I was pushing thirty. So I'd always been the employee. I had never had anybody work for me....And then suddenly, when *Beavis and Butthead* started, I had anywhere from thirty to as many as ninety people working for me. And so, I just suddenly became sympathetic to my former bosses. You know, I was just, like, God, these people don't appreciate anything. I've got to baby-sit them. They're always fighting with each other and me.

One eye-opening experience involved hiring someone to color in his line drawings. In a good-natured attempt to share the little bit of wealth he was finally accessing, Judge offered what he felt was a generous, above-minimum-wage rate for a job that didn't require any significant thought or creativity. At that time, mind you, he was working within a limited budget for an untried series of MTV shorts. Even so, Judge overheard, along with so many unprintable expletives, his employees complaining that he was getting rich at their expense. "I was, like, God, I can't win," he told Gross, obviously still surprised by the irony of his position.

This is the dark side of leadership. No one talks about it much, perhaps because most people would refuse to be promoted if they knew what to expect. Even worse, conventional training programs don't prepare new leaders, let alone visionaries, for the most infuriating challenges involved. Common advice for handling power stress is to "suck it up" and "get over it." Even the best books on emotional intelligence in the workplace only scratch the surface of the personal and social issues innovators face.

In negotiating the Cycle of Sacrifice and Renewal, for instance, renewal is not as simple as taking a vacation, eating dinner at home several times a week, and spending a couple weekends a month attending your child's soccer games. The inescapable pressure of unresolved interpersonal difficulties, high expectations and demands, heartless gossip, and the general lack of compassion people display for the leader's position follow you wherever you go, keeping you up nights, infiltrating your private thoughts and spousal conversations on even the most isolated Hawaiian beaches. In *Resonant Leadership*, authors Boyatzis and McKee create a strong foundation for interrupting the Sacrifice Syndrome through cultivating mindfulness, hope, and compassion; but real, lasting renewal also requires successfully managing a host of paradoxes simultaneously. Leaders must somehow balance individual and group needs within their companies and the culture at large. They must sacrifice personal comfort and short-term gratification yet avoid burnout, in part by setting effective boundaries with fans, foes, and the relentless energy of inspiration itself. To develop a thick skin, as new managers are so often tempted to do, is to lose the sensitivity necessary for creativity, and the compassion essential for effective leadership. To keep your heart open is to experience a certain amount of pain daily. Learning how to manage the discomfort without simply shutting down is possible. But the personal breakthroughs that are required resemble the transformations most often associated with religious or mystical experience.

Models for great leadership, in fact, read like recipes for sainthood. As Boyatzis and McKee observe, great leaders "deliberately and consciously step out of destructive patterns to renew themselves physically, mentally, and emotionally." These individuals "are able to manage constant crises and chronic stress without giving into exhaustion, fear, or anger. They do not respond blindly to threats with fearful, defensive acts. They turn situations around, finding opportunities in challenges and creative ways to overcome obstacles. They are able to motivate themselves and others by focusing on possibilities. They are optimistic, yet realistic. They are awake and aware, and they are passionate about their values and their goals. They create powerful, positive relationships that lead to an exciting organizational climate." And they're masters at helping colleagues and employees rise to similar levels of creativity, emotional intelligence, and social awareness simply for efficiency's sake, if not for altruistic reasons.

As I've so often asked myself, my colleagues, my mentors, and sometimes anyone within hearing range, where's the handbook for *that*?

The Horse I Rode In On

In the early 1990s, an initially frustrating attempt at renewal gave me the insight and later the tools to address some of these age-old dilemmas. I had recently resigned from my position as program director of a Florida public radio station to move to Arizona with my new husband, recording artist Steve Roach. After five years wrangling a group of energetic, highly opinionated, artistically motivated people, not only at the station itself but also during the numerous special events and music festivals I organized along the Gulf Coast, I was ready for a break. Working as a freelance writer, living in the desert with my own private composer creating new works of art in the next room, was a dream come true, fulfilling yet economically unpredictable for both of us. So it wasn't long before I also accepted a position as morning announcer at the local classical station. No longer dealing with the headaches of managing such an operation, I was expecting to hide out in the studio, enjoying a daily dose of Bach, Beethoven, and Brahms. The problem was, even though the station was technically a part of a major university's communications department, there was precious little communication going on. And so, after experiencing the employee/employer dynamic from the leader's viewpoint, I was suddenly thrust back into the labor pool to reevaluate both perspectives from the trenches.

In its public role, the station played sophisticated, soothing sounds. Behind the scenes, however, its administration was unnecessarily secretive and manipulative, playing political games, most often at the expense of female employees, who were rarely, if ever, promoted. As a nationally recognized music critic and former program director myself, I had a reputation that garnered a certain level of respect from the administration. But watching colleagues deal with a capricious, incongruent system tested my patience. Consoling these people inadvertently became part of my job, as several of my most creative work-related friends would burst into the announcing studio in tears, telling me ever more disturbing tales of maltreatment to the tempestuous accompaniment of Rachmaninoff, Wagner, and Ravel. As a lowly announcer myself, I was powerless to initiate organizational change, yet as an individual with a certain amount of leadership presence, I could occasionally turn the tide in my own favor. The ability to teach these skills to my fellow employees eluded me, however, mostly because I was unaware of key nonverbal elements influencing the most frustrating, as well as the most successful, of these pivotal interactions.

At the same time, I was perplexed by the famous musicians I encountered. Most people, radio station managers included, *suppress* emotion, hiding their true intentions behind bland smiles and passive-aggressive maneuvers, only to blow up at inopportune moments under stress. Yet artists rewarded handsomely for *expressing* emotion were likewise leading highly dysfunctional lives. It seemed that suppression and expression were two sides of the same dysfunctional coin, and my faith in the sanity of our species was deteriorating — fast.

And so in my midthirties, while my husband was off touring Europe with several other musicians, I impulsively bought a horse. My intention was to ride into the desert, to get as far away as possible from the human race on a regular basis. Yet this beautiful, willful mare refused to comply with my escape plan. Nakia, a striking Thoroughbred ex-racehorse, tested me every step of the way, showing absolutely no respect for my hard-won reputation. It didn't matter to her that a well-known music magazine flew me to Los Angeles to interview k.d. lang one week, then sent me to Japan a month later to write a cover story on Brian Eno. There was no way I could impress my mount with stories of how another publication was arranging dinners with classical violin virtuosos Isaac Stern and Anne-Sophie Mutter in between meetings with jazz great Wynton Marsalis and rock guitarist Carlos Santana. She didn't even care that I talked to Johnny Cash an hour before I drove out to the barn one day. Chatting with a country music legend did not make me a passable rider. All those years sitting at a desk, writing, listening to music, and talking into a microphone had cut me off from the fluidity, assertiveness, and balance in motion that even the most generous horse demands, and this mare was hell-bent on showing me exactly how my "prestigious" career made me weak and ineffective.

Yet a strange thing began to happen. As I became more adept at motivating my horse, focusing her attention, and gaining her respect, relationships at home and work improved. People commented on the change, yet no one could pinpoint what had shifted. I also noticed nonverbal dynamics at play in myself and others that were reinforcing dysfunctional patterns on both sides of the employer/employee relationship, though at first I had no idea how to change the situation. It was as if someone had suddenly turned a spotlight on interactions we'd been trying to maneuver through in the shadows, and yet for years I had been unable to even describe these observations to others. Over time, I realized that no matter how eloquently we humans advocated change, how diligently we debated the issues, how zealously we strategized, what we *couldn't* talk about was a much more powerful motivator of behavior than anything we could discuss. Working with horses quickly became much more than a diversion. It was *the* missing link in my education as a writer, musician, wife, friend, employee, and, increasingly, leader.

Psychologists have observed that only *10 percent* of human interpersonal communication is verbal. And yet in our culture, we've become mesmerized by words as our social and educational systems teach us to dissociate from the body, the environment, and the subtle nuances of nonverbal communication. More and more, our conversations don't even take place in person, as cell phones, email, and text messages proliferate. Where in the world do we go to master that other 90 percent?

For me, the most rustic of boarding stables proved a worthy setting. In fact, there was no end to the character-building exercises my growing herd saw fit to impose. Through a relentless series of experiential lessons, my four-legged companions transformed me into a more engaged, assertive, intuitive, adaptable, and courageous person, not so much by tutoring as by tuning me, helping me over time to hold a more balanced frequency. I was amazed to find that, like Pegasus, the mythical winged stallion who inspired poets, artists, and musicians, my horses could dispel the worst case of writer's block through the simplest interactions. Like Zen masters, these exquisitely mindful creatures helped me navigate paradox with increasing facility. They even held the key to effectively dealing with emotion, and it didn't involve suppression or expression. (For details, see Guiding Principle 1, in chapter 13 of the book.) I could act horselike in all kinds of perplexing human situations and completely change the outcome for the better. The barn took on a mystical patina as my equine friends taught me more in silence than anyone ever had in words.

It's taken me a good fifteen years to translate horse wisdom into spoken and written language, and yes, I can even inject significant logic into the discussion. Much of the research allowing me to do this didn't exist when I started this journey in 1993, so it seems I was born at the right time and place to take on such a project. Over the years, through much experimentation, I also developed ways of teaching these same skills to others. Yet while there is much I can now offer in conference rooms and lecture halls, my horses remain the true masters at transforming human behavior, illuminating ineffective habits and hidden strengths, and teaching awareness of, and eventually mastery of, that "other 90 percent" with remarkable ease and efficiency.

In this respect, it's absolutely no accident that the most effective historical leaders — from Alexander the Great to Katherine the Great, George Washington, Winston Churchill, and Ronald Reagan — were skillful riders, equestrians who had close relationships with spirited, arguably heroic horses. Regardless of policy and agenda, these people exhibited exceptional poise under pressure, clarity of intention, courage, and conviction. Their mounts were not mindless machines. They required — and continued to foster — an almost supernatural level of leadership presence capable of motivating others to face incredible odds and create innovative, highly ambitious empires. That Alexander the Great and George Washington each rode the same horses into battle year after year also demonstrates their ability to cultivate relationship as a source of power: to *tap* resources without taxing them, even in the most dangerous and desperate circumstances. Their horses returned the favor, saving their lives on more than one occasion.

Business, politics, education, and religion may seem like opposing forces at times, but they all share one significant, potentially fatal flaw: mistrust of the body. Civilization has thus interrupted the optimal flow of human evolution. Your body is the horse that your mind rides around on. It's a sentient being, not a machine. (See Guiding Principle 2, chapter 14.) Starve that horse, beat it into submission, ignore its vast stores of nonverbal wisdom, and it will fail you when you need it most, throwing you during a crisis, perhaps wandering into traffic at the most inopportune moment. Reawakening corporeal intelligence — learning to form a partnership with instinct, intuition, and emotion — these skills are essential in harnessing the strength, creativity, spirit, compassion, and endurance needed to manifest lasting, meaningful change.

There's a whole herd of horses in my cathedral, and they remain my greatest teachers. This is the course, the handbook they've dictated in so many subtle and powerful gestures.

Chapter Two

LEGACY OF POWER

The request for backup was unprecedented, especially so soon after the election — one Secret Service agent was injured, and the future president of the United States was taking care of him, waiting for assistance. Ronald Reagan hadn't even taken the oath of office, and already he was a security risk.

"I have a big problem out here," the detail supervisor reported during that subsequent, no doubt embarrassing, call to the White House. "I need someone who can ride a horse."

Turns out that Reagan wanted to spend time at his California ranch after a grueling election campaign, but it was difficult for him to relax with members of the Presidential Protective Division acting like Keystone Cops on horseback. As John Barletta reveals in his insightful, occasionally hilarious book *Riding with Reagan: From the White House to the Ranch*, no one on the secret service staff even knew how to tie a horse that first week at Rancho del Cielo, so the president-elect ended up saddling all their mounts. Things only got worse when they started riding. At one point, Reagan took off at a gallop, jumping fences through the rugged Santa Ynez Mountains. Members of the security team were having trouble keeping up, though it wasn't for lack of trying. Finally, one agent fell off his horse and broke his arm. The veteran of numerous cowboy movies dismounted and rushed to the man's side until the rest of the crew arrived on the scene. No doubt Reagan also supervised the rescue mission as his novice rider-agents figured out how to get their wounded comrade back to ranch head-quarters through a scenic yet confusing maze of trails where the deer and the antelope play alongside the scorpion, rattlesnake, and mountain lion.

"Our chief supervisor at the time rightly said that was not how things should work," Barletta wrote with his characteristic gift for understatement. "The President was not supposed to be giving us aid and comfort. That was what we should be doing for him." A quick, national search for the right agent to accompany the president on his rides produced the perfect combination — an army veteran, secret service agent, *and* experienced equestrian. Barletta spent the next decade accompanying Reagan on hundreds of rides spanning several continents.

Recreational Therapy

For Reagan, ranching was no publicity stunt. He built the fences in front of the rustic main house himself and was forever clearing his favorite riding trails of overgrown brush. When he'd head out to chop wood, he'd throw the saws into his old, beat-up red Jeep, even though his wife, Nancy, preferred he take the newer, safer blue Jeep she and some friends had bought for his birthday. In fact, the First Lady continually plotted with the secret service to rein in her husband's penchant for good, old-fashioned, mind-clearing, body-renewing hard work. Over time, through careful diplomacy, the security team convinced Reagan to refrain from jumping his horse and running the wood chipper. Then, of course, there was the question of firearms. One false alarm involved a simple attempt to control algae taking over the Rancho del Cielo pond. Reagan bought some goldfish to keep the water clear, which he inadvertently ended up feeding to a magnificent blue heron who surely thought he had stumbled upon a fish lover's paradise buffet.

Frustrated, Reagan marched out of the house one morning, pistol in hand, and started shooting, hoping to scare the bird away. "When the gunshots echoed through the air, the whole place went crazy," Barletta remembers. The author, who could see all the action from his post near the tack room, tried to calm everyone down with a brief, unintentionally inflammatory radio message: "It's OK. Reagan shot."

"Reagan shot?!" they screamed back. Barletta quickly explained what had happened, looking back at the president, who was already assessing the commotion he had caused.

"I suppose I should have told you I was going to do that, huh?" Reagan said. And that, Barletta revealed, was how the leader of the free world decided to turn over all his firearms to the Secret Service for safekeeping.

Despite these early mishaps, protecting the president on horseback was by far the biggest challenge Barletta's team encountered. When Reagan saddled his gray stallion, the security team had several hours of serious work ahead of them. It didn't help that the horse, El Alamein, was an Anglo-Arab, a half-Thoroughbred, half-Arabian combining the speed of the former breed with the intensity and endurance of the latter. He was so feisty, Barletta reports, that "the more you worked him, the more excited he got."

The stallion, a gift from the president of Mexico, had been taught to emerge from his stall, rear, and take several steps on his back legs, a spectacle designed to awe and intimidate even the most experienced equestrian. In fact, El Alamein's notoriously flamboyant nature was likely enhanced by trainers enamored of their Spanish conquistador heritage, a tradition producing proud, powerful, fiery horses, in part to scare the living daylights out of enemies, serfs, and common folk.

From antiquity through the conquest of the New World, a meticulously trained war stallion could rear, strike, and kick out his back legs on command to injure foot soldiers. He could leap to the side, slide to a stop, spin, and take off running without hesitation; he would also stand at attention in the midst of a raging battle if his rider dismounted to engage in hand-to-hand combat. Advanced competitors in the Olympic Games continue to demonstrate such feats, and these peacetime pursuits, too, require significant courage, fortitude, and risk to develop. The horse, after all, is an astonishing enigma, a prey animal willing to endure the horrors of war and the uncertainty of the unknown, carrying generations of riders, around the world, for reasons that still boggle the mind, sometimes receiving medals for exceptional bravery along the way.

Reagan, who started his military career in the U.S. Cavalry, no doubt felt history come to life on the back of El Alamein. He would ride for three or four hours at a time, rarely speaking to Barletta on the trail, totally immersed in the experience. Still, the president's favorite mount was a constant source of anxiety for those charged with the task of protecting their fearless leader. El Alamein was so intense and flighty that at one point Barletta had veterinarian Doug Herthel assess whether the horse was suffering from back pain or some other hidden injury. In a treadmill test, the stallion proved stronger than the average racehorse, reaching optimal respiratory levels in two minutes when it took most Thoroughbreds five minutes to hit the same threshold. Herthel, a seasoned equestrian himself, had some trouble controlling El Alamein in a subsequent ride. "I don't feel anything wrong with him," the doctor concluded after a good twenty minutes in the saddle, "but I can't believe you let the president of the United States ride this dingbat."

"Still, President Reagan loved that horse," Barletta observed. "It was almost as if this strong man and this strong horse really understood each other." Not that there weren't some close calls during the nearly ten years the president rode El Alamein. But Reagan's poise and athleticism, combined with his love of a challenge, saved him on more than one occasion. Nonverbally, he could conjure up a calming presence under pressure that was simultaneously firm and reassuring, focused yet agile. It's a skill that anyone who likes to ride a spirited horse develops through experience — or dies trying.

If Reagan had simply wanted to relax, he wouldn't have chosen a horse like El Alamein. The president was accessing something in that relationship, something elusive yet essential. Trotting off into the desert on a horse ready to bolt at the drop of a hat or the rattle of a snake, gaining the animal's trust and cooperation along the way, Reagan wasn't just clearing his mind; he was literally exercising abilities that would prove useful in the international political arena.

Detractors insisted the former actor and radio announcer was a figurehead, a charlatan launched into office through his extensive film and public-speaking experience, a political amateur controlled by more intelligent, covert, perhaps malevolent forces. As a skeptical college student at the time he was elected, I too was willing to believe this rumor, ready to dissect his every false move — and confounded by his increasing popularity. After all, what Reagan said wasn't so impressive. It wasn't even how he said it. Whatever "it" was, there was no logical explanation for it whatsoever in my mind, at least not until I bought my first horse at age thirty-two. Only then did I realize that what Reagan learned in the saddle was crucial to his success.

Night of the Lepus

Contrary to popular belief, riding a horse does not come naturally — for one infuriating reason: the most basic skills are counterintuitive to the flight-or-fight response in both species. Even mildly challenging situations cause the blood pressure to rise. Guts clench and muscles tighten as breathing becomes fast and shallow. Horses and other large prey animals evolved to sense these nonverbal danger signals in herd members *at a distance*. When you're sitting on the spine of such a powerful creature, his sudden, overwhelming urge to bolt, in concert with your body's involuntary alarm system, becomes a serious threat to your immediate survival. Within seconds, a deadly interspecies feedback loop of escalating arousal spirals out of control, creating a tornado of disorganized responses guaranteed to leave dust and destruction in its wake.

Take the classic amateur rider's initiation: managing a startled horse. If you could watch what happens to the nervous systems of both species in slow motion, ejection from the saddle stands out as the most logical conclusion.

However, seasoned equestrians learn to modify their own instinctual responses, causing their mounts to experience the *opposite* of fear. It's a nonverbal skill that comes in handy with humans too, as so many of my clients have discovered over the years.

"Stephanie Argento" runs a highly successful East Coast marketing firm. Tall, confident, effusive, the forty-nine-year-old mother of two teenage boys booked a last-minute New Year's Eve appointment with me through a mutual friend, hoping, as she put it, "to make sense of an unfortunate riding incident" that occurred during her family's Christmas vacation.

Stephanie's sister, Marie, had recently moved to Tucson and was inspired to buy a horse, which she kept at a small private facility near the Saguaro National Monument East, a scenic desert preserve with miles of trails. "Marie and I took riding lessons when we were little," Stephanie told me during our initial conversation. "Actually, we were so horse crazy, it was like we'd taken the postal service oath. You know, 'neither rain, nor snow, nor sleet, nor hail shall keep us from our appointed rounds.' And we were fearless, willing to ride any horse, anywhere, anytime. But then I went to college, got married, got practical. So I was really looking forward to visiting my sister over the holidays, doing some mindless touristy things, and maybe getting back into the saddle myself."

The opportunity presented itself the Saturday after Christmas. A group of Marie's fellow horse boarders planned to hit the trails, and one of them offered Stephanie the use of his daughter's horse. The lanky Thoroughbred gelding, an ex-racehorse, seemed a little feisty, but Marie had ridden with the family a number of times and had never seen Charger spook. Considering Stephanie's background, a fourteen-year-old girl's favorite horse "seemed like a no-brainer" to her and everyone else involved. The group headed toward the monument around noon, looking forward to a relaxing ride and a subsequent barbecue.

"So here it's this beautiful, sunny day in December, and I'm not even wearing a coat," Stephanie continued. "Charger's owner made me put a helmet on, which I resisted at first. I had these romantic visions of galloping through the desert with my hair blowing free under the big blue sky. I sure am glad he insisted, or I might be a drooling vegetable at this very moment."

The adventure started calmly enough. "The scenery was like something out of a John Wayne movie, all these gigantic cactuses, massive rock outcroppings, scruffy little trees, and majestic mountains. I was in heaven, seriously considering how to make the move to Tucson myself, when this huge jackrabbit ran out of the brush and sort of spooked the horse in front of me. Charger shied, and my heart skipped a beat. It actually felt like someone had kicked me in the gut for a moment. Then Marie shouted 'Night of the Lepus!' and we both burst into laughter."

Quizzical looks from the other riders prompted the sisters to explain as they headed on down the trail: "We'd been out to Colossal Cave the day before, and they had this little museum with, among other things, a display of some of the old Westerns that had been shot in the area. There was this poster for what looked like a really bad B movie called *Night of the Lepus* with Janet Leigh. That guy from Star Trek, the doctor [DeForest Kelley] was in it too. My husband had seen it at the drive-in years ago, and we were pretty much in hysterics as he described it, to the point where my sons looked it up on the Internet later that night."

The 1972 film depicts an ill-fated attempt at rodent birth control. When an Arizona rancher complains of rabbits overrunning his grazing lands, a local university professor injects some test subjects with hormones and genetically altered blood to curb their rampant reproduction. The whole thing backfires, of course. One of the lab rabbits escapes, creating a race of giant bloodthirsty, man-, cow-, and horse-eating bunnies.

As Stephanie and Marie related the details of this ridiculous tale, their mounts relaxed, and the trail ride continued without incident — that is, until their little posse turned back toward the stable and several of the horses seemed overanxious to get home. "Charger started jigging, pulling at the bit," Stephanie remembers, "but he wasn't the only one. It was exhausting trying to hold the horses back, so we all started trotting — but, my God, Charger had a rough trot. I was bouncing all over the place, trying to rein him in at the same time. Then we rounded the next bend, and this herd of deer came out of nowhere. Charger shot forward. I grabbed his mane and held on as best I could.

"The next thing I remember I'm on the ground and my sister's asking me if I know who the president of the United States is. Apparently, my horse ran all the way home before any of the other riders could catch up with him. Marie and I walked back because I refused to get on her mare, or anyone else's horse, for that matter."

Stephanie's helmet was cracked. She was bruised and confused. But the fact that she couldn't bring herself to get right back on a horse that day was, in her mind, "the most demoralizing part of all."

At the barbecue later that afternoon, Stephanie heard all kinds of gracious, ego-mending explanations for her fall, the most common theme involving the "fact" that, as prey animals, horses exist in a perpetual state of fearful anticipation. In their pea-sized brains, plastic bags blowing in the breeze are cackling, soul-stealing ghosts. Deer are fleet-footed, flesh-eating zombies. And jackrabbits, well, they're just plain mutant. Rider beware!

This all-too-common explanation gives way too much credit to the horse's imagination, a bizarre attribute to afford an animal you've just cited as mentally deficient. In truth, there's no scientific evidence for sinister B-movie plots rolling around in the equine brain — not that I would consider this mutant feature of the human storytelling instinct a sign of advanced intelligence. There is, however, a much better case for observing a finely tuned, empathic nervous system in action. When a horse spooks, he shows us something remarkable, and the latest research points to some surprising conclusions about our own hidden potential.

Having seen, and experienced, numerous close calls over the years, I can tell you exactly what set Charger off. Stephanie's tension, posture, and breathing (or her lack of breathing), her inexperience with the landscape, her rusty riding skills — and her own natural, unrecognized empathic talents — all conspired to catapult her off that horse, leaving her wincing in the dust and walking into the sunset on her own two feet. At the same time, I suspect her early equestrian experiences contributed to her success in business. Reawakening this nonverbal wisdom, bringing it to full consciousness, would give her an even more significant edge. Stephanie was thrilled to learn that the nonverbal fear-management skills she practiced with me that day would be useful in calming and focusing staff, clients, and family members once she returned home. (See Guiding Principle 7, chapter 19.)

Emotions Are Contagious!

Italian neuroscientists, studying the effects of movement on the brain, stumbled upon a strange and unexpected feature of the mammalian nervous system, one that quickly led to all kinds of research into the physiology of empathy. Not only are we hardwired to *share* experience; it turns out that sensations and emotions are more contagious than the common cold!

In the 1980s, researchers at the University of Parma placed electrodes in the premotor cortex of a macaque, hoping to figure out which neurons were activated by hand and mouth actions. They soon isolated a particular cell that fired only when the monkey lifted his arm. Apparently they did this over and over again just to make sure, as scientists are prone to do. But I would love to have seen the looks on their faces when a lab assistant lifted an ice cream cone to his own mouth during one of those sessions and *triggered a reaction in the monkey's cell.* Subsequent studies suggest that our brains are peppered with tiny *mirror neurons* that mimic what another being does, ultimately allowing us to detect someone else's emotions through his or her actions.

In their September 2008 *Harvard Business Review* article, "Social Intelligence and the Biology of Leadership," Daniel Goleman and Richard Boyatzis summarize the implications for those of us hired to motivate, inspire and basically move large numbers of people around in a coordinated fashion: "Mirror neurons have a particular importance in organizations, because leaders' emotions and actions prompt followers to mirror those feelings and deeds. The effects of activating neural circuitry in followers' brains can be very powerful."

In one intriguing study cited by Goleman and Boyatzis, researcher Marie Dasborough observed the effects of two management approaches. The first group of employees received negative performance feedback supported by positive emotional signals — ample smiles and nods. The other group experienced positive feedback couched in negative body language — frowns and narrowed eyes. As it turns out, those who emerged from good-natured *negative* feedback sessions felt more optimistic than those who received praise from cranky supervisors. "In effect," Goleman and Boyatzis conclude, "the delivery was more important than the message itself. And everybody knows that when people feel better, they perform better. So if leaders hope to get the best out of their people, they should continue to be demanding but in ways that foster a positive mood in their teams. The old carrot-and-stick approach alone doesn't make neural sense."

Like horses, who are keenly aware of nonverbal cues, people respond to the emotional atmosphere behind our words more profoundly than they do to the actual content and meaning. But vocal tone, body language, and mirror neurons are just the tip of the iceberg. Research into the human-equine relationship continues to uncover even more subtle interpersonal dynamics, and while no one understands the mechanism yet, it turns out that horses and riders don't have to *see* any evidence of movement or gesture to affect each other physiologically. While this may seem obvious when you're riding a horse — you can feel what's going on in his body and vice versa — emotions and sensations are contagious even when you appear to be walking calmly beside each other.

In a 2009 article published in the *Veterinary Journal*, researchers from the Swedish University of Agricultural Sciences performed a simple, elegant experiment designed to study the effect a nervous handler has on the heart rate of his or her mount. Twenty-seven horses of various breeds and ages were led or ridden at a walk by thirty-seven amateur equestrians. Wearing heart-rate monitors, each team traveled a thirty-meter distance between two cones a total of four times. Just before the final pass, however, the person was told that an assistant, who had been standing next to the path the whole time, would open an umbrella as the horse went by.

Now, as someone who's worked with a number of flighty horses over the years, my own heart skipped a beat just reading about this minor institutionalized threat. I mean, even right now, sitting at my computer, I actually cringe at the thought of the sound an umbrella makes when it flies open, especially when I visualize this happening five feet away from my Arabian stallion. If mirror neurons are involved in these palpable physiological responses, they're bouncing off a projection screen in my head. And the effect of imagination, interestingly enough, is what the researchers were ultimately measuring. Those scientific pranksters didn't open the umbrella (as any equine-liability insurance company would be relieved to know). Even so, the heart rates of both human and horse rose significantly as they passed the now suspect, inclement-weather-savvy lab assistant. Even more remarkable, no behavioral differences were observed in either horse or handler when the animal was being led, though there was a tendency for riders to shorten their reins after the dreaded news was conveyed. So, especially in the case of people leading their equine companions, the mere human *thought* of the umbrella's spooking power was enough to raise the arousal of the *horse*, who I'm pretty sure would not have understood the experimenter's warning in Swedish or any other language.

Let's not mince words here. What we're talking about is a mild form of telepathy, which, I might add, comes from the same root as *empathy* and *sympathy*. *Telepathy* literally means "feeling at a distance." Because we're methodically and relentlessly taught to dissociate from the environment and our own bodies, modern humans downplay rather than develop this ability, but the information still manages to leak through now and then in the form of "gut feelings" and other forms of intuition. While culturally conditioned minds work overtime to discount insights that bypass rational thought, the brain itself can't help but gather and process multifaceted somatic impressions with the split-second accuracy of a computer calculating a complex spreadsheet.

Logic, though useful at times, moves like a snail on quaaludes compared with the warp-speed conclusions coordinated by *spindle cells*. Four times larger than most brain cells, these neurons have an extralong branch allowing them to attach to other cells more easily, transmitting environmental impressions, memories, thoughts, and feelings at hyperspeed. "This ultrarapid connection of emotions, beliefs, and judgments creates what behavioral scientists call our social guidance system," Goleman and Boyatzis emphasize. "Spindle cells trigger neural networks that come into play whenever we have to choose the best response among many — even for a task as routine as prioritizing a to-do list.

These cells also help us gauge whether someone is trustworthy and right (or wrong) for a job. Within one-twentieth of a second, our spindle cells fire with information about how we feel about that person; such 'thin-slice' judgments can be very accurate, as follow-up metrics reveal. Therefore, leaders should not fear to act on those judgments, provided that they are also attuned to others' moods." (And, I must emphasize, provided these leaders are also aware of their own projections and prejudices, a topic I explore in chapter 12.)

It works both ways, of course. Spindle cells, mirror neurons, and horse heart-rate responses to threats imagined by humans add to growing scientific evidence that everyone — from your employees to your kids, your spouse, your mother-in-law, and your dog — is *designed* to read your mind. Kind of levels the playing field, doesn't it?

Here's an even more intriguing, or disturbing, bit of news, depending on whether or not you like to hide your emotions and intentions from others. In *Social Intelligence: The New Science of Human Relationships*, emotional-intelligence pioneer Daniel Goleman cites studies showing that not only does a person's blood pressure escalate when he tries to suppress feeling but *the blood pressure of those interacting with him also rises*. Lie detector tests, of course, measure arousal fluctuations. However, you don't have to be hooked up to a machine to reveal a hidden state of mind. Living beings are hardwired to transmit and receive this information at a distance. Our culturally induced emphasis on verbal communication lessens awareness of this valuable information over time, but anyone who retains or reclaims use of this natural ability appears downright psychic compared to the rest of the population.

The volume of this little-understood "sixth sense" is turned way up in prey animals such as horses, who become noticeably agitated in the presence of people who are incongruent, who try to cover anger, fear, or sadness with an appearance of well-being. This is not an equine judgment of our tendency to lie about what we're really feeling; it appears to be a reflection of emotion's physiology — and its contagious nature. In well over a decade of working with horses to teach human-development skills, I have regularly seen these animals mirror the precise emotion being suppressed, then calm down the moment the handler openly acknowledges that feeling — even if the emotion is still there. Let me say it again: The emotion doesn't have to change in order for the horse to show some signs of relaxation. By making the fear or anger conscious, by becoming congruent, the handler effectively lowers his own blood pressure, even if only slightly. But it's enough to drop the horse's blood pressure in response, which the animal demonstrates by sighing, licking and chewing, and/or lowering his head.

Unless you're a sociopath (which we'll get to later in this chapter), your blood pressure, heart rate, and breathing intensify when you're frightened or angry, even when you're wearing your best poker face. It takes extra energy to hide these feelings, which adds to the anxiety radiating from your body through a complex process that scientists are only now beginning to uncover. (It's important to emphasize that horses can detect *hidden* emotions that I cannot see in the client. Sometimes this person doesn't realize what he or she is feeling until the horse acts it out, oddly enough. Yet sure enough, when the client acknowledges this previously suppressed emotion, the horse will relax, sigh, lick, and chew. Something operating beyond the scope of mirror neurons is at work in humans as well, or the blood pressure of someone who's suppressing emotion would not affect the arousal of the people he or she is interacting with.)

The good news is that positive feelings are contagious too. A person who truly feels peaceful in situations that unnerve others can have a calming effect on everyone around her. This is a key skill in becoming a great rider or a great leader. In fact, with more time in the saddle, our Great Communicator, Ronald Reagan, might have just as easily become an accomplished horse whisperer. His ability to reassure and focus others during challenging situations had much less to do with words than most people would suspect.

Breaking the Spell

In 1990, psychologists Peter Salovey and John Mayer introduced the term *emotional intelligence*, defining it as "a form of social intelligence that involves the ability to monitor one's own and others' feelings and emotions to discriminate among them and *use this information to guide one's thinking and action*." Five years later, Daniel Goleman's influential book *Emotional Intelligence: Why It Can Matter More Than IQ* expanded on this concept, spawning widespread interest in the topic. Since that time, numerous studies have shown that, even among scientists, high "EQ" is more important than raw IQ and training in predicting career success, not to mention in building and sustaining strong personal relationships.

The most exciting research illuminates intricate biological processes at work in the simplest human interactions, prompting Goleman to recognize that leaders in particular must both manage their own somatic responses and learn to modulate these emotional-physiological cues and reactions in others. In the 2002 bestseller *Primal Leadership: Realizing the Power of Emotional Intelligence*, Goleman teamed up with Richard Boyatzis and Annie McKee to unveil the neuroscientific links between organizational success or failure. The authors argued that "emotions are contagious," a finding that "charges leaders with driving emotions in the right direction to have a positive impact on earnings or strategy." As the authors emphasize,

> Great leaders move us. They ignite our passion and inspire the best in us. When we try to explain why they're so effective, we speak of strategy, vision, or powerful ideas. But the reality is much more primal: Great leadership works through the emotions...
>
> In the modern organization, this primordial emotional task — though by now largely invisible — remains foremost among the many jobs of leadership: driving the collective emotions in a positive direction and clearing the smog created by toxic emotions.... Quite simply, in any human group the leader has maximal power to sway everyone's emotions. If people's emotions are pushed toward the range of enthusiasm, performance can soar; if people are driven toward rancor and anxiety, they will be thrown off stride.

Goleman further elaborated on this phenomenon in his 2006 book *Social Intelligence: The New Science of Human Relationships*. In his subsequent *Harvard Business Review* collaboration with Boyatzis, he offered a brief history and definition of this groundbreaking concept: "The notion that effective leadership is about having powerful social circuits in the brain has prompted us to extend our concept of emotional intelligence, which we had previously grounded in theories of individual psychology. A more relationship-based construct for assessing leadership is *social intelligence*, which we define as a set of interpersonal competencies built on specific neural circuits (and related endocrine systems) that inspire others to be effective."

Drawing on the work of neuroscientists, their own research and consulting endeavors, and studies associated with the Consortium for Research on Emotional Intelligence in Organizations, Goleman and his colleagues continue to search for ways "to translate newly acquired knowledge about mirror neurons, spindle cells" and other physiological findings "into practical, socially intelligent behavior that can reinforce the neural links between you and your followers."

Which brings me to the "PhD level" of emotional and social intelligence: managing empathic insights. Back when I wrote my first book, *The Tao of Equus*, in the late 1990s (published in 2001), the contagious nature of emotion was a controversial notion completely ignored by most people and vehemently challenged by skeptics, who saw it as some kind of psychic mumbo jumbo. Yet after repeatedly witnessing horses accurately mirroring the *unconscious* emotions of my clients, I began searching for scientific corroboration of what I called "shared emotion." At that time, I could find only one term for the phenomenon outside mystical and New Age circles: anthropologist E. Richard Sorensen's concept of "sociosensual awareness." In many ways, I still prefer this term because of the lilting, almost musical way it rolls off the tongue. *Sociosensual awareness* also has a decidedly positive connotation compared to *affect contagion*, a term I came across in the 2001 book *Healing the Soul in the Age of the Brain* by psychiatrist Elio Frattaroli. Not only did this phrase characterize how people sometimes feel victimized by others' emotions, but it also carried more weight with skeptics because of its medical connotation. Frattaroli's definition recognized that the hidden emotions of one person could infect another. While he framed this as something akin to a communicable disease, he recognized that it couldn't be explained away by conventional counseling principles like transference and countertransference. He subsequently learned to use affect contagion in his practice — in one case to accurately sense a patient's unspoken suicidal mood when standard psychological tests, and the opinions of respected colleagues, insisted the man had no self-destructive intent.

Frattaroli's realization that he could use his own body to sense his clients' emotions and Goleman's interest in capitalizing on neurological processes for the purpose of "driving emotions" of others "in the right direction" are two sides of the same empathic coin, one that equestrians have been tossing for centuries. If you specialize in training flighty, abused, or simply inexperienced horses, it's not just helpful to draw on these interrelated skills; it's essential to your survival.

Here's how it works. A second before your horse shies, bucks, or bolts, he sends what feels like an electrical charge pulsing through your body, causing your gut to clench and your heart rate to rise. Depending upon the severity of the situation, you might also feel your breath catching in your throat and the hair rising on the back of your neck as the information moves on up to your brain. When used effectively, this somatic alarm allows you to prepare for, and possibly avert, a troublesome spook. Remember, spindle cells can assess multiple inputs and choose the best response within *one-twentieth of a second*, giving you a brief window of time to modify the horse's reaction by consciously altering your own nervous system's response. Ultimately, how you handle this potent input determines whether you stay on his back (or in the case of leading a horse, whether or not he rears over you, kicks out, drags you to the ground, and/or leaves you with a painful case of rope burn as he breaks free and runs screaming around the farm working the rest of the herd into a frenzy, possibly setting in motion an even more unfortunate chain of events, including, but not limited to, unseating several unsuspecting riders in adjacent arenas).

An inexperienced rider can't help but respond to this massive dose of affect contagion instinctually, usually by collapsing into a (supremely unbalanced) fetal position, grabbing hold of the horse's mane, and wrapping her legs around his body. Leg pressure, being the cue to "go faster," is like hitting the "turbocharge" control on a race car, catapulting the horse forward. Those who manage to hang on through this little rite of passage get to experience the next round of responses — namely, a series of increasingly frantic bucks, which the horse employs mostly to regain his balance as the frazzled human dangling around his neck becomes an unfocused blob of dead weight. Actually the effect is worse than dead weight: a frightened rider's supercharged nervous system broadcasts its own breath-holding, gut-clenching, heart-racing alarm back into the horse's body, which intensifies the flight-or-fight response.

Breaking the spell of this dangerous feedback loop is a nonverbal skill. The words *whoa* and *relax* mean nothing to a horse when the rest of your body is screaming, "Let's get the hell out of here!" However, as Stephanie Argento discovered during that post-Christmas trail ride, hearing a companion shout "Night of the Lepus!" might make all the difference in the world.

The Opposite of Fear

Revisiting the details of that first rabbit-induced spook, Stephanie was intrigued to find that she'd experienced, viscerally, the dangers of affect contagion — and, accidentally, the power of its hidden potential. When a supersized bunny startled the horse in front of her, Charger too had shied, causing Stephanie's gut to clench and her heart to skip a beat. Had this process continued unabated, she probably would have rolled over into a fetal position and grabbed hold of his body with her legs, heightening Charger's impulse to turn tail and run. But quite unexpectedly, Marie had made her laugh, literally disarming a volatile physiological trend.

Fear, especially among social animals, is a sociosensual phenomenon, immensely efficient as an empathic alarm that shoots through the herd. Horses, after all, don't have to turn around and shout, "There's a lion in the grass; I think it would be prudent for all of us to flee in an easterly direction and reassess the situation on that hill over there." A split second before the threat-sensing horse can move his thousand-pound body into a flight-or-fight pose, let alone turn around and run, a shock wave of heightened arousal blasts through his nervous system — and the nervous systems of every horse, bird, rabbit, deer, and human in the vicinity. This potentially lifesaving form of shared emotion, however, can create a destructive hall-of-mirrors effect: any rise in blood pressure or muscle tension from the rider amplifies the horse's trepidation, needlessly inducing panic when, in the case of a jackrabbit, mild, momentary concern is the correct response.

Experienced riders learn, sometimes unconsciously, how to avert a spook by meeting the affect contagion of fear with the affect contagion of relaxation, focus, elation, and/or amusement. Physiologically, this means that when you feel that initial shock wave coursing through your body, you breathe into the tension, loosening your spine, unclenching your gut, releasing your jaw. Rather than bracing against the horse or grabbing his mane, you sit deeper in the saddle, maintaining an agile, balanced position. It actually helps to smile — if appropriate. Remember, incongruent emotion — such as covering fear with an appearance of well-being — causes your own blood pressure, and consequently that of the horse, to rise. However, the idea that a twenty-pound jackrabbit could pose a threat to the half-ton powerhouse of muscle underneath you is so ridiculous that the mere thought might produce an authentic chuckle or two.

It's particularly dangerous to dissociate at this point, because if you go blank and numb, you leave the choice of what to do and where to go up to a frazzled horse. You avoid the haze of indecision not by trying to disconnect from sensation overload but by *feeling* what's happening and *using those feelings as information*. This obviously takes courage and practice. To up the difficulty level, you must then modify your own physiological response to fear in order to drive the emotions and attention of your horse in the right direction. With mind and body fully engaged, breathing deeply, regaining balance if not total relaxation, you focus your mount toward the desired outcome — either away from a legitimate threat, like a royally pissed-off rattlesnake, or right on down the trail as that wild hare leaps across your path.

When it comes to *consciously* broadcasting the opposite of fear, *you must be present to win*. During that first spook, however, Stephanie's hide was saved by a timely joke. And laughter, it turns out, is one of the most efficient ways to turn a destructive emotional trend around. As Goleman and Boyatzis reveal, humans actually have a special subset of mirror neurons "whose only job is to detect other people's smiles and laughter, prompting smiles and laughter in return." Horses can't laugh, obviously, but the sudden mood shift that their handlers experience when amusement takes over is reliably contagious across species lines.

Whether you're a rider, a parent, a teacher, or a manager, a good sense of humor may well be the ultimate secret weapon, useful not only for disarming an out-of-control flight-or-fight impulse but also for achieving higher performance overall. Goleman and Boyatzis cite the research of Fabio Sala, who found that top-performing leaders elicited laughter *three times more often* in staff members than did midperforming leaders. "Being in a good mood, other research finds, helps people take in information effectively and respond nimbly and creatively. In other words laughter is serious business."

As with most forms of emotional intelligence, however, good judgment and sensitivity to nuance are essential in using laughter effectively. Sarcasm, for instance, is innately incongruent, allowing people to express contempt and anger in glib yet divisive ways, producing noxious by-products on both sides of a conflict. Those aligned with your perspective may be momentarily amused by your cutting remarks, but the end result is increased cynicism and scorn for the object of your derision, ultimately discouraging team work and negotiation. Those on the receiving end of your little joke experience a form of shame that quickly turns to rage. People who regularly use sarcasm *inflame* rather than defuse tense situations. And studies show that when blood pressure rises, intelligence and creativity drop.

Artful wit, on the other hand, packs a constructive contagious punch, disarming fear and anger with feelings of delight as well as amusement, encouraging people to work together more effectively. As Winston Churchill once said, "A joke is a very serious thing." During the darkest hours of World War II, the British prime minister harnessed the power of laughter to release tension while communicating inspiring, sobering, sometimes even critical, opinions and observations. Here's a sampling: "A fanatic is one who can't change his mind and won't change the subject." "[A politician needs] the ability to foretell what is going to happen tomorrow, next week, next month, and next year — and to have the ability afterwards to explain why it didn't happen." "An appeaser is one who feeds a crocodile, hoping it will eat him last." "Courage is what it takes to stand up and speak; courage is also what it takes to sit down and listen."

And courage he had, in spades, exercised to a large extent on the back of a horse, I might add.

Extreme Sports

Throughout his career, Churchill repeatedly demonstrated the ability to lower his own arousal in volatile situations, meeting the affect contagion of fear with the affect contagion of humor, courage, intelligence, and inspiration — centering and focusing large numbers of people who had good reason to panic. Yet nothing in his later years could compare with the intensity of his early cavalry experiences.

In the 1957 book *His Kingdom for a Horse*, Wyatt Blassingame describes, with hair-raising precision, what twenty-three-year-old Lieutenant Churchill faced during a cavalry charge in Egypt by the Twenty-First Lancers regiment. His horse, a gray Arabian he called Arab, was a former polo pony — polo was a game that Churchill himself played "extremely well. From a full run the little horse could whirl to the left or right or come to a sliding stop, keeping his balance like a ballet dancer." Those skills would come in handy during a Dervish army attack in September of 1898.

Sword drawn, racing toward the enemy with the rest of his troop, Churchill suddenly realized that a recent shoulder injury would prevent him from using the heavy weapon effectively. "At a full gallop," Blassingame marvels, "he managed to get the sword back into its scabbard and drew his pistol. This took time. When he looked toward the enemy again he was almost on them. The kneeling and crouching Dervishes in their blue robes were firing frantically, the smoke swirling over them." And just behind the front line, Churchill soon discovered, was a dry wash filled with thousands of fearsomely armed warriors. Dodging bullets he as raced through a cluster of kneeling riflemen, Churchill pulled hard on the reins at the edge of that sunken watercourse. "Arab skidded, then dropped catlike into the depression. If he had stumbled there, if he had fallen, a dozen swords and spears would have struck at the lieutenant. Once unhorsed he would have had no chance. But Arab stayed on his feet; he kept running; he broke through the swordsmen and leaped into the clear on the far side of the dry waterbed."

As horse and rider careened through the next wave of the khalifa's brave and fanatical army, Churchill saw a Dervish fling himself on the ground. For an instant the British officer thought the soldier had been shot. Then, even as Arab raced forward, Churchill "realized the man planned to slash at the gray's legs and bring him down, unhorsing the rider." With seconds to spare, "Arab turned as if he were on a polo field. The slashing swords missed. Leaning from the saddle Churchill fired two shots into the man. He barely had time to straighten when he saw another Dervish directly ahead, sword raised. But again the gray whirled, so close this time that even as Churchill fired, his pistol touched the face of the Dervish."

Not all of the Lancers were blessed with the same combination of skill and luck. When the charge ended, minutes after the attack was launched, they had lost almost one quarter of their force. Nearly ten thousand Dervishes had been killed or wounded by the time the rest of their ranks broke and ran. When the dust cleared, twenty thousand British and Egyptian soldiers had won the battle against sixty thousand of the khalifa's men.

After facing such an extreme form of "natural selection" at such a young age, it's no wonder that Churchill was able to remain centered and thoughtful in the conflicts to come. As Blassingame emphasized at the end of his breathtaking narrative, "without the leadership of Churchill, World War II might quite possibly have had a different ending."

From a Darwinian perspective, Lieutenant Churchill not only won the right to breed by surviving that pivotal battle, he demonstrated all the right stuff to lead: during a single cavalry charge, he exhibited poise in the midst of chaos, the capacity to negotiate massive amounts of sensory input, split-second accuracy in reading the nonverbal intentions of others, and — most important when your survival depends on remaining glued to a charging, skidding, twirling, leaping polo-pony-turned-warhorse — an advanced aptitude for coordinating movements with other team members.

The latter ability has a neurological component — namely, *oscillators*, cells that attune two or more beings physically by regulating how and when their bodies move together. Researchers see oscillators in action when people are about to kiss. These special neurons also help the cello section of the New York Philharmonic play in unison: if you could peek inside the musicians' heads, as scientists have figured out how to do, you'd see that the performers' right brain hemispheres are more closely coordinated with each other than are the left and right sides of their individual brains.

Optimal use of mirror neurons, oscillators, and other social circuitry allows leaders to engage what Goleman, Boyatzis, and McKee call resonance. Biologically speaking, a manager who worships objectivity, outlaws feeling, and hides in his office while handing down written policies and procedures, expecting followers to mirror his dissociative, stoic presence, is, at the very least, not using his brain properly — and preventing employees from reaching their potential as well. To activate the optimal team-building power of resonance, you have to actually care about others, sensing and coordinating with their feelings and motivations while, at the same time, turning destructive emotional feedback loops around by modulating your own empathic physical responses.

Two thousand years ago, people had no idea how many thousands of specialized neurons were firing during the complex social interactions of gifted leaders, but they recognized true talent when they saw it and even managed on occasion to write about it. The Greek historian Plutarch was particularly impressed with the exploits of a young prince named Alexander. Student of Aristotle, son of Philip of Macedon, the boy obviously had the opportunity to balance his rigorous intellectual studies with extensive equestrian training: at age ten, the future conqueror proved to be the only person in his father's entourage capable of riding an unruly horse named Bucephalus.

No one could mount the black stallion, and even the grooms were afraid to lead him. In one of the first historical reports of "horse gentling," Alexander noticed that Bucephalus seemed to be spooking at his own shadow. The young Macedonian prince took hold of the bridle and turned the quivering, snorting stallion into the sun. The boy spoke softly, stroking the horse for a while. Then, at the right moment, Alexander the Great leaped onto the stallion's sturdy back and took off at a gallop, reveling in the horse's phenomenal vitality rather than trying to rein it in. The connection between the two deepened over the years. Plutarch wrote that "in Uxia, once, Alexander lost him, and issued an edict that he would kill every man in the country unless he was brought back — as he promptly was."

Bucephalus died at the age of thirty, a long life for a horse even by today's standards. "During the final battle in India," observed Lawrence Scanlan in *Wild about Horses*, "the horse took spears in his neck and flank but still managed to turn and bring the king to safety before dying. Alexander was overcome with grief, and later named a city after Bucephalus." The legendary king relied on his mount's sensitivity, vitality, quick wits, and subtle warnings to help him survive many a battle. And Bucephalus relied on Alexander's ability to not only understand and respond to the horse's concerns but also interrupt the debilitating effects of escalating arousal, transforming the energy of fear into a power that neither member of this legendary team could have tapped on his own.

The Sociopath's Advantage

Arousal and relaxation — and the various emotions that arise from these autonomic nervous system cues — are the building blocks of a sophisticated, nonverbal language. Instantaneous, arguably telepathic, this feature of the "other 90 percent" (the nonverbal dimension of interpersonal communication) enhances relationships with coworkers and loved ones while offering protection from liars, thieves, and other malevolent characters. Yet there's always a shadow side to remarkable powers of communication and influence. By design, our natural empathic abilities sometimes cause us to defer to a peculiar feature of the sociopathic nervous system, allowing charismatic leaders like Adolf Hitler and Jim Jones to wreak havoc, especially among desperate populations.

The American Psychiatric Association considers *sociopathy* and *psychopathy* obsolete synonyms for the official clinical term *antisocial personality disorder*. Even so, the Psychopathy Checklist, developed by Dr. Robert D. Hare in the early 1990s, remains the diagnostic tool most commonly used to assess this condition. Major symptoms of antisocial personality disorder include the tendency to be glib, superficial, deceitful, and manipulative while also showing a *lack of empathy, lack of remorse or guilt,* and *shallow affect.*

In sociopaths, it seems, key emotional- and social-intelligence circuits are missing, while cognitive abilities remain intact. This high IQ–low EQ combination is confusing for the individual and toxic for those in his or her social circle. Hare reports that "psychopaths are often witty and articulate. They can be amusing and entertaining conversationalists, ready with a quick and clever comeback, and can tell unlikely but convincing stories that cast themselves in a good light. They can be very effective in presenting themselves well and are quite likeable and charming." However, they also "seem to suffer a kind of emotional poverty that limits the range and depth of their feelings. While at times they appear cold and unemotional, they are prone to dramatic, shallow and short-lived displays of feeling. Careful observers are left with the impression that they are play-acting and that little is going on below the surface."

People with antisocial personality disorder exhibit a severely impaired capacity to *feel,* let alone use emotion as information. Laboratory experiments employing biomedical recorders have shown that sociopaths actually lack the physiological responses normally associated with fear. Yet psychologists studying this troublesome profile have grossly underestimated the significance of this strange anomaly, which becomes a particularly dangerous talent in those with leadership ambitions.

For most people, Hare explains, "the fear produced by threats of pain or punishment is an unpleasant emotion and a powerful motivator of behavior. Not so with psychopaths; they merrily plunge on, perhaps knowing what might happen but not really caring."

From a personal-safety perspective, the disability is clear. But once you understand the importance of affection contagion in social interactions, the implications become downright disturbing. Cult leaders, for instance, prey on people who are easily overwhelmed by their feelings — from abuse survivors to highly sensitive adolescents to adults who've suffered a recent, debilitating loss. The ability to exude calmness, focus, and charisma in situations others find stressful — while telling them whatever they want to hear in a most charming, articulate, intelligent way — is matched by an equally ruthless impulse to whip followers into states of fear and anger whenever they show signs of regaining independent thought and will. With a bit of clever manipulation, a sociopath's impaired autonomic nervous system can also be misinterpreted as evidence of an evolved spiritual presence, one whose love connection with the divine has completely expelled all trace of fear. Perhaps this is why some of the most successful and ultimately *lethal* members of this population manage to secure leadership positions with a religious theme.

Give an emotionally disabled genius enough time, public exposure, and responsibility, and he'll eventually show his true colors by making a colossal mess of things. But how do you tell the difference between a Winston Churchill and an Adolf Hitler early enough to promote the talents of the former and avoid the mayhem of the latter? The answer lies in boosting your own emotional- and social-intelligence quotient as well as the EQ skills of everyone around you. This significant, multigenerational undertaking is the main supportive arch in all the cathedrals we are building. Without it, we'll forever be wasting time, money, and lives on faulty construction and psychopathic acts of terrorism.

Chapter Three

HIDDEN WISDOM

Imagine if a supervisor asked you to complete a project with only 10 percent of the information available to you, if schools were only committed to teaching 10 percent of what you would need to succeed in life. And yet that's precisely what's happening as we overemphasize the spoken and written word in business, education, and relationships. Once we realize that only 10 percent of human interpersonal communication is verbal, we can also recognize that telephone, computer, and text messaging innovations are deceptively seductive tools that *limit* human potential. Excessive dependence on these convenient devices creates voluntary learning disabilities in the realms of emotional and social intelligence that ultimately foster a kind of devolution if left unchecked over generations.

The tendency to treat the body as a machine already has a good four hundred years of history behind it, starting with René Descartes's influential philosophy in the seventeenth century and reaching its apex in the twentieth-century assembly line. Frederick Taylor's famous time-and-motion study technique, for instance, attempted to reach maximum productive efficiency by essentially turning workers into robots. Luckily the same scientific methods that, for a while, promoted a form of "mechanomorphism" in dealing with living beings have recently given us some very good reasons to reconsider the body's innate, richly nuanced intelligence.

In his book *The Other 90%: How to Unlock Your Vast Untapped Potential for Leadership and Life*, Robert K. Cooper actually predicts that the "dinosaurs of the future will be those who keep trying to live and work from their heads alone. Much of human brilliance is driven less by the brain in your head than by newly discovered intelligence centers — now called 'brain two' and brain three' — in the gut and the heart. The highest reasoning and the brightest ingenuity involve all three of those brains working together."

Physiologists now know that there are more neural cells in the gut than in the entire spinal column. As a result, the enteric (intestinal) nervous system can gather information and adapt to the environment. The heart also serves as an organ of perception. "In the 1990s," Cooper reports, "scientists in the field of neurocardiology discovered the true brain in the heart, which acts independently of the head. Comprised of a distinctive set of more than 40,000 nerve cells called baroreceptors, along with a complex network of neurotransmitters, proteins, and support cells, this heart brain is as large as many key areas of the brain in your head. It has powerful, highly sophisticated computational abilities."

"Gut feelings" can no longer be dismissed as whimsical or delusional: both the intestinal track and the heart have been shown to *generate* neuropeptides, molecules carrying emotional information. In this way, the body serves as a magnificent tuner, receiver, and amplifier for all kinds of information. It feels, learns, and has definite opinions that sometimes contradict those of the brain. As author and researcher Dr. Candace Pert asserts, *your body is your subconscious mind*. Imagine the edge, the power and insight, the sheer genius available to those who make this somatic wisdom conscious!

While science is finally embracing this concept, we already have a term for people who tap the wonders of those other two corporeal intelligence centers: we say they have "horse sense." The expression, dating back to the 1800s, refers to sound practical wisdom, a combination of finely tuned awareness, common sense, and gumption. People with horse sense pay attention to that "other 90 percent." They "listen to their gut" as well as their minds when making decisions and really "put their heart into it" once they commit to action. There's also an element of intuition involved, as in: "She's got too much horse sense to believe his story." For this reason, it's often thought of as a mysterious gift that certain lucky people possess from birth.

You *can* develop horse sense at any age, most efficiently through actually working with horses. In fact, it was that first spirited mare who taught me to stand up for myself and read the true intentions of others. I was in my thirties at the time, dealing with an aggressive yet secretive supervisor at the radio station. As I learned to motivate and set boundaries with a thousand-pound being, my two-hundred-pound boss suddenly seemed less intimidating. I not only found that I could effectively challenge unreasonable demands, I gained greater cooperation and respect as a result.

The practical applications were useful, of course. But something even more exciting began to happen. The training my horses provided encouraged me to gaze ever more deeply into the limitations of my own socially conditioned mind, allowing me to glimpse "civilized" human behavior through a wider lens. Staring at historical and current events from this new perspective, I realized that whether I was a left-wing Democrat, a right-wing Republican, a fundamentalist Christian, a radical feminist, a gay-rights advocate, a communist, fascist, creationist, or scientist, my effectiveness in the world was likely to be impaired by the same unconscious habits. Our ancestors had sailed across a potentially hostile ocean to escape the ravages of persecution and tyranny, hoping for a fresh start in the land of the free and the home of the brave, only to build the wildly hopeful structures of democracy on the same faulty foundation of long-buried, largely nonverbal assumptions and behaviors. For this reason, I doubted technology would save us; neither would liberal *or* conservative agendas based on the same worn-out neural pathways meandering through our fearful, body-phobic, increasingly dissociative, egotistical, machine-worshipping heads.

Pioneering Spirit

For thousands of years, people explored the world on horseback, charting territory they would have struggled to traverse on foot, reveling in a primal experience of freedom, strength, and speed so exhilarating that we still measure our most sophisticated engines in units of horsepower. But there was something much more profound happening in those interspecies associations. Learning to form effective, working partnerships with horses provided the most elusive yet important education a human leader could acquire — that "other 90 percent" exercised at a wholly nonverbal level. Now that the entire planet has been mapped, consciousness itself is the new frontier. Twenty-first-century pioneers are looking for ways to tap the vast resources of all three of their brains — those interconnected sensory and intelligence centers in the head, the heart, and the gut. In this respect, horses, once again, provide the ultimate shortcut.

I'm not talking only about developing balance, will, timing, focus, courage, and assertiveness. I'm talking about exercising intersubjective awareness. The fact that few people truly understand what intersubjectivity is explains why we have such a hard time understanding the "mechanics" of relationship and, ultimately, training innovative leaders of all kinds, whether they be CEOs, parents, teachers, or politicians.

In our culture, we prize and overdevelop objectivity, the ability to stand back and observe without affecting, or being affected by, what we are observing. Subjectivity is considered the artist's prerogative. We appreciate people who communicate their feelings, dreams, and views to us in evocative ways. Yet it's really intersubjectivity that we value in a fine work of art, the ability of the artist to depict a truth that we, too, feel deeply but may not have found the right poetry, visual symbol, or music to express. Artists in our culture are worshipped more widely than mystics, because no matter how practical we *think* we are, we're willing to pay good money for songs, films, photographs, books, and paintings that reflect what we crave to understand about deeper layers of nonverbal awareness and experience.

Intersubjectivity has an immensely more practical purpose as well, in daily relationships, in business, and most certainly in cultivating the skills associated with leadership and team building. Basically, intersubjective awareness involves paying attention to your own nonverbal experiences and body language cues and those of the people you're interacting with *at the same time*. It's easier said than done. Most adults, in fact, just aren't very good at this, because the skills associated with intersubjectivity have been seriously neglected in our culture. But when we become conscious of what we're communicating to others nonverbally, and what they're communicating to us nonverbally, a whole new universe of information is suddenly available to us. This information virtually demands that we develop the ability to improvise as we respond and adapt to these subtle cues on our way to achieving any goal.

With modern education overemphasizing intellectual and verbal arts, people who somehow manage to train all three of their "brains" become more influential in, even irresistible to, populations who lack this full-bodied charisma. Take Ronald Reagan, whose firm yet congenial, focused, larger-than-life presence was, in fact, the mark of a rider capable of harnessing power and intelligence without repressing the spirit that brings it to life. He so swayed public opinion that the phenomenon of "Democrats for Reagan" was cited by Barack Obama as an inspiration for cultivating cross-party support.

Photos of Reagan on horseback — heading across the range in any number of old Western movies, mounted on his regal gray Arabian at the ranch, and later, riding English-style with Queen Elizabeth — are plentiful on the Internet. Most people would consider this a colorful, perhaps elitist, pastime. Yet the fact that Reagan *loved* to ride speaks volumes about what kind of intricate, nonverbal training he received that led him to become the noteworthy leader history has since proven him to be.

During the election of 2000, I couldn't help contrasting the former president's engaging presence with the stiff, tentative, overintellectual style of Al Gore, a candidate whose ideas and policies I did, in fact, support in several key areas. While he has since gone on to win the Nobel prize, Gore's demeanor was unduly skewed toward the brain in the head. The "other 90 percent" was missing, at least during his public appearances. Whether or not the election was rigged, the race itself was close. George W. Bush's style of engaging with the public involved a bit more heart and gut, and that gave him a palpable edge in the nonverbal communication department.

Over time, however, the winner of that controversial vote did not demonstrate the level of horse sense that Reagan possessed. The most telling example was Bush's response to the news that New York City's Twin Towers were falling — a response caught on film while he was reading a story to some blissfully unaware schoolchildren. George W. had that deer-in-the-headlights look, which means he wasn't actively creating a calming presence; he was dissociating. Had he slipped into a similarly disconnected state on the back of a panicking horse, he would have ended up on the ground, temporarily unable to remember that he was the president of the United States.

What Would George Washington Do?

At this point it's important, enlightening actually, to appreciate the sophisticated combination of intellectual ability and horse sense possessed by our country's first president. George Washington was a prolific letter writer with progressive views on education and leadership even by today's standards. It wasn't nearly so easy to document his considerable nonverbal talents, of course, but many of his soldiers and colleagues wrote home about him, capturing intriguing anecdotes and observations of his particularly striking effect on others. Washington not only commanded respect, he moved people deeply, inspiring loyalty during periods of extreme hardship, mind-boggling uncertainty, and dramatic change. And he accomplished all of this with a reputation for being a man of few words, at least in public.

When I began studying Washington's career in earnest at the end of 2009, the country he fought so long and hard for was struggling with Wall Street betrayals, record unemployment, fear-mongering pundits, and hostile relations between, sometimes even within, the two political parties. Scared, angry people were burning the current president in effigy over health-care reform, shouting racial slurs, bemoaning the end of civilization itself. Uncompromising red-faced fanatics on both sides of the issue were threatening to move to Canada or Costa Rica if they didn't get their way. Like many people caught in the middle, I was disgusted with the greed, egotism, irresponsibility, manipulation, and extremism running amok in the name of patriotism. To say I was becoming jaded would be an understatement.

And then the spirit of George Washington rode up on his powerful steed. Little-known facts about the man's life captured my imagination, not only invigorating my research on leadership but renewing my faith in the sanity our country's original vision. I was, for a time, filled with such sincere and fervent feelings of patriotism that friends and family members would stare at me wide-eyed, leaning backward, glancing toward the door. "We were cheated by the public school system," I'd declare. "Our naive yet well-meaning teachers were making us memorize dates and names and superficial facts when they could have been teaching us the *process* Washington went through to become the ultimate leader and citizen of a free society. True democracy can't possibly thrive in this country until the abilities that Washington modeled become the rule rather than the exception, not just in politicians, but in the population at large!"

Then I'd practically shout, pounding the dining room table, "This ambitious yet essential goal cannot be achieved exclusively through verbal-oriented education!"

I've since calmed down considerably, but I still believe I was on to something. While my high school history teachers were devising coolly objective multiple-choice tests involving dates like 1776, names like Benedict Arnold, and events like the Boston Tea Party, essential facts about George Washington's true genius were languishing in obscurity, information that would have given me a road map to becoming a more courageous, adaptable, and insightful leader. I would have understood the hardships, mistakes, and betrayals he endured, how he rose above these challenges without losing his heart and soul. I would have glimpsed the power of charisma balanced by integrity and empathy. And perhaps most important, I might have understood the extent to which visionary leadership in particular demands qualities a lot more sophisticated and mysterious than passion, idealism, and a talent for risk management. Innovators charged with transforming society must develop a paradoxical combination of *conviction* and *adaptability*, demonstrating a level of *endurance* so high it's contagious while consciously engaging in the lesser-known, largely nonverbal art of fear management.

The Presence of Power

In the winter of 1777, George Washington somehow inspired a ragged group of soldiers not only to stick around for the Second Battle of Trenton but to actually win it. John Howland, a young private from Rhode Island, lived to tell the story. In an account published fifty-four years after the event, he struggled to remember what the general said but never forgot how it felt to borrow the man's courage.

"Lord Cornwallis was on the march from Princeton with, as it was said, ten thousand men to beat up our quarters," Howland reported, estimating that the "whole army of the United States" at that time was "supposed to amount to about four thousand men." And that wasn't even the worst of the news. The odds were against them in so many other, thoroughly demoralizing ways: "If any fervent mind should doubt this," he emphasized, "it must be from not knowing the state of our few, half-starved, half-frozen, feeble, worn-out men, with old fowling pieces for muskets, and half of them without bayonets, and the States so disheartened, discouraged, or poor, that they sent no reinforcements, no recruits to supply this handful of men."

As the British and their fierce allies, the Hessians, marched on Trenton, New Jersey, from their garrison in Princeton, Howland was one of a thousand troops assigned to delay the enemy's advance through a gutsy attack and retreat/ambush, across Assunpink Creek. "The bridge was narrow," he remembered, "and our platoons were, in passing it, crowded into a dense and solid mass, in the rear of which the enemy were making their best efforts." Yet in that moment of utter confusion and desperation, Howland touched a vision of power, gaining, in the crush of battle, a sense of steadiness, renewal, and awe: "The noble horse of Gen. Washington stood with his breast pressed close against the end of the west rail of the bridge, and the firm, composed, and majestic countenance of the general inspired confidence and assurance in a moment so important and critical. In this passage across the bridge rail, it was my fortune to be next the west rail, and arriving at the end of the bridge, I pressed against the shoulder of the general's horse, and in contact with the general's boot. The horse stood as firm as the rider, and seemed to understand that he was not to quit his post and station."

Washington alone did not create that transformational effect. It was the dedication and poise his mount exhibited that inspired the same in young Howland. Yet to fathom what an outrageous achievement it was for Washington to find and train an animal capable of enduring such a scene, you have to appreciate, first of all, the horror of the sound alone. For thousands of years, warriors fought with swords, spears, and arrows. The Revolutionary War seethed with musket fire and cannon blasts. And something else: "Horses were screaming on the battlefield," historian James Parrish Hodges reminded me during an interview in which we talked about Washington's leadership abilities. Riding a *prey* animal, a vegetarian, a species that much prefers flight over fight, anywhere near the scent of blood — let alone the din of absolute chaos and unmitigated agony — goes against every hardwired impulse the horse possesses. If the general's mount had been a machine programmed for survival, incapable of transcending instinct, such an act would have been impossible. Luckily, the general didn't believe this was true, or he wouldn't have been able to ride the same two trusted equine companions through the entire revolution with the odds stacked against them all, horse and human alike.

"It was a miracle," Hodges says of the colonists' success. "Washington tapped more in his people than they themselves thought they could give." And he never would have lived through the first of those battles if he hadn't inspired similar acts of heroism in his horses. After all, a good twenty years earlier Washington had received a promotion to the rank of colonel when Joshua Fry, commander of the Virginia Regiment during the French and Indian War, had died after falling from his horse.

The Silence of Power

While brief, eyewitness accounts of Washington's impressive riding skills were commonplace, historians past and present have failed to recognize the importance of his distinction as one of the finest horse *trainers* on either side of the Atlantic. To be sure, Thomas Jefferson characterized him as "the best horseman of his age, and the most graceful figure that could be seen on horseback." Yet few politicians and writers at that time understood the equestrian arts well enough to fathom the general's genius in that arena. Our only glimpse comes from the marquis de Chastellux, a French nobleman, military officer, and philosopher who served as liaison between Washington and the French forces that ultimately helped defeat the British during the Siege of Yorktown in 1781. Chastellux published his complete recollections of the American War of Independence five years later, including a description of his subsequent travels through the newly formed United States. Because of his literary talent and acute sense of observation, he produced what are still considered the most vivid descriptions of George Washington as an effective yet profoundly human leader in wartime. A peacetime visit to Mount Vernon gave Chastellux a still deeper understanding of his former comrade in arms.

Two crucial aspects of Washington's life and personality made it difficult for anyone to know him intimately, let alone write about him effectively: his preference for silence over casual conversation and the vast amount of time he spent in the saddle, for business as well as pleasure. As an accomplished equestrian himself, Chastellux was simply able to go where few men had gone before — riding with the Revolutionary War hero, on one of his exquisitely trained horses, no less.

"The weather being fair," Chastellux wrote, "I got on horseback, after breakfasting with the General. He was so attentive as to give me the horse he rode on the day of my arrival, which I had greatly commended. I found him as good as he is handsome, but above all well broke and well trained having a good mouth, easy in hand, and stopping short in a gallop without bearing on the bit. I mention these minute particulars, because it is the General himself who breaks all his own horses, and he is a very excellent and bold horseman, leaping the highest fences, and going extremely quick, without standing upon his stirrups, bearing on the bridle, or letting his horse run wild."

Washington could not have used abusive dominance techniques to create a mount of this caliber. In equestrian terms, he taught the horse to "carry himself" with the utmost grace and responsiveness. The general rode with a light yet persuasive touch, creating an agile, thoughtful partner rather than a dissociative, machinelike mode of transportation. And Chastellux, a man who'd visited the stables of European royalty, was impressed.

In addition to a long-standing, vigorous devotion to horse breeding, racing, and foxhunting (an athletic equestrian sport that involves racing cross-country and leaping over fences with packs of baying hounds), Washington's postwar *and* postpresidency "retirement" routine at Mount Vernon involved rising with the sun and literally rousting many of his own workers. After providing meticulous instructions on a variety of farm tasks and repairs, he ate a light breakfast at seven o'clock and then spent a good six hours in the saddle. In *His Excellency: George Washington*, Joseph J. Ellis describes him riding around the farm, "ordering drainage ditches to be widened, inspecting the operation of a new distillery he had recently commissioned on the premises, warning poachers that the deer on his property had become domesticated and must not be hunted, inquiring after a favored house slave who had recently been bitten by a dog."

What historians consistently fail to mention about his daily schedule (no doubt because Washington himself didn't discuss it much) concerns when and how he trained his horses, who would have needed years of careful development to reach the level of expertise under saddle that Chastellux reported, let alone exhibit the courage under fire Washington's favored war mounts possessed. The general trusted those horses with his life, and they proved worthy of his confidence in so many subtle yet remarkable ways. When he returned to the mansion around two o'clock each afternoon, Ellis reveals, "no one needed to take the reins off his horse. Washington simply slapped him on the backside and he trotted over to the barn on his own. (Horses like men, seemed disposed to acknowledge his authority.)"

That authority rested to a great extent on Washington's instinctual understanding of the leader's role as educator rather than dictator. He *cultivated* trust, courage, and devotion as much as he commanded it. It's a crying shame he didn't write a book on horse training, but the art form, being almost exclusively nonverbal, probably eluded his efforts to describe it in the brief journal entries he had time to record at the end of the day. Washington was too busy building an agricultural empire at Mount Vernon, fighting a revolutionary war, and negotiating the parameters of the very first U.S. presidency. Still, his success in all of those realms was without a doubt tied to his profound mastery of the human-equine relationship. As Thomas Jefferson later complained when he and Washington became political rivals, the persistent image of the elder statesman on horseback always seemed to trump the most eloquent speeches and persuasive intellectual arguments anyone else devised in opposition. Without saying a word, the man radiated dignity and power.

And there was no arguing with him. Not because he wouldn't listen — Ellis describes a crucial element of his presidential style as "leading by listening." He'd spend hours, even days, letting people speak their piece, sometimes to the chagrin of younger, more action-oriented members of his entourage. Once he considered the options and came to a strong conclusion, however, he had no problem herding large groups of people around with the infectious combination of poise, courage, energy, and conviction he exhibited in launching his twelve-hundred-pound war charger into a bloody battle with a thousand shoeless, half-dressed men running behind him.

This frustrated intellectually based idealists like Jefferson and James Madison to no end. The fact that Washington didn't talk a whole lot made them even crazier. As Ellis observes, "He possessed a nearly preternatural ability to remain silent while everyone around him was squirming under the social pressure to fill the silence with chatty conversation. ([John] Adams later claimed that this 'gift of silence' was Washington's greatest political asset, which Adams himself so envied because he lacked the gift altogether.)"

Washington's influence would forever remain a mystery to men with little horse sense, men who sat in chairs debating ideas while their colleague became "first in war and first in peace," literally riding through the richly nuanced, wholly nonverbal realms of that crucial "other 90 percent."

Empathy and Equality

As civilization progressed toward the Age of Reason, it became increasingly out of fashion, taboo even, for people to acknowledge animals as sentient beings, let alone companions, colleagues, or, heaven forbid, influences on human leadership potential. Add to this Washington's own penchant for keeping his feelings and thoughts under wraps until he was ready to make an official public statement on the many controversial topics of the day, and you begin to understand why little is written about the relationship he had with his most loyal and revered equine companions Old Nelson and Blueskin. At a time when most horses were not afforded palliative care, the fact that Washington's mounts were well nourished in retirement speaks volumes about how highly our first president regarded these four-legged war heroes.

In 1795, John Hunter, an English visitor to Mount Vernon, made the following casual yet telling observation in a letter to a friend:

> When dinner was over, we visited the General's stables, saw his magnificent horses, among them "Old Nelson," now twenty-two years of age, that carried the General almost always during the war. "Blueskin," another fine old horse, next to him, had that honor. They had heard the roaring of many a cannon in their time. "Blueskin" was not the favorite on account of his not standing fire so well as venerable "Old Nelson." The General makes no manner of use of them now. He keeps them in a nice stable, where they feed away at their ease for their past services.

This brief glimpse illuminates subtle yet important elements of Washington's philosophy. As he matured, his immense powers of influence, courage, endurance, and motivation were enhanced by an ever-widening, ever-deepening sense of compassion and appreciation for the contributions of others that crossed cultural, racial, and species boundaries. In Washington's world, respect for the *intelligence* of all life trumped concern for social norms and historical precedent, manifesting as a sort of empathy-in-action capable of sensing and tapping potential in unexpected places. Short-term gain became increasingly subservient to long-term goals, in terms of not just profit but also behavior, as Washington actively modeled how members of a free society would be expected to treat their colleagues *and* subordinates, even those who currently ranked as enemies or possessions.

Most soldiers and farmers, after all, considered a bullet to the head a humane, economically prudent way to retire an arthritic workhorse. Yet Washington's very survival during the war depended on choosing the best horse for the job, relying on that one animal in a million whose capacity for heroism matched his own. Seeing his prospective mounts as interchangeable machines to be used and discarded without conscience could actually have been fatal.

During the Battle of Monmouth Court House, for instance, his second in command, Charles Lee, panicked and began to lead a frantic retreat against firmly expressed orders. Washington relieved the man on the spot. Then, as Ellis observes, he rallied his troops to attack on more favorable terrain "while calmly sitting astride his horse in the midst of a blistering British artillery barrage." Old Nelson showed more courage and poise under fire than a highly experienced senior general like Lee, and Washington treated his loyal charger as an equine officer worthy of reward for exceptional service.

From there, the general's attitude toward "Negro slaves," "Indian savages," and the uneducated, often destitute immigrants who became his soldiers evolved as well. People who showed real talent, integrity, courage, and dedication were given positions of responsibility acknowledging their gifts and experience, regardless of race, religion, or social standing. Washington's valet, a slave named Billy Lee (no relation to the aforementioned senior general), assumed command of the servants and valets for all Washington's officers during the very same Battle of Monmouth Court House, leading them on horseback to safer positions behind the action. An exceptional rider himself, Lee also served as Washington's huntsman during peacetime fox hunts. In his memoirs, Washington's stepgrandson George Washington Parke Custis described Lee's formidable skills: "Will, the huntsman, better known in Revolutionary lore as Billy, rode a horse called *Chinkling*, a surprising leaper, and made very much like its rider, low, but sturdy, and of great bone and muscle. Will had but one order, which was to keep with the hounds; and, mounted on *Chinkling*...this fearless horseman would rush, at full speed, through brake or tangled wood, in a style at which modern huntsmen would stand aghast."

Lee had no trouble keeping up with Washington throughout the eight-year war, ready to hand over a spare horse or telescope in the thick of battle, facing every major threat, enduring the incredible hardships at Valley Forge, and enjoying the fruits of victory, including, eventually, his own freedom. Revolutionary War veterans visiting Mount Vernon often stopped by to reminisce with Lee, who was, in later years, disabled by a serious knee injury and fitted with a brace. While the formerly spirited, athletic man dealt with the physical and emotional pain through increasing alcoholism, his contribution was never forgotten. Washington's will provided him a stipend of thirty dollars a year and the option of remaining at Mount Vernon if he chose. Billy Lee lived the rest of his life as a free man on his former master's lush estate.

Washington's expanded view of human dignity and potential did not weaken his resolve to get the job done, however. High-born dilettantes who entered the war to make a name for themselves were given several chances to prove their worthiness — and unceremoniously relieved if they showed up lacking. This, of course, made Washington a controversial character at times, costing him considerable popularity among certain members of the upper classes. Still, he had no qualms about dismissing General Charles Lee (who had friends in high places and an inflated sense of his own importance) after the Monmouth Court House incident. Further acts of insubordination led to Lee's court-martial — and a certain amount of trouble for Washington to enforce it. Still, he managed to amass and train a multiracial, multicultural force of soldiers with the sheer nerve to achieve the impossible. Long before he ever took office, America's first president demonstrated, daily, the practical benefits of equality. It's doubtful he would have won the high-stakes War of Independence without such a radical sense of it.

Policy of Humanity

Of all the miraculous feats Washington performed during the war, surviving it was certainly one of them (considering his willingness to plunge headlong into the thick of battle, let alone lead such a seemingly lost cause to begin with). Even so, his ability to inspire others to transcend justified, deeply ingrained human impulses stands out as his greatest achievement. Hoping to quash any signs of rebellion, British soldiers had been systematically traumatizing the entire country, creating opportunities for the more sadistic members of their ranks to exercise their darkest instincts. King George's edict to provide "no quarter" to American troops must have been hard for some of his own men to stomach, however: Regulars and mercenaries were severely punished if they showed mercy to surrendering revolutionaries. Most colonial soldiers were killed on the spot as a result, though some were tortured, starved, and mistreated aboard prison ships.

Washington's troops, then, had good reason to exact revenge when the opportunity arose. Yet with the first major American victory came a wholly unexpected demand they do the exact opposite. Washington not only spared the lives of a thousand Hessians captured during the Battle of Trenton, he literally marched them toward the promise of a new life. "Treat them with humanity," he wrote in orders handed down to all his officers, "and let them have no reason to Complain of our Copying the brutal example of the British Army in their treatment of our unfortunate brethren.... Provide everything necessary for them on the road."

Through this extraordinary, thoroughly unprecedented move, Washington instilled tremendous self-control, and more than a hint of compassion, in his men. As James Parrish Hodges observed in *Beyond the Cherry Tree: The Leadership Wisdom of George Washington*, his reasons were both practical and idealistic. By introducing what John Adams later called a "policy of humanity," Washington was protecting his own soldiers, hoping the British might reciprocate in future altercations, if only to trade colonial troops for valued officers. He also correctly assumed that some of the Hessians might desert their cruel taskmasters and join the American cause. To encourage them, he "marched the prisoners through the German villages in Pennsylvania so they could see how prosperous their former countrymen were." Over time, Congress officially recognized the respectful treatment of enemy combatants as a *strategic advantage* that also exemplified the goals of the American Revolution.

"We were fighting for the rights of ordinary people," Hodges emphasized. By showing mercy when the British insisted on giving no quarter to his own troops, Washington set an example for the world, manifesting a new dream, a new way of being. The *experience* of the ideal profoundly affected his very first prisoners of war. Hodges reports that "about 40 percent of the Hessians stayed outright or went back to Germany, got their families, and came back over." As a result, Washington's eloquence of action demonstrated what Abraham Lincoln later so eloquently described in words: "I destroy my enemies when I make them my friends."

British leaders eventually conceded the negative effects of their own institutionalized cruelty. In 1778, Colonel Charles Stuart wrote to his father, the Earl of Bute: "Wherever our armies have marched, wherever they have encamped, every species of barbarity has been executed. We planted an irrevocable hatred wherever we went, which neither time nor measure will be able to eradicate."

Robert F. Kennedy Jr. observed in a 2005 *Los Angeles Times* editorial:

> In the end, our founding fathers not only protected our national values, they defeated a militarily superior enemy. Indeed, it was their disciplined adherence to those values that helped them win a hopeless struggle against the best soldiers in Europe.

In accordance with this proud American tradition, President Lincoln instituted the first formal code of conduct for the humane treatment of prisoners of war in 1863. Lincoln's order forbade any form of torture or cruelty, and it became the model for the 1929 Geneva Convention. Dwight Eisenhower made a point to guarantee exemplary treatment to German POWs in World War II, and Gen. Douglas MacArthur ordered application of the Geneva Convention during the Korean War, even though the U.S. was not yet a signatory. In the Vietnam War, the United States extended the convention's protection to Viet Cong prisoners even though the law did not technically require it.

The very fact that Kennedy had to write an article opposing torture in the twenty-first century shows how easy it is for people to slide back into old habits. But if scenes of American soldiers waterboarding suspected terrorists and humiliating naked Iraqi prisoners would have saddened Washington, recent acts of corporate greed would have inflamed his legendary temper. After all, when you consider that Washington fought the entire Revolutionary War *as a volunteer* — and I mean he literally did not collect a salary during the eight years he dodged artillery fire on horseback and begged for funds to feed and clothe his soldiers — well, you begin to understand how rarely the entrepreneurs and politicians who most profited from his efforts have bothered to follow his example.

And it is here, curiously enough, that Washington's long and varied career offers yet another revolutionary example, one of hope that people can actively change their ways despite aggressive personality traits and egregious past transgressions. In this respect, his horses may have provided the ultimate nonverbal education in the counterintuitive benefits of *nonpredatory* power.

Chapter Four

REVOLUTION AND EVOLUTION

George Washington's mother was an enigma: a true maverick, a pistol, a tough cookie, an *inconvenient* woman. Though well schooled in the genteel social graces demanded of a wealthy officer's daughter, she also knew how to shoot a gun, manage a boat, and, most exceptional for a woman of her era, train a horse.

An accomplished rider in her teens, Mary Ball dodged marriage until the ripe old age of twenty-three, when she became the second wife of a successful Virginia tobacco planter, sheriff, and politician. During Augustine Washington's frequent business trips, she proved capable of running one of his extensive properties, a seven-hundred-acre operation near Fredericksburg later known as Ferry Farm. Unlike most plantation wives, she refused to hire an overseer to help her. So when Augustine died in 1743, he left his wife in charge — until their eleven-year-old son, George, came of age to claim his inheritance or Mary found a new husband, whichever came first. Augustine's will specified that his widow would remain custodian of the farm until she remarried; at that point the man of the house would take over, as was customary in the 1700s. Many biographers believe she rebuffed all subsequent suitors to maintain her position.

By her midthirties, Mary Ball Washington cut a proud and imposing figure — backed by an unspoken power that people found unnerving. "She awed me in the midst of her kindness, for she was, indeed, truly kind," George's cousin Lawrence Washington marveled later in life, noting that he had been "ten times more afraid" of his aunt than of his own parents. "I could not behold that majestic woman without feelings impossible to describe.... Whoever has seen that awe-inspiring air and manner so characteristic of the Father of his Country, will remember the matron as she appeared when the presiding genius of her well-ordered household, commanding and being obeyed."

Mary's ability to protect her interests, voice her opinions, and run the plantation as she saw fit led to her subsequent reputation as a difficult woman. Modern historians, however, are more likely to see her as a strong, independent matriarch intelligent and assertive enough to nurture the untapped potential of a future war hero, entrepreneur, and statesman. Her enthusiasm for riding was pivotal, not only in exercising her son's nonverbal leadership abilities but also in exposing him to a rare yet influential phenomenon: a responsible, highly effective *feminine* approach to power. Long after George officially claimed his inheritance, she maintained an active role at the farm until she moved to a nearby townhouse at age sixty-four. (Augustine's son by a previous marriage, also named Lawrence, inherited the now-more-famous Mount Vernon, which became George's preferred home base after his beloved half-brother and role model succumbed to tuberculosis at age thirty-four.)

Reports of Mary's willfulness and short temper, especially later in life, reveal the ongoing frustration of a woman who knew that, no matter how accomplished and successful she became, she would always be a second-class citizen. Like the status of the slaves she oversaw at Ferry Farm, Mary's status was not changed by a Declaration of Independence declaring all *men* created equal. Her legendary crankiness, sometimes directed at her increasingly influential son, stemmed from an unsettling combination of pride in George's accomplishments and jealousy of the opportunities afforded him, especially when she had to ask *him* for money. The farm she so diligently managed for decades, after all, was never hers.

Still, Mary was truly revolutionary for her time. Historically, men rode, trained, and cared for horses. Women were more likely to travel in carriages. It wasn't until the nineteenth century that a modest but growing number of women began to exhibit some equestrian talent, at first mostly among the upper classes and usually riding sidesaddle. Joan of Arc, Katherine the Great, and Elizabeth I were rare exceptions. So was Mary Ball Washington, a fine rider who some historians believe taught her son how to train horses with a gentler touch. Though reliable documentation is sketchy, we do know that by the age of eighteen she owned three fine mounts, and she raised a number of feisty horses at Ferry Farm, including a sorrel colt that met an unfortunate end at the hands of her ambitious teenage son.

As the story goes, George was hell-bent on emulating Alexander the Great in his legendary horse-taming abilities. Knowing his mother would disapprove of rash and dangerous "training" techniques, he led the spirited, unschooled colt to an undisclosed location and attempted to ride the bucks out of him, cowboy-style. According to Marion Harland's 1893 book *The Story of Mary Washington*, "The experiment ended with the death of the fiery horse, who broke a blood-vessel in a futile attempt to dislodge the lad from his back."

It was Mary Ball Washington, not a farmhand or one of her son's older half-brothers, who subsequently noticed that the horse was missing. And, in a decidedly tragic, equestrian take on the old cherry tree story, George could not tell a lie. Harland reports that he admitted the facts "promptly and squarely. The widow struggled for a second with the temper she had not lost in passing it down to her child, then replied to the effect that she was sorry the horse was dead, but glad that her boy had spoken the truth."

Young George learned a grievous lesson that day — namely, that flashy, quick-fix dominance tactics end in destruction as often as glory — and that his own mother might very well know more about horse training than he did. Dealing with this strong-willed, cultured, fair-minded woman, he developed a respect for women as worthy companions and confidants, a then-unique perspective that would inform his marriage and his morale-boosting strategies at Valley Forge decades later. Washington also honed an ever-more-sophisticated version of his mother's awe-inspiring presence, most notably her ability to convey power, kindness, and integrity simultaneously. Developing that particular combination is common among expert riders. The proudest, most athletic horses seem to demand it.

When George accepted his first officer's commission at age twenty-two, against his mother's wishes, no less, Mary Ball Washington's independent streak, idealism, lucid problem-solving skills, and uncompromising morals were also well entrenched in her son, qualities that would be continuously challenged, and ultimately strengthened, through the unexpected, perplexing, sometimes truly horrific battles to come.

Half King

No matter how seemingly just the cause, war unearths labyrinths of trauma. Unrelated conflicts and tragedies from the distant past can affect the trajectory of current events in unexpected ways as human behavior becomes a minefield of opportunistic reactions to ancient pain.

George Washington learned this the hard way during his first tour of duty. In April 1754, the successful land surveyor and frontiersman gained a position as lieutenant colonel in the Virginia Regiment. Charged with leading 160 troops to help protect settlers in the Ohio Country, he inadvertently found himself exchanging the first shots in what later became known as the French and Indian War.

What seemed a straightforward mission — securing a strategic location where the Ohio Company, a land speculation company, was constructing a fort — turned into an unexpected conundrum when Washington trekked over the Allegheny Mountains, only to discover that more than a thousand French soldiers had already seized the half-built complex, renaming it Fort Duquesne. Alliances between French forces and various Indian tribes were already forming, and Washington's own closest Indian ally, Tanacharison, was frantically requesting support.

Known as the Half King to local settlers, the fierce warrior chief spoke fluent French. Still, he had good reason to mistrust the Duquesne contingent. As a boy, he'd been taken captive by the French, and while he was later adopted by the Seneca tribe, his early trials had become legendary in the region. Now in his midfifties, Tanacharison openly claimed that the Frenchmen who decimated his family had callously boiled and eaten his father during that tragic childhood encounter.

Washington was in a difficult position, fortless and vastly outnumbered to be sure. Still, what twenty-two-year-old officer could be expected to predict, let alone prevent, the additional havoc wreaked by an older, more experienced warrior's toxic past? A thousand foreign troops turned out to be the least of his worries as Washington christened his nascent military career with a most dubious distinction: within weeks, he would be praised and vilified on both sides of the Atlantic for overseeing a massacre.

The young lieutenant colonel's initial strategy seemed reasonable enough. He directed his men to build a makeshift fort near Tanacharison's camp, rallying whatever Indian allies they could find while waiting for reinforcements. Things quickly got out of hand, however, when the Half King rode up to warn him of a French patrol in the vicinity. On the morning of May 28, a combined force of colonial troops under Washington and a group of Indian allies led by Tanacharison surrounded thirty-two French soldiers encamped in a nearby forest glen.

Shots were fired. Though eyewitness accounts vary regarding which side actually started the skirmish, the French eventually realized they were outgunned and tried to surrender. Wounded yet lucid, their commander, Joseph Coulon de Villiers, sieur de Jumonville, insisted he'd come on a diplomatic mission representing King Louis XV.

Jumonville's motives were certainly suspect. After all, the French had just challenged English claims on the region by capturing Fort Prince George and renaming it Fort Duquesne. Even so, Washington was reportedly listening to the foreign officer's words, trying to decipher his intent through translation, when Tanacharison, who fully grasped the Frenchman's plea for peaceful resolution, walked over to where Jumonville lay. "Thou art not yet dead, my father," the Half King declared in French. Then he raised his hatchet, split the man's skull open, grabbed hold of his brain, and washed his hands in the blood-soaked carnage. Washington and his troops watched in horror as Tanacharison's warriors proceeded to scalp the remaining members of Jumonville's party, decapitating one and raising his head on a stake.

The Frenchmen who had slaughtered the Half King's father a half century earlier were long since dead and buried. Though they may very well have been criminals — rogue settlers running amok through the American outback — Jumonville paid dearly for their cruel actions, and his men were tacked on as interest. From that day forward, Washington had to wonder what other hidden debts were accruing in the minds and hearts of people he might encounter. After all, it was only a matter of time before he counted the French among his allies as the British challenged a colonial bid for greater freedom and prosperity.

Throughout the American Revolution, Washington was consciously trying to minimize the impact of the war, not only through the humane treatment of enemy captives but also by guarding the rights and property of nearby civilians, regardless of their shifting loyalties and mercenary efforts to profit from the war. In this undertaking, his *emotional* heroism was arguably more impressive than all of his battle strategies and courageous acts combined.

Test of Will

Valley Forge, a name synonymous with triumph over suffering, initially appeared to be a good location for winter encampment. With British troops comfortably occupying Philadelphia in December 1777, this nearby Pennsylvania town provided a strategic location, plenty of wood for warmth and cabin construction, and (theoretically) ample food supplies for American soldiers. The problem was that local farmers found it much more lucrative to sell their goods to the king's forces twenty miles away than to the shivering, shoeless, shirtless, blanketless troops under Washington's command. Not only did the Continental Congress have trouble raising funds voluntarily from the states, but its currency was depreciating, no match for the well-funded British, who paid in solid pounds sterling.

Washington had to concede that patriotic fervor was a fair-weather phenomenon. Regardless of the odds, many colonials had expected a fast and furious victory. After two years of conflict — with no clear winner in sight — revolutionaries were transforming into political fence-sitters faster than anyone had anticipated, and a dense fog of cynical self-interest was settling over the countryside.

In *Washington: A Life*, Ron Chernow sums up Washington's disappointment and outrage, illustrating that the general could, in fact, express himself effectively when the spirit moved him:

> Seeing the decay of public virtue everywhere, he berated speculators, monopolists, and war profiteers. "Is the paltry consideration of a little dirty pelf to individuals to be placed in competition with the essential rights and liberties of the present generation and of millions yet unborn?" he asked James Warren. "…And shall we at last become the victims of our own abominable lust of gain? Forbid it heaven!" Washington himself could be a hard-driving businessman, yet he found the rapacity of many vendors unconscionable. As he told George Mason, he thought it the intent of "the speculators — various tribes of money makers — and stock jobbers of all denominations to continue the war for their own private emolument, without considering that their avarice and thirst for gain must plunge everything…in one common ruin."

Washington's strong words fell on deaf ears. Efforts to shame fiscal predators, no matter how eloquently those justifiable sentiments were conveyed, did not save the day as men continued to die from starvation, disease, and exposure to the cold. The dream of freedom was kept alive that winter by Washington's own ability to endure one demoralizing scene after another. While letters reveal that he felt incredible anguish and despair at times, he continued to inspire those who were suffering for the cause.

Based on historical writings alone, Chernow finds it "astonishing" that the army didn't "disintegrate or revolt en masse." He remarks that he can only explain Washington's success by emphasizing, once again, that the Revolutionary War hero

> projected leadership in nonverbal ways that are hard for posterity to recreate. Even contemporaries found it difficult to convey the essence of his calm grandeur. "I cannot describe the impression that the first sight of that great man made upon me," said one Frenchman. "I could not keep my eyes from that imposing countenance: grave yet not severe; affable without familiarity. Its predominant expression was calm dignity, through which you could trace the strong feelings of the patriot and discern the father as well as the commander of his soldiers."

Fierce Sensitivity

As I pored over numerous books and colonial-era documents, looking for clues to Washington's extraordinary presence in the patterns of his actions, it struck me that his unique combination of fierceness, fairness, and compassion kept the troops together at Valley Forge and beyond. The general didn't coddle deserters or looters, ordering severe floggings of men caught stealing food. On rare occasions during his tenure, he executed soldiers planning widespread revolt. And finally, after months of tolerating profiteering by local farmers and merchants, hoping to resurrect their failing patriotic instincts, he allowed Nathanael Greene (considered one of the Continental army's most gifted officers) to organize a regional confiscation of all cattle and sheep fit for slaughter. Washington found this option innately reprehensible, however. He gave the order to forcibly obtain food for his starving troops only after two thousand men had perished not in battle but through widespread neglect from Americans who had charged him with raising an army in the first place.

And yet Washington never sacrificed empathy for effectiveness. Letters to trusted allies, friends, and family members reveal that he *felt* the plight of soldiers and settlers he encountered. "I see their situation, *know* their danger, and participate in their *sufferings* without having it in my power to give them further relief than uncertain promises," he had written earlier to British superiors, in 1756, asking for assistance during the French and Indian War. "The supplicating tears of the women and moving petitions from the men melt me into such deadly sorrow that I solemnly declare, if I know my own mind, I could offer myself a willing sacrifice to the butchering enemy, provided that it would contribute to the people's ease."

Martyring himself might have been an easier, seemingly courageous, though grossly less effective, option: the fear-management and emotional-resilience skills he mastered in hopeless situations ultimately gave him a razor-thin edge to win the most important battle of all, the War of Independence. Luckily for posterity's sake, Washington's talent for survival won out, allowing him to further develop the no doubt painful, eternally frustrating skill of appealing to the upper classes on both sides of the Atlantic for help through numerous conflicts to come.

Though he was able to renew himself in Mount Vernon's pastoral embrace after the French and Indian War, rest and success did not make him complacent. As Washington repeatedly reentered public life, supporting one desperate cause after another, the turmoil he endured *voluntarily* is truly staggering. Rather than shield his heart against the disappointment, anguish, and sheer horror he witnessed, Washington remained steady and thoughtful in the midst of feelings that would have short-circuited the average person's nervous system. His was not the coolness of the sociopath who felt no fear, but the authentic, hard-won calmness of a man whose emotional stamina was so great that he was willing to accompany people into the depths of despair, and *stay with them*, offering hope through sheer presence *because he had been there before and had come out the other side*. After all, by the time the Revolutionary War erupted, Washington was living proof that personal and professional tragedy could be accompanied by loyalty, love, and prosperity, that a brave, openhearted man could ride life's roller coaster with gusto — and even find a mate willing to share the journey.

In the dismal winter of 1777–78, he stayed, once again, with a group of brave though impoverished, weary souls at Valley Forge, doing what little he could to ease the pain of an impossible situation. The British were comfortably settled in Philadelphia with their servants and mistresses, their warm fires, soft beds, and silver place settings, waiting until spring to take up arms and finally quash that troublesome little colonial rebellion once and for all.

Washington was fronting his own money for war expenses and struggling to keep his plantation financially viable from a distance during a dangerous economic climate. His wife, Martha, was grieving the recent loss of her sister and one of her closest friends as the couple's second grandchild arrived on New Year's Eve. For a woman who'd already lost three of her own four children — one at age three, another at four, and most recently, a seventeen-year-old daughter who died from a violent epileptic seizure — birth was not a light and carefree occasion but a cause for continued hypervigilance. Washington could have delegated authority during the break in combat and gone home for a few weeks. Still, the general must have known that he possessed an extra "something" crucial to keeping the army together at Valley Forge. He deferred a much-needed, thoroughly justified trip to Mount Vernon and sent for his wife.

True Grit

Here's what you need to know about Martha Washington: she was one of the Revolution's secret weapons. The general hadn't called for his spouse exclusively because he was worried about her. He was enlisting the support of his most trusted confidant at a time when his considerable physical and psychological resources were taxed to the limit. And, as numerous historians have emphasized, he just plain missed her, terribly. As Chernow reports, "He pined for her presence" when family obligations delayed her trip to Valley Forge that winter.

If the long carriage ride on bumpy, frozen roads didn't exhaust her completely, what Martha saw upon arrival at this legendary encampment must have chilled her to the bone. Though she had visited her husband at previous military installations, she was visibly taken aback by his humble quarters. What's more, the general had lost his baggage a few months earlier, including his kitchen utensils, managing to hang on to a single spoon. But it was his haggard face and deeply troubled demeanor that unnerved her the most. "I never knew him to be so anxious as now," she confided to a friend.

Long after the war, the historic image of Martha as a dowdy, genteel grandmother comforted populations craving a benevolent and benign parental figure, but to the Revolutionary War general, she was a vital source of quiet power, empathy, practical wisdom, and stamina. "Not enough historians have recognized the importance of this portly, affable woman in George Washington's life," notes Thomas Fleming in *Washington's Secret War: The Hidden History of Valley Forge*. Her stalwart dedication to the cause in general — and to his well-being in particular — provided a crucial boost to the entire army's morale. As one admiring Frenchman put it, "She well deserved to be the companion and friend of the greatest man of the age."

These days it's common, and considered understandable, for couples to divorce under the pressure of losing a child or going off to war. What allowed George and Martha to face a relentless series of tragedies and continually jump back into the fray, together, literally betting the farm and their very lives on the slimmest possible chance for success — even when the vast majority of people around them were complacently standing by or unabashedly profiting from human misery?

We'll never really know enough about their relationship to answer that question definitively. Honoring her husband's request, Martha destroyed the vast majority of George's letters to her after his death, suggesting their correspondence revealed some painful, potentially embarrassing material, perhaps some rants and moments of indecision that could be taken out of context. But oh how valuable that information would have been in understanding the interpersonal difficulties they faced, the mistakes they made, and the complex emotional challenges they surmounted. For the eighteenth century, George's reliance on his wife as a confidant was unusual. Equally noteworthy was Martha's own leadership experience.

Even by modern standards, the couple exhibited an unusually high level of mutual respect and teamwork. Certain commonalities in personality and background suggest this was no accident: Neither George nor Martha went to college, yet both continually educated themselves. Both also possessed a strong work ethic as they managed the intricacies of several plantations together. An affluent, attractive widow at twenty-seven, Martha Dandridge Custis had clearly been a catch for ambitious young Colonel Washington when they'd married in 1759, but she was no dilettante. Her first husband had died two years earlier, leaving her in charge of a large working agricultural estate. A biographical sketch of her by the National First Ladies' Library reveals that "evidence of her business acumen in the lucrative tobacco trade is found in letters she wrote to the London merchants who handled the exporting of the large Custis crop output." Though Martha had been trained at home in music, sewing, and household management, the knowledge she later acquired in plantation management, homeopathic medicine, and animal husbandry "suggests a wider education than previously thought."

When she joined forces with her second husband, Washington, the responsibilities grew, exponentially. "With her extremely large inheritance of land from the Custis estate and the vast farming enterprise at Mount Vernon, Martha Washington spent considerable time directing the large staff of slaves and servants. While George Washington oversaw all financial transactions related to the plantation, Martha Washington was responsible for the not insubstantial process of harvesting, preparing, and preserving herbs, vegetables, fruits, meats, and dairy for medicines, household products and foods needed for those who lived at Mount Vernon, relatives, slaves and servants — as well as long-staying visitors."

So while Valley Forge was certainly no vacation, Martha's own sense of responsibility, her tenacity, and her problem-solving skills were already well established. "I never in my life knew a woman so busy from early morning until late at night as was Lady Washington," one wartime observer wrote, noting that she organized "the wives of the officers in camp, and sometimes other women" in offering various forms of assistance. (The extreme conditions at Valley Forge were endured that winter by more than five hundred women, mostly wives and sisters of the soldiers. Prostitutes were less common than most people suspect — an army lacking funds for food and clothing deferred salaries as well; hence no discretionary funds for extracurricular activities.)

A coddled, dominated woman could never have provided the fearless companionship and flexible, good-natured, activism on demand that Martha showed at Valley Forge. A spicy mistress could have relieved a bit of tension, but a man in Washington's increasingly tenuous position needed his own advanced emotional support system, someone with the nerve to face the truth of a situation while remaining centered enough to help him explore all the options, someone who was more concerned with the long-term, greater good of a project than with revenge, comfort, or obsessive social climbing. Martha's significant wealth and business experience were also balanced by humility and devotion. As the marquis de Lafayette revealed, she was a "modest and respectable" woman, who loved her husband "madly." That combination ensured she would travel to the ends of the earth for her heroic mate — as an asset, not a clingy, fawning fan.

Authentic Power

Historians often marvel that, despite ultimate victory in the American Revolution, Washington actually lost more battles than he won. In *His Excellency*, Ellis contends that "especially in the early stages of the war" the general's "defeats were frequently a function of his overconfident and aggressive personality." Close associates reported that they could feel him wrestling with strong emotions, a battle he sometimes lost in private displays of anger and frustration, suggesting that his legendary composure and patience were hard won.

Experts also agree that Washington had a rare talent for learning from his mistakes. When something went wrong, he didn't waste a lot of time and energy defending himself. According to Chernow, he "never walled himself off from contrary opinion or tried to force his views on his generals." He analyzed the situation, researched new options, and revised his approach, sometimes modifying his own beliefs, even altering long-entrenched personal habits that had been clearly beneficial in previous contexts. In this respect, his horse-training experience gave him a palpable edge. Throughout his life, Washington continued to refine his own potent instincts as deftly and methodically as he schooled the most volatile of stallions.

In *Dressage in the Fourth Dimension*, horse trainer Sherry Ackerman emphasizes that when both horse and rider exhibit self-mastery *and* responsiveness, their combined genius becomes fluid and adaptable. Even standing still, an expertly trained mount radiates power and suppleness as "the halt, in immobility, contains the energy of every movement. The horse is catlike, ready to spring from soft-jointed hindquarters through his coiled loins. As long as we do not disturb the collection, he remains prepared — powerfully positioned — for instantaneous movement in any direction, at any gait."

Collection is an important term in the equestrian arts. Technically, it means the horse is channeling his strength in an optimal way, not splaying his energy outward in a compulsive, uncoordinated fashion. When his neck is arched and his rear legs are positioned well under his body, his center of gravity moves toward the hindquarters, rounding and releasing his spine, allowing him to collect his power: to compress it like a metal spring, hold it, gather it, focus it, and release it purposefully. From this position, he can just as easily rear, move sideways, leap forward into a vigorous gallop, or quietly, artfully step backward.

In nature, a stallion wooing a mare will collect his energy to engage in dancelike movements that would be impossible to perform if he let his passion run wild. A well-educated saddle horse further develops this ability, combining increasing control of his own body and emotions with a finely tuned awareness of the rider's intentions, interpreting subtle weight shifts as meaningful communication. Serious equestrians uphold their end of the bargain by developing an "independent seat," meaning they're able to balance on a moving horse no matter what he does, directing that force toward a specific goal while continually adjusting to unexpected movements — without pulling on the reins, gripping with their legs, or hanging on to the saddle for support. Under the tutelage of a great trainer, each horse is carefully conditioned to increase the *impulsion* needed to realize his full athletic potential — while continuing to remain sound over time. (Rushing the process can cause injury.)

"Impulsion is a power surge that doesn't have anything to do with speed," trainer Ron Meredith reveals. "It means the horse is pushing more powerfully with his muscles, not moving them faster so he gives you more strides." The president of Meredith Manor International Equestrian Centre insists that "impulsion does not have anything to do with excitement, either. You don't use louder, more exciting aids to create excitement in the horse in hopes of getting impulsion. If you raise the horse's excitement level, then what you get is a horse that feels excited rather than one that feels the shape his rider is asking him to take."

Modulating power, centering and socializing it, is the equestrian's art, one requiring equal parts courage and thoughtfulness. The most talented colt is often the most explosive in the initial stages of training and can easily be mishandled as a result. When he rears or bolts out of fear, it's counterproductive to punish him, let alone try to shame him for misbehavior. The trainer simply shows her four-legged student a more effective alternative, a way to balance and focus his magnificent vitality, sensitivity, and energy. A mature, perceptive rider can tell the difference between her mount's confusion, apprehension, and aggression. In the latter case, correction is swift and appropriate. For instance, if the horse tries to bite his trainer, she might hold up her elbow so that his use of force meets a more pointed, unpleasant force in response. If he tries to bite again, she will up the ante, showing that she's fully capable of setting boundaries and protecting herself. The key, however, lies in her ability to move forward without resentment. When a defiant horse shows the slightest inclination toward cooperation, she calmly proceeds with the lesson, unruffled by the momentary interruption.

Inexperienced equestrians often mistake a stress response for an attack, needlessly escalating the situation. Violently punishing a frightened or frustrated horse *raises* his blood pressure, accentuating the flight-or-fight response, causing him to act out more dramatically. Immature trainers also tend to hold grudges, treating the horse as innately stupid or arrogant. This hopelessly critical attitude, reinforced by defensive, mistrustful posturing, virtually guarantees that the rider will continue to misinterpret the horse's behavior and overreact to perceived threats, resulting in greater confusion, fear, anger, and resentment — increasing the possibility of panic and injury in both "partners."

A seasoned trainer, on the other hand, demonstrates physical, mental, and emotional agility. This highly aware, inquisitive, centered form of human collection is simultaneously instructive, contagious, and comforting to the horse.

Calming a frantic youngster becomes an important way to bond with him and establish leadership, to earn his trust and cooperation. Disorganized, overstimulated horses sense that they're a danger to themselves and others. Even in the wild, they tend to seek out thoughtful, less-reactive individuals for guidance and support.

Survival of the Fittest

When someone feels the *need* to dominate, especially through force and intimidation, chances are he's inexperienced in the nuances of more mature forms of leadership. Dominance is a basic, albeit adolescent, claim for power, one that twentieth-century science interpreted as a law of evolution for all species. In the twenty-first century, however, researchers have come to realize that it's not the only law, nor even the most desirable law, of natural social behavior.

In a breakthrough article, "The Secret Life of Stallions," Kip Mistral interviewed Mary Ann Simonds, a wildlife and range ecologist who studied mustangs for thirty years. "Young dominator stallions — the type that most people associate with 'wild stallions' — might be able to break into and manipulate herds," she concedes, "but the mares try to escape. Mares want friendly stallions that can provide a sustainable herd environment. No one likes the dominator stallion types. Other stallions don't get along with them, which can be important, since sometimes stallions work together to attack or drive off a stallion they can't live with or that can't live within the larger community. Dominance doesn't go well in nature."

If this sounds overidealistic, check out the DVD *Such Is the Real Nature of Horses* by respected equine photographer Robert Vavra. He actually filmed an incident where several feral stallions broke up a fight between two feuding stallions, driving the perceived bully away from the bachelor herd until he agreed to calm down.

In the wild, stud colts rarely, if ever, oust their own fathers. Neither do they immediately find their own mares when they're encouraged to leave the original herd, somewhere between ages two and three. The vast majority of mustang stallions are in their teens before they're capable of attracting and maintaining a band of mares. In the horse world, as in the human world, leadership requires seasoning and experience. The initial urge to challenge authority is the first step in a long journey toward self-control, self-esteem, and self-mastery.

Karen Sussman, president of the International Society for the Protection of Mustangs and Burros, has witnessed bachelor bands temporarily protecting and sometimes cooperatively raising orphan colts and fillies. "We even have foals here that go back and forth between herds, and they are welcome everywhere," she notes. Apparently, the "survival of the fittest" impulse isn't set in stone among these horse communities. Or perhaps more accurately, their human observers are finally noticing that horses who are fit to *thrive* grow beyond the need for genetic and social dominance.

Equine Aikido

Over the past five thousand years or so, people have been striving to extricate themselves from a long list of oppressive religious, political, and economic systems. One of the most troubling misconceptions in moving toward greater personal empowerment is the idea that previously hidden feelings, opinions, or impulses are suddenly fair game for unbridled expression. Extremists by nature, humans tend to grab hold of the proverbial pendulum when introduced to a more open, candid form of social interaction. But the initial high of mutual freedom can quickly plunge into hurtful exchanges that damage relationships and discourage collaboration, inhibiting the lucid debate of challenging ideas that leads to innovation. A healthy dose of patience and equanimity helps create a fertile middle ground between suppression and expression, where honest, thoughtful communication thrives.

Merriam-Webster's Collegiate Dictionary, eleventh edition, supplies this definition of *patient*: "bearing pains or trials calmly or without complaint" and "manifesting forbearance under provocation or strain." Patient people remain "steadfast despite opposition, difficulty or adversity," the word *steadfast* referring to an ability to stay "firm in belief, determination, or adherence." This skill is an essential element of *equanimity*, defined as "evenness of mind, esp[ecially] under stress." In horses and humans alike, equanimity is *the* sign of a mature, well-balanced individual, one who stays centered when others become reactive, who sets reasonable boundaries without ordering everyone else around, whose clarity, composure, and poise are downright contagious.

We often assume that only humans are capable of developing these qualities — and only by transcending their basest animal instincts with great difficulty or self-righteousness. But this same highly evolved behavior exists, sometimes effortlessly, in nature. My horse Shadowfax, named for the wizard's magical mount in *Lord of the Rings*, was one such gifted individual. In 2004, he exhibited an uncannily supernatural level of emotional intelligence in socializing a couple of unruly stud colts.

I met Shadowfax at a breeding and training facility in Michigan. As a guest clinician at TN Farms, I was leading a variety of activities under a massive grove of oaks and maples when my attention was drawn to a nearby pasture. There an agile, well-muscled Appaloosa stallion was grazing and cavorting with his own weanling sons, something that few domesticated horses are allowed to do. (Most intact males are kept isolated for fear they might hurt their children.) Though only five years old, Shadowfax knew how to gently set boundaries with his feisty boys, playfully herd them around the pasture, and affectionately groom them. I was so impressed with his natural combination of power and gentleness that I bought one of his sons, a striking red-and-white yearling named Sage.

Several months later, when Shadowfax was up for sale, I brought him to Arizona. Sage remembered his father, calling out to him as soon as he got off the trailer. The first night, I was moved to see Shadowfax nuzzling his long-lost son over the fence. The next day, however, the younger horse attempted a brutal leadership coup. At that time, Sage and my two-year-old Arabian stud colt, Spirit, were going through the most fretful, inherently dangerous period of male adolescence, challenging their four-legged *and* two-legged elders. Hellbent on intimidating Shadowfax the first time they were turned out with him, they pulled out all the stops — kicking, striking, rushing in to bite.

The wise old man of six years didn't even panic, thoughtfully assessing the situation while staying out of harm's way. Then, as each colt reared over him, he lifted his front legs off the ground just high enough to lean into the youngster's shoulder, effectively knocking the aggressor off balance. Sage and Spirit ended up on the ground several times before they realized the move was intentional. Shadowfax seemed to be performing a kind of equine aikido, using the challenger's flamboyant yet unstable energy against him. Then he'd stand over the dazed and astonished colt, staring him down, pawing the earth right next to his head, clearly demonstrating his superior power, ingenuity — and restraint. By the end of the day, he was softly licking the face of his son and quietly milling around the corral with Spirit.

Trainer Mark Rashid might say that Shadowfax exhibited the traits of a "passive leader." Here the word *passive* refers not to inaction but to the fact that such a horse doesn't actively fight his way to dominance or obsessively try to control everyone else's behavior. Instead, as Rashid writes in *Horses Never Lie: The Heart of Passive Leadership*, he or she "leads by example, not force." This horse is "extremely dependable and confident, one that the vast majority of horses will not only willingly choose to follow, but actually seek out."

Studies of both wild and domesticated herds show that even though aggressive alpha-style leaders win the right to eat and drink first, these horses mostly succeed in alienating others. Their antics may be impressive to thrill-seeking humans, but if you sit down and really watch the rest of the herd, you'll notice most horses following more settled individuals around. Rashid once watched an alpha horse named Scooter "single-handedly keep no less than ten horses away from a water tank," launching full-blown attacks on a couple of horses and holding the rest at bay with menacing glances. The author saw a completely different dynamic unfold with satellite bands that approached the tank after Scooter finished. "In almost every case," he writes, "the passive leader would begin to drink while the others stood quietly nearby. Once the leader had taken several swallows from the tank, the others would slowly move in and they would all drink together. There were no threats, no attacks, and no fearful reactions. When the leader left the tank, the others willingly followed."

Watching one such mare effortlessly lead a herd of ten happy devotees, Rashid noted that she was "unfazed by her popularity and appeared to accept the others as if they had been buddies all their lives. The little band that followed her never seemed to get into arguments, living in relative peace whenever they were all together." In situations that would easily drive less experienced herd members into flight-or-fight mode, this mare truly knew how to "hold her horses."

Through my own experiences watching the intricacies of herd behavior, I've come to realize that "survival of the fittest" demands more than physical prowess. It involves the ability to conserve energy for true emergencies — or at least recognize and follow those who do. Most horses, Rashid insists, seek out a leader "that they know won't cause them unnecessary stress or aggravation," someone with "quiet confidence, dependability, consistency, and a willingness *not* to use force."

While Rashid calls this quieter style of herd management *passive leadership*, the term doesn't quite fit a horse like Shadowfax. Though he was eventually gelded as a form of birth control, the still-spirited yet poised Appaloosa continued to insist on a certain level of respect and deference: He didn't hesitate to up the ante when someone challenged his authority. Over time, I began referring to him as a *mature alpha*, a horse with the natural energy and inclination to assert dominance while also demonstrating restraint and concern for the well-being of others, one who balanced individual needs and group needs, using the least possible amount of friction or violence. After all, stallions who spend a good part of the afternoon beating each other up at the water tank are that much slower, and lamer, when running from a predator who's been lounging in the sun all day.

Conserving energy in this way may not seem like a vital survival issue for domesticated horses and civilized humans, but it's actually an important element in any successful endeavor. Businesses with significant internal strife have trouble *doing* business. Temperamental film directors go over budget and fall behind schedule. Bands of moody rock musicians break up at the height of their popularity. Politicians who inflame and manipulate public sentiments have trouble passing effective legislation. And horses who spook at every little thing lose in the show arena.

War and Peace

The good news is that while dominance and aggression may be hard-to-break habits, they're not necessarily hardwired. Primatologists have found that a lesser-known species of ape, the bonobo, can claim just as much kinship to humans as the chimp. Yet the bonobo prefers cooperative, conciliatory behavior; the females generally step forward to greet potential rivals with affectionate, peacemaking gestures and will often interpose themselves between males escalating toward a fight. Zoologist Frans de Waal calls it "survival of the kindest."

Even baboons, known for intensely aggressive behavior, seem to have less of a gene for dominance than a persistent custom of it. When the notoriously hostile alphas of a Kenya-based troop claimed, as usual, first dibs on the food, in this case a pile of garbage, they promptly died off from a nasty dose of tainted meat. The surviving low-ranking males, females, and children subsequently underwent what *New York Times* science writer Natalie Angier characterized as "a cultural swing toward pacifism, a relaxing of the unusually parlous baboon hierarchy, and a willingness to use affection and mutual grooming rather than threats, swipes and bites." The shift has persisted for two decades now. Even new males entering the group adhere to the unspoken guidelines of this gentler baboon subculture.

In his book *Field Notes on the Compassionate Life*, Marc Ian Barasch joins scientists like de Waal in speculating that "if bonobos instead of chimps had been taken as the prehuman model, the killer-ape crowd would never have gotten such traction. The scientific premise about our primate inheritance — and hence our modern assumptions about our basic nature — might have stressed equality of the sexes, familial bonds, and peacemaking rather than male dominance hierarchies and naked aggression."

Yet science itself may have been going through its own fretful adolescence when it latched onto examples in nature to justify our culture's penchant for conquest, competition, and dominion over all the earth's creatures. Since the equestrian arts were originally perfected for the ultimate dominance tactic — namely, war — horsemanship has also, at times, suffered from the same prejudicial perspective. In war, no one is exempt from being treated as a means to an end. Every soldier, and the horse he rode in on, must override fear, horror, grief, and compassion to serve a staunch hierarchy of masters who may — or more likely may *not* — have everyone's best interests in mind.

And yet, after centuries of rampant destruction, profiteering, slavery, and genocide, here comes George Washington, a man who kept his sensitivity intact on the battlefield, tempering great passion, power, ambition, and fierceness with personal restraint, adaptability, equanimity, and empathy. "Let your *heart* feel for the affliction, and distresses of every one," he advised.

That is *true courage*. That is *mature leadership*.

That is *evolution*.

Chapter Five

THE LION AND THE HORSE

*T*he human psyche is a *dynamic ecosystem*. Without the right balance of day and night, sunshine and rain, predator and prey, culture and nature, a landscape originally designed to support life turns into a desert, a dust bowl, an apocalyptic, postnuclear nightmare of desolation and alienation. In symbolic terms, daylight represents conscious awareness: what we can see and name, predict and command. Much of that "other 90 percent" operates subconsciously or unconsciously, moving stealthily through the night, resisting full explanation and domestication. Yet people don't just shy away from darkness in favor of the light. Some odd quirk of human behavior forces each generation to relive the fall of Adam and Eve in all kinds of crafty, covert ways.

Scientists and atheists are not immune. Practical modern minds tend to glorify what is "light" — that which is logical, socially acceptable, profitable, and/or controllable. Anything outside each person's current worldview is shrouded in darkness — not just unknown, not just suspect, but damned. This includes forms of perception. If you're fanatically religious, you're likely to revere faith and submission to established theological doctrine while distrusting reason, intuition, and feeling. If you're a genetic researcher, on the other hand, you're much more apt to promote reason and established scientific doctrine while discounting faith, feeling, and intuition. Either way, significant forms of nonverbal awareness are outlawed, remaining grossly underdeveloped. Families, tribes, and religious and political organizations accentuate this self-limiting tendency, socializing members to accept a particular set of static judgments, inspiring people to smugly dismiss, actively ostracize, threaten, or even kill those who operate from a different perspective.

No wonder so many of us reach middle age thirsting for something indescribable while feeling frightened or guilty about it. We've been reared by a culture of desert dwellers: obsessive, rain-phobic sun worshippers who shine massive spotlights at the stars to chase away the night. The mysterious, nourishing waters of emotion, empathy, instinct, artistic and mythic insight, gut feelings, and intersubjective awareness have all but dried up in many schools and professions. And it promises to get worse in the information age. After all, how do you quantify love or tweet your deepest, most elusive dreams?

To people who aren't particularly religious, the fall of Adam and Eve may seem like a quaint little folktale, but it's actually a brilliant teaching story, a perceptive, richly nuanced assessment of the flaw behind all human flaws: the *premature acquisition* of the knowledge of good and evil. The first man and woman, as you may recall, ate the forbidden fruit and were promptly expelled from paradise. But debates about why a benevolent God would put that disturbing tree in the garden usually ignore the possibility that it was planted for some future use: that the fruit would swell to ripeness as humanity itself matured.

Newly created and innocent to the core, Adam and Eve simply couldn't fathom the master plan of a fluid, multifaceted intelligence. From their pristine, undeveloped consciousness, parental cautions to stay away from that one compelling tree sounded stern and arbitrary. And so, like a couple of curious five-year-olds with no impulse control, they tasted the bitter knowledge of good and evil, resulting in the uniquely human compulsion to judge everything as either innately right or wrong, useful or useless, blessed or sinful.

Then, of course, they looked for someone else to blame. Adam complained that the woman tempted him to disobey God. And Eve became the first human to claim that "the devil made me do it." Waves of fear and shame followed these stunned, overstimulated little creatures out of Eden, leaving their descendants to manage the divine gift of judgment from a confused, hopelessly dualistic, dangerously limited point of view.

Historically and across all cultures, *groups* of people mutually reinforce the tendency to deny wholeness in favor of the light, forgetting that God is not the sun but the one who invented day and night, sound and silence, form and formlessness, freedom and restraint, male and female, heaven and earth, and a host of other opposites as tools of the creator's trade. Adventurous souls sometimes plunge into darkness, engaging in obsessively hedonistic, risky, or outright criminal behavior as a form of rebellion, but here again they fail to achieve balance — and usually look for a scapegoat (society, parents, divorce, drugs, or alcohol) to blame for their destructive, shortsighted ways. Only by exploring and integrating light and dark, spirit and matter, verbal and nonverbal awareness, predatory and nonpredatory power can we ever hope to reach our true potential.

I'm not saying anything new here. Thousands of books on psychology, mythology, art, religion, and symbolism explore ways to access parts of the mind that elude logic and language yet still prove essential to mental and emotional health. What I'm excavating in this brief history of power involves a lesser-known aspect of the optimally functioning psyche, one that has been repeatedly, sometimes dramatically, brought to our attention — then promptly ignored — for at least the past twenty-five hundred years. I'm talking about the inner, redemptive relationship between predator and prey, and, more specifically, the cultivation of nonpredatory wisdom as a key to, perhaps even a mandate of, human evolution.

Natural Horsemanship

I don't think I would have grasped the importance of the predator/prey dynamic had I not been investigating horse-training techniques in the early 1990s. Around that time, a small group of Western cowboys were actively bucking the system, promoting empathy and respect for the horse's perspective over traditional rough-riding, bronc-breaking practices. Through their increasingly popular books, videos, and public exhibitions, innovators like Bill and Tom Dorrance, Ray Hunt, Buck Brannaman, Pat Parelli, and Monty Roberts came to be known as founders of the "natural horsemanship" movement, influencing a new generation of trainers on both sides of the Atlantic.

Regardless of the individual methods these men created, a core principle they all share involves the notion that humans are predators and horses are prey animals. Difficulties arise when people unconsciously act predatory with animals designed to flee large cats and packs of wolves. The intensity of our gaze alone can be unnerving. Horses have eyes on the sides of their heads, emphasizing peripheral vision, while humans, like lions, look directly ahead, reinforcing a goal-oriented perspective originally designed for stalking. Some trainers also insist that, to horses, we move around in a perpetual rearing position, poised for attack with our grasping, clawlike hands. And we smell like what we eat: meat.

In the 1970s, when I was investigating vegetarianism, I read a number of books making the opposite case. Human physiology, they said, proved that meat eating was unnatural for us. After all, we have no fangs, and our nails can't rip through paper, let alone flesh. With the teeth and digestive system of an herbivore, we have to cook our steaks and cut them into bite-size portions. Some of us suffer colon cancer for our carnivorous sins.

The simple truth of the matter is that we are omnivores, with characteristics of both predator and prey. As a result, we all have Dr. Jekyll/Mr. Hyde moments as we struggle to bring these opposites into balance. The problem is that we've grown up in a culture of conquerors, where predatory behavior is reinforced in school and rewarded in business. Those who refuse to claw their way to the top often have trouble imagining an alternative, because the "wisdom of the prey" has been educated right out of them. Some accept the role of victim simply because they can't stomach becoming a tyrant.

Horses have much to teach us about the middle ground between submission and aggression. They're not cowardly weaklings designed merely to panic and run. Mature horses can seriously maim or even kill a mountain lion. They've served in countless bloody battles; some have been rewarded for unusual bravery. Psychologically, however, horses are designed to outsense, outguess, and outwit predators. Many behaviors people misinterpret as equine stupidity are in fact intelligent, highly successful evasion tactics.

In working with these animals, people find that predatory aggression is a colossal waste of energy, because a horse isn't giving full attention to a lesson when he's feeling threatened; he's figuring out how to escape. Anyone who relies on fear and intimidation will spend a great deal of time blocking the increasingly inventive evasion techniques their horses will devise. This dynamic creates the adversarial relationships many riders consider normal.

In *Almost a Whisper*, Oklahoma-born trainer Sam Powell summed up his own awakening to the limitations of master-slave, "power-over" paradigms, mirroring the journey that most of his colleagues took in achieving breakthroughs characteristic of natural horsemanship:

> I was a terrible kid, always into something. I was hot-headed and would fight at the drop of a hat. I'd fight a buzz saw if one challenged me. I had no interest in school or anything else; I just wanted to be a cowboy. By the time I was twenty years old, I was a full-time cowboy and all that entailed, including a catalog of broken bones that grew larger year after year.
>
> By my early forties, I had worked my way up to assistant manager of the horse division of a 128,000-acre ranch not far from Bartlesville, where I lost my passion for the cowboy ways, but fortysomething is a time when men take stock of their lives, weigh their successes and failures, confront their own limitations, sense their own mortality, and adjust their attitudes.
>
> I had broken just about every bone in my body, some more than once.

I had seen a lot of cowboys and horses injured or permanently crippled by the methods we were using and I knew I was getting too old for that. Out of curiosity and physical necessity, I began to wonder if there might be a better way.

Powell and other natural-horsemanship proponents began saying some radical things, *in public*. They talked about treating the horse as a being rather than an object, of communicating with his mind rather than controlling his body. They recommended learning about prey-animal psychology and equine *culture*, which many of these men were uniquely qualified to document for one simple reason: they were living out on vast tracts of land with horses who had reclaimed an autonomous herd-based lifestyle. There, among the wolves and mountain lions, the storms and droughts, the hot summers and cold winters, horses exhibited surprisingly agile forms of intelligence, collaboration, and leadership that their stall-bound counterparts, and the overcivilized people who rode them, had long forgotten.

As these cowboys learned to harmonize with their herds, some men hinted at profoundly transformational experiences, not because they were trying to hide the details, but because they couldn't translate their life-changing insights into words. Investigating equine culture meant traveling ever farther away from conventional human thought and behavior patterns, ever deeper into those mysterious realms of the "other 90 percent." Brave and dedicated students of the horse came back, however, with a shine in their eyes, a confidence in their gait, and a calm yet powerful presence, insisting that horses had more to teach humans than the other way around.

Keep in mind the courage involved in sharing this information with others: when the term *natural horsemanship* was coined around 1985, the movement's most basic principles were practically sacrilegious to fundamentalists who saw animals as soulless, God-given objects for human use, and to mainstream, twentieth-century scientists who treated animals as purely instinctual, emotionless machines. But the proof was in the pudding. Large numbers of professional and amateur riders began listening to these mavericks. At increasingly popular clinics and larger stadium exhibitions, people saw, unequivocally, that training techniques working *with* natural horse behavior were safer, more efficient, and much more enjoyable than fear and intimidation, dominance-submission practices.

And no matter how successful and charismatic these horse whisperers were, the very best of them were clear about one thing: the horses themselves had converted the original innovators, professional cowboys who came back from the open range with marked appreciation for the wisdom of the prey. As these men subsequently discovered, respectfully collaborating with a non-predatory species had expanded their minds and their hearts, giving them a leg up on human relationships as well. But the original motivation was purely practical, a better way to get the job done. As one Arizona-based cowboy told me, "I had a reason to change, and it was called *pain*."

The Yin Factor

We often think of the relationship between predator and prey as synonymous with that of perpetrator and victim. Horses, however, embody a different approach to *power*, modeling the *strengths* of nonpredatory behavior: relationship over territory, process over goal, responsiveness over strategy, cooperation over competition, emotion and intuition over reason. And yet, they can be focused and assertive when the situation calls for it. They quite literally follow the ancient Taoist recommendation to "know the yang, but keep to the yin," which often appears in translation as "know the masculine, but keep to the feminine." The Chinese sage Lao-tzu made this recommendation in the Tao Te Ching more than twenty-five hundred years ago; conquest-oriented civilizations emphasized the opposite. When a culture, like ours, keeps to the yang, discounting and degrading the yin, our ability to harmonize with other people, let alone nature, is seriously compromised.

At the same time, horses have little tolerance for timid, retiring, passive-aggressive people. If you sweetly ask for respect, without the conviction to hold your ground, they'll herd you around for sport and become increasingly dominant, even dangerous, over time. Horses demand a balance of strength and sensitivity. If you have too much predator in you, they'll become evasive. If you don't engage enough assertiveness, they'll treat you like a plaything. As nineteenth-century trainer Dennis Magner observed, working with horses requires "the delicacy of touch and feeling of a woman, the eye of an eagle, the courage of a lion, and the hang-on pluck of a bull-dog."

The dynamic interplay between a more considerate, empathetic form of masculine power and a rise in feminine power was crucial to the rapid success of natural horsemanship in the 1990s. "For the first time in human history, women dominated the horse industry," notes Robert Miller and Rick Lamb in *The Revolution in Horsemanship and What It Means to Mankind*. "The clinicians who pioneered this movement will tell you that without the prevalence of women in their audiences, they probably could not have stayed in business." According to the authors, it took "the emancipation of women in the twentieth century combined with an elevated standard of living" to create the now-common phenomenon of the female pleasure rider.

If this has been fortuitous for the equine industry — those who sell tack and riding habit, horses, horseshoes, and horse products — it has been a *blessing* to the horse. Why? Because most women are nurturing by nature and try to avoid conflict. They are less aggressive than most men, less intimidating in their stance, speech, or movements, and less inhibited about crooning to or petting animals. These are exactly the qualities to which horses are most responsive.

Yet, these qualities, which are less intimidating to the horse and less likely to precipitate the desire for flight, can also cause the horse to be less respectful and to feel dominant to the woman.

The authors conclude that "both masculine and feminine traits are needed for effective communication," that the "ideal" trainer "is a man who is in touch with his feminine side or a woman who is in touch with her masculine side."

Natural-horsemanship philosophy, however, went beyond reuniting yin and yang. It brought to light a long-neglected pair of opposites essential to an advanced understanding of power. Thanks to the outback revelations of a few open-minded cowboys, the practical, lifesaving, and life-*enhancing* advantages of prey-animal wisdom echoed the biblical prediction that the lion shall lie down beside the lamb in paradise.

Built on the spoils of conquest, our civilization gave rise to a situation in which the lion became a ruthless, unstoppable killing machine. These days, it's common for the predatory side of an individual's personality to devour the prey aspect early in life. People may go to church on Sunday and sit through tales of disciples taking up a gentler lifestyle, but when Monday morning arrives the beast rears its ugly head and the rabid carnivore is unleashed once again. For change to occur, the human psyche has to accept another matrix of wisdom capable of balancing the violent nature of the predator inside. Still, with modern humanity's potential for widespread nuclear and environmental destruction, the image of the hunted who outwits a hunter of such monstrous proportions is not likely to be the lamb, a much more innocent manifestation of prey philosophy. But the horse might capture the beast's attention as an innovation of this ideal in its most mature, most elegant, most powerful, most regal manifestation.

When we develop the complementary strengths of predator and prey, the lion transforms from aggressor to protector, from the murderer of sensitivity to its champion, helping us access the courage to feel *and* the willingness to act. A human who embodies the wisdom of lion *and* horse neither suppresses emotion nor becomes paralyzed by it. She uses her keen prey-animal instincts to sense aggression underneath the toothy smile of a colleague and employs her agile, nonpredatory intelligence to evade trouble without engaging in a carnivorous battle to the death. She holds her ground without ordering everyone else around. She embodies true assertiveness, becoming neither tyrant nor victim. She develops focused, goal-oriented thinking alongside a responsive, heartfelt, process-oriented mind capable of nourishing relationship.

Bringing our predatory nature back into balance is the challenge of a lifetime for individuals, and a multigenerational project for humanity. Luckily, we have living, breathing horses to help us reawaken the wisdom of the prey while demanding that we *own* our inner lion and put it to good use.

The Hidden Revolution

If might always made right, and survival of the fittest depended solely on competition and brute force, American revolutionaries could never have defeated the British. As the grossly outnumbered colonial army ran out of guns, food, clothing, shoes, men, and finally, morale, it was nonpredatory wisdom that *repeatedly* turned the tide, challenging widespread, long-standing notions about the nature of power, ultimately paving the way for a truly collaborative society of free men and women.

In this respect, George Washington was at the head of a hidden revolution, changing the face of leadership itself. Early in the war, he blatantly rejected flamboyant, alpha-style dominance tactics in favor of a more thoughtful and compassionate approach, leading by example rather than by intimidation, adopting a role similar to what trainer Mark Rashid calls the "passive leader" in a horse herd. Remember, this is the strong yet steady, collected leader that others choose to follow, one who conserves energy for true emergencies, who doesn't cause the group "unnecessary stress or aggravation," someone with "quiet confidence, dependability, consistency, and a willingness not to use force."

As Ron Chernow reveals in his intricate biography *Washington: A Life*, the general was consciously evolving a style of leadership the likes of which the world had never seen, working tirelessly to educate and uplift his long-suffering soldiers while dealing with constant assaults from a capricious, inexperienced, in-fighting Continental Congress and a skeptical public. Battling accusations that he was weak and indecisive (accusations by people who either wanted his job or were afraid that his popularity would make him too powerful), he nonetheless stayed the course, eventually proving himself worthy of the public's trust through the very act of valuing that trust to begin with.

Washington's tenure as commander in chief featured relatively few battles, often fought after extended intervals of relative calm, underscoring the importance of winning the allegiance of a population that vacillated between fealty to the Crown and patriotic indignation. The fair treatment of civilians formed an essential part of the war effort. Washington had a sure grasp of the principles of this republican revolution, asserting that "*the spirit and willingness of the people must in a great measure take [the] place of coercion.*" No British general could compete with him in this contest for popular opinion. With one eye fixed on the civilian populace, Washington showed punctilious respect for private property and was especially perturbed when American troops sacked houses under the pretext that the owners were Tories. *His overriding goal was to contrast his own humane behavior with the predatory ways of the enemy.*

Rejecting slash and burn, rape and pillage, techniques that the British still used at times, Washington guarded against needless trauma perpetrated by and on friends and foes alike. During those long stretches between battles, he recognized the value of a feminine presence in camp to counteract the despair and disillusionment of an army stretched to the limit, enlisting the support of women, not as prostitutes, but as social activists capable of providing comfort, care, and a host of other essential services to the soldiers. Even on the battlefield, his willingness to adopt a nonpredatory perspective saved the army on more than one occasion and, arguably, won him the war. In this respect, he managed to tame the inner lion of his own naturally aggressive, risk-taking, goal-oriented personality, resurrecting long-forgotten evasion maneuvers used by an ancient nomadic culture three thousand years earlier.

The Fool's Progress

Despite being vastly outnumbered, sometimes three to one, by the British, Washington made several bold attempts to win the war quickly, heroic efforts that ultimately cost lives and territory. Like the ill-fated plan to tame his mother's sorrel colt, a casualty of aggressive teenage idealism, Washington's initial wartime experiments in gutsy, overtly confrontational strategies backfired for the most part. By January 1777, American forces had lost New York City and were about to lose Philadelphia. Colonial troops, which had numbered twenty thousand a year earlier, had dwindled to less than three thousand when enlistments expired that winter, as did the kind of popular support capable of producing new recruits. As one French observer remarked, "There is a hundred times more enthusiasm for the Revolution in any Paris café than in all the colonies together."

Washington had two choices: surrender or adopt a "Fabian strategy." Named after Fabius Maximus — a Roman general who, in the third century BCE, fought off a much larger enemy force through less-confrontational, defensive tactics — the second option was still hard for Washington to embrace. In *His Excellency*, Joseph Ellis reports that the general had to grapple with his own self-image and long-standing beliefs, finally relenting "less out of conviction than a realistic recognition of his limited resources." As Ellis explains, "A Fabian strategy, like guerilla and terrorist strategies of the twentieth century, was the preferred approach of the weak. Washington did not believe that he was weak, and he thought of the Continental army as a projection of himself. He regarded battle as a summons to display one's strength and courage; avoiding battle was akin to dishonorable behavior, like refusing to move forward in the face of musket and cannon fire."

Washington also had to deal with the damage his reputation would initially suffer upon activating this obscure evasion strategy. It wasn't a matter of swallowing his pride so much as *volunteering* to be *misunderstood* — and knowing he would be mocked for it — *again*. A year earlier, Washington had managed to hold the British at bay on a ruse, suddenly and inexplicably showing restraint in battle, when in fact his troops had run out of gunpowder and didn't have the funds or connections to buy more for a good six months. And the general's reward for keeping this deadly secret from all but his closest associates? To be portrayed as a yellow-bellied, bumbling fool in a well-attended Boston theater farce, by an actor stumbling around in a big, floppy wig, waving a rusty sword.

So here he was again, in the winter of 1777, concealing yet another potentially fatal weakness: if the British had known he'd been left with a mere twenty-five hundred men, they would have attacked without mercy and easily won the war. Through no small amount of intrigue and posturing, Washington managed to obscure the facts while devising a strategy based on what he called "the melancholy Truths" — namely, that the states would never raise enough men or money to wage a conventionally successful campaign. In late March, Washington sent Nathanael Greene to brief Congress on the necessity of fighting an evasive war of attrition, luring the enemy away from port cities to exhaust their men and their supplies. (The British at that time had the best navy in the world, but they were less impressive on solid ground. And in the wilderness, those bright red coats made easy targets.) Yet as Greene subsequently reported, the idea "appeared to be new" to colonial representatives. Ellis notes that "Congress was apparently taken aback, because a Fabian strategy meant that Washington did not intend to defend Philadelphia at all costs if [British general] Howe chose to make it his target. His highest priority was not to occupy or protect ground, but rather to harass Howe while preserving his army."

Washington's political foes had to be salivating over this seemingly eccentric move, especially when the revised plan and the reason behind it — the sorry state of the Continental army — had to be kept secret from a fickle public to make sure the British stayed in the dark as well. Yet what no one, not even Washington, apparently knew was that the Fabian strategy was not a last-ditch, gamble of a move created by a desperate Roman dictator. It was a *proven* tactic used by a highly successful culture that incorporated equine wisdom into daily life. Fabius himself could have easily gotten the idea from a popular series of books by Herodotus.

In analyzing the Greek historian's brief yet telling accounts of an ancient horse tribe's behavior, we can see that Washington's plan actually had more in common with the strategy's original inspiration than the Roman's subsequent interpretation of it. Fabius had combined evasive maneuvers with a scorched-earth practice to prevent enemy forces from obtaining grain and other resources. Washington blatantly refused to engage in such destruction. Ellis's comparison of Washington's plan to the "guerilla and terrorist strategies of the twentieth century" also falls short in characterizing the Continental army's unusually constructive implementation of this long-neglected technique. Civilians, even those obviously aligned with the British, were never considered expendable for the cause. In this sense, the American general's restraint, compassion, and sensitivity to nuance brought a truly nonpredatory defense tactic back to life, changing the course of history forever.

Traveling Light

The first equestrians galloped across that vast sea of grass known as the steppes of Eurasia, and they put on quite a show. Adventurous souls who discovered how to ride about six thousand years ago (in the region now known as Ukraine) eventually took up the nomadic ways of their horses, abandoning the sedentary lifestyle of their agricultural ancestors for three thousand years of freedom.

Nomadic pastoralism, contrary to popular belief, was not a primitive condition. It was a specialization that developed out of settled farming communities, requiring horses and skillful riding techniques. It required the wheel to allow populations to migrate with their herds by cart and wagon, leaders able to make quick decisions in an emergency, and a variety of craftsmen and specialists, far more than family subsistence farming did. The early horse tribes even managed to raise crops without becoming enslaved by them. They simply planted wheat in patches of fertile soil and returned to reap the benefits during seasonal migrations.

Recent archeological findings also suggest that women were equal to men in many of these tribes. Skeletons of warriors at first thought to be young boys later proved to be female. Over time, it was estimated that nearly 25 percent of warrior graves contained women dressed for battle, some of them obviously bowlegged from years spent on the back of a horse. Yet these wild-riding ladies, mythologized as Amazons by the Greeks, were no less aware of their femininity. Their graves are filled with mirrors, scent bottles, and cosmetics of various colors. And like many women today, they *loved* to groom their horses. In burial mounds across Ukraine and southern Russia, up toward Tuva and the Altai Mountains, human and equine corpses lay side by side among a dazzling array of colorful saddle cloths depicting scenes from daily life. These in turn revealed a culture of decorative mane dressing and fantastic crested horse masks. Four-legged members of the tribe were dressed with as much enthusiasm as their two-legged counterparts.

And that's saying a lot, as it turns out: Contact with Greek colonies along the Black Sea brought a few, well-chosen luxuries. Since nomadic horse tribes only kept what they could carry, they wore their wealth in the form of elaborate, highly symbolic jewelry, gold weapon adornments, richly ornamented belts, and stylish riding clothes. Credited with the invention of pants, warriors of both sexes wore tight-fitting leggings tucked into leather boots, long-sleeved shirts and hip-length coats, all of which were embroidered with intricate designs, and some of which were trimmed in precious metals. In these tribes, later known as Scythians and Sarmatians, there was also a marked preference for "flame-colored" horses. According to Renate Rolle's *The World of the Scythians,* "The rich warriors on the gleaming red animals, with shining gold clothing and weapons, must have presented an impressive picture in the brilliant sunlight of the steppe."

More impressive, however, are reports of the nomads' behavior in battle, descriptions that have little in common with standardized legends of fierce barbarians out to vanquish the sacred innovations of the civilized world. Around 450 BCE, Herodotus, the Greek "father of history," wrote about a curious, highly frustrating encounter that King Darius I of Persia had with these tribes before deciding to take on a much easier project and invade Greece. Darius was chasing a group of Scythians who'd either attacked or offended him in some way, and he was apparently planning to punish them, but good. Gathering his troops together, he entered Eurasia for the first time in 512 BCE, but when he arrived at the edge of the steppes, none of his officers could figure out how to engage these so-called primitives in combat.

Whenever the troops got too close, the Scythians simply dispersed, riding into the grasslands, leading the king's rigidly disciplined military force farther and farther into the wilderness. For weeks, the horsemen watched from a safe distance, ignoring the king's provocative insults, infuriating him further by breaking ranks to chase a stray rabbit as the Persians made their threatening gestures. The Scythians were sleeping on horseback, drinking mare's milk and playing games along the way, while Darius's men were growing weak from starvation and exposure. Finally, the Persians were forced to turn around and march home as the Scythians cheered and chuckled in the distance.

The horse tribes maintained their culture and their territory by acting like the horses they rode. Choosing flight over fight was not a cowardly act but an obvious, thoroughly natural way to avoid unnecessary bloodshed. The enemy was ultimately irrelevant because there were no cities to defend. Warrior riders of both sexes led the challengers away from women with young children and mares with foals (who were mobile, though undoubtedly slower). It was only when increasingly materialistic members of these tribes began trading profusely with city dwellers that they sacrificed centuries of freedom. The more possessions they craved and acquired, the more their belongings weighed them down, and the more sedentary they became. Greek gold and wine and decorative vases eventually lured the nomads into a gilded cage of cultural amnesia. The ones who refused to forget fled farther into the grasslands until civilizations developing to the east and west expanded and overlapped right over their graves.

The assumption that nomads were more violent than their "civilized" counterparts has begun to evaporate in light of new research. The Danish archeologist Klavs Randsborg insists it wasn't marauding hordes of barbarians that led to the fall of the Greco-Roman world. Rather, these societies destroyed their environment and, in desperation, moved out to incorporate the lands and cultures nearby — Celtic, Germanic, Thracian, Scythian — "which until then had led an effective and long-standing existence in harmony with nature." Citizens of early cities were suffering from anxieties derived from the instability resulting from conspicuous consumption and unchecked population growth. Their only choice was to expand outward, taking over the territories of other peoples, subjugating those peoples and transforming them into the slave labor needed to build new buildings and reap greater harvests. Randsborg and his colleagues insist that, after nearly a millennium of expansion to compensate for repeated economic failure, this process had brought city dwellers to the point at which they had devastated the whole natural and political world around them.

The Gods of Adolescence

City life has marked advantages — and some inherently destructive disadvantages. Early civilizations experimented with gusto, constantly assessing what worked well and what demanded improvement, imagining increasingly sophisticated technical solutions, and constructing ever more impressive architecture, plumbing, food storage, and trade systems that were impossible to achieve without high-level social organization.

The problem was that modifying ineffective thought and behavior patterns turned out to be much more difficult than building the pyramids, especially when city dwellers the world over had already created their own colossal, archetypal conundrum — namely, an extreme, adolescent misuse of the knowledge of good and evil. To justify shortsighted, predatory practices that benefited the few at the expense of the many, ruling classes not only promoted the idea that nature was harsh and had to be subdued, they actively *demonized* nomadic cultures, especially those in which men and women shared power. To make matters worse, the monarchs *deified* themselves — at first probably to control slaves through shock-and-awe tactics. But soon enough, they began to believe their own publicity, which gave them even less motivation to admit their mistakes and analyze their own behavior. The gods, after all, *must* be perfect, their every command unquestionably followed, their every deed informed by a "divine" logic incomprehensible to mere mortals.

In effect, despite the multiple, seemingly unique cultures and religions, if you lived in a large Greek, Roman, Egyptian, Persian, Chinese, or later, European *urban* center, the hidden scaffolding of your belief system looked like this:

SEDENTARY	good, right, civilized
NOMADIC	evil, wrong, barbarian
PREDATOR	strong
PREY	weak
HUMAN/MALE	intelligent, rational, moral
NATURE/FEMALE	ignorant, instinctual, amoral

In extremely predatory societies like Rome before the time of Christ, competition and conquest were so ingrained they didn't even *have* socially recognized opposites. In this sense, to consider a concept weak, ignorant, wrong, or even evil is preferable to oblivion. After all, what we *can* name, we can at least debate and, over time, *cultivate* if it proves useful — when all the kings are dethroned and humanity is truly free to consider its previously suppressed, conveniently outlawed, or simply long-forgotten options.

George Washington's least-recognized and most impressive innovation hinged on his ability to transcend these long-entrenched opposites, drawing upon masculine and feminine, sedentary and nomadic, predatory and nonpredatory, verbal and nonverbal forms of power and intelligence — fluidly, as needed. A deeply spiritual man who felt a sense of divine calling, he nonetheless dodged the pitfalls of religious grandiosity. Not only did he refuse to be deified; he also avoided the much more common modern affliction of domineering self-righteousness, which, like deification, blocks lucid inquiry and constant behavior modification. Heaven and earth, faith and logic, culture and nature, vision and practicality, fierceness and compassion were all on his side, helping him to win an impossible war by tapping the balanced ecosystem of a fully functioning human psyche.

And at the crucial moment of victory, he did what no man had done before him, resisting the ultimate temptation of military success. British monarch George III was awed by reports of Washington's refusal to become king of a new country, saying that if the general did indeed hold to his promise, he would be "the greatest man in the world." After all, as Ellis points out in *His Excellency*, "Oliver Cromwell had not surrendered power after the English Revolution. Napoleon, Lenin, Mao, and Castro did not step aside to leave their respective revolutionary settlements to others in subsequent centuries."

In so many astonishing ways, George Washington was a revolutionary among revolutionaries. Two centuries later, we're still grappling with the gift — and the burden — of freedom he so generously entrusted to the future. It's time to dust off those stoic, faded images of the father of our country and live the example he set before us.

Chapter Six

THE MELANCHOLY TRUTHS

On an otherwise sunny Saturday morning in January 2011, Arizona congresswoman Gabrielle Giffords was shot during an informal meeting with her constituents. Eighteen innocent bystanders were also injured or killed by a single, deeply disturbed gunman.

The tragedy hit home — literally. Giffords and astronaut Mark Kelly had gotten married a few miles down the road from my latest home base, a small, wildly scenic horse property that my husband and I had recently purchased for a downsized version of our equine program. Among many other benefits this charming little ranching community afforded, I had been pleased to learn, our new Amado, Arizona, location put us squarely in Giffords's district.

I had long appreciated the congresswoman's intelligence, courage, and willingness to respectfully listen to people with opposing views. Giffords, not surprisingly, was also a lifelong horsewoman. In a brief career overview aired on National Public Radio's *All Things Considered* shortly after the attack, producers emphasized that working at a local boarding stable, cleaning stalls in exchange for riding lessons, had been her favorite childhood summer job. "I learned a lot from horses and the stable people," she told NPR. "There was a unique culture out there, and I think it provided good training, all of that manure-shoveling, for my days in politics ahead."

Political humor aside, Giffords's commitment and adaptability, her empathy, strength, patience, and poise under pressure echoed the skills of previously mentioned rider-leaders who had the nerve to take on difficult yet socially significant positions, putting their lives on the line, if necessary, for the chance to make a difference.

In the first confusing hours after the shooting at a Tucson supermarket, reporters were madly trying to determine if Giffords's wounds had been fatal. With CNN blaring on television and satellite radio throughout the house, I was feeling, like so many people that day, a combination of shock, sadness, and outrage. Yet somehow, the horses and the land outside seemed to temper these tumultuous emotions with an undercurrent of compassion and trust, as if the earth itself were vibrating long, subsonic chords of assurance that the world was not, in fact, coming to an end.

My upstairs writing office overlooks several corrals leading toward miles of open range, with Baboquivari, the sacred mountain of the Tohono O'odham tribe, rising up from the western horizon. On the opposite side of the house, much closer and to the east, a towering rock formation known as Elephant Head serves as a gateway to the Santa Rita Mountains. Only from a considerable driving distance does the trunk of the pachyderm appear, created by an elongated series of hills visible from Tucson, thirty minutes away on one side, and Tubac, fifteen minutes away on the other.

In Amado, the small rural town closest to the formation, Elephant Head looks nothing like an elephant. It's a massive, vaguely pyramid-shaped, cathedral-like structure that suddenly rises twenty-five hundred feet from its base. At first glance, you might think some ancient civilization carved it out of solid stone — except that the Empire State Building is only about half that tall and it took a good five thousand years of human ingenuity to reach *that* height.

Around five o'clock I turned off the television, convinced that Giffords would survive that first day and grow stronger with time. As I fed the horses in a melancholy yet appreciative silence, I watched the sun slowly melt behind Baboquivari, setting the elephant's head and the rest of the Santa Ritas ablaze in outlandish hues of crimson, gold, and lavender. And I wondered: What if scientists, politicians, *and* religious leaders stopped assuming that evolution and/or creation had already reached its culmination with the innovation of mankind? What if we realized that civilization was neither advanced nor terminally defective but a massive, worthwhile work in progress? That as visionaries in training, creatures designed to *create*, we might be on the edge of a quantum leap in our development — if only we would stop underestimating *and* overestimating ourselves and embrace our true collective potential?

In the days following the tragedy, local and national news reporters joined countless Internet bloggers and rabid radio callers in debating whether our society was becoming more violent. Every special-interest group seemed to have a different reason to stir up shame, fear, and self-righteousness. Advocates for and against gun control joined a much wider chorus of discussions on free speech, responsible journalism, and political rhetoric. As time went on, the anger and panic wandered further off topic with Christian televangelists waving the book of Revelation in concert (though certainly not intentionally) with psychics and spiritualists citing Nostradamus's prediction and Mayan calendar interpretations that the earth would experience some sort of savage devastation and divine reorganization in 2012.

If you happened to be researching human history from a cathedral-thinking point of view, however, you might be surprised, as I was, to find good reason to be optimistic. While we may never be able to eradicate isolated incidents of violence by people suffering from mental illness, we do have the tools to dramatically reduce trauma, terror, hate, arrogance, shame, and blame, grossly destructive by-products of civilization's dominance-submission stage of social development.

And we can learn to work together as equal, authentic, empowered beings — not by treating this ambitious task as a vague, hit-or-miss, extracredit project, but through a thoughtful, widespread educational movement to help humanity master the emotional and social intelligence, verbal and nonverbal communication, leadership, and visionary skills that will, finally, allow us to function effectively as free men and women.

Hidden Bias

Critics of our current system often talk about a "glass ceiling" preventing women and minorities from rising to significant leadership positions, an invisible yet palpable obstruction through which the next level of advancement can be seen but not reached. "I know there are still barriers and biases out there, often unconscious," New York senator Hillary Clinton said as she officially withdrew from the Democratic presidential primary in June 2008. Her loyal supporters were profoundly disappointed, but they eventually took her lead in moving forward constructively with a realistic appreciation for all she had, in fact, achieved. "And although we weren't able to shatter that highest, hardest glass ceiling," she emphasized, "this time, thanks to you, it's got about 18 million cracks in it."

Shortly after Clinton's concession speech, Barack Obama issued a statement praising his rival's "valiant and historic campaign" for helping his own daughters and "women everywhere" realize "there are no limits to their dreams." And he thanked Clinton for preparing him to break a similar barrier as he became the first African American to win the Democratic nomination. "Our party and our country are stronger because of the work [Clinton] has done throughout her life," he noted, "and I'm a better candidate for having had the privilege of competing with her in this campaign."

But there was another glass ceiling no one was paying attention to, one so high most people didn't know it existed, a hidden, evolutionary bias that the most ruthless alpha males had been bumping up against for centuries without so much as making a dent in the damn, confounding thing. In the fall of 2008, when a bunch of Wall Street executives, financial "geniuses," and real estate speculators hit this silent, unconscious barrier all at once, they bounced back to the ground so fast the seesaw effect catapulted a man of mixed race and unconventional background right smack into the presidency.

Barack Obama has been mitigating the fallout from this strange turn of events ever since, and, no, even at the start of his second presidential term he doesn't quite yet have the tools to succeed. *No one does* — mostly because our twittering, technically advanced, emotionally adolescent minds haven't fully grasped the core challenge underneath all the political rhetoric, free-floating fear, toxic frustration, and frantic cultural static.

The Higher You Go...

In the bestselling leadership book *What Got You Here Won't Get You There*, executive coach Marshall Goldsmith outlines twenty common yet troublesome habits that prevent successful people from becoming more successful. These career-stifling pitfalls have nothing to do with intelligence, technical skill, wealth, talent, education, or courage. They have to do with attitudes, interpersonal-communication difficulties, and personality quirks endemic to an incredibly inefficient, grossly outdated dominance-submission system. Quite simply, Goldsmith reveals, "The higher you go, the more your problems are behavioral."

In reading over the list, I couldn't help but notice that many of the behaviors in question are blatantly predatory, including the number one challenge: *winning too much*, which, according to the author, stems "from needlessly trying to be the alpha male (or female) in any situation." The vast majority of the remaining nineteen habits are related to the first, which he describes as "the need to win at all costs and in all situations — when it matters, when it doesn't, and when it's beside the point." Goldsmith emphasizes that our "obsession with winning rears its noisome head across the spectrum of human endeavor, not just among senior executives," culminating in a desire to win "even when the issue is clearly to our disadvantage." The amount of time, talent, and money wasted on this particularly insidious addiction is most obvious in our current political system, though it wreaks havoc in our churches, schools, humanitarian efforts, and family life whenever the need to "be right" is more important than being effective, let alone innovative, in solving the myriad challenges we face.

Humanity is evolving psychologically and socially through a process known as "civilization," and we've reached a collective impasse. *What got us here won't get us there.* Like the Fortune 500 executives that Goldsmith coaches, we need to look at our behavior, and we need to embrace some new skills. We *are* an incredibly powerful, successful species — with the ability to bankrupt the entire planet. Luckily we have some avatars to call upon, historically significant trailblazers who explored new territory while expending no small amount of blood, sweat, and tears. Several of these visionaries went on to become major religious figures (which I'll get to later). But we do have at least one thoroughly human innovator to consider. And he may very well be the best model to follow at this stage in our development.

Yes, you guessed it; I'm talking about George Washington. Like the well-intentioned general fumbling around the American outback with a ragtag group of ill-equipped troops, we need to reassess our concepts of power, develop fierce sensitivity, exercise emotional heroism, experience the frightening, confusing, thoroughly disorganized death of the old, and have faith that we are capable, simultaneously, of creating something new. Evolution and what Washington called "Divine Providence" appear to be on our side. An impenetrable glass ceiling on unchecked predatory behavior offers consistent historical evidence that some higher intelligence and/or process of natural selection is actively preventing us from moving forward until we can let go of our adolescent dominance fantasies and embrace a more mature form of social organization.

The turning point involves an unwieldy combination of humility, intelligence, empathy, courage, and transformation. Remember that while standing up to the British, the most powerful military force in the world, Washington had to concede that he would never be able to fight that juggernaut on its own terms. He had to try something new, incorporating, as it turns out, something very, very old: a long-forgotten, incredibly agile, nonpredatory wisdom to enhance the conviction, focus, and endurance he already had in spades.

In the twenty-first century, we are, once again, battling a force that threatens our freedom and survival, one that, unfortunately, has already proven much more powerful and insidious than King George's arrogant nobles and exquisitely trained soldiers. And yet I believe we've reached the point in our collective evolution where we can win this psychological war of independence with compassion, humanity, and perhaps even a certain amount of grace and delight.

Throughout history, we have met the ultimate enemy, over and over again, and he is the rabid carnivore in us. Working together — and only together — we can lure that dark beast out into the open and, not destroy it, but harness its incredible power, gentle it, and *civilize* it, once and for all.

Enter the Dragon

Psyche

Here's the rub: We're not just taming lions anymore. After five thousand years of conquest, genocide, and slavery, the predatory side of the human psyche has become a force of mythic proportions, a fire-breathing, landscape-destroying, coldhearted, flying reptile that lives for the hunt, goes for the jugular — and gets *high* from it.

To make matters worse, this dangerous, mutant species can talk. It uses intelligence as a weapon. And it *appears* to have magical powers, a kind of verbal bait-and-switch tactic that's little more than a perceptual parlor trick. Post-industrial dragons weave complex webs of pseudologic to mesmerize human prey, baiting them with promises of easy wealth, pretending to hold some innovative new secret to success that mere mortals can't possibly understand, deftly hiding the fact that these get-rich-quick schemes are filled with nothing more than hot air.

A particularly articulate and seductive beast named Enron offers the ultimate case study. Remnants of this modern dinosaur should be collected and displayed for posterity, perhaps in the Smithsonian museum as a cautionary tale for high school and college students to study, except that his bones are scattered throughout Texas, California, and India, among other unfortunate places, making the cost of such a massive reconstruction project prohibitory, especially in the currently depressed economy that Enron's demise foreshadowed.

The height of the company's rise in the 1990s, the speed of its fall in 2001, and the limitless depths of its deception are already legendary. In fact, the sheer audacity of the illusions Enron's top executives fed to investors, employees, and the public suggests that advanced intelligence and unchecked predatory behavior are a toxic combination, spawning a particularly delusional form of hubris that backfires, ironically, in a most disturbing mutation: a devastating, highly contagious strain of widespread human stupidity. If we want to know what sets us apart from all the "other beasts," Enron makes a strong case for the idea that our big crafty brains are not necessarily an evolutionary advantage, that when intelligence dissociates from empathy in particular, our very survival becomes questionable.

Up until the moment it declared bankruptcy, the Houston-based energy giant represented the sovereignty of unbridled capitalism. Appearing to increase profits year after year, Enron thrived on competition and deregulation, promoting its aggressive, "survival of the fittest" culture as evolution in action while simultaneously positioning its mutual-exploitation philosophy as a new economic religion.

Behind the scenes, however, the company was losing money at an alarming rate. Through the magic of an accounting system known as "mark to market," Enron would claim potential future profits on the very day a contract was signed, no matter how little cash came in the door. To make matters worse, deal makers would receive bonuses on speculative profits regardless of how accurate those initial projections turned out to be. For instance, the corporation spent a billion dollars building a power plant in India, realizing much later that the country couldn't pay for the power Enron's recently completed plant produced. Executives had already received several million dollars in bonuses based on imaginary profits that never arrived. In another, highly publicized deal, which Enron made with Blockbuster, the companies announced video-on-demand technology when developers were still struggling with the details. The plan collapsed when engineers failed to work out the kinks. Yet through mark-to-market accounting, Enron used future video-on-demand projections to book over $50 million in earnings — on a scheme that never made a cent!

Over time, it became clear that even mark-to-market tricks would be incapable of obscuring a fast-growing behemoth of debt. As a rising number of employees were encouraged to invest their retirement funds in Enron stock, outright fraud became the last resort of executives addicted to the company's "total domination" of trading in power, communications, and weather securities. CFO Andy Fastow came up with the ultimately fatal idea of creating special companies to hide increasing losses. With names like Raptors and Jedi, these deceptive financial entities symbolized Enron's adolescent fantasies of supercarnivores and space-age battles in which a supernatural "Force" was "with" executives, allowing them to defy the laws of financial gravity.

Soon enough, these wily wizards would be accused of black magic: At the end of 2001, tens of thousands of ordinary citizens and trusting employees lost everything. Several key players subsequently went to prison; one committed suicide. And the corporation's founder, a Baptist minister's son who mistook Enron's rapid rise as a sign that God was on the company's side, died from a heart attack weeks after receiving a guilty verdict that could have sent him to jail for forty-five years.

It's tempting to blame Enron's demise on avarice, pride, and deception, reading the entire fiasco as a moralistic passion play. We could just as easily present it as a case study of capitalism's failure. Or we could take a psychological approach and characterize company executives as sociopathic. Hell, we could even say the devil made them do it. But we'd be missing the point. Enron imploded because of a glass ceiling on predatory behavior that (as mentioned in the previous section and bolstered by research presented at the end of this chapter) seems to be a long-ignored principle of nature itself. This dangerous failure to recognize the profound limitations of predatory power was reinforced in the twentieth century by a gross misreading of Darwin's sorely incomplete "survival of the fittest" concept and a long-standing, culturewide inability to notice that the founders of three of the world's major religions, including Christianity, actively promoted *nonpredatory* wisdom. Until we as a species expand our perceptions, modify our beliefs, and alter our behavior in response to these factors, we *will* keep breeding dinosaurs like Enron, suffering the dire consequences of our own inability to evolve, despite constant warnings and helpful hints from God *and* nature.

The Smartest Guys in the Room?

A number of fascinating books on the Enron scandal have been written since the company declared bankruptcy in late 2001, including *The Smartest Guys in the Room* by *Fortune* senior writers Bethany McLean and Peter Elkind. *Power Failure*, by *Texas Monthly* editor Mimi Swartz, is a collaboration with Sherron Watkins, the Enron global finance executive who was named one of *Time* magazine's People of the Year for blowing the whistle on her company's illegal bookkeeping schemes. But the printed word alone doesn't do justice to the gestures, attitudes, and interpersonal dramas involved. For a taste of that "other 90 percent," I highly recommend the DVD documentary version of *The Smartest Guys in the Room*.

Among numerous standout moments, taped phone conversations documented callous Enron traders cheerfully encouraging California power plant managers to find "creative" excuses for interrupting electrical service. With Fastow's raptor tricks capable of hiding loss, not making money, Enron eventually felt the need to pirate its own hard-won deregulation of energy at the retail level, secretly causing rolling blackouts, manufacturing a phony California energy crisis to drive up the price of electricity.

As author Bethany McLean observes in an on-camera interview: "The Enron traders never seemed to step back and say, wait a minute, is what we're doing ethical? Is it in our best long-term interests? Does it help us if we totally rape California? Does that advance our goals of nationwide deregulation? Instead, they sought out every loophole they could to profit from California's misery," an incredibly shortsighted move that threatened to bankrupt the entire state, adding further momentum to Enron's cataclysmic downfall. A particularly pathological desire to manipulate the system for personal gain was at work, echoing Goldsmith's recognition that "even when the issue is clearly to our disadvantage, we want to win."

The corporate culture wholeheartedly supporting this mentality was methodically and consciously developed by Jeffrey Skilling, who served as Enron's president, chief operating officer, and finally chief executive officer during its most profitable years. Filmmakers contrast Skilling's cool, collected demeanor in court with scenes from daredevil motorcycle and Jeep expeditions he led through Baja California, Mexico, and the Australian outback, where small, all-male groups of executives and customers faced an adrenaline junkie's ultimate challenge: to risk bodily injury with the same death-defying attitude that informed Enron's outlandish business practices.

"Survival of the fittest" was Skilling's motto and religion. Richard Dawkins's 1976 classic, *The Selfish Gene*, was one of the CEO's favorite books, but it's clear that Skilling and his traders weren't interested in the nuances of evolutionary theory, acting more like rabid junkyard dogs than those high-functioning, mutually supportive species of masterful group hunters: the lions and the wolves. As McLean and Elkind observe in the book version of *The Smartest Guys in the Room*, those traders and executives "who stayed and thrived were the ones who were the most ruthless in cutting deals and looking out for themselves."

The traders eventually lost their jobs too, of course, though Skilling took the biggest hit. He was eventually convicted of nineteen counts of securities and wire fraud, sentenced to twenty-four years in prison, and obliged to pay $630 million to the government, including $180 million in fines. He and his ferocious colleagues subsequently joined a long list of clever, charismatic, unapologetically predatory leaders who've illustrated, over and over again *for centuries*, that this particular combination rarely sustains its perceived advantage in a single lifetime — and never, *ever* thrives in perpetuity, as so many fallen empires have illustrated throughout history.

Even in the innately competitive, profit-oriented corporate model, McLean and Elkind conclude, "no company can prosper over the long term if every employee is a free agent, motivated solely by greed, no matter how smart he is. No company can function if it only hires brilliant MBAs — and sets them against each other. There is a reason companies value team players, just as there's a reason that people who get along with others tend to do well in corporate life. The reason is simple: you can't build a company on brilliance alone. You need people who can come up with ideas, and you also need people who can implement those ideas and are well compensated for doing so."

In my own tenure as a leader, I've seen the value of educating myself, my students, and my entire staff to do both: find ways to help people develop visionary skills *and* master the art of implementation, further enhancing the reintegration of this previously rigid division of labor through mutual support and consensual leadership. Yet even idealists with the highest integrity and the best of intentions fall back now and then into the same worn-out patterns their ancestors learned as masters, slaves, and rugged individualists. In this effort, it's important to realize that in nature, cooperation trumps competition as an evolutionary force.

Missing Links

Well over a hundred years ago, a budding naturalist noticed that *mutual aid* within and even between species was a significant factor in determining fitness for survival. Prince Pyotr Alekseyevich Kropotkin started out as a huge fan of Darwin's influential theories. In fact, he was so excited about the concept of natural selection that he decided to use his significant influence and financial resources to launch research expeditions through eastern Siberia, northern Manchuria, and later, the steppes of Eurasia. The czarist-era Russian nobleman had high hopes for his first trip, planning to add his own observations to the scientific literature on evolution. In the late 1800s, he commandeered a group of ten Cossacks and fifty horses for the ambitious journey. But soon enough, he was confused and, initially at least, sorely disappointed.

"I failed to find — although I was eagerly looking for it — that bitter struggle for the means of existence, *among animals belonging to the same species*, which was considered by most Darwinists (though not always Darwin himself) as the dominant characteristic of the struggle for life, and the main factor of evolution," Kropotkin wrote on the very first page of his 1902 book, *Mutual Aid: A Factor of Evolution.*

He was even more disturbed by the fast-growing relationship between Darwinism and sociology, emphasizing that he "could agree with none of the works and pamphlets that had been written upon this important subject. They all endeavored to prove that Man, owing to his higher intelligence and knowledge, *may* mitigate the harshness of the struggle for life between men; but they all recognized at the same time that the struggle for the means of existence, of every animal against all its congeners, and of every man against all other men, was 'a law of Nature.'" In Kropotkin's experience, this potentially destructive view "lacked confirmation from direct observation." By then, he had witnessed significant instances of sociability, mutual support, and *competition avoidance* in the vast numbers of animals he encountered in the Siberian outback.

Watching huge herds of wild ruminants, including semiwild cattle and horses in Transbaikalia, Kropotkin challenged the notion that quantum leaps in evolution could ever have stemmed from sudden climatic change and other dramatic challenges. When "animals have to struggle against scarcity of food," he insisted, they come "out of the ordeal so much impoverished in vigour and health, that *no progressive evolution of the species can be based upon such periods of keen competition.*"

Retrogression, he argued, was more likely to result from extreme environmental stress and grossly limited resources. "All that natural selection can do in times of calamities is to spare the individuals endowed with the greatest endurance for privations of all kinds. So it does among the Siberian horses and cattle. They *are* enduring; they can feed upon the Polar birch in case of need; they resist cold and hunger. But no Siberian horse is capable of carrying half the weight which a European horse carries with ease; no Siberian cow gives half the amount of milk given by a Jersey cow." And, he was quick to point out, humans forced to eke out a meager existence under the pressures of natural disaster, impoverished ecosystems, or relentless war experienced slower intellectual development as a result of ill health and sheer physical weakness.

Competition for limited resources, he concluded, is not the rule either in the animal world or in mankind. In the frigid reality of Siberia, he observed birds, deer, and wild horses slowly, languidly moving south in the fall as squirrels cheerfully collected nuts, and bears became drowsy, preparing to hole up for the winter, emphasizing the wisdom of hibernation, food storage, and seasonal migrations as instinctual efforts to *avoid* fighting for limited resources. Riding across the vast expanse of the Russian steppes, Kropotkin and his contemporaries also compared notes on what he later determined to be the ultimate evolutionary advantage: sociability.

In one impressive instance, a naturalist named Syevertsoff documented nearly a dozen white-tailed eagles acting as a survey team. Spread across the sky at a considerable distance apart, they were together scanning an estimated twenty-five square miles. For a good half hour, individuals held their respective posts, tracing wide circles in silence, until one finally let out a piercing shriek.

Its cry was soon answered by another eagle approaching, "followed by a third, a fourth, and so on, till nine or ten eagles came together and soon disappeared." Later that afternoon, Syevertsoff arrived at the place where he had seen the group descend into the gently rolling grasslands hours earlier. There he discovered the gregarious birds gathered around the corpse of a horse. Some of the eagles, probably the older ones, who had eaten first, were perched on surrounding haystacks keeping watch while the youngsters dined in safety, surrounded by bands of crows.

A lone horse encircled by eagles, not wolves, was an unusual sight — the poor creature may very well have died from injury, old age, or illness. Adult herd animals, after all, are dangerous prey. As Kropotkin emphasized, the collective defense strategies of horses are highly intimidating to even the most ambitious predators: "In the Russian Steppes, [wolves] never attack the horses otherwise than in packs; and yet they have to sustain bitter fights, during which the horses sometimes assume offensive warfare....If the wolves do not retreat promptly, they run the risk of being surrounded by the horses and killed by their hooves."

Mutual aid, he insisted, was a significant factor on both sides of that classic drama, but the sheer numbers of nonpredatory species was an even greater revelation to the Russian prince. Surveying a wide variety of mammals, "the first thing which strikes us is the overwhelming numerical predominance of social species over those few carnivores which do not associate," he wrote, later adding that on the "great plateau of Central Asia we find herds of wild horses, wild donkeys, wild camels, and wild sheep. All these mammals live in societies and nations sometimes numbering hundreds of thousands of individuals, although now, after three centuries of gunpowder civilization, we find but the *debris* of the immense aggregations of old. How trifling, in comparison with them, are the numbers of the carnivores! And how false, therefore, is the view of those who speak of the animal world as if nothing were to be seen in it but lions and hyenas plunging their bleeding teeth into the flesh of their victims! One might as well imagine that the whole of human life is nothing but a succession of war massacres."

The Politics of Cooperation

Kropotkin's optimistic perspective on natural selection ultimately caused him a great deal of trouble, leading him straight to jail, as it turns out (though he eventually escaped). For a czarist-era nobleman to find so many incidents in nature of mutual aid and nonpredatory behavior was one thing. To become a vocal anarchist as a result of these observations was quite another. While some of his discoveries won him worldwide respect as a geographer, he subsequently took on a decidedly subversive mission, disguising himself as a peasant activist and lecturer named Borodin to spread nature-inspired visions of social reform, encouraging peaceful collectives of free, empowered people living in decentralized systems. His pseudonym was a blatant homage to Aleksandr Borodin, an early-nineteenth-century Russian composer who wrote the orchestral piece "In the Steppes of Central Asia," a lush tone poem with hints of oriental and eastern European folk melodies (an early version of "world music") that is still popular today.

Kropotkin's ideas, like Borodin's richly hued compositions, were enigmatic and stirring, promising something essential yet indescribable that might lure the unsuspecting listener off the beaten track. As Geoff Olson revealed in the 2005 *Common Ground* article "Kropotkin vs. Darwin: Cooperation as an Evolutionary Force," Kropotkin's nature-inspired philosophy not only rejected monarchy, it also challenged those later social experiments we've come to see as polar opposites: "the top-down models of communism's central planning and capitalism's free-market monopolies." To make matters worse, this wealthy prince had the nerve to challenge a fast-growing, international pseudoscientific-political philosophy that used Darwinism to justify the "natural laws" of war and predatory business practices, a movement that successfully lobbied to pass legislation in the United States *obligating* modern corporations to *profit* at the expense of any and all other social concerns. According to Olson:

> A particular essay by "Darwin's bulldog," Thomas Huxley, caught [Kropotkin's] attention during this time. "Life was a continuous free fight," wrote Huxley, "and beyond the limited and temporary relaxation of the family, the Hobbesian war of each against all was the normal state of existence." Huxley tempered these remarks to say that it is the duty of human culture to resist the brute violence of the animal world, but the Russian émigré was inflamed by Huxley's belief that the natural world is defined solely by struggle. *Kropotkin believed this to be an extrapolation backwards from human militarism and misery to the natural world.*

Huxley's comments inspired Kropotkin to write a series of rebuttals in *Nineteenth Century* magazine, which he eventually gathered together in his book *Mutual Aid: A Factor of Evolution.* Yet with his anarchist leanings offending royalty, fascists, communists, and free-market capitalists alike, Kropotkin found his work dismissed if not actively suppressed. His ideas would have felt especially threatening to the new industrialized elite, who embraced social Darwinism:

a debased interpretation of "survival of the fittest" concepts in which the rich become richer as a dictate of natural selection — with the powerful fully justified in exploiting the weak.

The entire multicultural history of the twentieth century provides evidence that widespread suffering and *retrogression* abound when opportunists delete mutual aid from the evolutionary program. "It's undeniable," Olson concludes, "that a one-size-fits-all reductionism, pushing the competitive aspect of the living world, helped pave the way for the monstrosities of eugenics and Aryanism. Even Darwin's better interpreters, like Huxley, unwittingly helped this legacy by playing up gladiatorial imagery in their description of life." In light of the Enron fiasco alone, Kropotkin's words ring true, now more than ever:

> [If we] ask Nature: "Who are the fittest: those who are continually at war with each other, or those who support one another?" we at once see that those animals which acquire habits of mutual aid are undoubtedly the fittest. They have more chances to survive, and they attain in their respective classes, the highest development of intelligence and bodily organization.... We may safely say that mutual aide is as much a law of animal life as mutual struggle, but that, as a factor of evolution, it most probably has a far greater importance, inasmuch as it favours the development of such habits and characters as insure the maintenance and further development of the species, together with the greatest amount of welfare and enjoyment of life for the individual, with the least waste of energy.

Life in supportive, nurturing societies, Kropotkin insisted,

> enables the feeblest of insects, the feeblest birds, and the feeblest mammals to resist, or to protect themselves from the most terrible birds and beasts of prey; it permits longevity; it enables the species to rear its progeny with the least waste of energy and to maintain its numbers albeit a very slow birthrate; it enables the gregarious animals to migrate in search of new abodes. Therefore, while fully admitting that force, swiftness, protective colors, cunningness, and endurance to hunger and cold, which are mentioned by Darwin and Wallace, are so many qualities making the individual, or the species, the fittest under certain circumstances, we maintain that under *any* circumstances sociability is the greatest advantage in the struggle for life.

The great thing about science is that, despite a glitch in the system that sometimes prevents valuable new perspectives from gaining acceptance, or even getting published in the first place, evidence eventually builds up and breaks through the personal and cultural biases of the international scientific community. Often this happens only after a rigid hierarchy dies off and a new generation takes over, but from a cathedral-thinking point of view, the process remains sound (though perhaps needlessly, sometimes dangerously, slow and ponderous).

Such is the case with twenty-first-century research that effectively challenges the "gladiator view" of nature, enhancing Kropotkin's mutual aid theory with an even more adventurous hypothesis. Compelling new evidence suggests that between ten and thirty thousand years ago, a new innovation — the human-animal bond — spurred a quantum leap in our own evolution through brain-altering biochemical responses and mutual behavior modification, leading to a shocking yet unmistakable conclusion: the species with whom our ancestors formed mutually beneficial relationships *gentled* and domesticated *us* as much as we domesticated them. What's more, the fields of animal-assisted therapy and equine-facilitated learning demonstrate that horses, dogs, and other companion animals are still upping the ante, empowering and training us in ways we are only now beginning to understand.

On a planet so intimately mapped through satellite surveillance, the last frontier may be hidden in our own barns and backyards. Our peaceful nickering and tail-wagging friends have been waiting, for centuries, for us to realize they're not just here to help us protect territory, trek through the wilderness, and master nature; they're *innately equipped* to assist us in tapping those higher levels of awareness, compassion, and leadership essential to fulfilling our role as *responsible* stewards of the earth, its myriad cultures, and its vast array of sentient, uniquely gifted life-forms.

Chapter Seven

ABEL'S GENIUS

*T*he *human-animal bond is shrouded in mystery*. We will never know who coaxed the first wolf to take a morsel of food by hand, who cuddled the first ancestral feline, or who rode the first horse. Not only did we form mutually beneficial partnerships with other species thousands of years before the invention of writing, historians and scientists didn't spend much time speculating how domestication occurred until the twentieth century. And the world's creation stories don't fare much better. It's as if, from the moment we first became conscious, the animals were already there, so intimately interwoven with human life that their presence was universally taken for granted, like rain, like the seasons, like breathing.

In Genesis, the beasts of the field and the birds of the air were named by Adam, who was created last, but there's no mention of how, why, or when the first man was inspired to form relationships with certain animals. There's that unfortunate episode with a crafty talking snake and the subsequent expulsion from paradise. The next thing we know, Adam's sons are reaping harvests, herding livestock, and fighting over which approach is better, a sedentary agricultural lifestyle or a nomadic pastoral one. The subsequent murder of one brother by the other depicts man's violent rebellion against God's *preference* and draws attention to humanity's forgetfulness of the real issue involved, one that, to this very day, promotes widespread human suffering.

Whether or not you consider yourself religious, and whether or not your orientation is Judeo-Christian, it is well worth analyzing the meaning behind this tempestuous tale. And it really doesn't matter if you interpret the Bible as literal, metaphorical, or a combination of both in this case. There's significant historical, psychological, and cultural information packed into the Cain and Abel conflict, which we would all benefit from remembering — that is, bringing to full, integrated consciousness. I originally touched on this subject in my first book, *The Tao of Equus*, in 2001, but recent theories on the human-animal bond suggest this ancient story may coincide with some compelling, newly emerging scientific research as well.

The Bible contains the collective wisdom, innovations, and historical dilemmas of a highly successful, seminomadic culture confronting the increasing influence of landowning, wealth-amassing, slaveholding civilizations throughout the Middle East. Much of what seems paradoxical in the sayings and writings of Moses and Jesus — and the countless others who contributed to this multifaceted volume — makes perfect sense in the context of a nonsedentary philosophy. It all started when God accepted Abel's pastoral offering over Cain's presentation of the fruits of his agricultural labors. The creator of the universe wasn't promoting meat over vegetables or satisfying some supernaturally demented thirst for blood. He was endorsing the shepherd's lifestyle, one that requires caring for and moving with the animals. But why would wandering around the countryside protecting sheep from wolves win out over peacefully tending to grains, grapes, dates, and flowers?

Here's where the idea of a divine intelligence comes in, the logic of which we are only now, in the twenty-first century, capable of deciphering through modern science and a good five thousand years of brutal trial and error.

East of Eden

For those who aren't familiar with this story, let's go straight to the source, in this case the New International Version of Genesis, chapter 4, which opens with Eve giving birth to Cain and, later, his brother Abel:

> Now Abel kept flocks, and Cain worked the soil. In the course of time Cain brought some of the fruits of the soil as an offering to the Lord. And Abel also brought an offering — fat portions from some of the firstborn of his flock. The Lord looked with favor on Abel and his offering, but on Cain and his offering he did not look with favor. So Cain was very angry, and his face was downcast.
>
> Then the Lord said to Cain, "Why are you angry? Why is your face downcast? If you do what is right, will you not be accepted? But if you do not do what is right, sin is crouching at your door; it desires to have you, but you must rule over it."

It's important to note that Abel doesn't engage in blood sacrifice, instead offering what he considers the most desirable parts of animals culled for his own sustenance. Cain's pride is visibly wounded, but God takes the time to explain his decision, encouraging the planter to follow a different path, foreshadowing some difficulties and temptations arising from this lifestyle over time.

Cain, however, takes the rejection personally. Unwilling to accept the drawbacks of his "career" choice, let alone change his behavior in response, he decides to get rid of the competition, luring Abel out to the field. In a fit of rage, Cain attacks and kills his younger brother, then lies when God asks him where Abel is.

"I don't know," Cain replies in this classic passage: "Am I my brother's keeper?"

"Your brother's blood cries out to me from the ground," God reveals, whereupon he punishes the first murderer, not by executing him, but by making it clear that the land "will no longer yield its crops" for Cain, essentially forcing him to leave his sedentary life and "be a restless wanderer on the earth."

Eventually, Cain does settle down again, "in Nod, east of Eden," where he marries, and builds a city named after his son Enoch. Yet the pastoral approach refuses to die out completely. Eve has another son, Seth. And even in Cain's line, the nomadic perspective emerges generations later, when his great-great-great-great grandson Jabal becomes "the father of those who live in tents and raise livestock," marking an exciting era for all sorts of innovations: Jabal's brother Jubal becomes "the father of all who play stringed instruments and pipes," and their half brother Tubal-Cain forges "all kinds of tools out of bronze and iron."

Abel-Bodied Vagrants

Back in the 1990s, when I was researching the domestication of the horse and the subsequent development of the ancient Eurasian horse tribes, I came across a number of intriguing books about other pastoral cultures and the benefits of this lifestyle in general. Daniel Quinn's award-winning novel *Ishmael* and Jim Corbett's brilliant yet lesser-known nonfiction work *Goatwalking* were particularly creative and insightful. Both cited the Cain and Abel story as marking a significant turning point in humanity's cultural evolution. In this sense, Cain's impulse to murder his sheepherding brother and build the first city represents the lethal animosity nomadic peoples have experienced in the presence of sedentary cultures since the beginning of civilization.

Quinn's fictional narrator discovers this bit of wisdom while engaging in telepathic debates with a gorilla who discusses the "Leavers," the hunter-gatherers, who live in harmony with nature, and the "Takers," the city dwellers, who arose with the agricultural revolution and aimed to conquer all other life-forms, destroying many species in the process. The book doesn't distinguish between a hunter-gatherer approach and the nomadic pastoral lifestyle, which as I mentioned in chapter 5, was an innovation that grew out of settled agricultural communities. The Bible *does* recognize Abel as Cain's younger brother, however, adding to the accuracy of this tale as a vehicle for retaining the memory of prehistoric events through eons of oral tradition.

While Quinn's novel artfully teases the modern mind with the first tendrils of a nomadic perspective, Corbett's 1991 book offers more specific information on the psychospiritual effects of pastoralism. *Goatwalking* resurrects Abel's wisdom by describing the profound realizations the author himself gained from wandering through the Arizona desert with herds of milk goats, engaging in the nomadic lifestyle for extended periods of time. Through this effort, he reconnected with the original meaning of the sabbatical, the ancient Jewish tradition of renewing the land — and most important, its people — by letting the ground "lie fallow" every seventh year.

The idea of the sabbatical, presented in the book of Leviticus, stems from a series of messages Moses received from God shortly before his people entered the Promised Land. After they were liberated from Egyptian slavery, the Jews, as you may remember, were sentenced to wander aimlessly through the desert for engaging in an embarrassing episode of idolatry. From a nonsedentary perspective, however, this wasn't so much a punitive move on God's part as a *necessary* correctional effort. After living with the ultimate pyramid-building, slaveholding city dwellers for untold generations, the demoralized, disempowered tribes of Israel would have needed to reawaken their rusty pastoral skills before they were capable of reinstating their unique culture in the Promised Land. Otherwise they might have built their own version of Egypt in Canaan. So they were compelled to meander through the wilderness, vagrants without a home, until they reclaimed Abel's wisdom and realized that nature was *designed* to nurture when treated with trust, affection, and respect.

To me, what follows marks a particularly fascinating moment in biblical history: On the eve of the Israelites' entry into Canaan, God decides to *collaborate* with his creation. Knowing full well that some members of these tribes would prefer, like Cain, to settle in one place, till the soil, and even build cities, he compromises with them, searching for a way to help them maintain balance. His solution involves, of all things, requiring people to keep at least some connection with the nomadic pastoral lifestyle, one that exercises the mutually respectful *interdependence* of human and nature, as opposed to the conqueror's human-*over*-nature mentality. Those who knew how to thrive in the wilderness would also be less prone to help others amass great wealth at the expense of personal freedom, and more likely to flee if things got out of hand and tyranny began to rule the land.

So, in addition to outlining all sorts of laws governing proper social behavior, the book of Leviticus introduces the idea of the *sabbatical*, a divine edict specifying that, every seven years, the people are obliged to shirk their workaday responsibilities and literally *go feral*.

A Recipe for Remembering

As a consequence of killing his brother and building the first city, Cain forgot the meaning of the Sabbath and lost his connection to the redemptive powers of nature, Corbett observes. Yet some manifestation of divine intelligence kept trying to jump-start humanity's memory, at times by compelling receptive individuals to leave the city, sneak out of the palace, or put down the plow and just start walking. Moses climbs Mount Sinai, receiving the Ten Commandments and later introducing the sabbatical. Lao-tzu, the Buddha, and Muhammad all spend significant time alone in nature before accessing their profoundly influential visions. Jesus wanders through the desert for forty days and forty nights before he returns to civilization, urging others to drop their fishing nets, abandon their businesses, and simply follow him to...God *knows* where. It's important to realize, however, that through this act the carpenter from Judea would have been reinforcing centuries of tradition. Judaism, until very recently, was remarkable in its long-standing commitment to ensuring that the entire population experienced the nomadic pastoralist's recipe for renewal, connection, and catharsis on a regular basis.

"For millennia," Corbett emphasizes in *Goatwalking*, "Semitic peoples have called wilderness 'God's land,' distinguishing it from settled areas possessed and remade to fit human plans.... The sabbath day is a time to quit grabbing at the world, to rest, and to rejoice in the Creation's goodness. During the sabbath year all are to cease making their living agriculturally, supporting themselves instead from the land's spontaneous, uncultivated growth. Debts are to be canceled and slaves are to be freed. Land ownership also reverts on the jubilee year [every seventh seven-year cycle]; no one shall permanently subjugate the earth or another person."

Part history, part philosophy, part law treatise and ritualistic handbook, the Judeo-Christian Bible also promotes collaborating with nature as a way of strengthening connection to spirit — explicitly in partnership with animals, no less. And this is where the story gets *really* interesting. Recent scientific studies suggest that living closely with their herds, rather than simply communing with the scenery, offered a developmental advantage to the people who undertook this lifestyle, increasing courage, trust, compassion, sociability, adaptability, and personal empowerment through a variety of hormonal and behavioral changes initiated and reinforced by the human-animal bond itself.

The fact that we've lost sight of these benefits in modern times marks yet another cycle of Cain's forgetfulness. It's not a moral failing. It's a pitfall of the sedentary, city-based lifestyle. Enslaved by ambition, we've pulled out all the stops this time, becoming a culture of obsessive overachievers, leading to a host of stress-related illnesses and greed-related acts of violence. But there are still pockets of the nomadic pastoral lifestyle scattered across the earth, and they do, in fact, hold the memory of something we can't afford to lose.

"Settled people," Corbett observes, "work relentlessly to remake and possess the earth because they can live only in man-made habitats where they are subjugated and used by whoever controls the land. In contrast, nomads take life sabbatically, as a gift from 'God's land.' Rejecting Cain's way, the prophetic faith recalls its nomadic origins when making its offering of first fruits, beginning with the words, 'My father was a cimarron Aramean' (Dt 26:5). From Tibet to Morocco, Kazakhstan to Baja, nomads identify with the cimarron, the domesticated animal that goes feral, the escaped slave who knows how to be at home in God's land[,]...opening nomadic consciousness to insights unknown to peoples who worship owner-masters because they can live only within the man-made world's make-believe boundaries....Learning to live by fitting into an ecological niche rather than by fitting into a dominance-submission hierarchy opens human awareness to another kind of society based on equal rights of creative agency for all."

Judeo-Christian philosophy has always been, and forever shall be, in conflict with civilization as we know it, creating a pesky incongruous feeling, a kind of nagging sandpaper of the soul, in any sincerely religious person forced to disrespect the earth by custom, circumstance, or the next paycheck. In the same book outlining the practice of the sabbatical, God makes it perfectly clear that "the land must not be sold permanently, for the land belongs to me. You are only foreigners, my tenant farmers" (Leviticus 25:23). And what landlord, after all, would knowingly lease a fine estate to a group of people planning to strip it, gut it, sell off its assets, and fill the large gaping hole with toxic waste and smoking garbage? In this sense, oddly enough, the Old Testament coincides philosophically with traditional Native American beliefs on respect for nature and the absurdity of buying and selling property, as no mortal man can truly own God's green earth — or rocky stretch of desert, for that matter.

It's time for *us* to compromise and collaborate with the divine for a change, to find ways of consciously integrating the twin innovations of Cain and Abel, accessing the benefits and lessening the weaknesses or inconveniences of both. God, after all, didn't execute Cain, surely seeing a stroke of genius in the eyes of that profoundly aggressive, deeply troubled soul — namely, a gift for technological and artistic advances that would have stirred a hint of hope and perhaps even pride in this vast yet compassionate intelligence.

Made in the image of our creator, we are, after all creatures designed to create, perfectly capable at this point in our development of reinventing ourselves and our society — if, unlike Cain, enough of us are willing to look at the destructive aspects of our lifestyle and change our behavior in response.

Adopting a nomadic pastoral lifestyle is no longer practical. Forming mutually respectful relationships with other species, on the other hand, is fully possible. Increasing research suggests that animal-assisted educational and therapeutic practices are both transformational and healing, helping people master the advanced human-development skills crucial to leadership and innovation. Translated into a twenty-first-century context, Abel's wisdom involves recognizing that animals not only nourish and protect us physically, they help us develop psychologically and socially through brain-altering biochemical responses and mutual behavior modification. The human-animal bond is one place where science, history, and religion firmly intersect — and inform one another. As myths and spiritual texts from around the world insist, horses, dogs, cats, and other domesticated companions are gifts from a creative intelligence that has been rooting for us all along.

We just haven't fully unwrapped the package yet.

Fox and Hound

Fossil records suggest that wolves were the first animals to be tamed and transformed — thousands, perhaps tens of thousands of years before other animals. Theories about how this happened abound, though everyone assumes it was a long, slow, precarious process. But a groundbreaking study at a Siberian research facility shows that the main physical and behavioral hallmarks of domestication could actually have been achieved in a single century — *if* a tribe of ancestral animal lovers had purposefully bred individuals who were less aggressive, less fearful, and more willing to engage with members of another species for reasons other than sustenance.

This evolutionary shortcut, of course, would have required a group of less aggressive, less fearful *people* who were interested in engaging with another species for reasons other than fur or sustenance. But the human side of the equation was actively suppressed in a Soviet geneticist's incredibly efficient experiment involving semiwild foxes. In 1959, Dmitri Belyaev launched a study to test whether animals with specific behavioral traits might become more amenable to domestication if they were bred to each other over numerous generations. Most researchers were interested in the physical characteristics common to domesticated animals: increased or decreased size, increased reproductive frequency, and pedomorphosis, the retention of juvenile traits by adults, including rounded skulls and floppy ears. The latter innovation was especially intriguing to Charles Darwin, who notes in his *Origin of Species* that "not a single domestic animal can be named which has not in some country drooping ears," a feature that isn't found among mature wild animals except the elephant.

Horses are occasionally born with floppy ears. Some of these individuals excel in competition despite their comical appearance, but they're rarely allowed to mate. Unlike in certain dog breeds where the characteristic is valued, drooping ears are not considered cute or desirable in the equestrian world. Yet despite millennia of selective breeding, the trait still shows up now and then, lending credence to the idea that floppy ears are a universal by-product of animal domestication, enhanced by humans in some species and vehemently discouraged in others. Belyaev's research confirms this notion, taking it one colossal step further: his Farm-Fox Experiment suggests that selectively breeding generations of animals for less fearful and/or less aggressive behavior quickly gives rise to the *entire array* of physical changes associated with pedomorphosis.

Born in 1917, Belyaev was an adventurous soul, intrigued by Darwin's theories but fully capable of putting his own imaginative, informed spin on them. Like Kropotkin, he occasionally suffered for his paradigm-busting insights, but that didn't stop him for long. In 1948, Belyaev lost his job at a Moscow laboratory for standing up to an anti-Darwin Soviet scientific movement. But moving to Siberia wasn't a depressing cliché for the controversial geneticist; it was a reality that spurred him to step out to the very edge of accepted evolutionary theory.

By the mid-twentieth century, growing evidence suggested that behavioral responses in all animals were regulated by a fine balance between neurotransmitters and hormones that affected the whole organism. Belyaev took this idea and ran with it. Working in the relatively sophisticated city of Novosibirsk (known as the "Chicago of Siberia"), he found support to test a novel proposition: he wanted to see if strengthening the *behavioral* traits associated with tamability might provoke some of the *physiological* changes associated with domestication.

So he chose the most courageous, naturally curious and gregarious foxes from a commercial fur farm in Estonia. To rule out training as a contributing factor, he kept human interaction with his test subjects to a minimum. And, as animal researchers are still prone to do, he housed them in an extremely stressful, unnatural environment — removing pups from their mothers at two months and putting them in small individual cages at three months. Even so, within a mere *six* generations, Belyaev succeeded in producing foxes that were easy to hand-feed and that would bark, wag their tails, and enthusiastically initiate contact with the experimenters. Some of these animals would whimper to attract attention, sniffing and licking their aloof caretakers like dogs begging for affection, melting the hearts of some of these scientists over time. Much more surprising was how dramatically the foxes changed physically through an experiment selecting for behavior, the low-fear and low-aggression traits that Belyaev theorized would lead to tamability and, eventually, full-fledged domestication if emphasized over thousands of years.

Only it didn't take thousands of years. Once a single scientist came up with the idea of breeding individuals with an *aptitude* for interspecies sociability, it took a mere *forty years* for a startling transformation to occur. The foxes began to *look* more like dogs, complete with curled tails, floppy ears, and striking multicolored coats offering no camouflage benefit whatsoever. The increasingly docile animals lost their musky smell, retained juvenile facial characteristics as adults, and were able to reproduce more often. Counterintuitively, selecting for behavior produced nearly *all* the physical characteristics associated with domestication, *instantly*: the thirty to thirty-five generations of selective breeding necessary to produce a hundred members of this recognizable new subspecies were literally a blip on the screen in relation to evolution.

Foxes considered truly domesticated didn't just look different, they were innately eager to please, competing with each other for the experimenter's attention when turned out in groups. Lyudmila Trut, who took over the experiment after Belyaev's death in 1985, believes their identity and continued development are now fully entwined with humans, a fact that the animals themselves understand instinctually. As she explains in her 1999 article for *American Scientist*, "Several of our domesticated foxes have escaped from the fur farm for days. All of them eventually returned. Probably they would have been unable to survive in the wild."

Some of these trusting, affectionate, incredibly beautiful animals are now sold as pets rather than callously slaughtered for their fur, but the move from cage to companion is much more than a humane option for reducing the pack and raising funds for the research center. The experimenters recognize the limitations of selective breeding in a vacuum (though the first fifty years of results were unexpectedly impressive). If funding continues, Trut and her colleagues plan to study what role the fox-human bond might play in the continued evolution of this species as it moves closer to the independent classification dogs received when their wolf ancestors transformed from *Canis lupus lupus* to *Canis familiaris*. She emphasizes that

> the domestic fox is not a domestic dog, but we believe it has the genetic potential to become more and more doglike. We can continue to increase that potential through further breeding, but the foxes will realize it fully only through close contact with human beings. Over the years, other investigators and I have raised several fox pups in domestic conditions, either in the laboratory or at home as pets. They have shown themselves to be good-tempered creatures, as devoted as dogs but as independent as cats, capable of forming deep-rooted pair bonds with human beings — mutual bonds, as those of us who work with them know. If our experiment should continue, and if fox pups could be raised and trained the way dog puppies are now, there is no telling what sort of animal they might one day become.

The Oxytocin Factor

Trut's acknowledgment of a "mutual bond" is significant. Film clips documenting this study at the Institute of Cytology and Genetics at Novosibirsk show how hard it must have been for staff members with the slightest scrap of warmth and compassion to resist their subjects' heartbreaking attempts to connect. To maintain the detachment Belyaev required, researchers had to ignore foxes reaching through the bars, crying out for attention (unlike their shy and fearful wild counterparts, who huddled at the back of those tiny wire enclosures). Once experimenters were allowed to hold and cuddle one of those furry little creatures, however, both species would have been hooked as surely as if they had been injected with one of the most potent, feel-good drugs known to man, or rather, woman. After all, as behavior-changing hormones go, oxytocin, released most reliably in humans when nursing babies or petting animals, is the ultimate bonding agent, one that creates a mind-altering combination of courage, focus, calmness, trust, and intense well-being, to boot.

Oxytocin both *inspires* and *rewards* connection. In part by reducing blood pressure and buffering the flight-or-fight response, this versatile hormone activates the physical, mental, and emotional receptivity needed for mammals to approach each other. Oxytocin then ups the ante, jump-starting social recognition circuits while reinforcing "tend and befriend" behavior through a release of dopamine, which can produce feelings of elation similar to mild doses of cocaine. Some scientists believe that dopamine uses this pleasure principle as "a teaching signal" to engage parts of the brain responsible for acquiring new behavior. In oxytocin's case, it's an explicit recommendation to form strong, mutually beneficial relationships. After all, when oxytocin works its magic, the caretaker or "befriender" receives as much or more of a dopamine boost as the object of her affection.

Both sexes produce this potent chemical, but in women estrogen enhances oxytocin's power. Testosterone, which men produce at high levels under stress, seems to reduce oxytocin's effects. In the chemistry of connection, women have a marked evolutionary advantage, making a strong case for the pivotal roles that females, human *and* animal, played in forging the interspecies bonds that led to domestication.

Oxytocin bears the unique double distinction of being the very first hormone to be identified in the early twentieth century and the first polypeptide to be sequenced and synthesized, more than forty years later. The American biochemist Vincent du Vigneaud won a Nobel Prize for the latter feat in 1955, but oxytocin's relationship-enhancing benefits weren't recognized until the end of the century, when a handful of women scientists became interested in its myriad effects. For a good eighty years after the hormone was isolated in 1902, it was seen as a purely mechanistic, birth-related phenomenon causing uterine contractions and milk release. It took a breast-feeding researcher on maternity leave in the 1980s to notice how dramatically oxytocin affected a woman's behavior, emotions, and perceptions of the world.

Kerstin Uvnäs Moberg had all the right stuff to excel in the academic world: the keen logic, relentless attention to detail, and innovative leaps of thought that, when combined with exceptional endurance and ambition, helped her complete an MD and PhD, gaining her a position at Uppsala University in Sweden. She also managed to start a family during that time. Thank God she had the inclination and sheer energy to become a supermom, because her subsequent reputation as a pioneering researcher rests on her direct exposure to the powerful, mind-altering effects of motherhood. "In pregnancy, nursing, and close contact with my children, I experienced a state diametrically opposed to the stress I was familiar with in connection with life's other challenges," she reveals in her book *The Oxytocin Factor*. "I was aware that the psychological conditions associated with pregnancy and nurturing fostered something entirely different from challenge, competition, and performance."

As Meg Daley Olmert summarizes in *Made for Each Other: The Biology of the Human-Animal Bond*, "Uvnäs Moberg returned to her lab at Sweden's Karolinska Institute to design a series of studies that would compare the mental and physical condition of breast-feeding and bottle-feeding mothers with the amount of oxytocin circulating in their blood. She found that in addition to having higher levels of oxytocin than nonnursing mothers, breast-feeding women feel less aggressive and less anxious, as well as less suspicious and less guilty. They also enjoy greater physical ease with fewer complaints of gut and somatic anxiety and experience less muscular tension than bottle-feeding mothers."

Uvnäs Moberg's uncommon ability to integrate the personal and scientific dimensions of her life spurred a host of studies, articles, and books on oxytocin. Her work finally legitimized the long-ignored yet intensely connective, arguably mystical states that women had been accessing, naturally, for eons. As science and technology journalist Susan Kuchinskas emphasizes in *The Chemistry of Connection*, "Many women find breastfeeding to be a deeply absorbing, meditative experience. The world seems to drop away as a mother gazes down at her baby. She's wrapped in a profound space, and may feel an oceanic joy and cosmic connection, not only with the infant but also with everything else."

If Sigmund Freud had lived a century later, he might have been less concerned with penis envy and more impressed with a woman's ability to mainline oxytocin. The good news is that men can experience the benefits of this wonder hormone too, and without a lot of effort — if they spend more time with women, children, and animals in ways that foster connection and affection over dominance and submission. And it is here, finally, where we begin to understand the ancient biblical preference for the pastoral lifestyle as an evolutionary force capable of balancing the more destructive tendencies of our immensely talented and incredibly dangerous species.

The Prime Directive

Over the past thirty years, studies involving rats, prairie voles, dogs, and humans have demonstrated that oxytocin makes mammals less fearful and more curious, encouraging individuals not only to form pair bonds, nest, and nurture their young but also to leave the nest and explore unfamiliar territory, most especially new relationships. "When given oxytocin," Uvnäs Moberg explains, "groups of rats of the same sex become more gregarious and less afraid of contact. As aggression in the group decreases noticeably, friendly socialization replaces it. Rather than avoid each other, the rats prefer to sit next to each other. This closeness leads in its turn to the release of still more oxytocin."

The hormone is increased on both sides of an interaction when mothers nurse their young, when animals of any age groom, lick, or stroke each other, and when they engage in mutually desired sexual activity (as opposed to aggressive, forced encounters). As a scientist, however, Uvnäs Moberg used oxytocin injections to isolate its effects in individuals. Subsequent experiments showed ever more startling results, including elevated pain thresholds, faster wound healing, and heightened learning capacity. But she could never fully separate oxytocin's influence on an individual's physiology from the hormone's prime directive: to calm and connect with others.

As she marvels in *The Oxytocin Factor*, "Surprisingly, to a lesser degree, *animals that live in the same cage but have not directly received the oxytocin also show the same changes.* The other animals in the cage become calmer and have lower levels of stress hormones." Astonished by this contact-high effect, Uvnäs Moberg gave the untreated companions a drug to suppress oxytocin. Sure enough, the hormone's inherently contagious nature was blocked, suggesting that those original oxytocin-injected rats were somehow able to activate the oxytocin systems of their cage mates. Subsequent experiments showed that oxytocin's benefits could be activated in others not only through nursing and direct touch but through smell, vocal tone, and other senses.

Oxytocin's continuously positive effect on the herd, not just the individual, prompted the Swedish scientist to emphasize that we "need calm and connection not only to avoid illness, but also to enjoy life, to feel curious, optimistic, creative. These qualities are hard to measure scientifically. What research does show, however, is that concentration and learning are also improved by a peaceful environment and nurturing relationships. Children under stress have a harder time learning than those who are calm and secure."

Research into oxytocin's benefits — along with the outrageous physical transformations of foxes selected for tamability in Belyaev's work — has made it clear that evolution does not promote an aggressive, fear-producing survival-of-the-fittest mentality. Rather, nature continually softens this most basic protective instinct behaviorally and biochemically through a preference for sociability and mutual aid.

Kropotkin's work stood alone in its recognition of this factor almost a century before it could be bolstered scientifically. But even while riding horses through the Siberian outback, the Russian prince seemed only vaguely conscious of *interspecies* relationships as the ultimate endorsement of his own theory. Here's where a growing number of modern researchers effectively come to *his* aid.

Powerfully Strong and Powerfully Nice

In *Made for Each Other*, Meg Daley Olmert explores the history, biology, and myriad benefits of the human-animal bond. Her groundbreaking 2009 book was the first to depict oxytocin as a crucial biochemical factor in domestication. Olmert's wide-ranging, multidisciplinary research also makes a strong case for the hormone's continued influence on pet owners and on people helped through animal-assisted therapy. Most significant is a 2003 South African study led by Johannes Odendaal and R. A. Meintjes showing that "when eighteen men and women interacted with their dogs (talking to them and gently stroking them) the owners' blood levels of oxytocin almost *doubled* — and their dogs were also twice as enriched with oxytocin!" Along with this rise in the hormone came a significant decrease in blood pressure and the stress hormone cortisol, as well as an increase in beta endorphins and dopamine.

Olmert has been in contact with Uvnäs Moberg over the years, and both of these women have deeply enriched my understanding of equine-facilitated therapeutic and educational practices that work, in part, by releasing oxytocin into the system. But there's another hormone that adds a bit more spice to the story, particularly in the context of leadership development. In *The Oxytocin Factor*, Uvnäs Moberg compares the "calm and connect" effect in rats with the effect of a similar substance, vasopressin, which differs by only two amino acids. This behavior-altering hormone also encourages pair bonding, especially during sexual activity, but in a wider social context it promotes a decidedly macho approach. Vasopressin, she says,

> instills courage by making the individual feel aggressive and fearless. The rat, male or female, is prepared to attack, mark territory, and vigorously defend itself. Oxytocin instead fosters courage by diminishing the feeling of danger and conveying the sense that there is less to be afraid of. Animal studies appear to show that oxytocin has a special ability to make animals "nice." Physiologically, therefore, a substance related to strength and readiness (vasopressin) is a close relative to one that produces friendliness and caring (oxytocin). They function in different ways, and we need them both. As the popular Swedish fictional character Pippi Longstocking says, "The one who is powerfully strong must also be powerfully nice."

Nowhere is this paradoxical combination exercised more dramatically than in traditional pastoral cultures. Here, the predatory side of human nature protects and culls the herd, while the nonpredatory side nurtures the herd. Cattle, sheep, goats, camels, horses, and other animals are treated not as slaves or commodities but as valued members of an interspecies society. Herders exhibit tremendous pride in and affection for their animals, who in turn trust their two-legged companions to lead them to greener pastures, oversee their mating, assist their births, and milk them — the ultimate oxytocin-producing activity.

Meat composes a surprisingly modest part of the pastoral diet. Modern tribes mix grains, roots, fruits, and vegetables (gathered, traded, or planted and reaped during seasonal migrations) with lots of dairy products, everything from butter and cheese to fermented mood-altering drinks like koumiss, which Mongolia's nomadic horse tribes make from mare's milk. Some cultures, such as Africa's cattle-oriented Masai and Siberia's reindeer-based Even people, occasionally consume blood from living members of the herd, though milk remains the staple. Moving with the animals keeps these people physically fit — electrocardiogram tests applied to four hundred young adult male Masai found no evidence of heart disease, abnormalities, or malfunction. Despite significant dairy consumption, their cholesterol levels were about 50 percent of the level of the average American.

Close interaction with powerful, nonpredatory animals also promotes mental, emotional, relational, and spiritual balance — as well as a form of empowerment that deftly combines fierceness and sensitivity. It is, after all, much more dangerous to herd, ride, or milk a large herbivore, even a domesticated one, than it is to hunt it from a distance. Interspecies affinity, attention to non-verbal cues, mutual respect, and mutual trust are literally survival skills for herding cultures.

Lost Knowledge

The human element also coordinates, thoughtfully and compassionately, with the realities of the ecosystem. Mongolia's highly successful pastoralists, who raise horses, sheep, goats, camels, and cattle, cull animals in the fall that aren't likely to survive the harsh winter ahead, drying the meat to sustain the herders' families until spring. In *Living with Herds: Human-Animal Coexistence in Mongolia*, Natasha Fijn effectively illustrates how deeply these cultures care for their animals. Oxytocin's social recognition circuits cross species lines, creating, as Fijn discovered, a nature-based philosophy of equality. The Mongolian pastoralists she encountered knew every animal by name. This, however, didn't affect their ability to make tough decisions. Rather, it reinforced "an egalitarian outlook, without favouritism or treating the animal as the equivalent of a pet. Likewise the attitude within Mongolian herding society is to take care of everyone within the herding community, not just singling out individuals for special treatment. Nonetheless, contingencies such as extreme weather conditions, parental survival, and other factors do require that some animals have differential treatment from others," particularly in the case of orphan foals, calves, or lambs who are brought into the tent, bottle-fed, then released back into the larger herd when strong.

Yet while Mongolian pastoralists are loving and nurturing, they're perfectly capable of standing up to an ornery bull, feisty colt, or rearing stallion. And they're fierce yet reverent in culling the herd. The human role effectively combines parent, leader, and predator through a sacred trust, ensuring that all the herders' animals have an opportunity to live a full life and, when the time comes, to die quickly, humanely, and meaningfully, as opposed to enduring extended suffering from weakness and starvation. Even so, "Mongolians do not eat animals that are under one year of age," she emphasizes. When she told one of the tribe members about the Western practice of consuming lamb and veal, tears welled up in the woman's eyes as she quietly said, "We love our young animals, so we couldn't eat them."

"She must have thought it a strange practice," Fijn concludes, "as she was being so careful to nurture some weak lambs that were sleeping beside the hearth in front of her. It would be counterintuitive for a herder to kill them and eat them before they had produced any young of their own, when the animals had not yet lived a full life. If a young lamb dies from weakness or illness, the herder then utilizes the hide but does not eat the meat." This reluctance to consume what our culture considers a delicacy shows how deeply bonded Mongolian herders become through the oxytocin-boosting activities of nursing and caring for the tribe's four-legged children.

Adults are also treated with reverence in death, but in a different way. Strict traditions ensure that individuals are killed humanely and quietly, away from the herd, the women, and the children. It's disrespectful to waste any part of an older animal. Only the bones, which Mongolians believe house the souls of all living creatures, are left untouched, so that the spirits of cherished herd members can be released according to their own timing, to be reincarnated. This means that dogs are prevented from chewing on bones. The Buddhist-influenced tribes that Fijn studied also believe that people sometimes reincarnate as "one of the five animals" (as horses, sheep, goats, camels, or cattle) and vice versa, lending an even deeper sense of sacrifice and communion to this symbiotic pact.

The close interspecies relationships that herding cultures develop, regardless of differing beliefs about the afterlife, can also be glimpsed throughout the Bible. The kosher code of the Jewish faith, in which a holy man actively blesses each creature before the slaughter, is the only remnant of this impulse that modern Western society has retained. Orthodox tradition strictly forbids cruelty to animals, outlining the specific procedures, prayers, and spiritual mind-set for mediating such a sacrifice. Interestingly, kosher laws also forbid the ingestion of blood on the grounds that this would commingle animal with human life streams. (When Christ offered his blood as well as his flesh at the Last Supper, this powerful gesture would have been readily understood as the act of merging his life stream with those of his followers.) The Even people of Siberia, who believe they are half human, half reindeer, do in fact ingest the blood of their animals, as do the Mongolian pastoralists, who are perfectly comfortable with the idea of humans and animals reincarnating across species lines.

The close association between two-legged and four-legged members of these tribes further explains why Jesus easily moved back and forth between metaphors in which he was depicted as a shepherd and a lamb. In fact, once you reconnect with Christianity's nomadic pastoral roots, the ritual of communion becomes a *multidimensional* symbolic act, designed not only to bring individuals closer to God but to keep Abel's perspective alive whenever and wherever city dwellers try to subjugate man and nature in support of a disconnected, materialistic cult of owner-masters. In this sense, Christ's paradigm-altering efforts to include non-Jewish people in the sacrament he created could also be seen as an attempt to balance the predation running amok in the Greco-Roman world, offering a potent transfusion of nonpredatory wisdom in the wake of increasing violence.

Extreme carnage wasn't just tolerated in Jesus's era; it was cultivated. The vast Roman Empire was managed by force and intimidation, reinforced by sadistic "games" at the Coliseum: gladiator exhibitions, public executions, and "beast hunts" (in which thousands of animals were slaughtered "with the right degree of cruelty"). The Roman historian Cicero praised this brutal style of entertainment for its ability to desensitize people to horrific acts, preparing them for battle. The fact that we now use our stadiums for football rather than blood sport is a testament to Christianity's effectiveness as an early form of social activism.

Whether or not you're moved to join the religion Jesus inspired, his life is historically and culturally significant, especially when you consider the wisdom of the pastoralist's perspective. Jesus actively reinforced a nomadic, nonpredatory philosophy at one of the most brutal times in history: He was born in a stable and laid in a manger. He encouraged people to give up their possessions and wander the earth, letting God through nature take care of their needs. He abhorred violence, even for self-preservation, yet he faced tragedy with a fierceness capable of challenging injustice without sacrificing compassion. Ultimately, his method of influence came, not through force, control, or even convincing intellectual arguments, but through communion — an act so intimate it was symbolized by the human consumption of his flesh and blood. These surprisingly effective gestures challenged the basis of Greco-Roman civilization, allowing Christ to turn the tide of increasing violence with a mere thirty-three years of earthly existence. If he and his followers had only accomplished the eradication of Roman blood sport, that in itself would have been an admirable achievement.

However, as Christianity was adopted by the sedentary, hierarchical culture Jesus felt called to change, the powerful movement he started began to lose something important, succumbing to "Cain's forgetfulness" as the religion was adopted by Romans, Greeks, and Europeans who had never experienced the pastoral lifestyle. Even so, the early Catholic Church was adamant that the Bible should be preserved as originally written, as the indisputable "Word of God," ensuring (perhaps inadvertently) that its deeper meaning remained accessible to anyone with "eyes to see and ears to hear."

Putting the Bible back into its psycho-social-historical context releases all kinds of information hidden from a predatory, conquest-oriented mind-set. Actually spending time with nonpredatory animals leads to further insight. With the resurrection of this ancient wisdom comes a host of sophisticated lessons on leadership, cocreation, and authentic community building — pastoral skills that are surprisingly progressive compared to the two-dimensional command-control model we inherited from early city dwellers. In the meantime, those old dominance-submission habits still hold sway over us, thwarting, daily, our attempts to realize anything close to a functional democracy, let alone a truly free society with liberty and justice for all. Cain's technical feats are brilliant and seductive, to be sure, but they remain disconnected, dangerous, and at times simply meaningless without Abel's fluidity, compassion, and earthy interpersonal genius. It's high time we wrest that long-suppressed knowledge from its current state of arrested development and, well, evolve, for God's sake.

Chapter Eight

HERD· POWER

True pastoralists are among the bravest, savviest leaders you'll ever meet. Not because they're trekking through the wilderness protecting calves from carnivores — though that's certainly part of the job — but because, from a very young age, these people learn to move with uncommon ease, power, vigilance, and grace among large herds of potentially dangerous animals.

The key word here is *herd.* Milking a cow or riding a well-trained Thoroughbred takes more nerve and skill than most people imagine, but negotiating with a group of gregarious herbivores demands an entirely different set of social competencies. When you step out of the saddle, you realize that all those horses could run you over or break your leg with a single anemic kick. Those steers calmly milling around the pasture could easily skewer you with their horns and toss you like a rag doll. Most of the time, they wouldn't mean to do serious damage. It's just that you happen to be a lot smaller and slower than they are. But if you play on their turf, you need to play by their rules, and that means you damn well better develop a stellar combination of assertiveness, mindfulness, and sensitivity to nonverbal cues. The good news is that the interspecies socialization skills used by pastoral cultures actually *uplift the intelligence* of the entire herd, resulting in behavior so coordinated, so sophisticated, it baffles the modern sedentary mind.

Take Africa's Fulani herdsmen, the pastoral equivalent of a high-wire act operating without a safety net. These nomadic northern Nigerian tribes have no fences to corral their cattle and no horses to help round them up. To raise the difficulty level, the Fulani must keep their animals from wandering into fenceless fields of grain, as the pastoralists raise their own crops during the rainy season and, at times, migrate through farmlands at the end of the drought season — when the herds are especially lean and hungry. And then there are the animals themselves. Crowned with long, piercing horns, even the cows can be fierce, and the massive white bulls are doubly intimidating.

The average Fulani herdsman faces a seemingly impossible task. He can't physically overpower his cattle with herding sticks and ropes, but he has to stand up to them. He can't outrun them or confine them, but he has to keep them together. And somehow, he has to convince them to orbit the tribe during its travels across the vast and sometimes treacherous African savannah. So it is no small miracle that in the Nigerian outback, you might run into a Fulani herdsman jogging back to camp at sunset with twenty cows and a couple of bulls merrily trotting behind him — in single file or two abreast! This impressive feat has less to do with taming, training, and restraining the animals than with inserting an entire tribe into the cattle social system, transforming the behavior of both species in the process.

In their 1979 article "Applied Ethology in a Nomadic Cattle Culture," researchers Dale F. Lott and Benjamin L. Hart describe the insights they gained studying the Fulani as "a two-species social system," viewing the culture's unusually sophisticated herding techniques "against a backdrop of bovine social behavior." And it is here that we citified Westerners might finally grasp the hidden nuances of natural group behavior and, upon reflection, discover the keys to an advanced understanding of leadership.

Don't Fence Me In!

Sedentary cultures control their herds primarily by technological means: fences, barn stalls, halters, yokes, ropes, and bits that, according to Lott and Hart, deprive "the animal of most of the alternatives that do not conform to human wishes." Factory farming is the ultimate example, as chickens, pigs, and veal calves are confined and harvested like vegetables in a greenhouse with no consideration for their needs as sentient social beings.

An alternative approach to restraint, Lott and Hart reveal, "is to actively select the desired behavior from the animal's own repertoire and evoke that behavior." This means you have to be influenced by the herd before you have any hope of influencing its members, an astonishing proposition for anyone living in an anthropocentric culture. This is why in "European and North American farming, the use of this approach has largely been limited to intimidation or subordination, in which man controls the animals by assuming the role of social dominant."

Many managers, teachers, parents, preachers, and politicians assume this same role when trying to influence people, of course, illustrating how limited our leadership repertoire has become through centuries of hierarchical, command-and-control models and various physical, psychological, and social restraints designed to rein in humans. But what's the alternative?

Consider, first of all, why we even have to ask this question. Through 5,000 years of conquest, slavery, serfdom, and, in modern times, the efforts of a privileged few to control large populations for profit and convenience, we've limited our own development of optimal social behavior. Yet if nothing else, events of the past 250 years prove that once the old fences fall down and the herd breaks free, rudimentary forms of dominance become impotent. The fact that we keep using these outmoded tools, despite their compromised effectiveness, underlines our current state of arrested development. We are free, and yet we are continually sliding back into old habits, struggling to find a way out of chaos into connection.

Like those feral horses we call mustangs, human refugees from all walks of life — escaped slaves, liberated women, religious and political dissidents, disenfranchised youth, anarchists, peace activists, and disgusted corporate employees — can't help but gather in groups, kicking, rearing, biting, and striving to reclaim their dignity in the outback of human experience. Until people somehow, over time, learn new ways to get along, to graze peacefully, protect each other, raise families, brave the elements, and endure the droughts while seeking, and eventually finding, those mythical greener pastures. The problem is that even the most sincere, potentially innovative groups have trouble collaborating, using their power effectively, and most important, airing differences constructively and respectfully. And so the same cycle of rebellion, conviction, optimism, conflict, shame, blame, hostility, disempowerment, and disillusionment starts up again in whatever "new world" the next round of rogues and visionaries hopes to mold into the perfect earthly paradise.

The solution does not hinge on more and better technology — though technology eventually aided and abetted our freedom even as it initially enslaved us as pyramid builders, cotton pickers, and sweatshop workers. In a society where "commoners" can now fly to Europe, drive to Montana, or move to Nebraska and buy a winter condo in Florida, it's simply harder to fence us in these days. With e-commerce gaining unprecedented influence, we don't even need to leave our homes to go to work, lessening the influence of oppressive, slave-driving bosses. And with cell phone cameras instantaneously broadcasting human rights violations to free spirits around the world, dictators are an endangered species. As a result, the very nature of politics is changing — so fast that our current politicians can't keep up.

In *The Third Industrial Revolution: How Lateral Power Is Transforming Energy, the Economy, and the World*, Jeremy Rifkin observes that young people raised on the expanded informational possibilities afforded by the Web "aren't much interested in debating the finer points of capitalist or socialist ideology or the nuances of geopolitical theory....Their politics are less about right versus left and more about centralized and authoritarian versus distributed and collaborative."

More specifically, the "two generations whose sociability has been formed, in large part, by Internet communications are far more likely to divide the world into people and institutions that use top-down, enclosed, and proprietary thinking, and those that use lateral, transparent, and open thinking." In essence, Rifkin goes on to explain, "the Internet slayed machismo," leaving future generations to imagine new forms of leadership as "the traditional, hierarchical organization of economic and political power will give way to lateral power organized nodally across society." At the dawn of the third industrial revolution, oddly enough, Pyotr Kropotkin's vision of free, empowered people living in decentralized systems has gained an unexpected boost through an invention he couldn't have imagined in his wildest, pre–Russian Revolution dreams!

"The collaborative power unleashed by the merging of Internet technology and renewable energies is fundamentally restructuring human relationships," Rifkin emphasizes, "from top to bottom to side to side, with profound implications for the future of society." Whether we like it or not, life in the twenty-first century demands unprecedented levels of emotional and social intelligence. Yet as all those rigid statues of conquerors past crash to the ground, we don't need more social-networking programs. What we really need is a dose of Abel's wisdom, an honest-to-goodness sabbatical from all the wonders that our cities do in fact hold.

In other words, we need to develop new leadership models to support authentic, empowered, transparent, collaborative communities. Luckily we don't have to completely reinvent the wheel. Many of these skills are hidden in far, far older forms of social organization, the nuances of which history failed to record because they were most efficiently accessed in the company of beings who cannot speak, let alone text...

Different Animals

First of all, let me clarify that the goal here is not to tear down all possible fences, fire every last CEO, and obliterate New York City and Washington, D.C., Sodom-and-Gomorrah-style. Distilled to its most basic premise, Abel's orientation stresses a thoughtful, caring, reverent *interdependence* between humanity and nature, traditionally through associations with nonpredatory animals who maintain a modified yet still satisfying social life of their own. This creates an interspecies culture in which the humans are influenced by the herd as much as the herd is influenced by the humans.

Since you're likely a stranger to this lifestyle, let's start our nomadic backcountry journey by exploring a familiar concept, dominance, from a pastoralist's perspective. First stop: a visit with the Fulani tribes.

As Lott and Hart reveal, these expert herdsmen "may be thought of as taking a social role such as a dominant or a herd leader. Yet it may be more precise to describe them as exploiting the predispositions of cattle to yield to a dominant and to follow a leader." Now that might sound redundant, but here's the clincher: the "dominant" and the "leader" are literally *different animals*.

A dominant cow or bull asserts authority by keeping other animals away from something desirable: food, water, females in heat, and so on. This most rudimentary form of alpha responds to the slightest hint of disrespect with immediate, sometimes outlandish, corrections. On the upside, he or she also gains respect by breaking up fights between herd members. But sometimes a dominant animal will charge others for no apparent reason, keeping everyone a bit on edge. As a result, the group gives such individuals lots of space, looking away while preparing to move away whenever the saucy cow or big bad bull approaches. This, however, makes it hard for the dominant to lead anyone, anywhere.

Herd members capable of rallying the troops, on the other hand, exhibit the characteristics of what horse trainer Mark Rashid calls the "passive leader," though as I originally mentioned in chapter 5, that term is somewhat misleading. The passive leader only appears passive to someone raised on the flamboyant, fear-producing intimidation tactics most aggressively displayed by adolescent alpha males, who are more often than not expelled from the herd until they learn to calm down and respect others. Which is why in nature, young stallions, bulls, and male elephants roam in bachelor bands of heavily scarred individuals. And even within the most skillful pastoral cultures, only a few carefully selected males reach sexual maturity; others become geldings, oxen, steers — or supper.

The herd leader is a much more balanced individual who conserves energy for true emergencies. Certainly no pushover, he or she knows how to set boundaries without causing others unnecessary stress. Such an animal often reveals his or her potential early in life through a paradoxical combination of independence and sociability — only in this case, it's truly more of a passive sociability. Others gravitate to this calm yet still charismatic herd member, orbiting like moons around this individual's intriguing combination of curiosity, poise, and good-natured alertness (as opposed to hypervigilance). While the leader enjoys company, he or she also exhibits a kind of take-it-or-leave-it attitude to the herd dynamics others seem so invested in, content to wander off languidly to investigate something new. Others trot over to check out what piqued his or her interest, causing the rest of the herd to follow in due course.

The easiest way to distinguish a leader in the making is to take each animal out for a stroll while the others remain confined. The individual most willing to move forward, enthusiastically and without looking back — whose absence at the same time inspires the greatest distress, even panic, in the rest of the herd — is your winner.

And then there's what Meg Daley Olmert characterizes as the glue that holds the herd together: oxytocin, that potent biochemical bonding agent that encourages connection and affection — enhanced through companionship, mating, nursing, mutual grooming, resting quietly together, playing, and moving in harmony.

Nurturers, companions, leaders, and dominants are all crucial to herd cohesiveness. Members tend to play more than one role, though rarely all four. The thing about being human among animals ten times your size is that you really do need to perform all these roles well to become a master herdsman, especially in the great unfenced backcountry where freedom abides.

And you need a drop, just a drop, of a cunning and ferocious lion in you to protect your extended interspecies family from the occasional carnivore lurking about — and, much more commonly, against excessively predatory members of your own kind. After all, if you combine the agility and evasive intelligence of the horse, the skill and sheer nerve to stand up to a stallion or a bull, and the power to rally an entire herd, any two-legged or four-legged animal at all concerned with self-preservation will run screaming in the other direction — if he's stupid or cocky enough to attack to begin with.

That extra hint of tiger is mostly just for show.

Backcountry Leadership

Mature Fulani herdsmen choose among the various skills associated with leader, dominant, parent or companion, and predator thoughtfully, for the good of the community. In this context, it becomes clear that the dominant's role, when balanced with other, more nurturing activities, is essential in two major areas: assuring human safety and keeping the cattle from getting into all kinds of trouble. Breaking up fights between animals is one of the most

dangerous yet productive ways of gaining the herd's respect as social dominant while also guarding against animal injuries that could easily get infected.
(Nomads have limited access to veterinarians.) To maintain safe relations with
bulls known for bold and unpredictable behavior, herders must also correct,
immediately and dramatically, the slightest hint of aggressive posturing, especially when it's directed toward a human. Boys well under age ten are taught to
recognize "broadside threats" and other more subtle signs that a bull is *thinking*
of charging, whereupon these young herders are obligated to respond with an
upraised herding stick and a yell, escalating quickly to a brisk charge and hearty
smacks with the stick if the massive long-horned animal doesn't immediately
back off. (Considering the size, speed, and power of an irritated bull, submissive behavior must be obtained *before* he decides to attack if the human has any
hope of surviving such an encounter. Remember, these people manage their
cattle on foot, not horseback.)

Even more impressive is the Fulani's ability to maintain fine control over
large groups without halters, ropes, or other restraints. At the end of the dry
season, when foliage of the uncultivated savannah is nearly exhausted, herdsmen allow grazing to the very edge of unfenced fields just as tasty shoots of
maize and other crops begin to grow. These men rely primarily on vocal threats
and occasional charges at errant animals to keep them off highly desirable
farmlands. In sharp contrast, Lott and Hart "observed several occasions when
non-Fulani cattle handlers had great difficulty managing even one cow."

This advanced ability to direct an entire herd depends less on training and
more on *generations* of interspecies socialization. From day one, Fulani calves
learn to respond respectfully to subtle changes in the body language of both
species. Tribesmen and -women must be brave, assertive, and alert around
animals ten times their size. Cattle must be gentle and respectful of children
smaller than their own newborns.

At age six, the boys begin learning how to wrangle their feisty bovine counterparts. While calves are nurtured and protected by both species, they're also
led away from their mothers each morning after feeding and tied to a "calf
rope" to keep them in camp as cows and bulls move out to graze until dusk.
After the adults leave, these four-legged youngsters are then turned loose, moving freely among the women, children, and older tribe members during the day,
interacting with humans through a combination of loose informal encounters and purposeful episodes of restraint (when secured to the calf rope). In
this way, social-intelligence skills and mutually supportive emotional bonds
are developed between the species. As the boys struggle to lead these initially
uncooperative calves, they also learn the wisdom of reining in and controlling

their own wild impulses while gaining strength, courage, and confidence. And impressionable young cattle learn to respect two-legged creatures who seem to grow smaller with each passing day: During the first two years of life, calves practically double in size for every inch their human companions grow.

And finally, the animals themselves relax into a cyclical, predictable, but varied lifestyle among their seminomadic human caretakers. While droughts can be harsh and stressful, adults of both species enjoy the differing terrain while orbiting camps that offer rest, security, and companionship at the end of the day. (Knowing that everyone will reunite at sunset, calves do not show the kinds of exaggerated fear responses that fillies and colts in the United States exhibit as a result of being weaned suddenly and then permanently separated from their mothers, causing the unnecessarily frantic behavior people consider normal in young horses.)

And then there's that glue holding the herd and tribe together. Cows feed everyone, blurring the lines of oxytocin's supreme bonding power through the daily act of milking and being milked. The hormone's calm-and-connect effect releases feelings of relaxation and affiliation across species lines, lowering blood pressure and suppressing the flight-or-fight response. Women tend to handle milking and dairy production, but even male herders spend a good part of each day grooming and massaging their cattle (who often initiate these encounters), causing both species to temper their fierceness with sensitivity and affection.

Lott and Hart observed Fulani men spending "considerable time moving among the cattle at the camps, stroking their heads, necks, and the inner surfaces of the rear legs. The cattle interrupt other behavior to stand quietly for this grooming and even approach herdsmen and 'present' themselves for grooming or petting. Of particular interest is the rubbing of the inner surface of the rear legs. Adult cattle rarely groom each other there, but calves are regularly licked in that area by their mothers as they nurse. Apparently the herdsman is exploiting a property that persists into adult life but normally functions to strengthen mother-calf bonds." The researchers were also fascinated to see "cattle approach and lick herdsmen as they would a conspecific," something that happened "both in the camps and after a herdsman had led his cattle at a run and then stopped."

Even among the Fulani themselves, however, "it is not clear how herdsmen become able to act as leaders. Some felt that the cattle naturally follow a leader and would as readily accept the Fulani herdsman as a conspecific in that role. Other Fulani said that they had to train the herd to accept leadership" through a cooperative leading and herding method undertaken by at least two people.

"In such training, one herdsman called while walking slowly away while the other drove the herd from behind."

Eventually, this technique results in reliable group behavior initiated by a single herder. "Once he has the cattle's attention, he turns away and begins to walk, or even run, continuing to call as he goes. The cattle follow him in single file or two abreast, sometimes vocalizing." That they're all heading back to their children at dusk is certainly part of the attraction, but the ability to rally these animals with "a unique call" and lead them in a specific direction at other times of the day (rather than drive them from behind with horses, containing the herd on both sides, as teams of cowboys do in the American West) is impressive.

As Lott and Hart conclude, "The adaptive value of following a leader seems likely that the follower benefits from the leader's knowledge of the terrain, food and water sources, and predators. At minimum, it favors group coherence while the animals are moving about."

And that, in essence, is the role of a leader in the great unfenced backcountry that favors mutual aid as an evolutionary force.

Aggressive or Assertive?

In an earlier article, "Aggressive Domination of Cattle by Fulani Herdsmen and Its Relation to Aggression in Fulani Culture and Personality" (1977), Lott and Hart did not seem to be aware of these leadership and socialization subtleties, concentrating instead on the herdsmen's fierce reputation and how working with cattle might have influenced the culture at large. It's also clear that, initially at least, the authors didn't quite understand the difference between aggression and the kind of committed yet controlled assertiveness needed to manage large animals — a misunderstanding most sedentary people share. Even so, the authors managed to *illustrate* that difference through brief descriptions of the behavior involved.

Though the Fulani's origins are sketchy, these tribes "apparently began their penetration of the study area in northern Nigeria between A.D. 1350 and 1450," Lott and Hart reveal. "At the time of the European colonization of the area they had achieved political domination of virtually all the local populations, although they were outnumbered at least four to one." History therefore suggests that the ability of a single herder to hold his own with an angry Fulani bull one minute, herd several dozen cattle away from tempting crops the next, and lead them all happily back to camp at the end of the day has significant repercussions for leading or dominating large groups of people as well.

The Fulani are also revered for their unusual courage, "both in the sense of lacking fear and being able to overcome it," a quality developed through practical cattle-herding methods and intense ritualistic traditions. From age six, boys begin daily herding chores with their fathers or older brothers, exercising their legendary bravery almost immediately. As Lott and Hart discovered through extensive interviews and observations, "At this time, they are encouraged to begin to display aggressive dominance towards the mature bulls and oxen. We are told that initially the boys are often afraid of the bulls. Nonetheless, they are obliged to discipline these animals by charging them or hitting them with herding sticks. Boys who refuse to beat cattle on instruction are usually considered cowards, threatened, and even beaten if they still refuse."

What sounds incredibly cruel on both sides of that interaction holds a certain rustic wisdom for herding cultures. In the first place, *grown men* would have good reason to shy away from these huge animals. Even worse, smacking a bull with a twig could easily antagonize him, *inviting* him to attack. Any stick a six-year-old is capable of wielding isn't much of a threat, either — it is the intensity of the child's commitment and courage that is being exercised here. As I noted earlier, for long-term safety the young herders must not only accurately read the first indications of a bovine challenge, they must also gain submission from an adult bull *before* he charges. And while I cringe at the idea of some families punishing the more sensitive boys for refusing to smack any animal, it's clear that their lives are in serious danger if they don't muster up the courage to face down those bulls.

It's important to remember that, in nature, a dominant animal *will* charge others for no apparent reason, apparently *trying* to keep everyone a bit on edge. This is especially true of adolescent alphas who haven't been recognized as dominant by the larger herd — and who haven't yet learned how to manage their power in more skillful ways. And so the boys are encouraged to follow suit, though they're doing so under the supervision of a more experienced herdsman who can either back them up or stop them from going overboard. Also, these tenderfoot herders aren't expected to *lead* the cattle, so subtlety in wielding their power is less of a consideration. And the boys are taught to stop when a submissive response is achieved. For a six- or seven-year-old boy, gaining respect from the bulls and dominant cows is more important than getting them to follow, even if it means causing cattle to look away and move away when these herdsmen-in-training approach, the very response dominant animals intend to solicit from their outlandish behavior.

At that stage, the boys' interactions *are* aggressive, in that the attacks are sometimes capricious and unwarranted, designed purely to gain advantage over others. However, Lott and Hart also observe that older herders do not punish animals undeservedly. And it is here that the authors neglect to make an important distinction between youthful aggression and a more mature form of assertiveness. To lead is a much finer art, and that means doling out acts of dominance for justified purposes only — namely, breaking up fights and keeping cattle away from farmers' crops. Also, once a herdsman establishes himself as someone that others *want* to follow, his authority is rarely challenged by adult herd members. Over time, any action he takes to set boundaries or move cattle away from something desired yet forbidden requires less and less force, becoming mere posturing for the most part.

In descriptions, master herders sound like certain older, vastly experienced but innately modest cowboys I've met: They're cool — in the deepest, most authentic, empowered sense of that word. They conserve energy for true emergencies, and at that point in their professional development nothing short of a tornado or lion on the prowl feels like much of an emergency. These quiet experts don't panic in response to herd dynamics, realizing that the most flamboyant attacks are launched by adolescents whose own lack of experience often trips them up. There's no need for mature leaders of any species to waste energy being surprised, offended, or afraid of these power plays; they need only be *aware* of the rash, sometimes impressive, sometimes uncoordinated yet still potentially dangerous antics of naive youngsters experimenting with their vitality, strength, and, at that age especially, sheer, unadulterated chutzpah.

A Ritual of Courage and Self-Control

In this same article, once again promoted as evidence of culturally endorsed aggression, Lott and Hart discuss the *sharo* tradition. From my perspective as a trainer of young horses, standing up to stallions who've literally threatened my life, I can't help but appreciate this strange, violent rite of passage as a forum for channeling adolescent male aggression into something greater: an advanced form of courage based on vulnerability, endurance, and self-control.

Fulani tribes come together once or twice a year for festivals that include music making, dancing, cattle exchange, courting or matchmaking, and clandestine romantic liaisons. One of the highlights is a celebration of a different sort, an exhibition of power enacted through ritualized public beatings. Young men between ages fifteen and twenty-five challenge others of a different clan to an intense and oddly egalitarian contest that has little to do with fighting skill and much more to do with demonstrating each individual's ability to endure fear and pain without cringing, crying, or lashing out in response. Lott and Hart report,

During the sharo ceremony, blows are delivered (with a stick that is typically ¾ inch in diameter and 3 feet long) to the torso of the person who has been challenged and who stands with arms upraised. The blows are given with the challenger's full strength. They produce large enduring scars of which the Fulani are very proud. The object, as far as the beaten boy is concerned, is to accept the blows without any sign of pain, and preferably no change in facial expression. In fact, to assure himself that he has not shown any sign of emotion, the individual being beaten holds a mirror to his face throughout the contest. At another sharo ceremony as soon as the next day, or as long as a year later, he is expected to beat his challenger in turn.

The boys are taught from a very early age to expect this contest, to meet its challenge, and to cherish the honor and the scars it brings to them. The traditional sanctions for failure to participate include social disgrace, humiliation from relatives, and a distinct disadvantage in obtaining wives.

The beating of the herd's dominant bull by a six-year-old is therefore couched in the knowledge that one day, when he approaches manhood, this same boy will volunteer to be whacked repeatedly and much more ferociously by a peer, who will by that very challenge invite the same treatment in return. The reciprocal nature of the sharo keeps it from degenerating into the hierarchical hazing rituals college fraternities promote, where older classmates abuse freshmen who have no recourse but to submit to the domineering behavior of elders or be expelled from the community.

True Mastery

But what else can we learn from the Fulani's dynamic passion play? About power, dominance, fear, courage, competition, and the violent surges of testosterone and vasopressin that every male — whether human, carnivore, or herbivore — must grapple with to reach his true potential? The sharo itself seems to supply an emphatic answer: one must face the aggressive acts of others, feel fear and pain without panicking, ultimately commanding and purposefully channeling one's own power and aggression for the good of the tribe.

That, in essence, is what the herd's dominant bull demonstrates with every new crop of six-year-old boys he encounters: that his massive power, while valued and admired, must be contained, that he must show respect to and collaborate with those obviously smaller and weaker than he — because the long-term survival, enjoyment, and evolution of the herd depend on it.

In the sharo ceremony, a boy becomes a man by taking on the role of a fully socialized bull, demonstrating his readiness to endure pain without fighting back. That willingness to be vulnerable at a more accomplished stage of life is what allows the community to trust that an adolescent will be able to develop his own power for the good of the tribe. After all, a bull who lacks self-control, who must dominate others at all costs and never back down, cannot be allowed to roam freely, let alone mate and be trusted to nurture his own children. A Fulani boy's bravery may be awakened through standing up to the herd's scariest, most dominant animals. But a man's worth to his future family involves the voluntary exhibition of his willingness to take the blows life hands him with self-control and pride, realizing that the tables *will* turn, and that soon enough, maybe tomorrow, maybe next year, *he* will be in the more powerful position.

In this way, generations of Fulani have been engaged in the mystical act of socializing power itself — not practicing how to *be* aggressive, but mastering how to *use* aggression in partnership with dominance, leadership, and daily acts of nurturing and companionship. The lessons they've learned over the past thousand years apply to modern sedentary people, male or female, who propose to use power effectively to support a larger cause.

As a parable for the development of visionary leadership, the Fulani life cycle suggests that no matter how old you are, when it comes to stepping out of your comfort zone and into the unknown, you will at times feel small and extremely vulnerable, like a six-year-old standing up to his first bull. The willingness to face life's challenges *before you have the skills in place* — without shrinking from the fear and pain involved — is courage personified. But it's certainly not the last act of bravery you'll ever perform. In fact, just when you think you have the answers, when you're clearly in your prime, some rangy, hot-headed teenager holding a big stick will call you out, and that's when the real challenge begins.

Our culture is defined by a severely limited understanding of dominance, leadership, and nonpredatory power. As a result, most adults operate from a state of arrested development, *especially* when it comes to the juvenile power plays we encounter at work, school, and church, and most definitely in politics. Even attempting to turn a duel into a sharo — in our case without the support or recognition of the tribe — demands *incredible* intelligence, courage, and self-control. But it's a skill we must hone and cultivate in society at large if we ever hope to develop the high tolerance for vulnerability that allows us to move beyond adolescence and into true mastery. (Techniques for updating the sharo, using it to develop *emotional heroism* in modern leaders, are featured in Guiding Principle 11; see chapter 23.)

Women's Work

There's little information on pastoral women — what they think and feel, how they experience life transitions, how they interact with their animals, what they're taught about love and power. Perhaps it's because most researchers are male, trying their best to keep an objective distance from tribal life. Perhaps it's because tribeswomen are shy around strangers — or actively sequestered from them. Probably a bit of all three: Lott and Hart, for instance, faced significant hurdles in gaining the trust of Nigerian herdsmen, relying on local veterinarians to provide introductions. The idea of two foreign white guys interviewing the herders' wives was either nixed or never broached to begin with. Articles by Lott and Hart focus exclusively on Fulani men.

Historically, our culture doesn't fare much better. Researchers in Western industrialized countries have been slow to consider the needs, perspectives, and contributions of women — physically, psychologically, and culturally. Women literally had to *become* scientists for science to understand women. Kerstin Uvnäs Moberg had to experience childbirth to notice that, in addition to causing uterine contractions and milk release, oxytocin affected behavior and mood, creating the "calm and connect" response. While a number of male researchers, including Cort Pederson, Barry Keverne, Keith Kendrick, and Tom Insel, added key elements to the study of the hormone's effect on social bonding, Uvnäs Moberg was a pioneer in studying oxytocin's antistress effects. Other female researchers made significant contributions to the field as well. In 2000, University of California, Los Angeles, faculty members Shelley E. Taylor, Laura Cousino Klein, and colleagues published an extensive study on the "tend and befriend" response to stress, which, they argued, women employed more often than "flight or fight."

Before 1995, stress studies were heavily based on male subjects, both human and animal. In their paper "Biobehavioral Responses to Stress in Females: Tend-and-Befriend, Not Fight-or-Flight," Taylor, Klein, and colleagues explained this bias. Female hormone fluctuations "present a confusing and often uninterpretable pattern of results" for clinical trials on diseases, drugs, and so on. This led scientists to believe that stress reactions would also be affected by reproductive cycling. And indeed, "evidence concerning a fight-or-flight response in females has been inconsistent."

But Taylor, Klein, and colleagues had the nerve to submit another theory to explain this discrepancy, one based on their own experience as women commiserating with and supporting each other during times of stress. Their theory coincided with research on oxytocin's "calm and connect" effect. What if, they

asked, inconsistencies in the female data were *not* due solely to hormonal fluctuations "but also to the fact that the female stress response is not exclusively,
nor even predominantly, fight-or-flight?"

Taylor and Klein's review of scientific literature on this subject is both extensive and fascinating. But survival-of-the-fittest logic alone supports the view
that women developed a tend-and-befriend response to stress for one very
good reason: Pregnant women with small children don't fare well in a flight-
or-fight context. Fighting puts both mother and child at risk, and running off
isn't easy when you're carrying babies or wrangling small children. Strategies
favoring mutual aid are simply more effective — for sedentary and nomadic
women alike.

Studies supporting this theory show that when female mammals feel threatened, oxytocin amplified by estrogen does in fact inspire tend-and-befriend
behavior. Women, in essence, are designed not just to *rely* on the power of the
herd but also to *create* and *cultivate* it through biochemical impulses that

1. buffer the flight-or-fight response;
2. encourage affiliation;
3. leave survivors basking in warm, expanded feelings of connection after
    the emergency passes; and
4. solidify the bonds that lead to mutually protective social behavior the
    next time a crisis occurs.

In pastoral cultures, this effect seems to be enhanced by the human-animal
bond, allowing men who lead and care for unrestrained animals to benefit from
the oxytocin effect, heightening connection and affection between human tribe
members. Not surprisingly, it was a woman researcher who first connected the
oxytocin response to the development of the human-animal bond.

In 1992, Meg Daley Olmert, an Emmy Award–winning documentary film
creator and writer, was developing a series on this subject. Her interdisciplinary findings and original insights into the role oxytocin plays in the formation
of the human-animal bond — and its therapeutic effects — were so intriguing that she was asked to join a research team headed by Dr. Carol Sue Carter
of the University of Maryland and Dr. Uvnäs Moberg, who was then based at
Sweden's Karolinska Institute. Olmert's lack of formal scientific training allowed her to think in ways that PhDs devoted to narrow fields are often unable or reluctant to do. Her vast experience integrating history, anthropology,
biology, and animal behavior for television, including such series as *National
Geographic Explorer*, Discovery Channel specials, and PBS's *The Living Edens*,

allowed her to make a leap of consciousness that brought to light a significant new theory on oxytocin's role in fostering the mutual domestication of humans and animals during the Ice Age. Olmert's years of dedicated research into the biology of bonding and, more specifically, the multifaceted biological and sociological nuances of the human-animal bond, eventually produced the 2009 book *Made for Each Other*, which I highly recommend reading for its amazingly accessible discussion of interspecies evolution.

It was Olmert who wrested Lott and Hart's 1970s studies of the Fulani from near obscurity, bringing them to a wider audience and, eventually, to my attention as well. Lott himself took an interest in Olmert's quest to find evidence of oxytocin's role in interspecies socialization, and he was impressed with how she reframed the Fulani in this context. Her recognition that the hormone creates the glue that holds the herd and tribe together pointed to the compelling biochemical basis for the power of affection and connection to alter consciousness and inspire leaps in evolution not just within but also *between* species.

Nature, Nurture, and Love

The Fulani are fierce, to be sure, but their understanding of power is much more sophisticated than that of the average modern city dweller, perhaps because their social structures are intertwined with those of prey animals who are also fierce yet trusting, sociable, and affectionate. For Fulani tribesmen, the courage to feel vulnerable is exercised explicitly in the drama of the sharo. Yet, as it turns out, this strange, counterintuitive ritual (and the interspecies lifestyle that gave birth to it) encourages these young men not only to endure hardship but also to experience love, beauty, and connection in ways that one researcher found immensely intimidating.

In his 1971 article "Defying Official Morality: The Example of Man's Quest for Woman among the Fulani," Paul Riesman describes what he learned from living with the Fulani, befriending them, and attempting to conform to their rules and customs. For nineteen months, he and his wife traveled with a tribe that became family, drawing him into an experience of emotional intimacy so powerful the itinerant anthropologist almost couldn't bear it. To be clear, Riesman remained loyal to his spouse, but his writings suggest that he had to become more poet than scientist at times to communicate life through Fulani eyes.

The young men especially, he reported, spent a large amount of time composing and singing songs combining the beauty of the landscape, the seasons, and the weather with the beauty of individual women, merging personal attraction with the timeless, archetypal ideal of romance in all its earthly and heavenly forms. In a few loose translations of lyrics, Riesman illustrates how nature, nurture, and love combine in the Fulani mind:

Late autumn over-cast
raindrops are sprinkling
splotch-necked cows are coming to drink
let us sing of Umaru's daughter....
Gusts of wind in the dusk
lightning at night
make us remember the season of rains
let us sing of Umaru's daughter....
Even the pang of the humming
of herdboys on a trek
does not equal that time when we talk
and we sing of Umaru's daughter....
Rainbows; and the blue bitter smoke of wood;
And radiant raindrops couching in cool flowers;
And flowers themselves, that sway through sunny hours,
Dreaming of moths that drink them under the moon;
Then, the cool kindliness of sheets, that soon
Smooth away trouble

Riesman felt strongly moved by the Fulani women, and he obviously relished his time with the whimsical singing herdsmen who loved them, sometimes from afar, sometimes through clandestine trysts that broke all the rules (and yet were somehow silently tolerated — in traditional Muslim tribes, no less). Ultimately, however, he resisted the charms of these pastoral sirens, not only to remain faithful to his wife but because he was overwhelmed by the intimacy of the culture itself. He believed that he would have reacted in the same way had he been single.

Our relationship with the villagers was one of friendship, though it was often described by them as a kind of kinship. It is true, older people all felt like parents to me, people my age were brothers and sisters, and younger people were our children. I was living in an atmosphere of warmth and security that I had never experienced in my own culture, and for which I was not prepared by my upbringing. It was like breathing pure oxygen. But the independence and freedom that I believe the Fulani experience in this atmosphere — I was afraid I could not [experience], for the independence that I am used to from my own life consists in being able to withdraw, separate, and differentiate myself from everyone else. I feared that I didn't have the strength that the Fulani do to maintain my sense of self in such a tumult of feelings, for my defense-mechanisms were designed for an emotional economy of scarcity rather than abundance.

Ironically, Riesman's experience suggests that the sharo ceremony does not shut down the hearts of the tribe's young men, as one might expect from descriptions of its goal to face pain and fear without flinching. Rather, this ritual exercises the willingness to resist the flight-or-fight impulse in favor of embracing something larger, including, as it turns out, the quest for love itself.

Fulani culture offers to its members a life that is supremely worth living. The individual is a member of the society from the day he is named (seven days after birth), but his adherence to it feels freely given rather than automatic or compelled, as I believe the quest for Woman shows. What this quest means to them cannot be put into words, except through their own poetry, for it is both specific and indefinite, limited and infinite. The important thing is that the Good in life is available to them within their culture and it calls from them the fullest expression of their individual personalities as they strive to obtain it. This quest cannot be mine, however, for there is nothing that calls me forth in the same way.

Riesman hinted at something key as he marveled at the Fulani's ability to cultivate *freedom through relationship*. As he saw it, this combination of power *and* connection created a platform from which an individual might soar and strive, not because he or she felt a nagging emptiness inside, but because the culture itself encouraged its members to love life, nature, and each other while also challenging people to grow beyond their own instincts and limitations. (The relationship between power, innovation, connection, and vulnerability is discussed in Guiding Principle 5 [chapter 17] along with strategies to increase tolerance for vulnerability.)

"I think that many Westerners feel that our culture does not offer anything worth striving for," Riesman concludes. "For myself and others who share this feeling, then, the search is for something to want, rather than for something we know we want." The author admitted that his search "begins from a feeling of essential non-relatedness to the rest of the world, while for the Fulani the beginning is in a set of relationships that the person finds himself to be in with other beings."

During his journeys through Fulani country, this adventurous anthropologist and his equally adventurous wife glimpsed a kind of emotional heroism we could all stand to develop, one that allows people to risk opening their arms wide to love and beauty with the same courage and strength they need to face fear and pain.

This is not a path for naive idealists, however. It involves developing the feminine arts of caring and nurturing in concert with the masculine energy of courage, power, and protection. It involves men and women who are willing to feel vulnerable, change, and become something greater through the sharos and pleasures of life itself.

Part II

THE NECESSITY *of* VISION

Chapter Nine

THE INVISIBLE

*H**ooves laced with steel* seemed to come at me from all directions as a coal-black stallion named Midnight Merlin ripped the lead rope out of my hands, bucked, whirled around, and lunged at me, rearing, striking, raging at a ghost. All I could do was hold my ground and pray that I was fierce enough to win his trust.

"I don't want to be this strong person," I kept saying over and over to myself, fighting the urge to run screaming out of the arena as he attacked me once again for no apparent reason. To contain this violence, I would need to tap a form of power I wasn't even sure existed. But first I had to get over my resistance to the by-then-blatant fact that gentleness, sympathy, and understanding couldn't begin to transform this savage, wounded force. Most important, I had to forgive. Forgive Merlin for threatening to kill me. Forgive myself for taking on such a ridiculously volatile case. And much more difficult, forgive the misguided training techniques, the clumsy, ignorant, unnecessarily aggressive approach that had turned him into such a monster.

And finally, I had to recognize, reluctantly, that it was a *woman*, not a man, who brutalized and betrayed this sensitive, virile horse.

Midnight Merlin was the most dangerous kind of stallion: powerful, agile, intelligent, and angry. His first owner, a New Mexico–based horse breeder named Shawnee Allen, appreciated his flamboyant beauty for its own sake. The horse was rarely ridden or exercised formally, as his black Egyptian Arabian bloodlines and stunning presence made him a valuable sire. His owner had other, much calmer horses to saddle up when she wanted to hit the trails. Most days, Merlin ran freely through grassy, tree-lined pastures, where he was able to play with some geldings over the fence when he wasn't mating mares.

The problem began when Shawnee sold him at age ten to "Lacey," a well-respected local trainer, through a deal that involved some cash and some trade in starting one of Shawnee's other colts under saddle. Yet when Shawnee stopped by this woman's stable a few weeks later to see how the younger horse was progressing, she found Merlin standing in the corner of a darkened box stall with his head tied between his legs. The stallion was spoiled and destructive, Lacey insisted; he needed to be taught a lesson.

Shawnee decided then and there to buy Merlin back, but the damage was already done. Her occasionally outlandish, yet good-natured, horse was fearful and aggressive, filled with rage and mistrust of anyone who walked around on two legs. Shawnee had no idea how to coax him out of his increasingly violent and unpredictable state. The horse seemed to have flashbacks similar to the extreme forms of posttraumatic stress that some soldiers experience. Eventually, Shawnee came across a confident, smooth-talking trainer who seemed to have some rapport with Merlin. With promises to safely rehabilitate the horse and market him throughout the Southwest as a stud, the man loaded Merlin onto his trailer and drove off, only to abandon him sometime later at a Tucson boarding stable called The Ranch.

Shawnee felt incredible remorse. More than once she had tried to do right by Merlin, only to have him return worse off than when he left. Though she loved the horse, she knew she couldn't handle him. After talking with The Ranch owners, who had introduced Merlin to me as a possible mate for my black Arabian mare Rasa, Shawnee decided to give it one last try. If I could develop a consistent and constructive rapport with the horse in one year's time, she would turn Merlin's papers over to me. If not, she would trailer him back to New Mexico and let him live out the rest of his life on pasture.

The Yang inside the Yin

Stallions like Merlin often rebel under our current system of domestication. Mares and geldings commonly live in herds, or at least touch noses over adjoining corrals. Most colts, however, lose any hope of a social life the moment some human deems them worthy of breeding. (To remain intact is to be sentenced to a stall, hence the word *stallion*.) People admire them from afar, yet the vast majority of studs in the United States lead lives incongruent with the passion, freedom, and magnificence they represent. They're worked on a strict schedule, turned out in solitary confinement, relentlessly showed and campaigned to bring in the best breeding price. And when they finally do get to mate, their every move is choreographed at the end of a chain "for their own safety." Because when profit is the only motive, it's too inefficient, too risky, too time- *and* imagination-consuming to help young stallions learn how to court mares on their own, let alone form relationships with their handlers other than through the most rudimentary dominance-submission protocols.

Merlin suffered in the clash between two worlds. Shawnee had given the young stallion a life of relative freedom. Sensitive to his needs and moods, she found ways of compromising with him. In part because she appreciated his flash and fire, she found the stallion amiable and, over time, trustworthy. She actually trained him to gallop across the pasture and rear over her to show off his agility and vitality to prospective breeding clients.

Merlin's subsequent trainer, however, read this same ritual as a threat. Seeing Shawnee as a "horse-lover" (a dirty word in some conventional training circles), Lacey decided to "correct" this "spoiled," presumptuous behavior, and not just by beating Merlin. Far worse for horses (who are naturally claustrophobic), she sentenced him to the most demeaning, blatantly spirit-breaking punishment possible, a trip to the dungeon: a darkened stall where his head, tied between his legs, made him bow down to his mistress, and hold that position, not just in submission but in shame — and no small amount of pain.

Perhaps his spirit would have been broken if Shawnee hadn't recovered him. Knowing Merlin, it's more likely that he would have injured Lacey, or broken one of his own legs in the process, either way invoking an equine version of "Give me liberty or give me death!"

And yet the moment he was given a second chance, Merlin's journey as my teacher began. For with this supremely damaged, vengeful horse, I learned that kindness wasn't enough to heal the wounds of misused power. I had to become powerful myself, yet in a much different way than most people would expect. I had to access the *yang* inside the *yin*. And I couldn't do it on my own.

Though I tried all kinds of conventional and innovative training and therapeutic strategies, my only hope of healing Merlin's traumatized, mal-socialized masculinity involved harnessing the power of an entire herd and finding the right people to help me in this unconventional project. During the decade I worked, played, and lived with Merlin, until his death in 2009, I became something akin to a master herdsman as circumstances forced me to balance the roles of dominant, leader, midwife, nursemaid, and devoted, trusted companion to a growing black-horse family.

Because he was so dangerous to ride, I was forced to relate to this volatile male presence exclusively on the ground, like the Fulani with their cattle. And though Merlin didn't have horns (thank God), his previous trauma made it dicey to even think about letting him live and mate off lead with my beloved mares Rasa and Comet. After all, he hadn't been raised in a culture that socialized intact males from an early age with the help of an entire interspecies tribe. If anything, the sedentary "civilized" approach to horse breeding and training created the destructive combination of unchecked dominance and disconnection that led to Merlin's insanity.

Most people thought I was equally crazy for even attempting to rehabilitate him and were skeptical of my every move. As a result, I felt renewed and supported when I encountered descriptions of the Fulani through Meg Daley Olmert's pivotal book *Made for Each Other* in 2011, quickly absorbing as much research as I could find on this interspecies society. Lott and Hart's insights helped me better understand the transformative skills I developed with my black-horse family. Socializing Merlin, and later his sons, taught me many of the same lessons about dominance, leadership, and companionship that created a balanced approach to male power in Fulani culture — although my colleagues and I accessed these principles through much confusion, grief, frustration, and, at times, sheer terror. Equally important were Riesman's accounts of the profound intimacy and freedom-through-relationship this lifestyle engendered. (I highly recommend reading his 1974 book, *Freedom in Fulani Social Life*, not only for its detailed descriptions of Fulani life and philosophy, but for the author's perceptive contrasts between the nomadic pastoralist mind-set and his own intrinsically isolated, starkly mechanized modern psyche.)

Ultimately, I was saddened, though not surprised, to find that the Fulani culture Lott, Hart, and Riesman had chronicled forty years earlier was approaching extinction in 2012. Like the Apaches who once roamed freely through southern Arizona, across the very lands where my horses and I recovered a hint of this ancient wisdom, Africa's nomadic tribes were systematically being assimilated into a sedentary life that offered them poverty, disconnection, confusion, and depression (an emotion that, Riesman noted, the Fulani didn't have a word for in the 1970s).

Like the Apache in the late 1800s, twenty-first-century Fulani have their own Geronimos who violently rebel at times. And they seem destined to suffer a similar fate. If the rampant, worldwide prejudice against the pastoral lifestyle isn't arrested in the eleventh hour, Cain will kill Abel in Africa well before the century comes to a close.

Black-Horse Wisdom

Still, I'm strangely hopeful that some of this pastoral wisdom might be resurrected, distilled, and incorporated into our own culture. After all, my horses created an interspecies tribe by calling a handful of accomplished and adventurous souls together, and we learned some sophisticated, long-neglected lessons about power in the process. Yet unlike the Fulani, we had no models to follow, no ready-made support system. Those who took on the Merlin project were rogues and pioneers willing to feel their way through the dark, falling into ditches and stepping on each other's toes at times. In this effort, the symbolic synchronicities of working with a black-horse herd did not escape me, not for one minute.

In dreams and myths from around the world, the black horse heralds the reassertion of qualities difficult for the well-groomed persona to handle, revolutionary insights and energies that can't be readily tamed by the rules of polite society. To those courageous, humble souls who ultimately aspire to ride the black horse, this explosive force becomes a vehicle for expanded consciousness, inspiration, and innovation. To those who suppress or ignore its talents, fear its passion, or try to harness its energy without compassion and integrity, the black horse becomes an impetuous and compulsive element inflicting mood swings and bizarre cravings on people who once seemed the epitome of good sense and reason.

Black-horse wisdom challenges people to step off the well-worn paths of civilized thought. It is wisdom shrouded in mystery, wisdom that's felt more deeply than can ever be explained, wisdom we often ignore, unfortunately, until some difficulty in life opens us up to other possibilities. This universal archetype champions knowledge rejected by the mainstream: instinct, emotion, intuition, sensory and extrasensory awareness, and the human-animal partnership associated with tribal cultures. Science may never be able to dissect this wisdom, to bring it into the light of conscious understanding, but through the metaphor of the horse, and through real-life interactions with these animals, we can learn to track these mysteries, maybe even ride them if we develop the right balance of trust, discernment, skill, abandon, and power.

The tools my culture gave me for rehabilitating a real, honest-to-goodness, royally pissed-off black horse were severely limited: rudimentary, grossly incomplete scientific theories on dominance hierarchies and survival-of-the-fittest/competition-for-limited-resources models of evolution, combined with behavioristic horse-training methods — all of which Merlin promptly mule-kicked right out of the arena. Even natural-horsemanship principles and other more enlightened riding or therapeutic techniques treated the horse as an instinctual being with little consideration for his social needs. Yet seeing Merlin as an intelligent, social being was the first of three crucial missing pieces.

I gained other important clues from watching several experienced stallion trainers work with Merlin during the first six months of our tempestuous association. One of these women, Shelley Rosenberg, was open-minded enough to lend her expertise to my goal of socializing, rather than isolating, Merlin. Still, no matter what she and her equally experienced colleagues *told* me about their methods, I could see that some pivotal nonverbal element was at work, something even they weren't fully conscious of, let alone capable of translating into words. This something seemed to light Merlin up, engaging an intangible sense of promise. And it had to do with their ability to remain calm and centered no matter what he did, while exuding power: courageous, controlled, *nonpredatory* power.

Over time, Merlin also lived up to his wizardly name, imploring me to recognize what most people dismiss as invisible, drawing my attention to principles now finding legitimacy through the field of energy medicine. These three factors — social intelligence, nonpredatory power, and the reality of subtle energies exchanged in relationships between living beings — were Merlin's greatest gifts to everyone brave enough to study with him under the guise of saving a damaged horse.

Somewhere along the way, I gained the courage to admit that Merlin's most profound lessons had parallels in ancient religious writings — and that the rest of my herd had been leading me down this same strange path for years.

Power and Religion

Certain key aspects of Taoist, Christian, and Buddhist teachings were useful to me in wrangling Merlin and, subsequently, in better training and socializing his sensitive, vivacious sons. Still, developing so-called spiritual skills at the barn didn't lessen the effects these skills had on the rest of my life: exploring nonpredatory power and subtle energies, experientially, created an involuntary transformation that raised my courage, altered my perception, and opened my heart, constantly confronting me with the ineffectiveness of words to describe what I was learning.

I could also see that writing or speaking about such insights engendered a great deal of misinterpretation. Still, I was undaunted, filled with the conviction that any ensuing drama or confusion was worth the price of admission if my sketchy verbal approximations inspired even *one* other person to notice what had previously been hidden. Standing at the edge of a vast desert wilderness with an increasingly empowered herd by my side, I was struck by the immensity of what could *never* be spoken — and the dubious history of power and religion suddenly made sense to me.

While their personal histories and cultural contexts were very different, Jesus, the Buddha, and Lao-tzu were masters of nonpredatory wisdom. All three left civilization as they knew it and spent time in the wilderness grappling with big questions related to life, death, and the meaning of both. They returned with a counterintuitive view of power, one completely unrelated to brute force.

These social innovators were unusual in that not only did they embody nonpredatory behavior during a particularly violent stage of civilization's worldwide development, but Jesus and the Buddha, in particular, isolated and consciously taught advanced emotional-intelligence principles that are naturally activated in pastoral cultures, encouraging people to

1. resist the flight-or-fight impulse in favor of tend-and-befriend behavior;
2. emphasize mutual aid over competition for limited resources;
3. develop the high tolerance for vulnerability needed to endure fear and pain as well as risk love and connection; and
4. recognize that the individual psyche matures in deep relationship with others, most especially through the consistent, freely given support of others.

Over the centuries, however, the insights of these three teachers became overshadowed by another factor related to the visionary aspect of leadership: religions grew up around these pioneers, primarily because all three emphasized, in various ways, that the human mind was embedded in a larger matrix of intelligence, one that, if accessed, could provide innovative solutions to the challenges people faced. Their alliance with this mysterious source of inspiration was palpable: contemporaries of Jesus, the Buddha, and Lao-tzu noticed that these men had become wiser, braver, more poised, and more peaceful as a result, that these charismatic teachers *exemplified* an expanded view of human potential.

Yet because their most profound experiences occurred in the realm of that "other 90 percent," attempts to describe their discoveries sounded vague and mystical, couched in metaphor, parable, and experiential rituals or techniques designed to jump-start a transformational process that was primarily nonverbal. Even so, some of their followers were able to integrate and *live* these principles, in direct contrast to the brutal conquerors of their day.

Early Christians and Buddhists in particular were so effective in spreading their life-changing perspectives that predatory cultures had to acknowledge and eventually absorb their teachings, if only to control their influence. So while insights on nonpredatory power tempered humanity's aggressive tendencies, civilization's hierarchical, intensely opportunistic focus also affected how these religions were interpreted and practiced over time.

This confusing state of affairs has been amplified over the past four hundred years or so by an *over*reliance on verbal communication and logic, not to mention increasing disconnection from nature and animals, and a resultant mechanistic view of life. During that time, mainstream science vehemently dismissed ritual, myth, and metaphor as superstition, when, in fact, these high-context forms of communication were the only means people had to *point* to nonverbal insights that couldn't be translated into linear, logical language.

Influenced by the Age of Reason and the growth of technology, modern religious people grapple with the flip side of this same issue: searching for ways to prove or justify the *literal* truth of ancient texts. But two thousand years ago, the scientific method hadn't been invented yet, books were rare, information was passed primarily by word of mouth, and scribes weren't educated to separate concrete reality from emotional and spiritual realities. Consequently, religious writings mixed actual historical events with symbol, poetry, parable, dream interpretations, transformational sacraments, and other methods for recording and exploring ineffable mysteries that nonetheless influenced people in powerful ways.

The Unsayable

Much information categorized as "spiritual" is nonverbal or unphotographable, not supernatural. Nonetheless, there will always be an element of mystery to the invisible, unnameable forces that move people to perform great deeds, leaving a sense of awe and wonder in their wake. This is especially true of men and women who tap the triumvirate of power, vision, and innovation, spurring leaps in human consciousness and behavior that affect generations. The soulful, palpable, yet elusive presence such people embody is always greater than their personal histories convey, which is why symbolic and mythic elements are often added to their biographies by followers and observers who were deeply affected by direct encounters.

Yet nuances tapped on the other side of sound are notoriously hard to sustain after the original innovator moves on, especially when a culture encountering this wisdom functions in opposition. No matter how inspiring and eloquent the pioneers may be, they can only leave their words, methods, stories, and images behind — hoping, but not guaranteeing, that people will use these maps to travel the same territory.

Insights on nonpredatory power that Jesus, the Buddha, and Lao-tzu accessed provide a classic example. Because an exceedingly small portion of their wisdom could be written down, millions of city dwellers have been able to worship these innovators while continuing to be influenced by hierarchical, predatory, competitive, emotionally disconnected modes of behavior. And so, historically, we see large numbers of Christians, Buddhists, and Taoists act in aggressive ways completely at odds with the examples set by the founders of their faiths.

Even more disturbing, the inexact nature of techniques developed to explore and record that "other 90 percent" allows these same tools to be misused at times, especially when people are pressured to follow a subsequent, usually dominant, authority figure's interpretation of the original rituals and metaphors. Organized religion is not the only transgressor in this regard: science and politics too have suppressed experiential exploration and constructive debate on spiritual matters. As a result, our modern rights to freedom of speech and freedom of religion have been used to create subcultures of believers and nonbelievers who deride each other rather than exchange ideas, competing for followers — and the votes, funds, and other resources that come with them.

We don't crucify people anymore, at least not literally. But because issues related to vision, creation, and charismatic presence also have to do with power, those invested in the status quo feel threatened by anyone who accesses an expanded view of reality, even if he or she is simply drawing on invisible and nonverbal insights that others ignore, inventing something "new" out of information that was already there. Abuse almost always follows: innovators in fields ranging from business to art, religion, science, and politics are initially, and usually ruthlessly, ostracized, discredited, controlled, or overwhelmed — by competitors *and* peers — through rejection, sarcasm, lack of funding or publication, institutionalization, or most recently, medication. It takes a brave, intelligent, committed, and inspired human being to stand up to this pressure without losing his conviction and, in some cases, his mind. When it comes to enduring the animosity most pioneers experience, introverted and highly sensitive visionaries don't have a prayer.

And so we've reached the point where U.S. politics appears to be ruled by aggressive fundamentalists on one side and humanistic atheists on the other, despite the fact that millions of citizens aren't represented by either of those narrow views. Yet crucial insights continue to be washed out of alternative debates as many social activists see spirituality and religion as outmoded dominance tactics employing the ultimate hierarchical trump card to manipulate the masses. After all, ambitious men and women have used God to justify everything from torture, witch burnings, and "holy" wars to modern acts of terrorism, racism, sexism, environmental destruction, and the eradication of indigenous cultures worldwide to seize territory and resources.

But what if we invoked our right to freedom of religion for another purpose, neither *rejecting* nor *blindly worshipping* influential figures like Lao-tzu, Confucius, the Buddha, Jesus, and Muhammad? What if we suspended our beliefs and disbeliefs, just for a moment, to look at these innovators as *visionary leaders*, paying special attention to their insights on power, creativity, and social intelligence, and their awareness of invisible or nonverbal forces representing a much wider view of evolution and human potential? What if we studied — outside the confines of conventional science and religion — their ability to tap revolutionary, thought- and behavior-altering states of consciousness that, in all cases, inspired culturally significant movements that long outlived their founders?

How might our world look different? How might we then respond to our world? How might the world change in response to us?

For our purposes here, I'd like to focus on one long-neglected topic: nonpredatory wisdom. In this case, while Confucius and Muhammad were significant visionaries with much to offer on other topics, let's concentrate on three religious figures who changed the world by explicitly recommending and, most important, *living* a "yin" approach to power.

While characteristics of predatory versus nonpredatory power in nature are discussed in Guiding Principle 8 (see chapter 20), it's important to recognize that we still live in a culture where brute force, predatory behavior, and opportunistic dominance hierarchies proliferate. As a result, the very idea of nonpredatory power initially seems elusive, overoptimistic, even mystical — mostly because the emotional- and social-intelligence skills involved are hard to photograph, dissect, or translate into words. Perhaps this is why nonviolent alternatives to civilization's predatory orientation were initially exemplified by religious leaders who, as mentioned earlier in this chapter, promoted mutual aid over competition for limited resources, tend-and-befriend behavior over flight-or-fight, and the ability to calm and focus others over the age-old practice of scaring people to gain control (Guiding Principle 7; chapter 19). These men also exemplified emotional heroism (Guiding Principle 11; chapter 23) and the related ability to feel vulnerable without becoming aggressive or defensive (Guiding Principle 5; chapter 17).

As oxytocin research suggests, some of these qualities are instinctual in women. But in relation to *social evolution*, it was a significant, paradigm-busting move for *men* like Lao-tzu, the Buddha, and Jesus to further develop these principles, urging large groups of people to temper aggressive, knee-jerk survival mechanisms for the short- and long-term benefit of the *entire human race* (not merely the local tribe). That all three expressed this goal as being inspired by a "higher source of wisdom" is appropriate considering how dramatically these innovators strayed from the callous, destructive, sometimes blatantly murderous behavior that was both common and often lawful during their lifetimes.

A compassionate, mutually supportive approach to power was, and still is, counterintuitive for many humans. Yet — whether by divine intervention or by a strange evolutionary mutation that occurred, virtually simultaneously, in China, India, and the Middle East between twenty-five hundred and two thousand years ago — it's clear that these ancient innovators somehow made the idea of following a nonpredatory path compelling, influencing billions of followers who have, throughout history, tried to understand and live up to the potential their leaders tapped millennia ago.

Orient Express

There's a serious lack of information on the Chinese sage Lao-tzu. Some historians suggest his name, a pun that simultaneously means "old master" and "old child," may have been the pen name for a group of anonymous sages who wrote the Tao Te Ching in the sixth century BCE, but there's no question that someone associated with that book had a vision. Taoism represented a dramatic, unprecedented departure from the philosophy of the warring tribes and equally aggressive city-based monarchies running amok in ancient China.

At a time when women, and most men for that matter, were made slaves to whoever was strong and ruthless enough to seize power and struggle to hold it, the Tao Te Ching recommended that people "know the yang" (the active, masculine principle), "but keep to the yin" (a nurturing, feminine principle). With this seminal statement, Lao-tzu was quietly urging his followers to temper their predatory tendencies by emphasizing the supportive, benevolent qualities inherent in nature. What's more, by aligning with the Tao, the "way of things," the primordial essence of the universe, people could achieve peaceful coexistence with each other, not through rigid human laws, but through a fluid connection with life-giving forces, unified somehow through a coordinating intelligence that was both purposeful and adaptable.

Lao-tzu avoided characterizing the Tao as a deity; it was infinitely larger than all the ancestors, nature spirits, and gods in the Chinese pantheon combined, encompassing the qualities they personified and so very, very, very much more. Even so, the Tao wasn't flashy, bombastic, or vengeful, and it didn't play favorites. In his many metaphors on the subject, Lao-tzu described this elusive principle as the *root* of existence working quietly underground to seed, stabilize, and nourish the growth that appeared, flowered, and shriveled, only to flower again and again. Lao-tzu often referred to the Tao as the "mother" of creation, without forgetting that it also contained the yang, the father. He also emphasized that each created being was simultaneously an expression of a certain aspect of the Tao and, at a deeper level, a holographic image of the Tao's most basic principle: "Everything has both yin and yang in it," the Tao Te Ching revealed, "and from their rise-and-fall coupling comes new life."

Human holograms were, in essence, mini-universes. Still, they gained power not by striking out on their own but by aligning with the original source of what they mirrored. Lao-tzu observed that sacrificing one's petty concerns and willful, shortsighted ways to harmonize with the Tao allowed individuals to achieve "effortless action" in concert with an innovative yet primarily non-verbal force of creative ebb and flow. People couldn't misuse the Tao, because they had to give up their human ambitions to follow it. The Tao was inherently virtuous because it enfolded the needs and talents of the individual into the trajectory of the whole, giving rise to everything seen and unseen, spoken and unspoken, through a constant, eternally morphing play of opposites symbolized by the yin/yang circle itself.

The author of the Tao Te Ching spent much time distinguishing this nameless, formless "way of things" from the countless nameable things, forces, and ideas that are manifestations of it. Descriptions of the Tao place it *firmly* in the realm of the "other 90 percent," in that it can never be defined or expressed in words. And yet, Lao-tzu insisted, it could be *known* and *experienced*. Its primary operating principles could be observed and most efficiently accessed in nature, which is why early Taoist sages were always emerging from the wilderness radiating immense peace and wisdom, saying a few choice words, gathering a few students, and disappearing back into the trees, sometimes never to be heard from again.

As a force of social evolution during the rise of city-based cultures, however, Taoism had limited appeal. People had to be adventurous *and* sensitive, willing to *feel* rather than force their way through life. They also had to leave the security of the known, spend some time away from the herd, and be transformed in ways that would make it hard to reenter their old lives. So while I personally would rather be a sage than a slave, I must also appreciate the reality of what people are willing to endure — and give up — to stay with family and friends.

Taoism had no overt, tangible social context for the wider view of freedom and connection it represented. But it did give people a glimpse of an egalitarian, nonpredatory form of power. Everyone had direct access to the Tao. It wasn't thriving at anyone's expense; it was sustaining each unique being born into the world while also acting for the good of the whole. No one had to serve a tyrant to get close to the Tao, or become a bully to protect his stake in it. It was like traveling a river downstream: all you had to do was lift your feet out of the sand and float. You didn't even have to jump in and catch a wave, because the Tao was already flowing everywhere around you. You only had to relax into this buoyant force and a wave would catch *you*.

For most humans, this deceptively simple concept was incredibly threatening. Throughout the Tao Te Ching, Lao-tzu observed how civilization's most cherished habits of perception and social organization worked in opposition to the "way of things." Unfortunately, the *unproductive* forms of leadership, competition, and self-interest Lao-tzu described are as common now in the West as they were in China twenty-five hundred years ago. This does, however, make it easy for modern humans to understand the classic Taoist dilemma: When you've spent your entire life trying to possess and control the river, frantically swimming upstream, any advice to let go is an affront to your human ego and, most likely, the habits of your ancestors. More distressing is the *sensation* of release: The moment you stop struggling and allow the current to carry you, you not only seem to be sliding backward, the sudden rush of power feels like certain death.

At that point, most people panic, dog-paddling ferociously, struggling to regain their balance by pushing against the river again. What they don't realize is that by refusing to trust this much larger fluid force, they're striving, ponderously, strenuously, desperately, to swim back toward the *past*, to where the river has *been* — and not getting very far in the process. Because as the current surges relentlessly downstream, sparkling in sunlight, glistening in moonlight, singing softly in the darkness, those who fight the Tao are mostly treading water.

Power and Presence

When I first encountered the words of Lao-tzu in a college religion course, they sounded so whimsical, so paradoxical, so delightfully mystical. But his advice turned out to be incredibly practical when it came to training horses, prompting me to realize that this shrewd and compassionate Chinese master was actually offering helpful, *grounded hints* on how to succeed in life with the least amount of grief and effort possible. From this perspective, the Tao Te Ching was clearly an ancient improvisation on the theme of "what got you here won't get you there," written for the entire human race. (See my discussion of the book by this name in chapter 6.)

But Lao-tzu's words, no matter how intriguing, didn't come close to teaching me what I needed to know. They were a thin layer of icing on one massive cake. In my early thirties, I was compelled, more by necessity than philosophical curiosity, to explore the deeper, experiential wisdom of the Tao — focusing, as it turns out, on the opposite of Lao-tzu's advice for feuding Chinese war lords.

Growing up in the 1960s, before the women's liberation movement, I had been trained to submit, to be a "nice girl," to intuitively feel what others were too proud to ask for in order to soothe, support, and please them, to let beauty speak louder than words while saving sex for marriage. My yin had been over-emphasized, and distorted, stretched in seemingly opposing directions by fashion magazines, movie stars, and conservative, understandably paranoid parents. Well into adulthood — despite one divorce, a brilliant second marriage, and, at a professional level, numerous management opportunities — I realized that I most certainly did *not* know the yang. Outside the pleasures of romantic relationships, I didn't even *want* to know the yang: the competitive, survival-of-the-fittest, adolescent-alpha models of leadership I witnessed actually made my stomach turn.

And that's where horses, masters of nonpredatory power, became my greatest teachers. Through years of frustration, trial, and error, they helped me understand what power really was — and, initially at least, what it was not.

When I bought my first mare, Nakia, in 1993, I assumed, like many people, that riding horses would somehow be easy, natural. As a child, I found my equestrian ambitions thwarted by parents, who sprang for music lessons instead, hoping I would grow out of that horse-crazy stage. Even so, I was allowed to assist a friend at fairs and horse shows and occasionally ride her pony in exchange for cleaning stalls. But it wasn't enough to satisfy my urge to spend time with these soulful animals, alone, on my terms.

And so for years I lived a secret life, sneaking over to a nearby horse trader's farm after school to cavort with members of his transient herd. The old man caught me a few times and threatened to tan my hide, but I persisted. Like a deer, cautious and observant, camouflaged by the brush, I became increasingly invisible to him as I slipped through barbed wire into a secluded back pasture, knowing that the herd would alert me to his predatory gaze in a thousand subtle ways.

There I'd lure the calmest, friendliest horses to the nearest fence or tree stump and ease onto their backs. But without a bridle or lead rope, I had to go wherever the spirit moved them. Most of the time, they simply grazed, unconcerned, effortlessly hauling me about, indulging the tiny two-legged creature who brought them carrots in exchange for informal rides. I spent hours stroking their shiny coats and hugging their big strong necks, feeling peaceful, connected, expanded, aware, and ecstatic all at once, addicted, I now realize, to an oxytocin high contagious to the entire herd.

On days the trader went to auction, I tested the trust growing in my skittish, younger companions by encouraging them to run and leap next to me, sometimes enticing them to the fence and getting them to stand still long enough to slip onto their backs for a clandestine trot or gallop. And I'd laugh, flopping about, hanging on to their manes, sliding off and squealing when they made an unexpected turn. For five years, I let my parents believe that I was out climbing trees, catching butterflies, eating blackberries, and picking wildflowers, which I truly was doing — on my way over to the farm. Had they known about my real hobby, they surely would have locked me in my room or invested in a much safer course of riding lessons.

As an adult, however, I discovered that horses held me to a different standard. Or perhaps more accurately, I was holding *myself* to a different standard in presuming that these proud, agile, thousand-pound animals would accept me as their leader. Massages, apples, and walks through the desert helped my first mare and me bond — as companions. But that didn't mean she thought I was in charge, not by a long shot.

Nakia, a dark bay Thoroughbred ex-racehorse, was nervous, pushy, and obstinate under saddle. We'd occasionally have nice rides, when it suited *her*, and while she never tried to buck me off, she scared the crap out of me in all kinds of heart-stopping ways on the ground, sometimes rearing and spinning around, other times jerking back when tied to the hitching post, breaking the lead rope and running wild around the barnyard. Luckily I didn't wait too long to get some help. But *good help*, as it turned out, was hard to find.

My earliest trainers told me ad nauseum that I had to "be the alpha of my two-member herd" while demonstrating all kinds of special bits, whips, and restraints. They also promoted a surprisingly uniform series of stern looks, well-timed smacks, and gruff, shaming phrases I was supposed to mimic — in a mild southern drawl, no less. Amazingly, whether my teachers and fellow boarders grew up in Ohio, Indiana, New York, or California, they all sounded like they hailed from Texas or Alabama when they used the word *Quit!* to correct some form of undesirable behavior. And they didn't take too kindly to questions about how humane their methods were. "Horses aren't too bright," they insisted. "Downright dangerous if you don't teach them who's boss." (These phrases too were underlined with "the drawl," apparently communicating a kind of cowboy logic that silly, sentimental women like me shouldn't argue with.) So, while I had bought a horse to relax, to escape the pressures of work, I was engaged in all kinds of power plays at the barn that I had no idea how to handle.

By that time, I had been a leader or manager in a variety of situations. People, for the most part, responded well to my enthusiastic, supportive, nondominant style. But I had been promoted or nominated into positions that already existed. My title as "director" or "chairman" of whatever professional organization or nonprofit committee I was working on preceded me, enhanced immeasurably by my notoriety as a music critic and journalist. I was only vaguely conscious of the fact that people respected me, in part, because they wanted something from me — press, connections, airplay, funding, a lucrative gig at the next jazz festival — and so it didn't take much for me to motivate them. What power I did have was related to reputation, position, words, and inspiring ideas. But Nakia didn't want any of these things from me. I could also see that she didn't respond well to intimidation and punishment, and that efforts to shame her into compliance had absolutely no effect whatsoever. Nakia, like many horses, was confused, and even a bit crazy, because the methods trainers past and present employed were at best sorely lacking and, at times, downright abusive.

To succeed in a human-equine subculture, this spirited mare craved *real* direction, connection, respect, and leadership: a powerful, centered, trustworthy presence that could calm and focus her, helping her to face her fears, modulate her energy, and over time, develop her talents. But that kind of power, that kind of presence, was a lot like the Tao, a force beyond words and concepts that drew its greatest strength from the invisible dimensions of existence, combining yin and yang to *lead* by *following* the horse's own natural instincts, channeling them in a more productive, more masterful direction.

Je Ne Sais Quoi

It literally took me *years* to understand this, let alone write about it. But when I published my first book, *The Tao of Equus*, in 2001, I wasn't chronicling my conversion to an oriental philosophy. I was emphasizing that people needed to consider the nonverbal and unseen forces of power, feeling, mind, and relationship if they hoped to excel in life. And I was unabashedly promoting horses as the most efficient teachers of nonpredatory wisdom, exercising those elusive yet profound intelligence centers in the heart and the gut that are so crucial to developing leadership presence and emotional and social intelligence. Twelve years ago, however, I didn't have the vocabulary to sum this up succinctly, mostly because the research necessary to say what I just said didn't exist. As a result, my first book had an air of mystery to it that was somewhat accurate — and somewhat misleading, causing some readers to believe that my horses and I had developed supernatural powers; there were, however, elements to our journey that I still can't explain. Artists, innovators, and horse trainers have been dealing with this same challenge for centuries.

In an article on Ray Hunt, one of the fathers of "natural horsemanship," the interviewer marveled at his techniques, outlined the basic concepts he could summarize in words, and then quoted Hunt as saying that there was an indescribable "*one other thing* that makes it all work. And I don't know what that is." The writer said she was "glad" this "one thing couldn't be packaged and put on a menu and ordered up like some brand of beer. It was real though; and it could be known, but only in the moment."

I've since learned that this *one other thing* is actually a combination of several, wholly nonverbal skills involving the effective use of timing, focus, assertiveness, intersubjective awareness, and somatic cues, including changes in blood pressure, muscle tension, and breathing (yes, breathing is a language to horses). It also entails the even more impressive ability to fluidly adjust to those cues from moment to moment — all while keeping the original riding or training goal in mind.

A great trainer sees what others ignore, and responds to subtle feelings even he isn't fully conscious of, which is why it's so difficult for him to teach what he knows. The resulting aura of charisma, wisdom, and mystery such a person generates can be awe inspiring, which is why some people speak of equestrian innovators with the same deference and admiration they normally reserve for religious leaders.

The territory is similar in many ways. Nineteenth-century horse whisperers seemed to harness magical forces, embodying both saint and sorcerer. Some trainers played this up for notoriety and profit, perhaps even believing their own press. (Before the late twentieth century, similarly gifted women, on the other hand, would have kept their talents quiet, as their social standing, in some cases their very survival, depended upon *avoiding* rumors of unearthly powers.) Mastery of that "other 90 percent," however, did not mean these people were channeling supernatural forces. Even so, it took a special person to wrangle the unseen, unspoken elements of existence into a reliable set of skills that could tame unruly horses.

In recent years, equestrian clinicians like Linda Tellington-Jones, Mary Wanless, Sally Swift, Pat Parelli, and Pat's equally accomplished wife, Linda, have spent significant time researching how people learn somatically as well as cognitively, developing sequences of riding and training techniques broken down into easily digestible chunks. And even then, it's hit or miss, especially with horse owners looking for a quick fix. Some students go through a predictable stage of talking, walking, and dressing like the innovator as they buy the special equipment, read the books, and study the videos. Yet people often experience significant frustration when these same rituals don't immediately work with intensely discerning horses. Efforts to mimic the leader are not at all silly, however — as long as people eventually realize that the example they're following goes deeper than clothes, quips, tack, and gestures. What students really need to emulate is something indescribable: a whole constellation of nonverbal insights, feelings, and responses that the clinician can only dimly approximate with the most sophisticated words and methods.

As the Buddha once said to an eager disciple, teachings of real significance are "similar to a person pointing his finger at the moon to show it to someone else. Guided by the finger, that person should see the moon. If he looks at the finger instead and mistakes it for the moon, he loses not only the moon but the finger also." In other words, anyone who fixates on the methods, metaphors, mannerisms, and equipment the teacher uses to draw attention to invisible or nonverbal forces or insights misses the entire point.

 True visionaries don't just notice what was previously hidden or ignored by the culture at large; they help others to see it and use it. Communicating the unspeakable becomes an essential part of the innovator's job, as does handling the frustration of being misunderstood and struggling, constantly, to create more clarity. We're not just talking art and religion here. The classic "finger pointing at the moon" dilemma most certainly applies to countless other disciplines, especially those related to leadership presence and social intelligence. In this respect, horses are emerging as reliable catalysts for expanded vision, empowerment, and the recognition of other, currently unnameable skills necessary for people to excel.

Ulrike Dietmann — a talented writer who established her own Epona-based equine-facilitated learning practice in Germany — teaches creativity, leadership, and personal-development skills that help others sense and follow their own unique callings. Her translated book *On the Wings of Horses: A Hero's Journey into the Heart of the Creature* says it best: "Animals reflect our internal states. Their behavior follows an invisible energy. This is something that astonishes me again and again. They make the invisible visible." As strong, intensely mindful, nonpredatory, social beings, horses are the ultimate guides on our quest to discover a more balanced form of power while cultivating freedom-through-relationship, a pastoral innovation related to what English-speaking Buddhists call "dependent co-arising."

So at this point, would it really surprise anyone to learn that, before he became enlightened, the Buddha was revered as an exceptional horseman?

Chapter Ten

MOON DANCE

Gaining the trust of an angry stallion is an ancient power story, one that predicts greatness. But what does it mean? What skills and intrinsic personal qualities does this archetype promote?

Alexander the Great outshone his father's officers in gentling the unruly Bucephalus, a spirited horse who subsequently carried his one and only master through numerous conquests, helping him subdue the known world all the way to India. There Alexander named a city after his loyal companion, who was reportedly killed at age thirty during the Battle of the Hydaspes (in what is now known as Pakistan) in 326 BCE.

Similar horse-taming tales are told about a young prince who lived in northeast India over two hundred years earlier, though his brand of power turned out to be much different from Alexander's. Siddhartha Gautama too was raised to become an emperor-warrior. And indeed, shortly before his birth in 563 BCE, oracles told his father, King Suddhodana, that Siddhartha would become a great leader. But there was one nagging hitch. A sage named Asita sensed a crossroad in the prince's path, one that shook Suddhodana to the core. If the young prince contemplated the nature of suffering, Asita predicted, Siddhartha would renounce his kingdom and instead become a saint, one capable of leading others to peace.

As the story goes, Suddhodana tried to combat this possibility by shielding his son from witnessing death, disease, and old age. But life, being what it is, made that impossible when Siddhartha came of age and wanted to explore his kingdom. Learning of realities outside the palace walls, Siddhartha could no longer enjoy his insulated, privileged existence and sneaked out of the castle one night, fulfilling Asita's prophecy. For six years, he wandered the countryside studying with a variety of hermits, mendicants, and holy men and experimenting with all kinds of spiritual practices, becoming the Buddha, "the awakened one," at age thirty-five.

The Power of Gentleness

It's hard to separate myth from history, as there are literally thousands of legends that rose up around the Buddha in the centuries following his peaceful death at age eighty. One feature of his biography that persists in the more reliable, as well as the more fanciful, sources involves reports of outstanding horse-training abilities.

As the firstborn son of a wealthy monarch, Siddhartha received the finest education available in all disciplines, becoming a bit of a renaissance man before his sixteenth birthday. Accounts describe him as a perceptive philosophical student, talented musician, skillful chariot driver, and cool and daring horseman who was nonetheless known for his unusual kindness to animals, preferring to lose a race rather than whip his mount toward the finish line. He exercised his princely authority to discourage cruel behavior in others as well. Popular tales chronicle his successful efforts to stop one boy from beating a snake. He also rescued a swan wounded by a cousin's arrow, going before a council of elders to win the right to heal the bird and set him free, over the hunter's right to claim his quarry, an episode that clearly illustrates the Buddha's innate nonpredatory orientation.

Another telling anecdote suggests that Siddhartha's sympathy was further awakened by observing beasts of burden, human and animal alike. One afternoon, when he was nine years old, his parents took him to the ritual first plowing of the fields. While most people were entranced by colorful parades, tempting food displays, immaculately dressed dignitaries, and holy men chanting Vedic scriptures and wearing flowing robes and stunning headdresses, Siddhartha sat down at the edge of the fields to watch another, more perplexing spectacle unfold. As the Buddhist monk and author Thich Nhat Hanh describes in *Old Path White Clouds: Walking in the Footsteps of the Buddha*, Suddhodana subsequently became so distressed by his son's behavior that the king left the celebration early — not because Siddhartha was acting up but because his interest in the interconnected struggles of all species he encountered that day foreshadowed the fulfillment of Asita's prophecy:

[Siddhartha] watched a buffalo straining to pull a heavy plow, followed by a robust farmer whose skin was bronzed from long work in the sun. The farmer's left hand steadied the plow while his right hand wielded a whip to urge the buffalo on. Sun blazed and the man's sweat poured in streams from his body. The rich earth was divided into two neat furrows. As the plow turned the earth, Siddhartha noticed that the bodies of worms and other small creatures were being cut as well. As the worms writhed upon the ground, they were spotted by birds who flew down and grabbed them in their beaks. Then Siddhartha saw a large bird swoop down and grasp a small bird in its talons....

When the king and queen passed by sometime later, they discovered Siddhartha still sitting in deep concentration. Gotami [his stepmother] was moved to tears seeing how beautiful Siddhartha looked, like a small, still statue. But King Suddhodana was seized with a sudden apprehension. If Siddhartha could sit so solemnly at such a young age, might not the holy man Asita's prophecy come true? Too disturbed to remain at the picnic, the king returned alone to the palace in his royal carriage.

Some poor, country children passed by the tree speaking and laughing happily. Gotami motioned them to be quiet. She pointed to Siddhartha sitting beneath the rose-apple tree. Curious, the children stared at him. Suddenly, Siddhartha opened his eyes. Seeing the queen, he smiled.

"Mother," he said, "reciting the scriptures does nothing to help the worms and the birds."

Siddhartha...then noticed the children observing him. They were about his own age, but their clothes were tattered, their faces soiled, and their arms and legs piteously thin. Aware of his princely attire, Siddhartha felt embarrassed, and yet he wanted very much to play with them....He asked Gotami for permission to invite the children to the picnic feast. At first she hesitated, but then she nodded in assent.

This incident marked a turning point in Siddhartha's young life, demonstrating not only his sensitivity to the suffering of others but his growing awareness of the impotency of most religious and social structures to address this issue. Siddhartha's perceptive, compassionate nature was unsettling to his father, who wielded power to insulate himself and his extended family from life's uncomfortable realities. This, as the Buddha would later observe, was ignorance in action, and it had nothing to do with low IQ. Rather, it was a *misuse* of intelligence for people to *ignore* what didn't fit into their limited self-serving views of life. Ignorance was both a by-product of and a necessary ingredient in the increasing human obsession with creating ever more elaborate cocoons that supported the lavish comfort of the few at the expense of the many.

Siddhartha's father was the king of this strategy. From the festival day forward, Suddhodana insisted that his son be educated and entertained within the carefully controlled setting of the palace grounds. There Siddhartha enjoyed every possible socially sanctioned pleasure, continuing to develop exceptional archery, music making, and riding skills enhanced by his patient, empathetic nature. Luckily for posterity, Suddhodana didn't realize that the equestrian arts, which most royals employed for pageantry and war, were also capable of exercising an expansive, nonpredatory power, one that would transform Siddhartha's sensitivity into mindfulness, courage, and poise in the midst of chaos, giving him the tools he would need to leave his comfortable life and attempt the impossible.

Kanthaka

In one classic coming-of-age story, Siddhartha tamed a wild stallion to win the hand of Yasodhara, daughter of a neighboring king. This oft-cited anecdote is remarkably similar to the Alexander-Bucephalus tale, in that the horse was incredibly defiant and extremely dangerous.

Details vary, but in many accounts, Siddhartha was competing with other young noblemen to impress the beautiful princess and, perhaps more important, her powerful, exacting father. One by one, suitors tried to mount the horse as terrified grooms restrained the enraged animal with ropes. In some versions, an initially successful rider was thrown and nearly trampled to death before guards pulled him to safety in the nick of time. Still, Siddhartha showed no fear. Like Alexander, the Indian prince took a more thoughtful, compassionate approach, calmly walking to the agitated animal, speaking softly, and eventually stroking his face and sides. When the stallion began to lick Siddhartha's hand, a tentative sign of trust and submission, the young man quietly eased onto the animal's back, winning the contest. Yasodhara became a royal horse whisperer's wife, mother of his son, and much later, one of her husband's spiritual followers, joining the first order of Buddhist nuns.

Like many authors who've written about Siddhartha over the past twenty-five hundred years, Deepak Chopra included a horse-gentling episode in his novel *Buddha: A Story of Enlightenment*, artfully combining the sketchy facts about the prince's favorite horse, Kanthaka, with reports of the young man's ability to tame a wild stallion to win Yasodhara's hand in marriage. This anecdote, however, takes place when Siddhartha is a bit younger, and much more interested in horses than in girls:

> When he got to the stables he found Channa holding the reins of his favorite white stallion. The horse had come to the king from the wilds, and at first nobody could tame him. But Siddhartha spotted the animal's fear and used it. Every time he brought a stick of sugar cane for the stallion, he would sit and wait as long as it took for the horse to walk over to him. He never approached on his own, even if it took an hour for the animal to calm down.
>
> When he was tempted enough, the horse wanted to snatch the treat and run off, but Siddhartha made sure that his hand always touched the horse before he released the food. Gradually the white stallion began to accept being touched as part of being rewarded, until the day came when Siddhartha approached him in public and put a bridle on him, a feat nobody else had accomplished. From that point on it was only a matter of time before word went about that the prince had tamed an untamable wild stallion. On the day when the horse allowed himself to be mounted, Siddhartha named him Kanthaka.

Buddhist histories specify that it was Kanthaka who, years later, carried his master away from the palace under cover of darkness, through the countryside and across the Anoma River, where Siddhartha embarked on the ultimate journey of freedom — from suffering, craving, hate, and delusion. Some ancient texts insist Kanthaka died of grief when Siddhartha struck out on his own that night. But the horse was subsequently reincarnated as a Brahman (a member of India's priestly caste) who, after attending talks by a then much older Buddha, easily took the teachings to heart, eventually becoming enlightened himself.

Lunacy and Skepticism

It's not necessary to believe in reincarnation to glean useful insights from this tale, if we look at the more fantastic elements as *fingers pointing to the moon*. In this respect, I must return to the strange story of "taming" my own black stallion Midnight Merlin. To tell it honestly, I share, at times, pivotal experiences I can't back up with scientific research, at least not yet. But in subsequent chapters I'll offer some working theories on these principles that help leaders lead, trauma survivors heal, and visionaries in training navigate the unknown.

Innovators must walk a razor's edge, entering the great unmapped territory of human experience without getting lost or going crazy. Here skepticism becomes a healthy tool — if it isn't used to disregard feelings and forces that defy the current worldview. It's important to remember that, from a limited sensory perspective, the *appearances* of most phenomena are misleading. Increasingly sophisticated telescopes and microscopes have already shown us wonders we could never have accessed with our limited vision.

Even so, life's mysteries shouldn't be worshipped or dismissed because we can't see the whole picture. The moon, after all, seems to wax, wane, die, and be reborn each month, because it's reflecting a temporarily hidden sun in relation to the earth's shadow. And it is here that art, science, and *utility* merge. Lunar cycles inspire poets and control ocean tides. The soft, blue light flowing over the nighttime landscape is aesthetically stirring and deeply comforting — perhaps even more so because we now know that the harmonious interaction of *three* celestial bodies gives rise to this subtle nocturnal luminosity, motivating us to explore other areas where relationship creates functional, mutually supportive realities that are, at the same time, magnificent to behold.

Still, midnight travelers don't need a working knowledge of astronomy for the moon to light their way. And so it is with the invisible, inexplicable forces that horse trainers and other leaders can draw upon to reach their goals, and even help change the world, *before* cutting-edge science, let alone culturally accepted thought, can even begin to catch up.

Desert Dojo

People searching for soulful ways to unlock the mind often look to Buddhist and Taoist principles. But Midnight Merlin didn't require that I find a guru or subscribe to any belief system to practice mindfulness. He did, however, insist — upon the threat of death at times — that I develop this ability, fast. Yet I also knew that anytime he became too much for me, I had a whole herd of much gentler, highly experienced teachers munching hay in my own backyard. I often enlisted them as patient tutors for remedial skills that my thick human brain found challenging — and that my stubborn human ego was doubly reluctant to accept.

Horses embody many of the attitudes people access through more formal meditation techniques, including the ability to engage fully with reality. What seems so difficult for a grasping, hoarding, controlling, competitive human being comes easily to these highly social, intensely aware, nomadic prey animals. Horses are actually hardwired for the state of nonattachment championed by the Buddha. In the wild, they don't defend territory, build nests, live in caves, or store nuts for the winter. They move unprotected with the rhythms of nature, cavorting through the snow, kicking up their heels on cool spring mornings, grazing peacefully in fields of flowing grass, despite a keen and constant awareness of predators lurking in the distance. While they react quickly in the face of danger, they also show remarkable resilience in recovering from traumatic events. They don't ruminate over and over and over again about the injustices of the past, clouding their vision and their enjoyment of life with ceaseless internal dialogues about how cruel it is that God invented lions.

But traumatic events in nature are different from the inescapable stress some horses endure in captivity, where they're forcefully pulled away from their mothers at six months, restrained, confined, and in many cases, isolated, if not physically abused. Many horse owners, influenced by behavioristic views of animals, treat their mounts like machines, becoming resentful, even violent, when they act "unpredictably." Other people coddle these massive, agile creatures, talking to them like babies, never allowing them to grow up and claim their dignity as powerful, intelligent beings. Either way, limiting, preconceived notions cause both amateur and professional equestrians to disregard important nonverbal cues that come from the horse and their own bodies. When these valuable, in some cases lifesaving, communications are habitually ignored, unnecessary accidents and injuries invariably follow. It's not uncommon for riders to go through horse after horse, trying desperately to find that rare animal physically and mentally capable of fulfilling some lifelong competitive or recreational goal.

I myself was on this path when I realized I didn't have the skills to handle my first horse, Nakia. Even more disheartening, my first trainer's techniques escalated her confusion and frustration, creating an increasingly defiant, flighty horse. Several people advised me to sell this "dangerous, uncooperative" mare. Luckily, I found a gentle, experienced woman — with a small farm of her own — who appreciated the ex-racehorse's high-spirited nature. As Nakia stepped on the trailer and rode off into the sunset, I undertook a quest to find the right trainer and the perfect horse.

As it turns out, I never did find perfection. I found something much more interesting. In working with a series of horses who defied conventional training techniques and agendas, I stretched far beyond my own limited beliefs and perceptions about not only the human-equine relationship but the nature of reality itself, particularly in regard to "shared consciousness," expanded awareness, surrender, and innovation. Along the way, I began to understand (viscerally, emotionally, and much later intellectually) what those ancient horse-taming tales tell us about the nonverbal genius of gifted leaders.

Wu-Wei

Lao-tzu observed that "it is upon disaster that good fortune rests," pointing to what is perhaps the most potent Taoist paradox, one that my own growing herd challenged me to embrace over and over again. After twenty years living, working, and studying with these remarkable animals, writing about them through births, deaths, triumphs, and hardships, I can honestly say that the most profound transformations happened precisely when things didn't go my way — when my most reliable tools, ideas, training methods, and coping strategies failed and I had, well, *nothing* left to do.

Taoism, more than any other philosophy, recognizes that such impasses, while initially frustrating, even demoralizing, can be life changing in the best sense of the word — *if* we adopt a more innovative approach. And for Lao-tzu, the most powerful strategy, oddly enough, involved *wu-wei*, which translates as "not doing," "not forcing," or "not striving." Wu-wei is *not* advice to "do nothing." It's not a recommendation to pack up and go home, and it's most definitely not achieved by glossing over the challenging elements of a situation. It's about suspending the all-too-human fixation on what *should* or *shouldn't* happen to notice what *is* happening — without flinching, running off, engaging in wishful thinking, or trying to aggressively control the situation.

At first, this *looks* like you're doing nothing because, after exhausting your repertoire of quick-fix solutions and habitual patterns, you're finally open to analyzing the previously ignored dynamics standing in your way: feelings, behaviors, and other, more subtle nonverbal energies, processes, and insights. Wu-wei also requires more courage than most people expect. It's actually a lot like being challenged to a sharo, only in this case, you're not being whacked with a big stick; you're being asked to stay present, endure, and think clearly through the utter confusion and humiliation of not knowing what to do next.

Yet in marshaling this acutely aware, fully engaged form of patience, you begin to notice "what *wants* to happen." Unexpected solutions appear on the horizon of consciousness, seemingly of their own accord, creating the mystical sense of a higher intelligence taking over. And, given your previously conditioned responses, which can only function in the context of a limited worldview, it appears that something larger than your ego *is* being activated.

Artists often describe this pivotal shift as being "visited by a muse." Lao-tzu explained it as "aligning with the Tao." Judeo-Christian innovators characterize it as an act of "surrender" that allows them to be "guided by God." In the influential PBS series *The Power of Myth*, Joseph Campbell and journalist Bill

Moyers discussed this same phenomenon as feeling "helped by hidden hands" or having an "invisible means of support."

Scientists, too, hit the wall, reporting that unexpected theories emerge when they've exhausted all logical conclusions and conventional strategies, admitting a kind of defeat. People later hailed as geniuses are not necessarily smarter than their peers. They've simply broken through whatever old paradigm holds everyone else back — by sacrificing some cherished belief or acknowledging the incompleteness of some widely accepted scientific "truth," letting new information in, and patiently waiting for an organic, subconscious integration to take place. These people may seem to give up, for days, weeks, or even years. But deep down, their drive to find a solution, their sheer fascination with the subject, never wavers.

It was my horses who taught me to relax into this irritating limbo stage between letting go of the old and envisioning the new. They also revealed that the art of wu-wei requires releasing attachment to a conventional or idealistic *outcome*, not *being detached* from the situation. Caring about the other beings involved was essential. It also helped to have faith: in myself, in humanity's as-yet-unrecognized potential, and in the benevolence and intelligence of nature. In essence I had to acknowledge that the universe operates on principles that invigorate the mind *and* the heart. If I defiantly held on to any belief system — from scientific survival-of-the-fittest notions to fundamentalist religious precepts, New Age utopianism, and the disconnected, mechanistic, nihilistic perspective characteristic of some modern atheists — I would have missed important opportunities to evolve, let alone deepen my knowledge and sheer enjoyment of life.

Let me give you an example of how a "problem horse" plunged me into a fruitful period of wu-wei, expanded my awareness, and inspired a subsequent innovation. What the heck; let me give you two or three.

As detailed in my previous books, and summarized in Guiding Principle 2, "Listen to Your Horse" (chapter 14), the first, most painful incident occurred with my promising young Arabian mare Tabula Rasa (from the Latin for "clean slate"). With the help of a sensitive, adventurous trainer, I had the privilege of starting this intelligent, affectionate horse from the ground up, after I let Nakia go. My first year with Rasa was sheer heaven, a dream come true, as we took long walks in the desert together on foot and, eventually, to my great satisfaction, under saddle. And then came a pivotal trail ride in August 1994: a huge black Rottweiler chased us down a deep sandy wash, permanently injuring Rasa's right back leg, which X-rays subsequently showed was already weakened by a congenital joint condition.

I was officially grounded by the universe that day, tossed off my high horse, forced to make a crucial decision. Would I cut my losses and sell Rasa as a brood mare, as most people recommended I do? Would I buy another, better, sounder horse and start over?

A series of compelling dreams and indescribable emotions encouraged me, against all possible logic, to keep this mare whose soulful eyes spoke more profoundly to me in silence than anyone ever had in words. I could not shake the feeling that she had something important to teach me. Still, her injury initially made it impossible for me to even lead her on walks through the desert or do the simplest ground training exercises. After some progressive therapeutic interventions, I was advised to board her on pasture for six months, cross my fingers, and let nature take its course.

We were, by that time, deeply bonded, which might easily explain my reluctance to sell her. Our mutual affection also made it impossible for me to turn her loose and walk away for half a year. At the time, however, few people respected our connection. Horses were considered unintelligent, purely instinctual beings, incapable of feeling or expressing emotion. Some local ranchers didn't even name their horses, believing these animals weren't "smart enough" to respond — a misconception Rasa, and every other horse I've ever met, disproved. Still, people continued to joke about my "thousand-pound pet." And so for years, we basically hid out, interacting in places where the smirks of other horse owners could, for the most part, be avoided.

At the same time, I continued to boost my horse-training skills, first by apprenticing at an Arabian breeding farm where I kept Rasa in a back pasture with my former cow horse Noche and several boarders' horses. By day, I learned conventional ways of handling stallions, breeding mares, weaning foals, and training young horses. After the humans left for the day, I learned just as much by interacting with Rasa and the rest of her makeshift herd on their terms.

Because I couldn't train or ride my injured horse, I was forced to do nothing *with* her for six months, which meant I spent hours milling around the pasture with her and a half dozen other horses. There I observed all kinds of surprising behavior that completely contradicted what my trainers were teaching me about "hardwired" equine instincts and dominance hierarchies, behavior that foreshadowed my understanding of how the horse-human relationship could be used to elevate the mental, emotional, and social intelligence of both species.

For a description of the herd behavior that initially led me to entertain this possibility, see Guiding Principle 2, "Listen to Your Horse" (chapter 14). In fact, thinking back on the experience, I see clearly now that I conceived most of the "Power of the Herd" Guiding Principles in that wu-wei pasture nearly twenty years ago, though it subsequently took that long to (1) bring these unconventional yet ultimately practical insights to consciousness, (2) name and define them, (3) communicate their benefits to others, (4) create reliable experiential activities that exercise these abilities in equestrians and nonequestrians alike, (5) find scientific research to validate at least some of these principles, and (6) streamline them into an equine-inspired twelve-point program for developing advanced leadership and emotional- and social-intelligence skills. (My original list included over twenty guiding principles.)

In this chapter, however, I want to emphasize that my *connection* to Rasa, my desire to be with her whether or not she would ever be "useful" as a riding horse again, took me down an unexpectedly fruitful path. I originally bought this mare to escape the pressures of modern civilization, and what I learned in being forced to give up that still-limited human agenda opened my eyes to a whole new way of being, not just with horses, but also with people.

By embracing the hidden gifts of what initially seemed a tragedy, I gained confidence in opening my mind and heart to life's unexpected lessons, and I relaxed into the Tao, feeling the current carry me toward oceans of potential.

Good Fortune

There were two guiding principles (4 and 11) that I wouldn't have isolated had I not faced the advanced power struggles I encountered with Midnight Merlin. And yet to even get to the point where our association was productive rather than frustrating or even deadly, I needed every scrap of information, every conscious and unconscious, verbal and nonverbal, conventional and unconventional skill I had developed as a result of Rasa's injury.

Without my initial stroke of "bad luck" with this promising mare, I never would have apprenticed at the Arabian farm. I would have been out riding Rasa in the desert after work and entering horse shows on weekends, becoming fully indoctrinated in standard ways of riding and training horses for diversion, escape, financial reward, and ego gratification. While certainly not a part of my own master plan, the basic skills I developed handling stallions, mares, foals, and yearlings through conventional breeding, birthing, weaning, and training strategies were essential in even entertaining the idea of adopting Merlin five years later.

My motivation was, like my original quest to buy a horse, conventional and somewhat superficial. As a registered black Arabian stallion, Merlin was the perfect mate for Rasa, who was also a registered black Arabian. On paper, they couldn't have been a better match. Among experienced stallion handlers, Merlin's value as a sire alone generated support for my little project. The timing was also right in terms of my own skill and interest levels. Even after Rasa's six-month convalescence, I was never able to ride her to any significant degree, though we were learning to dance together through modified ground training exercises that could easily continue through pregnancy and childbirth. By the time we met Merlin in 1999, Rasa and I had developed a profoundly satisfying, continually educational, nonriding relationship that changed my life in other areas, and I was beginning to teach some of these skills to people intrigued by the idea of working with horses to enhance their own personal and professional growth.

Perhaps most important of all, I was immensely more experienced in navigating the unknown. A whole "new," previously invisible world had been made visible to me through my unconventional association with Rasa. Understanding how horses use emotion as information; how our bodies act as tuners, receivers, and amplifiers for nonverbal signals; how feelings, sensations, heart rate, blood pressure, and breathing are contagious was essential to my ability to stay safe with Merlin. As was the idea of wu-wei, not doing, not striving, but waiting patiently, mindfully for a new solution to emerge seemingly of its own accord.

When I began working with Merlin, I quickly saw that forcing the stallion back into activities he associated with his abusive trainer could easily end in serious injury for us both. More frustrating was the fact that gentler, more progressive therapies, such as equine massage, acupuncture, and T-Touches (a somatic training and rehabilitation technique developed by the horse trainer Linda Tellington-Jones) were completely useless to me as well for one surprising, incredibly irritating reason: touching Merlin was the most dangerous thing you could do to him, the thing that repulsed him the most.

As a result, I plunged into a whole new episode of wu-wei that taught me something much stranger than I could have imagined had the stallion been amenable to a nice, oxytocin-boosting massage. In the process, I learned several unexpected skills useful to trauma survivors and their family members, most especially soldiers coming back from war.

Time and Space

There's a disturbing scene in the film *Buck*, a widely watched 2011 documentary on the author and horse trainer Buck Brannaman, who consulted with Robert Redford during the making of *The Horse Whisperer*. Near the end of the film, a young woman brings her three-year-old colt to a clinic hoping Buck can alter the animal's intensely aggressive behavior. The flashy palomino stallion hadn't been abused. Rather, his increasingly dangerous antics arose from a series of hardships related to his mother dying in childbirth, possible oxygen deprivation as the owner pulled him from the mare's womb, the need to bottle-feed the orphaned foal, and an apparently unrelated back injury that took the woman herself out of commission for months during a crucial early training stage when she could have taught the horse some lifesaving manners. (However, it also appeared that even if she had been physically capable of working with the horse at that time, the woman wouldn't have known how to teach these skills to her special-needs horse.)

Judging from his behavior on-screen, the horse didn't show any signs of brain damage from oxygen deprivation. He was alert and responsive. The challenges seemed related to a different kind of developmental issue: Bottle-fed colts treat humans as their peers and elders, which is endearing for the first few months. When testosterone kicks in at age two, however, this association becomes increasingly problematic as the colt begins to challenge people with the same outlandish power plays you see mustangs engage in with each other. In the wild, a crucial adolescent socialization process takes place, managed by older, more experienced mares and stallions, who can easily handle a kick, bite, or charge that would kill the average human being.

The plot thickened when the woman mentioned that she had *eighteen* stallions at home, and that she'd turned the colt out with some of these other males at times, perhaps hoping to create a "bachelor band" experience for her orphaned colt while she was convalescing. However, in domesticated horses — who haven't been properly socialized by *generations* of seasoned *equine* leaders — this can result in ganglike behavior among stallions. Imagine encountering a group of *thousand-pound* Crips or Bloods racing toward you at thirty-five miles an hour, rearing ten feet up in the air, striking at you with hooves as hard as brass knuckles, then mule-kicking you down the street after taking all your money. It's easy to understand why Buck initially conveyed shock, then fear for the woman's safety.

In the film, no information was given on these other horses, where they were kept, or how the woman ended up with so many of them, though Buck gently scolded her for what he, and the vast majority of experienced equestrians, would perceive as a naively idealistic addiction to stallions. Buck told the woman that she needed to take a look at her desire to have so many of these wild and powerful males in her life, emphasizing that horse problems mirrored the handler's unresolved issues. But as a horse trainer, not an equine-facilitated therapy specialist, Buck was powerless to offer his client support in this area. His conversation with her involved little more than a few shaming statements, a hint of empathy, and no real solutions for the palomino who, during the documentary at least, was presented as too far gone to help.

Let me make one thing perfectly clear: *most* of us are powerless in these situations. As we emerge from five thousand years of slavery, dominance, and submission, we don't yet have the skills to pull ourselves up by our own bootstraps and heal the trauma that humans experience as often as horses in our current system, sometimes in war, sometimes as orphans, sometimes through parental abuse like Buck Brannaman faced as the child of a violent father. We're just now learning how to heal the emotional, psychological, and spiritual wounds of the past, how to cultivate power in nonpredatory ways, and how to compassionately support others on this quest. In this respect, no horse whisperer, teacher, counselor, or spiritual leader has all the answers, magically transforming pain and confusion into clarity and peace.

To solve these complex problems, we must engage in *consensual* leadership (Guiding Principle 10, chapter 22), which means "sensing together," ideally tapping the expertise of experienced and compassionate people in multiple disciplines, analyzing what works and what doesn't — without shame, blame, power plays, or sarcasm. As a culture and as a species, we also need to change our perspective on troubleshooting, welcoming periods of wu-wei over quick-fix solutions, enhanced by the social-intelligence skills needed to collaborate, experiment, and explore the unknown together.

Was the colt too far gone? Watching the admittedly erratic behavior exhibited on-screen, I don't think so. There were a number of positive signals from the horse, some surprisingly successful moments during the first training session (which included a team approach by Buck, the experienced horse he was riding, and a training assistant). There were also some misinterpretations regarding the roots of the colt's aggression, and a disciple-like, method-oriented lack of awareness on the part of the assistant, who got mauled when he was asked to go into the corral alone with the horse while Buck saddled up for a second training session that never happened, at least not on film. Justifiably concerned for the bleeding assistant, the woman decided to put her three-year-old colt down. He was quietly loaded back onto the trailer, and the two drove off into a different kind of sunset.

Based on experience with an even more violent stallion, I was saddened to see that the palomino wasn't given what he needed most at that moment: time and space. I'm not using these words in their usual sense — the frantic, frustrated, mal-socialized animal most certainly did not need six months of freedom to run amok on pasture. He needed to experience *mutually respectful* boundaries, learning how to respect others' space while also realizing over time that *people would respect his space* when he showed signs of escalating arousal, a still-controversial premise in the mainstream equestrian world. (See Guiding Principle 4, chapter 16.) Because the woman did not understand this crucial missing piece, however, her safety was seriously compromised. When Buck made it clear he couldn't fix her horse in a week, the difficult decision she made, while tragic, may have saved her life.

The issues involved were much too complex to address in a workshop designed for preparing conventional riding, showing, and cattle-herding horses to become safe mounts for the average Western rider. Because of initial circumstances beyond anyone's control, this spirited young stallion had been raised to see humans as herd members. In that sense, the orphaned palomino was inadvertently launched on a Fulani-like path, but in a culture that was absolutely clueless regarding the intricacies of interspecies socialization. No wonder he was frustrated and confused. He needed assistance from a master herder in developing physical, mental, and emotional self-control, rather than mindless submission to humans who had no knowledge of the difference between dominance and leadership, let alone between boundaries and assertiveness.

To reach the potential hidden inside this challenge, the golden-haired colt needed at least one mindful, adaptable, empowered advocate who (1) exhibited high levels of his or her own emotional self-control, (2) could recognize which normally beneficial natural-horsemanship methods weren't working and, just as important, which methods *were* working, (3) knew how to solicit and continuously evaluate help from other sources when he or she ran out of ideas, and (4) was willing to endure a particular kind of sharo, the kind in which you're brave and experienced enough to hold your own with a troubled teenager, soldier, or trauma survivor — without indulging, or lashing out at, an individual who is dangerous purely because, one way or another, *he* was injured by life circumstances exacerbated by humanity's lack of emotional and social intelligence.

Heroic Wu-Wei

When I accepted Shawnee Allen's offer to rehabilitate Midnight Merlin in 1999, I wasn't prepared for the many ways he would attack horses and people alike. Initially, I couldn't even walk into his stall and put a halter on him without a serious fight. Whenever I actually succeeded in getting close enough to touch him, he would jerk back and rear as if he'd been shocked by a cattle prod. By that time, it was also clear that the conventional use of saddles, bits, and lead

ropes, and even the free-longing protocols used by natural-horsemanship afi-
cionados like Monty Roberts, Ray Hunt, and Buck Brannaman, intermittently
and unpredictably caused a massive escalation in arousal that would send the
horse into a blind fury. The trainer who abandoned the stallion in Tucson had
employed these techniques with dangerously inconsistent results. (Merlin must
have scared the tar out of the man one day, as he suddenly left town, not even
bothering to call Shawnee to tell her where the horse was. It took The Ranch's
owners several months of research to find out who she was and where she lived.)

I too ran the Merlin gauntlet as I assessed his response to many of these
same methods. In observing his behavior over time (well, really more like enduring and surviving his behavior over time), I found the trauma pattern to
be "consistently erratic." Merlin seemed to try, sincerely, to keep it together. He
was at times engaged and filled with promise, intelligent, and even enthusiastic about learning something new. Then suddenly, seemingly without warning,
he'd trip off into a rage, whereupon he'd either lunge toward the handler, rearing and striking with teeth bared, or pull away and run around so frantically
he'd lose his balance and slide on his side, sometimes ten or fifteen feet across
the arena into the fence, scraping his hide, lying there for ten minutes covered
with sweat, staring blankly as if he'd given up the ghost while his pulse was racing frantically. These tantrums were heartbreaking to witness, and absolutely
horrific if you happened to be in there with him.

At the same time, touch was so offensive to Merlin that experienced equine
massage therapists, T-Touch specialists, and veterinary acupuncturists couldn't
get near him. While the stallion's response to training techniques would send
him into an occasional, unpredictable rage, putting your hands anywhere near
his hide sent him into an instantaneous, guaranteed rage. To avoid further injury and trauma for the horse, not to mention all the humans involved, I gave
into a period of what I can only characterize as *heroic wu-wei* because, for the
first week or two, doing nothing *with* Merlin involved a high level of vigilance
and some serious self-defense skills.

The strategy seemed simple enough. I decided to see how far away I needed
to stand from Merlin in order for the horse to calm down. My goal was to start
from this place, and move closer, day by day, inch by inch, until I was finally
touching him. Instead, I found that Merlin demanded I stand in the same place
day after day, about five feet from his body. If I even leaned in, he would pin his
ears and begin to show the first signs of flight-or-fight. So I simplified the goal
even further. Thinking that perhaps I would have to stand there until Merlin
finally trusted me, I spent ten to thirty minutes each day standing in the corral
with the stallion, five feet away from him, holding a whip in a neutral position

in case he decided to attack, which he was progressively less motivated to do. After a week, it seemed like he looked forward to a form of companionship that asked nothing from either of us.

Standing there for days on end, I developed a relaxed yet heightened state of awareness — out of necessity. If I held my breath or tensed my body in any way, Merlin would do the same, which meant he would either move away or attack. In terms of his or my rising physiological arousal, however, it was actually difficult at times to tell "who started it." Because Merlin's demeanor could change so quickly, it didn't *matter* who started it. I had to address the situation immediately or it would get out of hand. And so I began to think and react not in terms of *who* was afraid, angry, or agitated but more along the lines of assessing *when fear, anger, and/or agitation were present in the horse-human system.* By noticing the slightest rise in my own blood pressure, heart rate, or tension, then immediately adding breath and relaxation while simultaneously holding my ground, I could calm Merlin at a distance of five feet, often without lifting the whip — *if* I noticed the shift in its earliest, most subtle form and took immediate action to calm my own body while simultaneously conveying strength and power.

Talk about the benefits of stallion-induced mindfulness training! It wasn't just about noticing what was happening. It was about sensing, then quickly altering, my own body's response to escalating tension while simultaneously paying attention to another being, calming him in the process. Merlin needed someone who could physically, at a distance, help him modulate his own out-of-control, traumatized nervous system. And by learning to do this for him, I was mastering this ability in myself.

It subsequently became clear what many of the horse-taming tales throughout history were pointing to: the nonverbal, somatic genius of exceptional leaders able to control fear and aggression in large animals and, consequently, in large populations. Think of Washington's horse standing through cannon and musket fire, inspiring hundreds of shoeless soldiers to do the same when every fiber of their being was shouting "Retreat!" Consider the already advanced physical, mental, and emotional self-control Siddhartha would have needed to gentle the enraged stallion he faced in winning Yasodhara's hand in marriage.

In working with horses, the Buddha literally had a leg up in developing important nonverbal skills he drew upon to make that final leap toward enlightenment at age thirty-five, striving over the next forty-five years to teach these life-enhancing mental, emotional, and social-intelligence principles to other people. His sometimes clear and logical, sometimes vague and mystical teachings pointed to a reality that could never fully be translated into words.

From this perspective, it's clear why his program for self-mastery was called the *dharma*, a Sanskrit word characterizing practices that illuminate universal principles interweaving natural phenomena and the human psyche, ultimately creating a dynamic, harmonious interdependence.

In accepting the challenge to heal Merlin, in somehow finding the courage to face this ridiculously dangerous task, my own mind-body awareness was elevated beyond anything I knew was possible. Over the next decade, a slowly progressing, positive feedback loop began to reach fulfillment. As Merlin forced me to stretch beyond my conventional human perceptions, habits, and skills, *he* stretched, the herd stretched, and the other humans in his life began to stretch as well. This was not always an easy path to follow, as I sometimes felt as though we were bushwhacking through cactus in the dead of night. And yet, we evolved in concert with each other, shedding our limiting fears and beliefs to *believe in each other*.

Two years after Merlin died at age twenty-three, I came across accounts of the Buddha and Kanthaka, and it struck me that this story could easily represent the first recorded case of mutual evolution between a human and a horse. What if the stallion that Siddhartha so skillfully and compassionately trained had also been training *him*, psychologically as well as physically carrying his master away from the heavily defended, insulated palace of a hierarchical, materialistic father? In the process, the legend specifies, Kanthaka himself moved beyond instinct, further developing his species' natural gifts for nonattachment, for expanded individual and herd awareness, and for nonpredatory power, later becoming enlightened as a student of the fully realized Buddha.

In working with Merlin, I developed a few valuable rehabilitation techniques and a deeper understanding of the horse-human connection, accessing insights I could later teach experientially and sometimes, though not always, translate into words. But acknowledging that we were simultaneously *separate and not separate* was the most powerful and elegant black-horse mystery of all. The Buddha described this principle as "dependent co-arising." Thich Nhat Hahn called it "Interbeing." But Merlin gave me a dramatic, direct experience of it when I became humble and patient enough to stand *with* him, waiting not simply for a training solution, as it turned out, but for a transformation of consciousness I had no idea any four-legged creature could inspire.

Distant Signals

Long after Midnight Merlin gained the self-control to live with Rasa and Comet, sire three sons, meet his granddaughter, and even teach my human students how to combine power with relaxed, yet heightened awareness, I would stand next to him, usually at sunset, sometimes watching the full moon rising over the mountains. After a few minutes of peaceful connection at a distance, he would often walk over to me, gently, respectfully asking for a scratch or even a lengthy massage, still demanding that I remain sensitive to his not nearly so sudden shifts in mood. In breathing into the first hint of tension, I would silently urge him to simply move away when he'd had enough. And once again, he'd stand nearby.

In the absolute silence of one cool desert night, I felt a vague yet unignorable sensation gathering force in the space between us, as if an idea, inspired by our association, were struggling to express itself. I took a deep breath, letting it fill my heart and filter up to my brain, where it exploded into an image that quickly dissolved into words. A still, small voice whispered in concert with a delicate evening breeze, and it was hard to tell whether this insight was coming from Merlin, me, the soft blue light surrounding us, or all three at once: "We are like moons, waxing and waning, darkening and shining through relationships with other celestial bodies that, at first glance, seem remote and self-contained. And yet, we move oceans on these planets, reflecting light we cannot hide or hoard, aiding travelers on nighttime journeys through distant lands."

My body jolted ever so slightly in response to this unexpected poetry. Merlin shook his mane and looked right at me, his black eyes at once earthy and otherworldly.

"This," he silently conveyed through waves of appreciation surging between us, "is the theme of a universal song."

Chapter Eleven

STICKS AND STONES

I magine asking a group of financial advisers with chronically high blood pressure to perform tricky arithmetic calculations — without their computers. Then imagine upping the ante by having these already agitated people rehearse speeches to a client whose money they've just lost.

That's what Karen Allen calls a stress test. In the late 1990s, her intentions were neither punitive nor sadistic. The award-winning research scientist simply wanted to assess what effect a new pet might have on people who didn't already share their lives with one. So she picked a particularly tough crowd: unmarried, hypertensive stockbrokers.

As expected, the blood pressure of each participant spiked during the initial math tests. Phase two of the experiment required that *all forty-eight* of Allen's stressed-out subjects take an ACE inhibitor called lisinopril, a drug used to treat high blood pressure, which successfully brought their resting heart rate within normal range. Half of the brokers were then randomly selected to adopt a cat or dog from a local animal shelter.

Six months later, they returned for another round of cranial gymnastics, to which, this time, the researchers added the decidedly uncomfortable element of breaking "the bad news" to an imaginary client (which no doubt proved to be good practice for Wall Street's as-yet-unforeseen future). The blood pressure of all the traders rose when performing these mentally and emotionally challenging tasks. But the medication-only group experienced *double* the stress response of those lucky stockbrokers who took the same tests with their furry friends present. And these people weren't even petting their pets! The unrestrained animals were sitting quietly nearby or wandering loose around the room.

Upon hearing the astonishing results, several subjects in the control group decided to even the score by adopting a dog or cat soon after the experiment ended, taking full advantage of the calming, supportive presence that an animal companion — and *only* an animal as it turns out — can provide.

Best Friends

Based at State University of New York in Buffalo, Allen had been studying the physiological responses generated by social interactions for over a decade. By the time she rounded up that group of frantic stockbrokers, she'd already conducted experiments to determine whether a trusted *human* companion might have the same effect on stress and performance. In one study, forty-five women took similar mathematical tests, first in the laboratory with an experimenter present. Then, at home two weeks later, they endured three more rounds of testing, one in the presence of a female friend, another with a beloved pet dog present, and a control session with only the experimenter present. During each round, the subjects were connected to machines measuring pulse rate, blood pressure, and skin conductance responses. The friends were instructed to be supportive in any way they preferred, but no one touched or spoke to the women at any time during the test. And although the subjects might have stroked their dogs when they first brought them into the room, the animals were allowed to roam freely. Participants did not pet their four-legged companions during the task itself, so touch was not considered a factor.

Keep in mind that the human companion was a close *friend*, not a co-worker or competitor. Even so, the stress readings were far and away the highest in the presence of those friends, noticeably less in the presence of the experimenter alone, and *significantly* lower with the test subjects' pets milling around. The average pulse rate of subjects performing the tasks with a supportive female friend in the room was close to 120 beats per minute, around 105 with the experimenter, and *less than 75 beats per minute* when a beloved dog was present. Blood pressure and skin conductance readings showed similarly dramatic differences.

As Allen and her colleagues revealed in their 1991 article published in the *Journal of Personality and Social Psychology* that outlined the results, "It's clear that the pet dog did not act merely as a pleasant and familiar distraction. Given that task performance quality did not differ between subjects in the pet present and control conditions in the home or among subjects in the laboratory setting, one can assume that subjects in the pet present condition were not particularly distracted by their pet dogs and remained engaged in the tasks." The women, however, were less accurate when their friends were present, starting over more often and moving more quickly through the tasks, supporting previous studies showing that "the presence of others increases drive and decreases performance on relatively novel or unlearned tasks."

In cool scientific fashion, Allen speculates in a footnote to the same article that "the stress buffering role of pets may, in part, explain their functional significance for humans and, hence, their historical presence in homes." But the women themselves were more effusive. In postexperiment interviews, "several divorced women said that whereas husbands may come and go, and children may grow up and leave home, a 'dog is forever.' We were told that pets never withhold their love, they never get angry and leave, and they never go out looking for new owners." Somehow, this allows people who share their lives with animals to not only relax during off hours but to accurately perform irritating math problems with unusual ease — while hooked up to wires and electrodes, no less.

The (Emotional) Cost of Doing Business

Through "performance anxiety" is the popular expression, there's a more revealing scientific term for the kind of stress we experience when executing a task, especially something new, in front of other people: *evaluation apprehension.* Involuntary physiological responses reveal how deeply we're affected by the subconscious assumption that every person we encounter, friend or foe, is evaluating everything we do. Even more maddening, those pesky elevations in blood pressure and pulse rate cause us to speed up and make more mistakes as a result, heightening the discomfort of learning just about anything, let alone experimenting with truly innovative ideas and behaviors, reinforcing our reluctance to try something unfamiliar — no matter how ineffective, or even destructive, old habits prove to be. The high level of evaluation apprehension we experience in the presence of other members of our own species, family included, also explains why creative geniuses tend to be reclusive, and why the most widely influential agents of social change, including the Buddha, Jesus, and Muhammad, spent significant time alone in nature before returning to the city with messages and methods of hope, connection, and transformation. (See Guiding Principle 10, chapter 22, for a simple way to lessen the effects of evaluation apprehension in groups.)

The increasingly intense scrutiny that modern culture amplifies mercilessly, especially through the media, compromises our ability to think clearly, let alone creatively. Regardless of the lip service paid to democracy, intensely competitive forms of capitalism favor the most domineering, naturally predatory leaders who *enjoy* a good fight. But that's not even the bad news: Sociopaths have an even greater advantage in our current system. Because of their compromised ability to feel fear, their lack of remorse for hurting others, stretching the truth or outright lying, and their marked gift for glib and entertaining put-downs, sociopaths are *best* suited to combating the personal effects of evaluation apprehension — while using the same phenomenon to manipulate and intimidate others. It takes an almost supernatural level of courage and self-sacrifice for a compassionate person with vision and integrity to step into the fray. As a result, we don't need complex conspiracy theories to worry about selfish, dictatorial leaders taking power. The farther away we move from the oxytocin-boosting and stress-buffering effects of nature and animals, the more easily civilization *selects* for aggression and sociopathy.

Politics is the ultimate chamber of horrors in this regard. "Evaluation apprehension" doesn't come close to characterizing the debilitating effects of all the infighting, backbiting, sarcasm, character defamation, and sheer mean-spirited vehemence our leaders endure in carrying out the simplest tasks. Yet the situation hasn't changed much in the past 250 years. The same old interpersonal dramas, knee-jerk reactions, calculated deceptions, and capricious, hypercritical judgments are just broadcast more widely and rapidly — set to music, with better visual aids.

Long after enemy forces surrendered and sailed back to England, President George Washington experienced vicious personal attacks, betrayals all the more shocking to him because they were carried out by fellow countrymen, some of whom had encouraged him to take office in the first place. The details are both fascinating and enlightening, especially concerning the creation of a two-party system that Washington abhorred. (For a succinct, engaging overview read the "First in Peace" chapter in Joseph Ellis's *His Excellency*.) One intricate example illustrates the now-classic pressures he faced.

In the mid-1790s, heated debates occurred over a treaty to continue trade with Great Britain, an important income source for American merchants and farmers alike. Some people quite simply hated their former oppressors and wanted to cut all ties. Any attempt to form a postwar relationship, they argued, was a betrayal of the Revolution itself. The French, who also had New World interests, didn't like the idea, either. Washington, however, supported negotiation, not only for economic reasons, but as a way to keep tabs on an imperialistic regime that might someday strike again. (The War of 1812 proved him prescient on this account.) With compelling reasons, backed by Washington's unusually effective leadership presence and, let's not forget, his hard-won reputation as the war hero who refused to be king, the president's opinion carried considerable weight, and the Jay Treaty was passed. Detractors, still hoping to turn the tide, felt they had no choice but to launch a direct assault on Washington's character, which was hard to do without fudging the truth, spreading rumors, and whenever possible, gloating over any challenges the country faced rather than rallying behind the commander in chief to solve problems that might arise as a result of the admittedly imperfect trade agreement.

People who essentially liked Washington yet disagreed unsuccessfully with key policies began circulating rumors that billed him as a good-natured has-been, a naive, senile old man who was clearly out of his league. Letters by Thomas Jefferson to this effect were "leaked" to sympathetic members of the press who didn't mind going public without revealing their source, at least initially. Jefferson denied this covert betrayal for months, until one of his more offensive letters condemning Washington's leadership was actually printed in several newspapers, effectively ending all correspondence between the two former friends.

Even more aggressive personal attacks ensued, according to Ellis, in the summer of 1796: "In response to the Jay Treaty, the French Directory had declared commercial war on American shipping, and one of the first prizes captured was an American cruiser coincidentally named the *Mount Vernon*. Editorials in the *Aurora*, taking a line that would have been regarded as treasonable in any later international conflict, saluted the French campaign on the high seas and chortled over the capture of a ship associated with Washington's reputation."

Benjamin Franklin Bache, publisher of the Philadelphia-based newspaper the *Aurora*, smelled blood in the water. Gaining notoriety as *the* voice for traumatized, or simply opportunistic, colonials who feared centralized power in *any* form, Bache stretched his newly guaranteed right to freedom of the press by resurrecting a malicious rumor, unabashedly and quite purposefully misleading the public. Based on some old forgeries of Washington's signature, part of a British scheme to have him removed as commander in chief during the Revolutionary War, the *Aurora* put a blatantly deceptive "spin" on the enemy's failed attempt to discredit him decades earlier. Bache somehow acquired these documents, gleefully printing "evidence" that the former general had accepted a bribe, creating the impression he'd been a British spy all along. Washington tried to laugh off this anemic ploy. After all, in his mind, he'd already been proved innocent. "But in the supercharged atmosphere of the time," notes Ellis, "all political attacks, no matter how preposterous, enjoyed some claim on credibility." Ultimately, the president had to spend several days arranging for an official record of the British forgeries to be filed in State Department archives.

Over time, these infuriating little dramas wore Washington down, producing the desired effect: removal from office. There's good reason to believe that the two-term tradition he initiated by voluntarily stepping down after eight years had more to do with his disgust at how politicians and journalists were using their newfound freedom than with any plan concerning the optimal number of years future presidents should serve for the good of the country. According to Ellis, "Washington described the Republican campaign against the Jay Treaty as a blatantly partisan effort masquerading as a noble cause," characterizing "the vicious personal attacks and willful misrepresentations that dominated the debate" as "ominous signs of a new kind of party politics for which he had no stomach."

As Washington confessed in a letter to a colleague, "These things, as you have supposed, fill my mind with much concern, and with serious anxiety. Indeed, the trouble and perplexities which they occasion, added to the weight of years which have passed over me, have worn away my mind more than my body; and renders ease and retirement indisputably necessary to both during the short time I have to stay here."

A Deepening Chasm

The Jay Treaty "exposed a major fault line running through the entire revolutionary era," Ellis concludes. "On the one hand stood those who wished America's revolutionary energies to be harnessed to the larger purposes of nation building; on the other side stood those who interpreted that very process as a betrayal of the Revolution itself." The most fanatical proponents of both the pro-central-government and the anti-central-government arguments quickly fell prey to the classic Adam-and-Eve dilemma, each presenting his or her perspective as obviously good, then right, then right*eous*, while rejecting the opposing view as inherently evil, wrong, demented, or simply unintelligent. It was much easier to promote one side and demean the other than to respectfully negotiate the nuances of both: the latter task, after all, involved sophisticated emotional- and social-intelligence skills that eons of predatory, winner-take-all regimes had suppressed in both leaders and followers.

The founding fathers, contrary to popular belief, were not uniformly opposed to government and taxes. They were trying to invent a fair system that could support individual and group needs simultaneously. Yet due to pressure from a newly freed yet profoundly traumatized public, two political parties began to form around a simplistic, amygdala-based debate: whether or not a democratized government would protect them or take advantage of them. Washington tried in vain to balance the two interrelated perspectives and was caught in the crossfire — struck, according to Ellis, "in the spot he cared about most passionately, his reputation as the 'singular figure' who embodied the meaning of the American Revolution in its most elevated and transcendent form."

Ever mindful of the freedom for which he sacrificed so much time, energy, personal safety, and money, he was also dedicated to forming a coherent, considerate, and empowered government, one that could stand up to the opportunistic European interests hovering relentlessly offshore. Washington confidently straddled that fast-widening chasm until he finally had to leap to one side or the other to serve what he saw as the most urgent priority: nation building. As commander of an unlikely army, the former general had experienced firsthand (most notably at Valley Forge) how debilitating a lack of centralized power and shared financial responsibility could be when coordinating large groups of people to achieve significant goals. Many soldiers were never paid for their service in the struggle for independence, as a postwar Congress remained ineffective in raising the monies necessary to make good on military commissions faithfully fulfilled by thousands of long-suffering men years earlier. America's first president ultimately realized, much to his horror, no doubt, that leading a group of untrained, underfunded men into battle was much easier than leading a country of autonomous individuals with opposing ideas, regional interests, short-term memories, and loyalties so capricious that some rebelled against paying taxes on principle, even to honor back salaries owed to the very soldiers who freed the population to begin with.

The Jay Treaty incident also revealed a disturbing by-product of freedom that wounded our first elected leader more deeply than musket and cannon fire ever did: the power of the unbridled press. It is both oddly comforting and incredibly disheartening to realize that the same smear tactics employed by modern politicians and reporters represent a time-tested American tradition. Comforting because it's clear that people are *not* becoming more violent, catty, or distrustful; they've been that way since the beginning. Disheartening because, even with more than two hundred years of democracy under our belts, the population as a whole hasn't learned a damn thing about working together respectfully and effectively.

And yet from a cathedral-thinking point of view, the dilemma is understandable. After thousands of years of servitude and victimization, the vast majority of people who emigrated to the United States not only were trauma survivors with good reason to mistrust their leaders, they quite simply had no idea how to collectively manage their freedom. With few nonpredatory leadership models to follow and few or no emotional- and social-intelligence skills to pass down to their children, generations have been fumbling in the dark, reacting to the simplest challenges like a group of confused and angry teenagers.

Striking a balance between questioning our leaders and supporting them has never been easy. In a democratic society, we are simultaneously the bosses of, shareholders in, collaborators with, and followers of the officials we elect. Few of us, however, possess the EQ skills to excel at two or three of these jobs, let alone combine all four, because the responsibilities of *effective citizenship* have been grossly downplayed in an attempt to rein in leaders we still suspect will abuse their power like the kings and conquerors of eras past.

Politicians and pundits perpetuate our current state of arrested development. They may wear designer suits and mesmerize the public with complex legal jargon and sophisticated computer-generated graphics, but with respect to emotional and social intelligence, the vast majority of them have yet to grow up themselves. Adolescents, after all, exercise power by *dis*empowering others — obsessively rebelling against authority, establishing their own exclusive cliques, and finding creative ways to demean outsiders — and that's exactly what a vast number of vocal Americans have been doing since they sent King George packing in 1783.

Old Lion

As bosses go, American democracy operates more like a shortsighted, underhanded, bipolar dictator than an enlightened voice of collective wisdom. People don't need guns to grossly misuse power. U.S. history is filled with savage verbal and written assaults that brutalized our leaders, preventing them from tapping anywhere near their true potential in office. Perhaps more disturbing, these same undermining tactics took out innocent bystanders, even when the main target was strong and ornery enough to withstand the pressure. One of the most graphic examples involves yet another accomplished equestrian who became president: Andrew Jackson.

Arguably the roughest, toughest backwoods character to ever take office, Jackson was brave and talented in many areas, but seriously lacking in emotional-intelligence skills: easy to insult, quick to fight, and ruthless in defending a cause once committed. Unlike George Washington, who tempered his aggressive tendencies with empathy, restraint, and nonpredatory wisdom, Jackson took on the moniker "Old Lion" with pride. He could be ferocious, taking tremendous risks and enduring considerable pain to win any challenge — at any cost. Lauded as a national hero for winning the Battle of New Orleans, the final action of the War of 1812, he was feared and revered for his furious temper, which he routinely used as a management tool. Jackson, therefore, was uniquely equipped to prevail in the election of 1828, which, even by modern standards, was the dirtiest campaign in history.

In part because Jackson was so contentious, supporters of his opponent, John Quincy Adams, pulled out all the stops, openly calling Jackson a murderer for his past involvement in a duel and his decision to execute six wartime deserters. In response, the Jackson contingent began spreading rumors that Adams, while serving as ambassador to Russia, had presented the czar with a despicable gift: a young American prostitute.

But it was Jackson's wife, Rachel, who ultimately paid the price, as her rocky first marriage to another man became a major political issue. The couple was publicly grilled over the murky details of when her previous husband had divorced her and when she began living with Jackson nearly forty years earlier. While Jackson insisted that he and Rachel believed she had been divorced when they were married in the early 1790s, official records were (and still are) sketchy. The campaign escalated with Adams's followers accusing Rachel of adultery and bigamy. Jackson was pegged as a murderer, an adulterer, *and* a home wrecker, but these accusations only inflamed his intensely competitive nature. Refusing to back down for a second, Jackson supporters intensified their allegations, openly calling Adams a pimp, insisting that his ability to procure women for sexual favors explained his success as a diplomat.

Jackson somehow won that election. Shortly before the inauguration, however, Rachel died of a heart attack, reportedly dreading four years of insults, jokes, and sneers in Washington society. At that moment, Jackson's savviest adversaries must have felt more fear than remorse or cruel satisfaction. There was that duel after all, and whether or not it could be considered murder, the fact remained that Jackson had shot a man for insults less severe than those the new president was now insisting had literally killed his wife.

"Sticks and stones may break my bones, but words can never hurt me." So goes the old saying that Jackson either didn't believe or had actively set out to disprove twenty years earlier. In 1805, shortly before his fortieth birthday, he had defended his honor at gunpoint, mortally wounding a man who called him a coward. The incident involved a Thoroughbred breeder named Joseph Erwin, who had backed out of a horse race featuring Jackson's stallion Truxton. The event was eventually rescheduled — with Truxton winning and Jackson pocketing a significant sum. Even so, petty tirades exchanged in letters, and eventually in the press, resulted in a duel between the future president and Erwin's son-in-law, Charles Dickinson, who was not only publicly deriding Jackson but privately demeaning Rachel. In alleged conversations impossible for historians to substantiate, Dickinson spread early rumors of adultery and bigamy that gathered force over time, apparently proving fatal to Jackson's sensitive and devoted wife twenty-three years later.

Now here's the astonishing part about that duel: Jackson *knew* his opponent was a better marksman. But the Lion of Tennessee was crafty, cantankerous, and truly, if somewhat misguidedly, courageous. He decided he'd have a better chance of winning the fight if he fired second, so he braced himself and let Dickinson take that frantic first shot, hoping that no matter where the bullet struck, he would be able to withstand the pain long enough to focus and execute a much more deadly aim. According to his biographer H.W. Brands, Jackson "had the supreme confidence of will — in his capacity to get off a shot even with a pistol round in his own body." As he later boasted, "I should have hit [Dickinson], even if he had shot me through the brain." That wasn't too much of an exaggeration, as it turns out. In *Andrew Jackson: His Life and Times,* Brands describes the details of this revealing altercation:

> Dickinson raised his pistol and pulled the trigger in a smooth, experienced motion. The crack of the discharge was lost in the surrounding trees as the smoke wafted away. Dickinson stared in amazement as Jackson stood his ground, apparently unhit. Jackson, his face as grim as death, raised his own pistol, looked implacably into Dickinson's eyes, and pulled the trigger. Nothing happened. Jackson examined his pistol and saw that the hammer had been but half-cocked. He completed the cock, aimed again, and fired. The bullet penetrated Dickinson's abdomen below the ribs. Dickinson slumped over and fell to the ground.

Jackson *had* been hit. The bullet, missing his heart by little more than an inch, "shattered itself against Jackson's breastbone and rib cage, inflicting a painful and bloody but not life-threatening wound — assuming infection didn't set in." He actually mounted his own horse and rode back to a nearby tavern as Dickinson was carried off to a friend's house where "he lingered for several hours" and "died with the dusk."

Grace and Rage

That Jackson had the self-control to take a bullet, but not an insult, speaks volumes. I can't help but wonder what kind of leader he would have been if he had developed the *emotional* heroism to match his larger-than-life personality, massive ego defenses, and sheer physical strength. (See Guiding Principle 11, chapter 23, for a procedure for exercising emotional heroism.) To this day, he's considered one of our more successful presidents because he was able to push through significant policy changes that influenced the country over the long term, despite the mean-spirited attacks that plagued American politics in the early 1800s. But since he always gave as well as he got, he was also incredibly destructive, an iron-willed, intimidating executive with little regard for public opinion, let alone informed opposing viewpoints. What's more, layers of unresolved personal grief, outrage, and resentment continued to fester under the surface of his already volatile temper, causing him to lash out unpredictably at people and causes he might otherwise have managed fairly. For this reason, Jackson's rise to power reveals important features of the *modern* American psyche, characteristics that fall into the "what got us here won't get us there" category of social evolution.

As Jon Meacham contends in his intricate biography of Jackson, *American Lion*, "Andrew Jackson is in many ways the most like us," an observation that, while compelling, is anything but complimentary:

> In the saga of the Jackson presidency, one marked by both democratic triumphs and racist tragedies, we can see the American character in formation and action. To understand him and his time helps us to understand America's perennially competing impulses. Jackson's life and work — and the nation he protected and preserved — were shaped by the struggle between grace and rage, generosity and violence, justice and cruelty.... The America of Andrew Jackson was a country that professed a love of democracy but was willing to live with inequality, that aimed for social justice but was prone to racism and intolerance, that believed itself one nation but was narrowly divided and fought close elections, and that occasionally acted arrogantly toward other countries while craving respect from them at the same time....A champion of extending freedom and democracy to even the poorest whites, Jackson was an unrepentant slaveholder. A sentimental man who rescued an Indian orphan on a battlefield to raise in his home, Jackson was responsible for the removal of Indian tribes from their ancestral lands. An enemy of Eastern financial elites and a relentless opponent of the Bank of the United States, which he believed to be a bastion of corruption, Jackson also promised to die, if necessary, to preserve the power and prestige of the central government. Like us and our America, Jackson and his America achieved great things while committing grievous sins.

The Cherokee Trail of Tears was not only Jackson's most grievous sin; it was a blatantly unethical, if not illegal, maneuver by a president powerful enough to ignore the law if he saw fit. To placate gold-mining interests in Georgia, Jackson refused to support a federal judge's ruling that the Cherokee tribe could *not* be driven from its mineral-rich lands. However, since no one proved influential or strong-willed enough to compel the president to enforce the decision, an anti-Indian movement gathered force with Jackson's blessing, eventually resulting in the eviction of several southern tribes. Sixteen thousand people were subsequently rounded up at gunpoint and ordered to move west; four thousand men, women, and children died along the way. (To this day, some Native Americans refuse to use the twenty-dollar bill, with Jackson's portrait on the front.)

Jackson is sometimes referred to as the American Hitler for his involvement in this tragic episode, but he wasn't a true sociopath. History suggests that he was instead an impulsive, hotheaded man with a chip on his shoulder and an addiction to winning at all cost. Normally these character flaws would have hindered his ascent to the highest public office. Jackson, however, had a good portion of that "other 90 percent" on his side.

An accomplished rider from an early age, he spent years in the saddle honing a powerful leadership presence. Two qualities in particular — Jackson's well-known ability to stand his ground intractably, despite public opinion (or even the law itself), and his marked talent for herding large groups of people toward a common goal (whether they liked it or not) — were no doubt enhanced immeasurably by his penchant for spirited stallions and high-strung Thoroughbreds. Unlike some of the gentler, naturally cooperative workhorse breeds, racehorses can be alternately aggressive, flighty, and obstinate in the early stages of training. Jackson learned how to nurture their stellar athletic qualities — without letting these intimidating animals bully him with their incredible energy, size, and strength, giving him the confidence to wrangle willful, feisty people.

But this particular set of skills — which would have served him well as dictator, king, or conqueror — could take him only so far in the more sophisticated interpersonal context of democracy. The citizens he proposed to lead were not high-performance horses, slaves, or women with socially sanctioned limitations. A significant portion of the population actually had rights and opinions that Jackson didn't know how to manage. What's more, free men liberally, and legally, used words as weapons, engaging in constant verbal duels that stirred up Jackson's most contentious, competitive qualities. He was incapable of turning this counterproductive trend around among members of his own species. After all, while his favorite Thoroughbreds might rear and strike in the early stages of training, they responded well to firm yet fair treatment — and they had no hidden agenda. They didn't grudgingly comply with Jackson's wishes while engaging in underhanded power plays, secretly organizing other herd members against him. They didn't spread malicious gossip, and they really didn't care that Rachel had been married before. The Old Lion was truly kinder, more affectionate, and more protective of these animals as a result.

According to Brands, "Nothing angered Jackson more than mismanagement of the horses." He went out of his way to ensure that his colts and fillies were given the best possible start in life, taking care not to push them too hard too soon. But his increasingly harsh and resentful treatment of people suggests that, for all his hard-won horse sense, he failed to absorb the collaborative, nonpredatory wisdom that these powerful animals also embody. As a result, Jackson never achieved the balance of a mature alpha-style male, and he had absolutely no idea how to relate effectively to peers. In this sense, he had more in common with Alexander the Great, another aggressive, eternally adolescent, charismatic leader-horseman who had an addiction to winning, than with equally talented yet immensely more compassionate and adaptable innovators like George Washington — and the man who had become the Buddha two thousand years earlier.

To be fair, however, it's important to realize that Jackson was operating from a serious developmental disadvantage. The son of a destitute pioneer family, he didn't experience anything close to the stable, near-idyllic childhood that Washington, Siddhartha, and later Jackson's own horses enjoyed. Jackson's father died several months before he was born, reportedly from a backwoods accident combined with sheer exhaustion. To make matters worse, young Andrew endured unimaginably brutal treatment in a British prison camp at age fourteen, becoming an orphan as a result of the Revolutionary War. That he transcended this tragic upbringing is a credit to his intelligence and spirit. But Jackson was a serious wartime trauma survivor, plain and simple, and his erratic behavior, while understandable, caused significant widespread suffering as he came to power.

Chapter Twelve

THE CHALLENGE

*F*rom command-and-control leadership models and predatory business practices to the current ways people misuse their much-valued freedoms of speech, religion, and the press, destructive behavior abounds in twenty-first-century life. It's notoriously difficult for any species to change instinctual or deeply ingrained habits without a strong outside force acting as a catalyst. Modern, well-educated human beings are no different in this regard, which is why any effort to change unproductive attitudes and reactive patterns initially feels as if we're pulling ourselves up by our own bootstraps. Despite our best intentions and proven brilliance in solving technical challenges, we keep making the same grossly inefficient interpersonal mistakes over and over again.

And yet, if we approach social-intelligence issues with the curious, problem-solving stance innovators routinely adopt in addressing computer design flaws, missile-building conundrums, and home construction dilemmas, we find that the *sequence* involved is similar: Most people, in recognizing they've hit a block, get stuck in the inevitable first stage of fruitlessly trying all possible variations on the same habitual themes. Frustration builds, eventually resulting in rage or powerlessness. Experienced artists and inventors, on the other hand, do something different after hitting the same wall a half dozen times. They surrender — without giving up — entering a constructive phase of "not doing" that Lao-tzu called wu-wei. In this limbo between letting go of the old and imagining the new, innovative thinkers notice previously ignored or hidden factors standing in their way. They ask for help and/or do some research outside their field. The breakthrough that follows represents a leap of consciousness, but there's still much work to be done. From that moment on, anyone with a pioneering insight is catapulted into the multifaceted realm of visionary leadership.

Drawing culturally significant solutions from the amorphous world of ideas involves much more than imagination, genius, or sheer chutzpah. Adventurous souls must activate some serious people skills. To succeed, even shy, introverted, tongue-tied inventors must learn to communicate the vision effectively; inspire, motivate, and collaborate with others; and, most important, convince a wider public to give up their own deeply entrenched, ineffective habits in order to try something new.

Take the relatively benign yet still challenging process of building a better mop. In his controversial 2012 book *Imagine: How Creativity Works*, Jonah Lehrer describes the surprisingly intricate, perception-altering journey Procter and Gamble undertook to wrestle buckets and lemon-scented detergents from the chapped hands of billions of disgruntled homeowners. Over the years, the company had spent millions of dollars trying to develop better floor-cleaning products, yet their most brilliant chemists couldn't solve an age-old dilemma: Soaps strong enough to dissolve dirt had a similar effect on wood varnish and human skin. Nearly fifty years after astronauts first walked on the moon, people were still fighting with the same unwieldy, medusa-headed device their great-great-great grandparents used. (An American patented the first mop *holder* in 1837; references to the mop itself go back to fifteenth-century Europe.)

And so Procter and Gamble, which employed more PhDs than several major university faculties combined, did something outrageous; it suspended research and asked for help. The company hired the Boston- and Los Angeles–based design firm Continuum, urging researcher Harry West and his team to "think crazy, to try to come up with something that all those chemists couldn't." West, who later became Continuum's CEO, didn't hire more scientists, however. After realizing that Procter and Gamble had already tried every molecular combination known to humankind, West spearheaded one of the strangest and certainly most boring periods of high-tech wu-wei in modern history: He sat down, pen in hand, and watched people sweep, vacuum, and mop their floors. West's team took voluminous notes on the most tedious, mundane cleaning activities that the average person endures, even setting up video cameras in homes, capturing hundreds of hours of housework. "I wanted to forget everything I knew about mops and soaps and brooms," he told Lehrer. "I wanted to look at the problem as if I'd just stepped off a spaceship from Mars."

After several months of observation, West's team realized that the mop itself was one of the most inefficient tools imaginable, that people spent more time rinsing out their mops than they did cleaning their floors. "You've got this unwieldy pole," he explains. "And you are splashing around this filthy water trying to get the dirt out of a mop head that's been expressly designed to *attract* dirt. It's an extremely unpleasant activity....Once I realized how bad mopping was, I became quite passionate about floor cleaning....I became convinced that the world didn't need an improved version of the mop. Instead, it needed a total *replacement* for the mop. It's a hopeless piece of technology."

Coming up with an alternative, however, stumped the design team, which, as Lehrer reports, "returned to making house visits, hoping for some errant inspiration. One day, the designers were watching an elderly woman sweep some coffee grounds off the kitchen floor. She got out her hand broom and carefully brushed the grounds into the dustpan. But then something interesting happened. After the woman was done sweeping, she wet a paper towel and wiped it over the linoleum, picking up the last bits of spilled coffee. Although everyone on the Continuum team had done the same thing countless times before, this particular piece of dirty paper led to a revelation."

That now-obvious insight resulted in the Swiffer, a disposable dirt magnet attached to a pole, blending the efficiency of the paper towel with the back-saving technology of the mop. Still, it took nearly five years for this seemingly simple innovation to hit the market. Procter and Gamble initially nixed the idea. The company, after all, had created a massive market selling mops and floor-cleaning detergents. When showed sketches of the Swiffer, early focus groups exhibited a similar reluctance to sacrifice their mops. After "a year of pleading," however, Continuum persuaded Procter and Gamble to let another focus group play with a prototype, and as a result "the product scored higher in focus-group sessions than any other cleaning device Procter and Gamble had ever tested." When the Swiffer was launched in 1999, it generated more than $500 million in sales the first year.

Stone Age Power Tools

The resistance West and his team faced is minor compared to the emotionally charged, sometimes violent reactions we face in urging people to change their outmoded approaches to leadership and interpersonal challenges. Everyone, regardless of culture, religion, nationality, or social status, is essentially grappling with the same antiquated "power tools" their distant ancestors were using millennia ago. These social-intelligence faux pas are like grimy, smelly old mops, incredibly inefficient, *attracting* dirt we must clean up later, in the form of resistance, resentment, and trauma (personal and multigenerational).

In this chapter, I briefly outline the four most destructive tactics we commonly, and stubbornly, employ to influence others' behavior. Call these moldy old habits whatever you like. My only recommendation is that you pick something humorous or absurd to further diffuse their power. We don't need any more commandments or deadly sins. (The devil, above all, hates to look ridiculous, as does the average dictator.) How about the Four Sacred Mops, Stone Age Power Tools, Interpersonal Sink Holes, or Behavioral Mud Slides?

It's also helpful to note that these unproductive power strategies are universal, existing below the surface of ideology. Even so, they're sometimes reinforced in the name of tribal tradition, religion, or social pressure. In reality, major world religions explicitly discourage most of these behaviors, but they are incredibly insidious. Over the past three thousand years or so, religious, cultural, moral, and even legal efforts to curtail some of these harmful habits have been only marginally successful, as people continue to cling to what they know. I've grappled with them myself. I've seen devout Christians, Jews, Buddhists, Muslims, Native Americans, atheists, politicians, scientists, educators, entrepreneurs, horse trainers, New Age idealists, openhearted social activists, and predatory sociopaths all use them over the years, with predictably damaging results, providing short-term solutions that stir up more trouble in the long run, often causing significant suffering that subsequent generations are forced to mop up.

History has shown, over and over and over again, that telling people "thou shalt or thou shalt not" do something is the *beginning* of a long, difficult road to alter even the simplest, most mundane behaviors. As in the case of Procter and Gamble and its early focus groups, providing people with research on how inefficient a tool is, even showing them a picture of a better way, is not enough to change old habits. We need to hold the new prototype in our hands, experiment with it, move beyond the strangeness of using it, to *feel the ease and delight* in using it.

I could write an entire book on these archaic social "intelligence" skills and how they've done us wrong, providing voluminous case studies from all cultures and eras, but it's more important to make these dubious habits conscious and move on, practicing new habits, creating new strategies, some of which are outlined in the "Power of the Herd" Guiding Principles, some of which you or your colleagues might someday invent in much the same way that Continuum developed the Swiffer. In any case, here they are, in all their irritating and ridiculous glory. I've organized these juvenile, in some cases devastating, tactics into four classes of similar behaviors, offering brief definitions and examples followed by related approaches that are more productive. (You'll notice that it's difficult to talk about any of these counterproductive strategies without bringing in at least one or two others.)

Take a few notes on these antiquated tactics, how they show up in your personal and professional relationships. In the future, whenever you use one of these clumsy power tools, notice how much additional time you spend cleaning up unforeseen interpersonal difficulties that arise as a result. But don't wallow too long in all this muck. Keep on reading. I promise you, new visions of leadership and empowered relationship are close at hand.

1. Predatory Dominance: Thriving at Others' Expense

Predatory dominance overemphasizes a "competition for limited resources" mentality. It employs hierarchical, command-and-control leadership models combining intimidation, entitlement, violence, and fear escalation to enslave or prey upon others.

As shown in previous discussions of natural herd behavior, the dominant and the leader are often two different animals. In pastoral cultures, master herders learn to combine the roles of leader, dominant, caretaker or companion, and predator, acting for the good of the entire interspecies tribe. However, in civilized, sedentary cultures, we've lost this richly nuanced understanding of power. Through humanity's increasing disconnection from nature, many of our social structures have become unbalanced, *overemphasizing* dominance and, even more dangerous, pairing it with predatory behavior.

Carnivores and adolescent alpha-style dominants use intimidation and violence to confuse, disempower, control, and, of course, eat others. In nature, however, predators perform a valuable service. If the world had no lions and wolves, then horses, cattle, gazelles, zebras, and wildebeests would overpopulate, consume all available resources, and die of starvation. Ambitious human dominants — who are smart enough to manipulate nature and isolate themselves from it — are not yet smart enough to balance their ever-increasing appetites in service to the greater good. Emphasizing short-term, personal gain, they deplete ecosystems while preying on people in legal and illegal ways. While slavery has been outlawed in most countries (though it still exists in criminal subcultures), predatory dominance proliferates any time people use fear, intimidation, or deceit to thrive at someone else's expense, hijacking the physical and emotional resources others need for survival, in order to bolster an insulated, increasingly luxurious lifestyle.

Predatory dominance includes forms of bullying and more subtle ways of disempowering people to maintain control. As socializing factors, for instance, fear and intimidation have been shown to inhibit intellectual development and creativity. At first, this appears to be a plus for conquerors who intend to enslave large populations and breed dim-witted, compliant worker drones for the ruling classes. Yet, as discussed in the first section of this book, these techniques don't even provide the leader with long-term satisfaction or peace. There's always someone younger and hungrier waiting in the wings, ready to pounce at the first sign of weakness. As a result, dictators — whether political, corporate, or familial — must become vigilant and increasingly mistrustful to survive, qualities that easily devolve into paranoia.

To make matters worse, descendants and innocent bystanders must also watch their backs with servants, employees, and family members who've been victimized by this system. People and animals suddenly and unpredictably become violent when they have nothing left to lose, creating land mines of personal and generational trauma. George Washington gained the dubious distinction of starting the French and Indian War when he was unable to control Tanacharison's sudden urge to massacre a group of Frenchmen, who were clearly unrelated to the sadists who had killed the chief's family forty years earlier. Similarly, the stallion Merlin repeatedly attacked me for no apparent reason during the first six months of our association. The abuse he suffered in the name of training nullified his immense potential as a show horse, which further underlines the waste of time, energy, and resources this approach reliably produces.

People who lead through fear, intimidation, and deceit must anticipate revenge and constantly manage the hair-trigger responses to minor threats that untreated trauma survivors experience *and* pass down to their children. Conquerors see themselves as sword-wielding supermen, but they spend more time mopping up blood and grime than enjoying the fruits of victory.

CONSTRUCTIVE ALTERNATIVES. Historically, some nomadic pastoral tribes have engaged in conquest and slaveholding, including treating women like cattle to be traded or stolen. These cultures have also suffered from the noxious by-products of uncontrolled predatory behavior. (See the brief discussion of Genghis Khan in the following section.) Yet there are numerous examples of pastoral tribes that have tempered their aggressive tendencies through daily interactions with large nonpredatory animals. Master herders use dominance consciously and sparingly, for specific, peacekeeping purposes: protecting the group from predators, setting boundaries with adolescent stallions and bulls, and keeping their herds from damaging valuable crops. (Effective boundary-setting techniques are featured in Guiding Principle 4, chapter 16.) When larger populations develop these leadership skills, people can use *the power of a fully empowered herd* to stand up to organized aggressors in business, education, religion, and politics. (See Guiding Principle 8, chapter 20, for an overview of predatory versus nonpredatory power styles in nature.)

One of the most fascinating modern examples of nonpredatory power in action involves John F. Kennedy's war-averting strategies during the Cuban missile crisis. The president's self-control, ability to model the difference between aggression and boundary setting, and inclination to reach out to the enemy, appealing to Khrushchev's humanity, arguably saved the world from massive nuclear destruction.

2. Retaliation: Turning Victims into Perpetrators

Retaliation includes all kinds of knee-jerk reactions to physical violence, insults, and disrespect, including revenge and grudge holding, as well as hair-trigger responses to minor threats that cause some people to overreact, sending them into disorganized fight-or-flight modes that stir up more trouble than necessary.

Retaliatory behaviors initially seem like justified reactions to the physical or emotional violence proliferated by predatory "might makes right" leadership models. Revenge in particular, however, turns victims into perpetrators, channeling creative energy and ingenuity into destructive pursuits. Cultures that fall into the conquest-and-revenge cycle produce erratic innovators who never reach their true potential.

Genghis Khan and Andrew Jackson are great examples of brilliant, charismatic leaders whose skills were compromised by intense childhood exposure to war and abuse. Exceptional horsemen, their mastery of the "other 90 percent" made them formidable, highly influential agents of social change — for better *and* for worse. Hailed as saviors by some and devils by others, Khan and Jackson were both, wreaking immense, unnecessary havoc that still breeds resentment and grief in the descendants of those who suffered most.

These troubled geniuses were products of a defective worldwide belief system, still prevalent yet slowly eroding, one in which survival-of-the-fittest, "power over" leadership models are giving way to mutual aid and mutual empowerment. When we look at the pastoral roots of the Judeo-Christian tradition, at nonpredatory philosophies like Taoism and Buddhism, at Kropotkin's long-ignored observations on mutual aid as a factor of evolution, and at recent research on the biology of the human-animal bond, it's easy to argue that, from a cathedral-thinking point of view, aggressive, opportunistic social structures are constantly being challenged by multiple sources. Despite human attempts to find ever more clever ways to use religion and science to justify the continued use of predatory dominance hierarchies, God and nature appear to be on the same side in tempering these destructive practices. Still, there is much healing to be done, a process continually interrupted by revenge and all the toxic waste that results from indulging this counterproductive response to injustice, violence, and pain.

Khan grew up in a culture where tribes were constantly raiding, pillaging, and exacting revenge upon each other as men were killed, women kidnapped, and children orphaned. When his father captured his mother in one such skirmish, Khan himself was produced by rape. Mother and son later endured abandonment by their "adoptive" tribe when Khan's father died. As a teenager, Khan himself had to rescue his own young wife under similar circumstances, never knowing if his first child was truly his own.

Still, modern historians puzzle over Genghis Khan's dual nature: his ruthlessness in war was offset by a certain amount of generosity, religious tolerance, and cultural innovation compared to the behavior of other kings and conquerors. This suggests that the nomadic pastoral lifestyle offered him some support in developing empathy and self-control amid extreme circumstances, perhaps because of the oxytocin produced while caring for large animals. Mongolian creation myths also emphasized a union of predatory and nonpredatory characteristics — the first man was believed to have arisen from the mating of a wolf and a deer. Khan's ability to fluidly move from savage fierceness to thoughtfulness and sensitivity appears to be as much a cultural and philosophical influence as a personal talent.

Andrew Jackson's fits of rage, predilection for revenge, and extreme sensitivity to insults hindered his ability to govern fairly as America's seventh president. Yet considering his background, it's amazing he was able to function at all. As a fourteen-year-old prisoner of war, he was beaten for standing up to his jailers, and forced to live in a room filled with dying men and rotting corpses. His mother, upon hearing that both of her sons had been captured, talked British officers into releasing the boys; but after their grueling journey home, Jackson's brother and mother both died, leaving him an orphan.

Like many wartime trauma survivors, Jackson was counterphobic when it came to fear, able to face extreme physical pain, danger, and violence, while at the same time he alternately exploded in response to and retreated from the emotional challenges of peacetime relationships. This seriously compromised his ability to collaborate with others, respectfully air differing opinions, and negotiate thoughtfully.

Where revenge was concerned, Jackson's destructiveness was overt. He was like a bull in a china shop. If you offended him, he challenged you to a duel or came after you in some other obvious way. Equally difficult to deal with, however, are covert forms of revenge, particularly grudge holding. People who use this tactic are more like vandals who visit the china shop at night, break a few items, then loosely glue them back together, hoping a pricey plate or saucer will break apart in the owner's hand when he shows it to a customer. The floor looks clean, of course; no violence seems to have occurred. But like more obvious forms of revenge, holding a grudge also compromises our ability to collaborate with others, respectfully air differing opinions, and negotiate thoughtfully.

Studies on grudge holding in the workplace suggest that women use this technique more often than men. Members of either sex who favor this strange little power tool feel disempowered or simply lack the crucial emotional-intelligence and negotiation skills to use their power effectively. Trauma survivors and highly sensitive people who experience hair-trigger responses to minor threats can rack up a long list of grudges in no time at all, moving from job to job in extreme cases. At the very least, they're sometimes passed over for promotions despite high IQ and great ideas.

As new employees, grudge holders are hard to spot. When challenged or wronged in some way, they don't "fight it out" in person; they retreat and undermine offenders from a safer distance. People who engage in this passive-aggressive form of revenge are highly effective at blocking communication, innovation, and problem-solving efforts. This compromises team building, hurting the grudge holder and everyone associated with him or her in the long run.

While overt revenge results in violence and more trauma, grudges draw on a different arsenal of "mops," spreading dirt around in quieter, more subtle ways through sarcasm, cynicism, the silent treatment, and gossip. The latter sometimes involves pathologizing coworkers perceived as adversaries, a now-popular technique in which amateur psychologists diagnose offenders with any number of personality disorders. This twenty-first-century version of objectification and demonization, boosted by gossip disguised as concern, spreads slowly yet effectively through clandestine conversations questioning a team member's mental health.

It's important to remember that no matter how satisfying it initially feels to exact revenge, hold a grudge, or lash out at someone who has offended us, these efforts backfire, stirring up more trouble in the long run. This is doubly true for leaders who tend to enlist others in these nefarious pursuits, producing numerous casualties.

On this issue, George Washington stands out, once again, as an unusually evolved character. His courage was matched by an emotional strength that allowed him to maintain sensitivity on and off the battlefield. He actively de-escalated volatile situations, calming and focusing others while exuding power and authority, *preventing* American soldiers from exacting revenge on British prisoners of war. In this way he reduced trauma and turned many captive mercenaries into supporters. Yet Washington remains the exception to the rule. Andrew Jackson's aggressive, knee-jerk reactions to threats of any kind are relatively common among modern leaders. His erratic behavior provides a classic example of how destructive people can be when they're unable to match physical strength, intelligence, conviction, and endurance with *emotional heroism*. (See Guiding Principle 11, chapter 23.)

CONSTRUCTIVE ALTERNATIVES. Over the years, I've found that when someone tries to undermine my authority, hurt, betray, or insult me, it helps to treat the ordeal as an impromptu sharo, a skill I initially exercised with my stallion Midnight Merlin. With this fiery horse, I found that if I held my ground with a strong yet inquisitive attitude when he suddenly became aggressive (rather than running off or striking out in anger), I avoided causing further abuse while gaining his respect and trust. I've yet to experience a human attack that produces anything close to the terror I felt the first time Merlin raced toward me rearing and striking. Even so, this same technique works with intimidating, antagonistic, panicking, or enraged people as well.

If someone literally came after me with a big stick, I'd surely run screaming in the other direction or try to defend myself. But at an emotional level, the sharo is an incredible tool for modulating interpersonal conflict. To take a bit of a verbal beating — waiting for the right moment to respond constructively rather than reacting with hostility — is a profound act of self-control that pays off in the long run. With regard to social intelligence, this is not about playing the victim. It's about overriding unconscious flight-or-fight impulses to stay present during extreme situations. In this sense, it's also a heroic form of wu-wei, allowing you to assess what's happening before you react. (See Guiding Principle 11, chapter 23, for specific procedures that transform the sharo concept into an emotional-intelligence tool.)

Several additional skills are involved in turning potential enemies into colleagues, friends, or at the very least, *respectful* competitors. First, you must increase your tolerance for feeling vulnerable (Guiding Principle 5, chapter 17) without panicking. But enduring acts of aggression or disrespect is not in itself enough. You must also address the reasons behind such attacks *with* the person who attacked you, approaching the difficult conversation that follows from an empowered, compassionate stance. In this effort, it's helpful to understand how to set boundaries with aggressors (Guiding Principle 4, chapter 16), use fear-management skills (Guiding Principle 7, chapter 19), and discuss uncomfortable topics in thoughtful, nonshaming ways (Guiding Principle 9, chapter 21).

There is absolutely nothing new or exotic about this advanced social-intelligence skill. The term *sharo* may be Fulani, but it's not an original idea. A good fifteen hundred years before these master herdsmen arrived on the scene, Jesus took this same concept to the absolute limit, and not only by encouraging people to turn the other cheek when challenged. He fought extreme violence with uncompromising nonviolence, performing the ultimate sharo, suffering with arms wide open while nailed to a cross, preaching compassion and forgiveness to the very end. That many Christians throughout history have had trouble activating this principle under pressure shows how truly extraordinary Jesus was. Yet the evolution of human consciousness and behavior demands that people adopt this counterintuitive approach to power in daily life, no matter what religion they practice.

3. Objectification and Projection: The Deadly Duo

Objectification involves characterizing other living beings, groups, or cultures as unevolved, unintelligent, defective, or even innately evil. Projection involves punishing, rejecting, or persecuting others for the same weaknesses and darker qualities we refuse to acknowledge in ourselves.

Because there's no need to consider an object's feelings or needs, objectification allows opportunists of all kinds — from politicians, preachers, teachers, pundits, entrepreneurs, and scientists to conquerors, terrorists, child abusers, and psychopaths — to justify ostracizing, destroying, or exploiting people and animals. The more archaic practice of demonizing people is still popular among religious extremists. The modern "arts" of racial profiling, sexual stereotyping, and pathologizing those we don't get along with are also forms of objectification.

According to philosopher Martha Nussbaum, objectification occurs when we treat a living being in any of the following ways: as a tool, as a possession, as lacking in agency or self-determination, or as interchangeable (and therefore easily expendable). In all twenty-first-century cultures, animals are legally objectified, though laws specifying humane treatment temper extreme cruelty in some countries. The related technique of characterizing a human being as an unintelligent, instinct-driven animal is still used to oppress women and deny rights to certain ethnic groups worldwide. As advanced as we may think we are in this regard, Western civilization has only very recently begun to emerge from the trance of this age-old practice. In 1906, the London zoo featured an African bushman as an exhibit. Hunting licenses for aboriginal tribes were available as late as the 1930s in some countries. In other African and Middle Eastern subcultures, selling women, beating them without reprisal, and controlling their sexuality through the brutal practice of female circumcision are still enforced by religion, shame, and tradition.

When we feel strong emotions like hate, disgust, or extreme mistrust in relation to people, cultures, or animals we've objectified, there's usually an element of *projection* involved as well, which means the person or group is acting as a mirror for darker qualities we don't want to see in ourselves. Hardly a day goes by that we don't witness people projecting their own shadow onto others: A conservative male senator venomously opposes gay rights, only to be caught having an affair with a man. A notorious Middle Eastern terrorist speaks out against the decadence of Western society by day and watches Internet porn at night. Four close-knit coworkers commiserate about a colleague's "gossipy," undermining nature, insisting she can't be trusted, unconscious of the fact that *they* are talking behind her back with no intention of addressing their concerns constructively.

Catching ourselves in the act of objectifying or projecting is hard to do — and extremely unpleasant when we actually succeed in making this behavior conscious: The initial awareness of what we've done unleashes waves of shame and guilt, especially if we've hurt someone with this "tool." But as discussed in the following section, there are constructive ways to move through shame, blame, and guilt, allowing us to use these admittedly problematic agents as stepping-stones to a more balanced, empowered state. When we stop employing shame and guilt as weapons to punish and control others, these grime-attracting processes actually fertilize new growth.

Of all the antiquated power tools in our closets, however, the combination of objectification and projection is by far the most destructive. The Deadly Duo, as I like to call it, causes even gentle, well-meaning people to feel justified in whipping out a host of other nefarious tools, rallying revenge, dominance, intimidation, shame, blame, guilt, rejection, persecution, and exploitation in service to literal and figurative "holy wars." Leaders who employ the Deadly Duo stir up incredible trouble, leaving generations to mop up all kinds of trauma, mistrust, and retaliation. Hitler is the ultimate modern example. His devastating, incredibly effective, exceedingly well-organized ability to objectify the Jews, projecting all possible human weaknesses onto a single ethnic group, is enacted to a lesser degree daily, in offices, schools, playgrounds, churches, homes, and most definitely political discussions where any individual or group is treated as a hopeless cause worthy of ridicule.

Conservatives *and* liberals are apt to employ objectification and projection when they feel frustrated or threatened, usually adding voluminous amounts of shame and blame, invigorated by heart-stopping doses of sarcasm and exaggeration. This creates a most unhealthy stew of angst and outrage that many people, me included at times, actually find entertaining when it's (ironically) done well: politically based comic strips and radio and TV programs thrive on this technique. Yet I have to ask myself: What price do we ultimately pay for these divisive forms of humor? Perhaps in small doses they're a guilty pleasure, but only if we realize we're ultimately making fun of the foibles, frustrations, and cartoonishly ineffective habits that humans throughout history have struggled to release without significant success — at least so far.

INDIVIDUAL CONSIDERATIONS. *Recognizing* when we're objectifying or projecting *instantly* reduces the destructive potential. The worst effects occur when people engage this Deadly Duo unconsciously. It's also important to realize that objectification spreads like an infectious disease in all kinds of unexpected ways. People objectified in one context often objectify others, adding projection to the mix, adopting a form of "selective empathy." This combination, for example, allows victims to mistrust or punish anyone who reminds them of the original perpetrator (who took advantage, in part, by objectifying *them*.)

While this sounds like an issue best handled in a counselor's office, the incredibly irritating truth of the matter is that objectification and projection often occur in the workplace, throwing a serious wrench in everyone's ability to get the job done. For instance, I've encountered female abuse survivors who, despite counseling in some cases, still suspect that all men are insensitive, untrustworthy, potentially violent predators. At work, some of these women engage in emotionally aggressive behavior with colleagues of both sexes, feeling justified in lashing out over minor threats or interpersonal mistakes.

And that's just the tip of the iceberg. Since it's so difficult for former victims to admit that they too have the potential to act insensitively, they refuse to see that they've overreacted in certain situations. To make matters worse, they sometimes pick a particular team member to demonize, usually the most naturally aggressive male or female on staff, projecting all their own darker qualities onto this person, shutting down communication and innovation on all sides. Since the scapegoat is considered evil and hopeless, he can never apologize profusely enough for legitimate faux pas, let alone discuss the possibility that someone may have overreacted in other situations. And any improvements he may show as a result of emotional- and social-intelligence coaching are either completely dismissed or considered superficial and suspect by people projecting their own shadows onto him.

This complex scenario is activated in the horse world as well, particularly with stallions and highly sensitive, fiery breeds like Arabians. I've met some cowboys who insist that all Arabs are crazy and dangerous, when it's clear that these proud, defiant, sometimes emotionally explosive trainers have much more in common with the "demonized" breed than with the calm, submissive quarter horses most ranchers prefer. Aggressive trainers actually seem to draw out and then punish a horse for the same qualities they possess.

This might very well have been a factor in Merlin's brutal training. Lacey didn't simply correct behavior she found unproductive. Tying Merlin's head between his legs in that darkened stall was a form of torture that had no training value whatsoever, making him even more dangerous and unpredictable. It would be easy to characterize Lacey as cruel or inept, but it's more likely that her judgment was hijacked by the exaggerated feelings and reactions all people exhibit when they're projecting their darker qualities onto others. She may also have been engaging in "transference," a special term describing how we sometimes overreact to people (or in this case horses) who remind us of family members, friends, clients, or colleagues who have hurt us in the past. In this way, projection and transference can pack a double whammy of uncontrolled emotional responses that have little to do with the current situation.

To clarify: projection is the act of attributing your inner feelings, perceived weaknesses, and even unrecognized strengths onto others because you're simply unable, or stubbornly unwilling, to see these qualities in yourself. Transference is a more specific type of projection that occurs when your thoughts and feelings toward someone are strongly influenced by attitudes originally developed in a significant past relationship. Both projection and transference can inspire intensely negative or deceptively positive emotions and reactions.

Yet even positive transference can wreak a certain amount of havoc: If a new employee has a hairstyle, smile, vocal tone, or more subtle mannerisms that remind you of your favorite college roommate, you may "intuitively" trust this new person because she reminds you of a long-lost friend. Then, when she acts differently (because she's *not* your college roommate), you may suddenly, "intuitively," feel betrayed.

In Lacey's case, negative transference and/or projection prompted abuse that she would have felt justified enacting at the time. Who knows what tripped that trigger? Lacey may have been hurt by a black horse in the past. Or, as is often the case with stallions, she may have been acting out all her unresolved feelings about aggressive male energy in general, perhaps because she was abused by a father, uncle, husband, or lover. Had she simply woken from the trance that kept her from seeing Merlin as an individual with his own unique history and needs, she could have stopped herself from unnecessarily harsh treatment that in the long run didn't benefit *her* in any way, let alone the "student" who became her whipping boy.

CONSTRUCTIVE ALTERNATIVES. People who face the Deadly Duo with courage and awareness turn potentially debilitating weaknesses into strengths. When we stop objectifying other people, species, and cultures, we can tap their unique abilities and perspectives to perform ambitious goals. It's doubtful that George Washington would have won the Revolutionary War if he hadn't been able to do just that: putting people with real talent, integrity, courage, and dedication in positions of responsibility, regardless of race, religion, or social status. And, as observed in chapter 3, if he had treated his war mounts as unintelligent, instinctual, interchangeable objects, he might never have recognized and further developed the talents of Old Nelson, that one horse in a million capable of withstanding cannon fire, inspiring panicking troops to stay in the fight on more than one occasion.

Projection has a silver lining as well. The people who inspire or irritate you the most are often mirroring qualities that you've rejected in yourself, spotlighting hidden talents or unrecognized skill deficiencies that would be useful if developed — and dangerous when left undeveloped. I highly recommend reading Debbie Ford's *The Dark Side of the Light Chasers* for some simple yet powerful exercises in this arena.

Transference may also be at work. Whenever you experience unusually strong feelings arising in response to any person or group, take a moment to consider whether you may be triggered by past betrayals, difficulties, or traumas. Rather than lash out in anger or flee in absolute terror, analyze which emotions belong to the current dilemma and which belong to the past. You may realize, for instance, that a colleague innocently used a phrase that your father often uttered sarcastically right before he fell into a rage. The moment you make this conscious, you can avert an unnecessarily heated argument. If you unconsciously punish your coworker for something a parent said to you twenty years ago, however, you could easily damage a valued work relationship and spend weeks mopping up the mess.

When projection or transference infringes on interpersonal interactions, it helps to notice the phenomenon, then focus on the present situation, wrapping the meeting up early if you're too agitated to think clearly. Make an appointment with a coach, confidant, or counselor to deal with transference from past relationships or explore any undeveloped personal qualities your colleague may have been mirroring. It also behooves you, as a leader, to notice when others are triggered and to help employees manage the confusion professionally. (Techniques for handling strong emotions, projection, and transference in others are featured in Guiding Principles 3 [chapter 15] and 9 [chapter 21].)

A CULTURAL CHALLENGE. "Collective transference" adds a particularly destructive dimension to the Deadly Duo when activated in larger populations. Some people have been taught to treat an entire group as innately defective because of war-related trauma or an ancestor's negative past experiences with one or two members of that group. Yet the initial awareness that one subculture is objectifying, demonizing, or exploiting another marks the beginning of a long, often difficult process. Economic and political structures that allow people to benefit from objectifying others must be altered, which means enduring the discomfort of revising antiquated practices to meet the needs of everyone involved. Those acting as conquerors or dominators will initially resist giving up the few dubious advantages they receive from exploiting others. Those social groups oppressed through objectification and/or projection will have to regain their autonomy and self-esteem while resisting the urge for revenge.

Because most socially sanctioned forms of the Deadly Duo take generations to alter, cathedral thinking is also essential. Without a long-term approach in mind, sensitive, well-meaning people can become frustrated and complacent, blaming the oppressors while doing little or nothing to help the oppressed.

Yet every little bit does in fact help. George Washington saw that the objectified populations of his era (including slaves, Native Americans, women, and horses) possessed intelligence, self-determination, and individual (noninterchangeable) talents, literally saving his life at times. As discussed in previous chapters, he made some dramatic efforts to treat these populations humanely while realizing it wasn't possible to change their legal or social status during his lifetime. In this way, he modeled behavior that others were inspired to emulate, making a difference to countless marginalized individuals, who, as they felt valued and increasingly empowered, positively influenced others in turn.

Washington's evolving response to slavery in particular offers insights into our own limitations in altering widespread, culturally reinforced forms of objectification. His family and friends were slaveholders immersed in a plantation system that traded African captives as cheerfully as twenty-first-century Americans buy and sell high-performance horses. Yet after Washington fought for the British in the French and Indian War and allied with the French against the British during the Revolutionary War, his ability to objectify any culture was seriously eroded. By the time he retired his favorite warhorses, high-born officers had betrayed him, and talented slaves like Billy Lee had served him loyally, sometimes in intermediary leadership positions.

As a result of his increasing awareness, Washington refused to callously sell off the family members of his own slaves. Over time, of course, this meant that he was feeding and clothing more people than he needed for labor, and losing money in the process. Toward the end of his life, he realized that slavery had one major strike against it: the practice wasn't economically feasible if you treated slaves as intelligent beings with their own social and emotional needs.

So why didn't President George Washington promote legislation eradicating slavery? Letters suggest that he thought it was inevitable, though unrealistic at the time. During the tempestuous postwar era, he couldn't even inspire Congress or the American people to raise funds to pay the back salaries owed to soldiers who freed the country to begin with. He just barely passed the Jay Treaty while dealing with severely contentious attacks from the press and the public alike.

And though he wouldn't have been able to put his finger on it at the time — as the terms weren't invented until the early twentieth century — Washington's effectiveness as a leader was seriously compromised by positive *and* negative projection and transference. More than any president since, Washington was praised as a savior by the very same people who feared that he was, at any minute, likely to become an American version of King George or Genghis Khan. The horrors that some immigrants had experienced with conquerors and inquisitions simply could not be soothed by the promise of a new democracy, especially with slavery proliferating in the South.

During Washington's presidency, Americans also began engaging in the now timeworn tradition of projecting their darker qualities, and deepest transference-related fears, onto the United States government. To this day — even among those who haven't been directly oppressed — the association of *central control* with *tyranny* appears to be a collective concern passed down from immigrants to descendants, carrying an intense emotional charge of fear and mistrust that takes generations to fade. After all, in the United States, we have a mere 230 years' experience with a tenuous, sometimes violent, sometimes enlightened democracy — compared with 5,000 years of overtly oppressive social structures. Yet, just as some female abuse survivors objectify all men as predators, we must be careful not to scapegoat a government that has, from the beginning, been trying to find a better way.

Public figures *and* social structures serve as projection screens, worshipped and vilified as people work out their previously unresolved experiences with authority figures (transference) and their own personal power (projection) on the models they have in front of them. Anyone promoted to a leadership position must realize this. Knowing up front that the extremely positive reviews and violently negative reactions you encounter daily are not necessarily about you goes a long way in helping you decipher and endure the chaos that accompanies success.

4. Shame and Blame: Agents of Oppression, By-Products of Transformation

When used as a weapon to defend ourselves, intimidate others, or control their behavior, shame is the most archaic and heavy-handed of all the conversational power tools. Injecting shame into a discussion is like hitting someone over the head with a club during an otherwise reasonable negotiation, causing people to become confused and defensive and shutting down communication, empathy, understanding, and thoughtful problem solving on both sides of an interaction.

As a personal emotional message, the related feeling of guilt helps us recognize when we're overstepping boundaries, manipulating, hurting, or neglecting others, helping us "course correct" and learn from our mistakes — if we're willing to alter unproductive behavior. If we're not willing to take responsibility for our actions, however, we look for others to blame, a practice that discourages personal accountability and quickly leads to projection and objectification.

We often think of shame as a personal-development issue or a tribal, religious, or cultural issue, but this social emotion wreaks all kinds of havoc in professional, educational, and political contexts too. The human habit of shaming others to influence behavior or to discredit or disempower them is so ancient and insidious that many people honestly don't notice when they're using this tool in business-related conversations — or when it's being used on *them*. Yet studies have shown that shame does not change behavior in productive ways. In fact, it adds unnecessary resistance, mistrust, and resentment, causing people to attack or humiliate each other or to stay quiet when others need help.

Social worker Brené Brown calls shame the "silent epidemic." In her best-selling 2007 book *I Thought It Was Just Me (but It Isn't): Telling the Truth about Perfectionism, Inadequacy and Power*, she draws together numerous studies and anecdotes showing that "shame is much more likely to be the source of destructive behaviors than it is to be the solution."

Like other shame researchers, Brown compares this problematic emotion with the more constructive feeling of *guilt*, illuminating the difference between the two with the following contrasting statements: "I am bad" (shame) versus "I did something bad" (guilt). When shaming people to gain control, we convey similar sentiments: "You are bad" versus "You did something bad." Brown observes,

> Shame is about who we are and guilt is about our behaviors. If I feel guilty cheating on a test, my self-talk might sound something like "I should not have done that. That was really stupid. Cheating is not something I believe in or want to do." If I feel shame about cheating on a test, my self-talk is more likely to sound like "I'm a liar and a cheat. I'm so stupid. I'm a bad person."
>
> Guilt is holding an action or behavior up against our ethics, values, and beliefs. We evaluate that behavior (like cheating) and feel guilt when the behavior is inconsistent with who we want to be. Shame is focusing on who we are rather than what we've done. The danger in telling ourselves that we are bad, a cheat, and no good, is that eventually we start to believe it and own it. The person who believes she is "no good" is much more likely to continue to cheat and fulfill that label than the person who feels guilt.

In working with leaders, innovators, community and nonprofit organizations, parents, educators, and professional teams of all kinds, I find the rampant use of shame as a power tool to be the most shockingly unproductive behavior I encounter. Of course, we see this technique used in politics, with each side looking for all kinds of ways to shame the other. And the intent is truly to show that the other side *is* bad, in other words *hopelessly defective*.

It's common to hear insulting, shaming statements in corporate contexts. Many religious leaders use shame to control the behavior of congregation members and most certainly to discourage people from exploring other faiths, even those based on the same original founders and holy texts. Atheists shame believers, and vice versa. Doctors shame their interns. Academic experts use shaming statements to assert dominance over students, colleagues, and innovators. Riding instructors commonly shame their students into submission. And although animals are highly resistant if not immune to this uniquely human power play, I've seen many equestrians try to shame their horses. (The subsequent lack of response to this "tool" usually precipitates a severe beating.)

But even among "enlightened" social activists, mental health professionals, and leaders in the human potential movement, shaming statements abound. I've observed thousands of shaming phrases and gestures used in planning and team-building contexts, each time undermining trust, creativity, communication, and problem-solving efforts. And I've worked with numerous clients whose careers have been needlessly derailed by shaming attacks from bosses, colleagues, and subordinates. Shaming people in the workplace is more than a silent epidemic; it's a powerful, incredibly hard-to-break *addiction*.

Let me give you one, unfortunately typical but rather mild, example: The CEO of an internationally recognized healing and wellness center recently told one of the facility's founders: "You're no longer relevant." He did this in a full staff meeting, effectively ending a twenty-year relationship. He could have easily said, "I think we need to update some of the healing modalities in your department." Instead he callously depicted *her* as old, outdated, and incapable of revision. She wasn't the first valued team member to leave the organization after enduring the CEO's insensitive, competitive, purposefully demeaning remarks. And she certainly won't be the last, under current management at least.

CONSTRUCTIVE ALTERNATIVES. Many of the guiding principles offer strategies for removing shame and blame from interpersonal and group interactions — without compromising the need to discuss difficult topics, increase personal accountability, and change unproductive behavior. These include Guiding Principle 3 (managing contagious emotions; chapter 15), Guiding Principle 4 (mastering boundary setting and assertiveness techniques; chapter 16), Guiding Principle 5 (developing a higher tolerance for vulnerability in oneself, and refraining from using others' vulnerabilities against them; chapter 17), Guiding Principle 7 (defusing panic; chapter 19), and Guiding Principle 9 (preparing for difficult conversations; chapter 21).

Of these, Guiding Principle 4, oddly enough, is *key* to shame-avoidance training, according to Brené Brown's pivotal research. In her 2010 bestseller, *The Gifts of Imperfection*, she deftly illustrates how "the fear of setting boundaries and holding people accountable" is the unexpected root cause of many personal and work-related shaming tactics.

The author herself was "stunned" to find that "compassionate people are boundaried people," yet Brown's subsequent personal transformation informed her understanding of the link between the two. Earlier in her career, she admits, she was "sweeter — judgmental, resentful, and angry on the inside — but sweeter on the outside." Today, she describes herself as "genuinely more compassionate, less judgmental and resentful, and way more serious about boundaries."

How does this work, exactly? "The better we are accepting ourselves and others," Brown reveals, "the more compassionate we become. Well, it's difficult to accept people when they are hurting us or taking advantage of us or walking all over us." She insists that "if we really want to practice compassion, we have to start by setting boundaries and holding people accountable for their actions." The related tactic of blaming others, she observes, is also related to boundaries and accountability:

> We live in a blame culture — we want to know whose fault it is and how they're going to pay. In our personal, social, and political worlds, we do a lot of screaming and finger-pointing, but we rarely hold people accountable. How could we? We're so exhausted from ranting and raving that we don't have the energy to develop meaningful consequences and enforce them. From Washington, D.C., and Wall Street to our own schools and homes, I think this rage-blame-too-tired-and-busy-to-follow-through mind-set is why we're so heavy on self-righteous anger and so low on compassion.
>
> Wouldn't it be better if we could be kinder, but firmer? How would our lives be different if there were less anger and more accountability? What would our work and home lives look like if we blamed less but had more respect for boundaries?

Answers to these questions demand an advanced understanding of power, backed up by significant emotional and social intelligence. Brown goes on to show how one business leader she worked with was initially perplexed by the idea that he was shaming his employees because of a reluctance to hold people accountable. It's clear that we're dealing with a *skill set* that most people simply don't have, no matter how high they climb up the corporate ladder — or how intelligent, religious, moral, or caring they otherwise prove to be. Brown writes,

> Shaming and blaming without accountability is toxic to couples, families, organizations, and communities. First, when we shame and blame, it moves the focus from the original behavior in question to our own behavior. By the time the boss is finished shaming and humiliating his employees in front of their colleagues, the only behavior in question is his....
>
> It's hard for us to understand that we can be compassionate and accepting while we hold people accountable for their behaviors. We can, and, in fact, it's the best way to do it. We can confront someone about their behavior, or fire someone, or fail a student, or discipline a child without berating them or putting them down. The key is to separate people from their behaviors — to address what they're doing, not who they are....We have to stay away from convincing ourselves that we hate someone or that

they deserve to feel bad so that we can feel better about holding them accountable. That's where we get into trouble. When we talk ourselves into disliking someone so we're more comfortable holding them accountable, we're priming ourselves for the shame and blame game.

When we fail to set boundaries and hold people accountable, we feel used and mistreated. This is why we sometimes attack who they are, which is far more hurtful than addressing a behavior or a choice....It's also impossible to practice compassion from a place of resentment. If we're going to practice acceptance and compassion, we need boundaries and accountability.

The use of shame as a power tool is epidemic in the professional world. As a result, skills associated with managing its effects — and ultimately eradicating shame in the workplace — need to be incorporated into any serious leadership training program. Yet people without overt leadership aspirations also must address this frequently ignored emotional- and social-intelligence issue. I've seen many talented, creative people face needless hurdles in realizing their personal and professional goals because they lacked shame resilience.

According to psychologist and Eponaquest instructor Pamela Zamel, "repeated and unprocessed encounters with shame can erode your self-esteem and sense of wellness. While the temporary feeling of guilt or embarrassment can lead to positive self-correction, shame is accompanied by the profound message that *you are not fit to belong*. Shame also interrupts curiosity, enjoyment, creativity, and the desire to connect with others."

In one of her workshop brochures, she summarizes Gershen Kaufman's pivotal insights in *The Psychology of Shame*. Pamela emphasizes that shame is often followed by fear, distress, and anger. "The potential for shame exists in every interpersonal encounter. When an individual's expectations or needs are deemed as wrong, unattainable or 'too much,' shame is experienced." Shame can also be a "private phenomenon," Pamela writes, accompanying "a failure to measure up to our own internalized view of how we should *be, do, act* or *perform*. These internalized standards come from early life experiences, significant relationships, cultural values, and societal messages."

In 2012, Pamela joined two Eponaquest faculty members — horse trainer Shelley Rosenberg, author of *My Horses, My Healers*, and psychiatrist Nancy Coyne — to create an equine-facilitated personal-development workshop titled "The Cage of Shame." The seminar helps abuse survivors who face significant blocks in dealing with home- and work-related interpersonal challenges develop "shame resilience." As the course description reveals, unprocessed shame "can become an organizing principle in one's personality, shaping and coloring all perceptions and expectations, and essentially making one more and more prone to future shame experiences." This powerful equine-facilitated intensive offers skills to interrupt the "vicious circle" set in motion when people become "imprisoned" by their own shame-based feelings and experiences.

A DEEPER CHALLENGE. There's another side to shame that becomes even more problematic for visionaries, particularly innovators seeking to inspire widespread social change. Throughout history, and quite literally in the biblical sense, shame appears to be an inescapable by-product of transformation — with blame and guilt following close behind. As discussed in chapter 5, the Adam-and-Eve story offers one of the earliest depictions of this archetypal pattern. After the first man and woman ate the forbidden fruit, engaging a higher state of consciousness as a result, they didn't suddenly feel God-like. Instead they experienced a shocking surge of emotions associated with self-reflection and personal responsibility. They felt guilt for disobeying God and shame upon becoming aware of their nakedness. To release the intense pressure of these uncomfortable new sensations, Adam blamed Eve for their trouble, and Eve blamed the snake, setting in motion a guilt-shame-blame cycle that every human faces upon reaching the age of reason.

The now-standard definition of shame as a rejection of someone's state of *being* — as opposed to the definition of guilt as a critique of unproductive, hurtful, irresponsible, or immoral *behavior* — is still relevant here, but the issue takes on a wider scope in the context of social evolution. It appears that anytime we move from a limited worldview, accepting new information, expanding and transforming in response, we encounter feelings of shame for the previously constricted, perhaps selfish or even childish, state of being from which we just emerged. This is often accompanied by guilt for the hurtful things we may have unknowingly done to other people, cultures, animals, the environment, and perhaps even ourselves. Recognizing that we were operating from a narrower state of consciousness is essential to moving through this form of shame, allowing us to take personal responsibility for our actions, change our behavior, and fulfill the promise of a new, more empowered state of being.

I often encounter this uncomfortable yet necessary sequence of events with equestrians who attend my workshops. Once they see that horses can act as sensitive, highly adaptable teachers — that some of these animals show a greater capacity for compassion and healing than most *people* these students have encountered — many conventionally trained riders feel not just guilt but also incredible shame for the ways they previously treated these intelligent, openhearted beings. The same thing happens to scientists who've engaged in conventional animal research activities that involve extreme confinement, pain, and death.

If we have any hope of moving from practices associated with predatory dominance, which thrives on objectifying animals, women, slaves, and so on, we must temper the urge to shame or punish those who've recently "woken up" from the culturally induced trance that promotes these dubious power tools. People can more easily and efficiently change their behavior when realizing that *they* are not *evil, callous,* or *abusive,* but that the system they grew up in *taught* them to engage in these destructive practices. Helping people sort through the shame and guilt they feel while supporting them in learning to use or invent more productive tools allows them to embrace a new way of operating in the world. Acceptance, understanding, and forgiveness are *essential* to transformation.

Timeworn Evasions

The initial jolt of awakening to a higher level of awareness and responsibility is so jarring that those of us who don't receive the kind of unconditional support mentioned in the previous section (and, hopefully, some new behavioral skills to go with it) tend to slide backward, desperately grasping at timeworn evasions. We may try to hide, medicate, or lash out rather than embrace the initial feeling of nakedness and vulnerability. We may blame others instead of looking at our own behavior and acknowledging what role we played in some questionable situation.

From there, we can quickly digress to the deadly arts of objectification and projection, easily receding back into the ancient human habit of punishing, enslaving, or preying upon "lesser beings" who aren't "sentient" enough to warrant consideration, empathy, and care. It's a vicious circle. After abusing objectified populations, sometimes simply to release the pressure of our own shame, we must either wake up and finally change our behavior (and both forgive ourselves and make amends for an even longer list of callous, sometimes horrendous acts) or *project* the additional guilt we feel ever more vigorously, making others pay for the mistakes and weaknesses we struggle desperately to disown. The latter option leads to multigenerational cycles of punishment and revenge. At the extreme end of this spectrum, we find serial killers who dispatch women, men, or even children with incredible cruelty, acting out unresolved betrayals or abuse scenarios in all kinds of "imaginative" ways.

Most shame-avoidance techniques, however, are nonviolent, a dubious side effect of human intelligence: despite significant potential for innovation and expansion, our big brains can be used to actively suppress feelings, experiences, scientific evidence, and personal observations that challenge our limited, selfish agendas. The Buddha called this mental evasion tactic "ignorance," recognizing that, while it may initially feel more comfortable than letting new information in, this impulse keeps people in an arrested state of mental, emotional, and spiritual development. (Metaphors and techniques for breaking through intellectual blocks to innovation and transformation are outlined in Guiding Principle 6, chapter 18.)

Modern civilization often reinforces the notion that ignorance is bliss, but cultural and political structures designed to help us ignore what challenges us only keep us in limbo. Once innovations and life circumstances crack the comfortable shell that was incubating a much larger, more compassionate, creative, responsible state of consciousness, we can never truly go back to that previously insulated state of being — one that, truly, "knew not" what it was doing, and *must* be forgiven as a result.

Around 500 BCE, the Buddha offered mindfulness and meditation techniques to address this multifaceted issue. Five hundred years later, a dramatic effort to move humanity through an even more fitful stage of intellectual, emotional, social, and spiritual adolescence inspired the first four books of the Bible's New Testament. At the height of the Roman Empire, an innovative social activist and religious leader named Jesus spent three years on the "lecture circuit" encouraging people to evolve beyond an extremely violent, predatory way of operating in the world. While he offered parables and overt directives on the causes and recommended solutions, he also understood the concept of shame as a block to transformation.

Jesus knew that people would feel intense, debilitating shame and guilt as a result of "waking up" and recognizing the "sins" perpetrated daily by anyone adhering to a predatory-dominant lifestyle. The skills he outlined verbally and the behaviors he modeled nonverbally were so sophisticated that civilization is still trying to catch up.

Reading accounts of his words and deeds, we see the following skills and principles in action:

1. An ability to reach out to objectified, marginalized populations
2. A courageous, uncompromising use of nonpredatory power
3. Rejection of all retaliatory behaviors, including revenge, grudge holding, and aggressive or defensive responses to insults, shaming tactics, betrayal, and, during the last few days of his life, physical violence and pain
4. Compassionate engagement with all cultures and social classes, which

encouraged people to change hurtful *behaviors* without rejecting their deeper state of being or their potential to become something greater

5. Emotional heroism
6. Extremely high tolerance for vulnerability
7. Unwillingness to use others' vulnerabilities, mistakes, and "sins" against them
8. Forgiveness in the face of injustice
9. Unwavering faith in the ability of humanity to move beyond fear, aggression, oppression, shame, blame, and pain to a compassionate, awakened, harmonious state of being and behaving
10. A graphic, multifaceted, highly symbolic use of what the Fulani later called the sharo — an act of physical, mental, and emotional endurance that, in Jesus's case, engaged a compassionate form of power that could embrace death itself

The last tactic was so complex and multilayered in meaning and intent that it is often misunderstood. For instance, I've heard skeptics say that if Jesus had actually been a divine incarnation of God, he would have magically conquered his enemies and avoided death on the cross. Some Christians, on the other hand, have used this episode to scapegoat the Jews for the role that a few Jewish individuals played in the events leading up to the Crucifixion. When we read the sketchy details outlined in the Bible, however, it's clear that Jesus did everything possible to guarantee that he would endure this challenge — with an incredibly sophisticated, group-consciousness-altering goal in mind.

Riding between the Worlds

Throughout history and across all cultures, significant innovations in emotional and social intelligence have often been accessed through what we now call "shamanic acts," techniques that induce altered states of consciousness bridging the gap between consensual physical reality and the more fluid, creative, spiritual realities that visionaries tap to bring something new into existence. While some shamans use trance drumming, dancing, or psychedelic drugs, others employ fasting, physical endurance, isolation in nature, or a combination of these to jump-start significant transformative states. Major religious innovators, from Lao-tzu to Moses, the Buddha, Jesus, and Muhammad, appear to have done this with a wider social agenda in mind, moving from personal shamanic acts (such as wandering through the desert, fasting for forty days and nights) to creating group shamanic experiences that help others see and process life challenges from a more expanded perspective.

Whether you see Jesus as a divine incarnation or not, it's clear that he had an unusual talent for drawing large groups of people into transformative experiences, particularly those promoting nonpredatory wisdom, mutual aid, and emotional heroism. From his birth in a barn to the sacrament of Communion (in which he offered his "flesh and blood" to disciples, encouraging them to carry this highly symbolic ritual forward), Jesus underlined his intent to act as a "sacrificial lamb" for all of humanity, not just his own culture or tribe.

Enduring the *public spectacle* of the Crucifixion, however, was an even more brilliant, intensely courageous move. By performing an extreme sharo of *conscious* self-sacrifice — demonstrating compassion and self-control in the face of death itself — Jesus transformed Rome's ultimate intimidation-torture tactic into a symbol of triumph over oppression. From a cathedral-thinking point of view, embracing the cross served yet another purpose: By encouraging people to project their shame, weaknesses, and darker qualities onto him, he invited these painful by-products of transformation to "die with him," promising a clean, pristine rebirth into a more expansive, empowered existence. In this effort, he literally offered to diffuse shame and guilt for the people who participated in the events leading up to his crucifixion. At the same time, he made it clear that he was ritualistically offering to release these same debilitating emotions in future generations — through the timeless archetype he enacted in the passion play of death and resurrection.

In researching his life on a more practical level, however, I was surprised to realize that during his brief time on earth, Jesus actively preached against and/or avoided all four of the Stone Age Power Tools covered in this chapter. Not everyone was willing to embrace his innovations, of course. But history shows that as news of his words and gestures spread beyond the Middle East, they tempered the "conquest and revenge" cycle proliferating throughout the world.

While countless individuals and communities have taken to heart the principles he introduced, civilization still condones and even promotes predatory behavior, despite attempts to outlaw it. Sometimes, ironically, dominant individuals adopt Christianity as a social control to oppress and shame large populations into submission. The good news is that anyone can access the original text directly — engaging with Jesus's innovative parables, sayings, and behaviors while also using the ever-present archetype of his death and resurrection to release shame and embrace transformation.

New Moon Rising

But what happens after we remove fear, shame, blame, objectification, projection, revenge, and predatory dominance from the equation? What does power look like when the shackles are removed?

Here's where an all too often ignored dimension of history foreshadows an unexpected answer: Among Alexander the Great, the Buddha, Genghis Khan, Joan of Arc, George Washington, Katherine the Great, Geronimo, Winston Churchill, and many other influential leaders, a pattern emerges. For thousands of years, the invisible forces of charisma, bravery, poise, focus, endurance, and conviction have been most reliably bolstered by a silent, nonpredatory tutor. Recognizing the horse's multicultural importance, not just as a beast of burden, or even a companion of kings, but as a *teacher* of kings, conquerors, heroes, and pioneers, is an essential first step in wresting this wisdom from obscurity and purposefully exercising it in the future.

The horse stands at the place where all trails come together, and a new moon shines upon us. To retrace the steps of sorrow and injustice, courage, compassion, and innovation — elevated by a being that has been used for both conquest *and* freedom — is to know the dark and light of power.

To become a student of the horse — rather than a calculating, disconnected master — is to master our own predatory tendencies, reclaiming our original calling to move beyond instinct in *partnership* with nature, tapping our potential to become visionary leaders capable of rallying the endlessly evolving, fully conscious forces of a truly empowered herd.

Part III

HORSE SENSE *at* WORK

The Twelve "Power of the Herd"
Guiding Principles

GUIDING PRINCIPLE OVERVIEW

For Optimal Group Performance,
Innovation, Endurance, and
Deep Personal and Professional Satisfaction

1. USE EMOTIONS AS INFORMATION (CHAPTER 13)
   Employing this Four-Point Method for Emotional Agility — in combination with the Emotional Message Chart, a key to the constructive messages behind fear, anger, frustration, sadness, grief, depression, jealousy, shame, and disappointment — allows you to access feeling and intuition in service to your goals.

2. LISTEN TO YOUR HORSE (CHAPTER 14)
   Your body is the horse your mind rides around on — a sentient tuner, receiver, and amplifier for all kinds of nonverbal information. Use the body scan, a six-point method outlined at the end of this chapter, to gather information in unfamiliar situations, develop fresh approaches to challenges, and "read a room," sensing the unspoken feelings and concerns of others.

3. MANAGE CONTAGIOUS EMOTIONS (CHAPTER 15)
   People unconsciously transmit and amplify emotions during group interactions. Conscious leaders help followers decipher the useful messages behind troubling feelings. Masterful leaders can change the emotional tone of an entire group, driving others' emotions in a more productive direction.

4. **Master Boundaries and Assertiveness (Chapter 16)**
   It's essential to understand the difference between setting boundaries (holding your ground or protecting territory, space, and resources) and motivating others (using assertiveness to influence others' behavior or direct them to take action in pursuit of a specific goal). Both activities involve a skillful use of power. You can avoid adding aggression, shame, blame, and resentment to these activities by dialing your power up progressively (*crescendo*) and then acknowledging achievement of the desired response with *immediate positive feedback*. In this way, boundaries are set with nonverbal cues, cultivating safety, cooperation, clear thinking, and greater trust between team members. And goals are achieved through a simple formula for assertiveness: Commitment + Crescendo + Immediate Positive Feedback = Increasing Motivation, including greater self-motivation in others, freeing leaders up for other pursuits.

5. **Develop a High Tolerance for Vulnerability (Chapter 17)**
   This long-neglected key to emotional strength training uplifts the trust, courage, intelligence, and creativity of the entire group.

6. *Choose* **the Programs;** *Be* **the Programmer (Chapter 18)**
   Habits handed down by parents, teachers, and society, though useful at times, can limit personal growth and organizational innovation. Great leaders know when to employ established methods and policies, when to import "programs" from other sources, and when to create new ones.

7. **Conserve Energy for True Emergencies (Chapter 19)**
   Mature leaders know that long-term survival and success depend on the ability to tap resources without taxing them and to calm and focus others in challenging situations. Use these advanced fear-management protocols to defuse panic and rally the troops, engaging courage and thoughtful problem-solving skills.

8. **Employ Nonpredatory Power Liberally, and Predatory Power Sparingly (Chapter 20)**
   Power does not have to be harsh, exploitive, oppressive, or shortsighted if you master the skills associated with this guiding principle.

9. *Prepare* for Difficult Conversations (Chapter 21)
True innovation depends on having uncomfortable yet productive conversations on difficult topics. Use this method to turn interpersonal conflicts into opportunity.

10. Engage in Consensual Leadership (Chapter 22)
Teams of experts excel when they can fluidly exchange leadership roles according to who's calmest, clearest, most experienced, most inspired, or most invested in the outcome. Consensual leadership depends on developing teams who display a high tolerance for vulnerability (Guiding Principle 5). While their technical expertise may vary, people capable of sharing leadership must also know how to conserve energy for true emergencies (Guiding Principle 7), respectfully discuss difficult topics (Guiding Principle 9), and actively diffuse "evaluation apprehension."

11. Cultivate Emotional Heroism (Chapter 23)
Great deeds depend on keeping your heart open through the ten thousand joys and ten thousand sorrows of life. To face tragedy, betrayal, and injustice with the compassion, creativity, bravery, endurance, and power necessary to effect change in the world, you must use impossible or seemingly hopeless situations as opportunities to strengthen your heart. This advanced emotional-intelligence skill parallels an ancient rite of passage performed by traditional herding cultures, which have much to teach us about a courageous, balanced approach to leadership used by people who live with animals ten times their size.

12. Enjoy the Ride (Chapter 24)
No matter what's happening around you, emotional-agility, social-intelligence, and fear-management skills allow you to deal efficiently with technical difficulties and interpersonal challenges and then go back to "grazing." Over time, as you learn to ride life's roller coaster with ease, an underlying sense of deep peace emerges and grows stronger. You find that you can let go of the stories that tie you to the injustices of the past. And you can fully enjoy the present, knowing that you are courageous, empowered, and agile enough to meet the future with the relaxed and expanded awareness of a mature herd leader.

Chapter Thirteen

GUIDING PRINCIPLE 1
Use Emotions as Information

*M*ost of us are taught to suppress troublesome, inconvenient, or socially unacceptable feelings. But wearing a mask of confidence or compliance to hide fear, anger, jealousy, or sadness only works in the short term. Over time, the internal pressure of unresolved emotion builds, causing seemingly sane, well-adjusted people to explode at inopportune moments, reinforcing the belief that these "irrational" sensations are by-products of a "lowly animal nature" that overrides cool, objective reason for some nefarious purpose.

This idea goes back, way back, to the ancient Greeks, particularly the stoicism movement established in the third century BCE. Early explorers of human potential, these men thought that negative emotions resulted from errors in judgment, and that a sage who reached perfection would no longer experience such disruptions. Over time, an outright war of reason against feeling developed, suppressing positive emotions as well. As Jay Griffiths observes in her book *Wild*, René Descartes and the rationalists of the late-seventeenth and eighteenth centuries cultivated "a hatred of 'enthusiasm,' for its emotional, wild surges of knowing were too natural, too bodily, too animal. Rationalism demanded superiority to, and separation from, nature and nature's ways of knowing."

Around the same time, a Protestant Christian sect known as the Puritans adopted a similar philosophy toward nature and the emotions, inadvertently creating a strange stoic alliance between science and religion during the settling of the New World. Considering the influence of these powerful movements on U.S. history, you have to wonder how the "pursuit of happiness" slipped past their stern, uncompromising gaze to become one of three inalienable rights cited in the Declaration of Independence. As H. L. Mencken famously observed, Puritanism is the "haunting fear that someone, somewhere might be happy," a perspective that still influences people whether or not they have an obvious scientific or religious orientation. This is especially true of hierarchical authority figures in some business and political organizations, schools, and even families who model a physically rigid, intensely critical, unfeeling approach to life and work.

And yet…the same culture that mistrusts emotion rewards actors, dancers, poets, painters, and musicians. These lucky people not only are encouraged to feel the full range of what everyone else denies, they inspire us in the process, bringing us back to life at the end of a stressful or exceedingly boring workday, reminding us that logic can never touch the mystery, passion, beauty, and power of what it means to be fully human.

As the excesses of famous artists throughout history so aptly illustrate, however, civilization's fear of unbridled emotion isn't entirely unjustified. I spent my formative years playing in orchestras and chamber music groups, eventually making a living as a music critic and marrying a talented composer in the process. And I can tell you, from years of observation and direct experience with musicians in all genres, that people trained to express emotion do not lead more functional lives than those taught to suppress emotion.

Unlike the rationalists, Puritans, and a good portion of the modern general public, artists certainly aren't afraid of intense emotion. As a result, they're less likely to hide their true feelings, explode at inopportune moments, and feel profoundly embarrassed about it afterward. Still, they do suffer, often on purpose. With respect to emotional intelligence, this creates its own equally disturbing, counterproductive pattern.

Think about it for a moment: Which emotions dominate rap and heavy-metal music? Rage, lust, and rebellion, right? What about blues, or traditional, crying-in-your-beer country music? Sadness, frustration, jealousy, and, well, once again, lust or even love, but usually with a "he or she done me wrong" kind of twist.

To create a hit song — let alone the next, and the next, and the next — great musicians and mediocre wannabes alike have been known to immerse themselves in situations that give rise to these tempestuous feelings. Classical and jazz artists express a much wider range of emotions, but music history books are filled with accounts of all the ill-fated romances, tragedies, and glimpses of insanity that inspired these people to compose masterpieces. Suffering for one's art may lead to success, it's true, but it's suffering nonetheless — not only for the artist but for everyone in his or her general vicinity.

Answers and Antidotes

By the early 1990s, I was so tired of the overt drama and sublimated conflict I encountered in the worlds of music and business that I came to an unmistakable conclusion: suppressing emotion and expressing emotion are two sides of the same dysfunctional coin. Luckily, around that same time, I bought a horse, hoping to ride into the desert to blow off steam and find a little peace. And it was at a rustic Tucson boarding stable that I glimpsed a surprising alternative to the turmoil civilized humans unnecessarily endure when they treat logic and emotion as uncompromising opposites. The answer, quite simply, involves taking action informed by the melding of both.

While observing horses and doing plenty of follow-up research, I realized that there were predictable, rational messages behind emotions like fear, anger, frustration, sadness, grief, disappointment, and even depression, information I shared for the first time in the 2003 book *Riding between the Worlds*. Horses *use emotion as information* to engage surprisingly agile responses to environmental stimuli and relationship challenges. Rather than suppressing uncomfortable feelings or outlandishly expressing them, these powerful animals employ a simple four-point method that any human is smart enough to learn, one that provides an antidote to the stress we mistakenly create by denying the body's intelligence and its incredibly efficient use of emotion as a nonverbal communication system.

It took me several years to translate this aspect of equine behavior into a process that seems obvious to me now. But the split second I began to use emotion as information, my life became much saner and more enjoyable. Over the past decade, my colleagues and I have taught this Four-Point Method for Emotional Agility to thousands of people on five continents with similar results.

Here's how it works: by becoming more horselike in your responses to emotion, you can successfully align thought, feeling, and action for optimal performance, enriching your personal and professional relationships in the process. Horses, especially those who haven't been traumatized by abusive human handling, are models of emotional agility. They

1.   feel the emotion in its purest form;
2.   get the message behind the emotion;

3. change something in response to the message; and
4. *go back to grazing.* (In other words, they let the emotion go, and either get back on task or relax, enjoying life fully. They don't hang on to the story, endlessly ruminating over the details of uncomfortable situations.)

The vast majority of humans never get past step 1. Suppressors do everything possible to refrain from feeling a troublesome emotion to begin with. To some, even positive emotions are anathema to logic and are outlawed as a result, creating a subculture of emotional flatliners who act like robots. For these people, the intersubjective, emotional- and social-intelligence skills needed to nourish fulfilling relationships "don't compute," remaining grossly underdeveloped.

In business, those who obsessively promote logic over feeling also have trouble succeeding, either remaining in technical jobs, repeatedly passed over for more lucrative management positions, or sometimes simply failing as leaders if they are promoted. As an oft-cited UCLA study showed, even in scientific fields, high emotional intelligence is *four times* more important than raw IQ and training in overall professional success. After all, to get a major grant, you have to network, inspire, and influence others. And to carry out a large-scale experiment once it's funded, you have to build a winning research team, which includes managing, motivating, and in some cases wrangling others, many of whom know more about their jobs than you do and have egos to match (or exceed) their level of expertise.

At the opposite end of the spectrum, drama queens (or kings) and artists rewarded for expressing emotion tend to wallow in their feelings without moving to step 2. In other words, expressers rarely get the message behind the emotion, let alone change something in response. These people can be equally ineffective in leadership positions. While suppressors tend to ignore important nonverbal cues, appearing disengaged, even clueless at times, expressers are more prone to overreact to challenges, stir up emotion, and hold grudges. At the very least, some have significant trouble with step 4 (going back to "grazing," meaning getting back on task) as they replay — over and over again in emotional Technicolor — tempestuous scenarios of conflict, betrayal, injustice, jealousy, disappointment, and triumph, usually against a background of ecstatic love affairs, tragic endings to those relationships, and the deep despair, transcendence, or longing that follows. This impulse, which might serve someone well as a playwright, actor, or singer, tends to wreak havoc in daily life. Bands that break up at the height of success also suggest that emotional expression and artistic talent do not necessarily coincide with the development of effective leadership and interpersonal skills.

Four-Legged Emotional Prodigies

Horses, by comparison, are models of emotional sanity. By collaborating with the nonverbal wisdom of feeling, they conserve energy for true emergencies. At a distance, they can sense whether a mountain lion is on the prowl or simply passing through. In the former case, the herd races to safety without hesitation. In the latter, alert yet relatively relaxed horses will often continue grazing as the cat saunters through the field on his way to an afternoon nap. These animals don't waste time fretting when they have to run from a predator.

Same with anger: horses use this momentarily uncomfortable rise in energy to help set boundaries. A stallion may get a little feisty and try to push his mares around. If they're not in the mood for his shenanigans, they'll pin their ears and warn him to back off. If he doesn't listen, they'll become more emphatic, kicking out and squealing if necessary. When he finally gives them space, they'll relax, joining him later for a nap under a favorite tree. These horses don't need hours of counseling to work out their resentment and disappointment. Both offender and offended get the message behind the anger, change something in response, let the emotion go, and resume their enjoyment of life.

As it turns out, letting the emotion go is easier than you might expect. Contrary to popular belief, fear, frustration, and anger are actually quite reasonable if you know how to work *with* them. When you get the message behind these "negative" feelings, and change something in response, they dissipate on their own. Psychotherapy and sainthood are not prerequisites for emotional mastery. Most people can learn the necessary skills in a weekend, and life itself provides plenty of practice.

The problem is that most adults have been suppressing emotion for so long that these simple warnings have fused into monstrous complexes that truly are disturbing when they rear their ugly heads. We've grown up fearing feeling itself, and *that* is the root of our discontent. To put this strange human habit into perspective, imagine the check-oil light coming on in a teenage girl's first car. Rather than encouraging her to check the manual to see what it means, her parents strongly advise her to ignore it. A week later, she covers this deviant signal with duct tape and continues to drive around, hoping none of her friends will notice. She begins to smell smoke, but she's afraid to check under the hood and too embarrassed to bring the issue up at dinner. When the engine starts to seize, her father tells the confused and frightened young woman that she better get control of that unruly vehicle, or else. In their purest forms, feelings are no more sinister or irrational than dashboard warning lights, and our attempts to reject them no less ridiculous.

And here, perhaps, is the best news for people new to the field of emotional intelligence: When you learn to use emotion as information, *you don't actually look emotional*, at least not in the classic sense. You appear engaged, thoughtful, and present. Since you're not reacting to feelings of fear, frustration, anger, or disappointment in unconscious, unproductive ways, you begin to adopt a poised, problem-solving stance in relation to the somatic signals arising from interpersonal challenges and occasional threats in the environment. Over time, you literally lose your fear of fear itself, gaining the ability to calm and focus others in situations that would normally breed panic and conflict. And finally, because you no longer waste energy suppressing emotion, you free your body, mind, and spirit for creative pursuits and innovative solutions to problems that overwhelm others. Your passion for life and work becomes contagious, as does an underlying sense of deep peace developing from the confidence you gain in riding life's emotional roller coaster with grace, ease, and at times, even amusement.

Using the Emotional Message Chart found at the end of this chapter, in conjunction with the horse's Four-Point Method for Emotional Agility outlined earlier in this chapter, helps you stay centered and think clearly when uncomfortable feelings arise. Inspired in part by the work of Karla McLaren (particularly concerning her innovative insights into sadness, grief, and depression first presented in her audio book *Becoming an Empath*), the Emotional Message Chart is a key to the valuable messages behind the most troublesome emotions. It has been updated and expanded for use in the workplace, though it's equally effective in navigating personal relationships. (If you want more information on how to use emotions to navigate personal challenges, I highly recommend McLaren's most recent book, *The Language of Emotions*.)

Context and Intensification

In spoken language, the same word sometimes expresses multiple meanings according to the context. Similarly, emotions like fear and vulnerability feel comparable yet hold different messages. The same goes for anger and frustration, sadness and grief, and envy and jealousy. Also, keep in mind that on the Emotional Message Chart, the definitions of these highly informative feelings relate specifically to *emotional intelligence*. So while you may find ten different meanings for sadness in the dictionary, the only definition you'll find here is one that you can use as a reliable message to help you make informed decisions and take effective action to move forward productively.

Some people, particularly those who have suppressed emotion for so long they have trouble feeling these somatic messages in their initial stages, find that they don't notice an emotion arising until it intensifies into a much stronger signal. If this happens to you, you may find yourself skimming the "Intensification" column and reading the related entry in the "Message" column to discover the message that coincides with whatever current situation has given rise to an emotion you can no longer ignore.

The Emotional Message Chart and commentary presented here offer brief examples of how the meanings behind these potentially volatile signals can help you manage your own and others' emotions in professional situations at work, at school, in community organizations, and in political and social activism contexts.

A more succinct outline of the chart is featured at the end of this chapter, which you might want to copy and post above your desk, in the break room, or on your home and office refrigerators for quick reference. Subsequent guiding principles build on this information in preparing for productive conversations on difficult topics, advanced fear-management skills, and emotional-strength-training principles.

Fear and Vulnerability:
Emotional Keys to Risk Management

Horses show a remarkable talent for managing risk and negotiating change — without suffering the chronic anxiety many humans endure. In taking cues from the ways these powerful animals respond to and recover from encounters with predators, I realized that it's helpful to discern between an external threat in the environment, which is fear as nature's warning system, and the kind of fear I now distinguish as *vulnerability*, which is an internal threat, a challenge to your self-image, belief system, or comfortable habits. The two feel similar, and most people treat them as the same; but fear and vulnerability call for different responses, though both can be relevant in times of significant change and innovation.

With an external threat, you need to move to safety. With vulnerability, you're not in immediate danger, but circumstances are asking you to expand out of your comfort zone. Take the recent financial crisis. Some people are facing the very real threat of losing their jobs and homes. Others are dealing with the vulnerability of having to modify the ways they do business, of having to step into the unknown and try something new.

Humans sometimes don't protect themselves when they should, and they sometimes go into flight-or-fight mode when there's no real danger. It's as if we're more reactive to and fearful of change than an actual physical threat. Much social strife is caused at home, at work, and between countries by our inability to recognize the difference between fear and vulnerability. Horses, on the other hand, embrace change and enjoy life even as they keep track of all the lions and wolves wandering through their neighborhood.

Like other large herbivores, horses use speed, size, agility, and power to protect themselves and their young, drawing additional security from the group. But they also benefit immeasurably from their ability to read the intentions and emotional states of predators *at a distance*. Nature documentaries sometimes overemphasize successful kills, no doubt for sensational purposes (and perhaps because of humanity's overidentification with predatory dominance). But it's important to realize that thousands of hours of film depicting a relatively peaceful coexistence between predator and prey are left on the cutting-room floor. In Africa, it's common to see lions lounging less than a hundred feet from grazing herds that can clearly assess from moment to moment whether these giant cats are dangerous. Video clips also show single adult horses, zebras, and wildebeests attacking and driving off predators who've managed to pull down another herd member. And after that close encounter with death? Both rescuer and rescued shake off the encounter quickly and get back to grazing, back to *life*.

Fear *resilience* is a lesser-known feature of natural herd behavior that many humans have lost. Social structures based on predatory dominance encourage people to prey upon each other, creating inescapable stress in abusive work, home, or school environments. Developing nonpredatory power helps people boost their courage and combine forces to transform the four Stone Age Power Tools and other needlessly destructive practices that currently wreak havoc beneath the surface of virtually all cultures, religions, and business and educational disciplines.

Like lions, tigers, and wolves, our more "carnivorous" coworkers can learn to balance their talents and needs to support the healthy functioning of any organization's ecosystem. This is only possible, however, when savvy, emotionally and socially intelligent leaders and team members learn how to set boundaries, manage fear, and defuse aggression — without shaming people or holding grudges. (See Guiding Principles 3 to 11 in chapters 15 to 23.)

Remember: in pastoral cultures, expert herders combine predatory and nonpredatory power to direct these opposing forces for the good of the entire interspecies tribe. Rather than stirring up fear to gain control — which creates dangerous stampedes in large groups of loose animals — master herdsmen calm and focus the animals in emergencies while joining forces with fellow tribesmen to fight off predators if necessary. (See chapter 8.)

Nomadic animals like horses also exhibit a marked talent for adapting to change. Carnivores fight over territory, sometimes to the death. Herbivores harmonize with the landscape and the seasons. If water and grass become scarce, they search for greener pastures with their family groups, often migrating with other nonpredatory species. There's a real sense of adventure in the herd when it's time to move on, not fear or resentment. Horses show incredible endurance migrating over vast distances precisely because they know how to enjoy, and be nourished by, the journey.

Subsequent guiding principles offer specifics on how to use fear and vulnerability in negotiating risk and navigating change. (For an in-depth look at fear-management skills, see Guiding Principle 7, in chapter 19. To understand the important role that vulnerability plays in team building and group creativity, see Guiding Principle 5, in chapter 17. To understand the importance of emotional heroism in leadership, see Guiding Principle 11, in chapter 23.)

In the meantime, here's a quick look at the functional messages behind these two interconnected emotions:

EMOTION	MESSAGE	QUESTIONS TO ASK OF THE EMOTION	INTENSIFICATION
Fear	Intuitive, focused awareness of a threat to your well-being	What is the threat? What action must I take to move to a position of safety?	Worry, anxiety, confusion, panic, terror, dissociation, dulling of the senses

In its purest form, fear is nature's warning system of an external threat in the environment. Intensifications like worry, anxiety, and confusion result from trying to explain fear away or control what scares us while ignoring a deeper message we don't want to face. For instance, it's common for people to override fear in order to enter into an abusive relationship, disregarding early evidence that something's not quite right in order to reap some other benefit, such as a wealthy lifestyle or prestigious marriage. (In this case, a perpetually anxious wife might worry about keeping the house clean and making sure dinner is served on time to avoid a beating.)

Panic and terror are the result of true and urgent endangerment that is being ignored, often pointing back to and accentuated by an injury or trauma the person wasn't allowed to work through. Peter Levine, author of *Waking the Tiger*, and other psychologists active in the field of somatic psychotherapy have some important insights to offer people who work with trauma survivors, including military personnel suffering from post-traumatic stress disorder.

Dissociation ("going blank and numb" under stress) is a state that can initially result from not being able to flee a situation perceived as deadly, such as a serious accident, rape, physical abuse, or war. However, survivors of extreme experiences sometimes get stuck in this mode, freezing in mildly stressful situations when they're not in physical danger, such as in conflicts at work or when speaking in front of groups. This leads to the "perpetual assistant" phenomenon, in which an otherwise brilliant person is unable to realize her true potential.

Experiential education can help dissociative people retrain their nervous systems to handle increasing stress and recognize that they are no longer in physical danger. (Long-term abuse survivors sometimes experience dull senses at the beginning of their treatment, as their nervous systems were essentially short-circuited by extreme stress and violence.) Equine-facilitated therapy is particularly effective in this regard because it capitalizes on the oxytocin (calm-and-connect) response in the presence of a large, nonjudgmental animal, inspiring people to develop relaxed yet heightened awareness, boundaries, assertiveness, and other skills associated with power and relationship.

Emotion	Message	Questions to Ask of the Emotion	Intensification
Vulnerability	Something significant is about to change or be revealed.	What belief, behavior, perception, or comfortable habit is being challenged? How might my life change if I accept this new insight?	Panic, rage

Vulnerability is an emotion that feels like fear on the surface, but it represents an internal threat, a threat to your self-image, belief system, or comfortable habits. The key lies in separating it from fear, our natural warning system, which points to external threats. If, upon checking in with the mind-body awareness system, you find no discernible threat in the immediate environment, check to see if the threat seems to instead arise from a conflict within the self.

Vulnerability marks the point at which an old coping strategy, behavior pattern, or perception of the world is being challenged — or a previously repressed part of the self is being revealed. People with a low tolerance for vulnerability tend to develop a rigid identity based on established methods, degrees, or familial or societal norms. This false sense of self, or "conditioned personality," is merely a collection of habits and has no creative power to imagine a new way acting in response to change or unexpected information. (See Guiding Principle 6, chapter 18, for strategies you can use to move beyond limiting thought patterns.) Panic results when the conditioned mind feels a need to "run away" from the insight. Rage arises when the personality tries to fight or violently suppress the insight. (See Guiding Principle 5, chapter 17, for ideas on how to develop a higher tolerance for vulnerability.)

When vulnerability becomes an external threat. Here's the tricky part about fear and vulnerability. In some highly competitive environments, and most certainly in overtly predatory social structures, people are encouraged and sometimes even taught to use a colleague's or competitor's vulnerabilities against him in order to boost their own status.

(Vulnerabilities include lack of training in a new area, skill deficiencies, miscommunications, honest mistakes, unpopular concerns, high sensitivity, shyness, and interpersonal weaknesses.) Guiding Principles 3 (chapter 15), 5 (chapter 17), and 7 (chapter 19) address how to deal with this destructive aspect of group behavior.

Anger and Frustration: Mastering Boundaries and Assertiveness

When anger arises, it signals that someone has invaded your physical or psychological space, perhaps unconsciously, perhaps with the intention to control or take advantage of you. Either way, the surge of energy that accompanies this emotion helps you stand your ground when someone pushes your boundaries. Anger feels similar to frustration, and both can intensify into rage. Frustration, however, emerges when you meet resistance in changing someone else's behavior, or when you're ineffective in handling a technical difficulty. Anger encourages you to hold your ground (without ordering others around). Frustration emerges when you've reached a block that prevents you from achieving a goal.

The problem is that most people don't understand what a boundary is — let alone how to set one effectively. To make matters worse, highly dominant leaders appear to use anger as a management tool (Andrew Jackson and Steve Jobs come to mind), intimidating others into submission, undermining teamwork and creative thought in the process. In this case, however, it's most often frustration intensifying into rage that creates these adult temper tantrums. (A person trying to influence others' behavior is not setting boundaries; he's being assertive. Frustration in leaders most often arises when employees or colleagues don't respond to initial efforts to motivate them, change their behavior, or keep them on task.)

Workplace rageaholics lack boundary-setting, assertiveness, motivation, and problem-solving skills. The same can be said, oddly enough, of the even larger number of people who "retire in place." Well-meaning employees who lack boundary and assertiveness skills, or feel disempowered by volatile bosses and coworkers, will choose boredom and apathy as nonviolent coping strategies for their own unresolved anger and frustration. But these meeker personality types also undermine teamwork and innovation over time, using sarcasm and cynicism to release the pressure. In keeping their own steadily intensifying feelings under wraps, these people are also likely to blow up when the pressure rises too high, though usually at an innocent bystander, creating a phenomenon I call "deflected rage."

Most people refer to this unexpected loss of control as the straw that broke the camel's back. While many instances are inspired by work-related challenges, most people have enough self-control to wait until they get home to explode, essentially making a loved one pay for their inability to set boundaries and motivate others at the office. Here's a classic example: John's boss, Brenda, is making unreasonable demands on his time because of a coworker's negligence, asking him to handle tasks that aren't a part of his job. This coworker, Ginny, always makes excuses for ignoring crucial aspects of her job that she finds tedious. Even Brenda can't seem to motivate the errant team member, finding it easier to call on John to pick up the slack, using his desire for a promotion as leverage. John feels increasing anger at having his workload unjustifiably increased and his personal life reduced. He's also frustrated because of the entire team's inability to motivate Ginny and hold her accountable.

After weeks working overtime on a never-ending stream of projects and feeling both anger and frustration rise, John sits down to yet another late dinner with his family — after missing his son's soccer game once again. Then it happens: the nine-year-old spills a glass of milk, and something just snaps. Suddenly John is screaming at the devastated child, who already felt neglected by his father's seeming lack of interest.

This loss of control, of course, fuels the entire family's belief that "anger is bad," when it's really the *misdirection* of this emotion that causes so much trouble. The guilt that ultimately follows such an outburst seems to confirm the need to keep this primal feeling under wraps, but continued suppression is not the answer. Rage is a needlessly destructive intensification of anger and/or frustration, both of which are useful emotional signals when accessed early and employed intelligently.

The difference between anger and frustration is so straightforward that even a child can understand it. Let's say your son is throwing his toys around in a rage. Helping him decipher the message behind this violent intensification causes both of you to become thoughtful in the midst of a tantrum. Breathing deeply while talking in a matter-of-fact tone of voice, ask him situation-relevant questions: "Allen, are you mad because your little sister came into your room again and took something without asking? If so, that's anger, and I'll back you up in setting a stronger boundary with her. Or were you just trying to force that square peg into a round hole? Well, then, that's frustration. Do you want help with that puzzle?"

Deflected rage, the unconscious diversion of anger onto an innocent by-stander, may seem complex, but it's little more than a relic of the dominance-submission paradigm. This archaic mentality doesn't recognize the concept of personal boundaries, so it outlaws anger. Slaves with a strong sense of self, after all, don't act like slaves. To force them to give up their lands, relinquish their culture, squelch their dreams, and work without just compensation is a gross boundary violation solidified through relentless demoralization. The descen-dants of serfs and preunion factory workers carry the rage of generations, with no models for sensing or setting boundaries in the present. Climbing the social ladder by accumulating wealth or advanced degrees becomes the most obvious way to escape the underling's fate.

Kings who wield the power of life and death over their subjects have evolved into managers who take advantage of employees, tenured professors who put PhD candidates through hell, doctors who shame and intimidate their interns, and parents who treat their children like possessions. Those subdued by this demented version of authority take comfort in the promise that some-day, if they play by the rules, they'll have their own flunkies to torture.

And so the cycle continues. People groomed for this lifestyle never learn to stand up for themselves thoughtfully and appropriately. They become victims or bullies, usually a combination of both. Even those who try to break the pat-tern may lack the skills to pull it off. Conscientious cowards engage in drugs, sex addictions, and other self-destructive behavior to diffuse the rage turned inward. Yet anger in its purest form is nothing less than a call for self-respect and integrity — and for the courage to reinforce them both.

Skills associated with assertiveness and setting boundaries are discussed in Guiding Principle 4, in chapter 16. However, there's an additional emotional message that often feels like anger, one that becomes crucial in managing oth-ers' emotions (Guiding Principle 3, in chapter 15).

Over the years, I've noticed that children and highly sensitive adults, as well as horses, dogs, and other companion animals, become agitated in the presence of someone who's incongruent. People usually interpret this sensation as anger, when in fact it's an alarm signaling that they're interacting with someone who is not what he appears to be — who may, in fact, be wearing a mask of happi-ness, friendliness, courage, or control, when he's actually feeling aggressive, sad, or fearful.

The most efficient way to read anger is to first sense if someone has stepped over a boundary. If not, check for frustration. If neither of these messages seems relevant, this uncomfortable feeling may indicate that you're interact-ing with an incongruent person. Someone who wears a mask of happiness, compliance, indifference, or stern control to hide vulnerability, disappointment, frustration, jealousy, or grief may or may not be lying per se. Some people have been so conditioned to suppress emotion that they no longer know *what* they're feeling. By asking yourself a question — "What is the emotion behind the mask, and is it directed toward me?" — you can determine whether this person is hiding something in order to take advantage of you, or if he's simply sad, angry, or fearful for personal reasons. In the latter case, this "incongruence alarm" (which feels like anger to some people, and more like agitation or anxiety to others) often subsides when you notice the incongruity and realize the person may act unpredictably because of his conflicted emotional state.

Emotion	Message	Questions to Ask of the Emotion	Intensification
Anger	A physical or emotional boundary has been crossed.	What must be protected? What boundary must be established or restored?	Rage, fury, deflected rage (exploding at an innocent bystander), boredom, apathy (masks anger that can't be dealt with; a nonviolent coping strategy)

Karla McLaren's insights into boredom and apathy as repressed anger are intriguing. Someone who uses boredom or apathy as a coping strategy for dealing with anger can be resentful and sarcastic without causing anyone serious physical damage, but the emotional toll on coworkers, family, and friends can be seriously damaging — covert expression of anger through sarcasm and complacency is toxic over time.

It's important to note that sadness and anger are sometimes used to mask each other. Women will sometimes cry and assume they're sad when they're actually feeling anger because they're afraid to stand up for themselves. Men are more likely to express anger when they actually feel sad, because they've been taught that "real men don't cry."

This is not a hard-and-fast rule, however. Sometimes men are afraid of the explosive forces of their own repressed anger and will opt to show sadness instead. Some women would rather get angry than feel sad because they're afraid they'll never stop crying if they allow the tears to come forward.

EMOTION	MESSAGE	QUESTIONS TO ASK OF THE EMOTION	INTENSIFICATION
Frustration	The action you're taking is not effective.	Where is the block? What can I do differently? Who can I ask for ideas or assistance?	Rage, powerlessness

Commonly mistaken for anger, frustration does in fact feel similar to anger, and both emotions can intensify into rage. The difference, however, lies in the message. Frustration arises when we employ a technique in work or life that simply isn't effective, or try, but fail, to influence another being with whom we have a relationship. Rather than look for alternatives, or ask for help, we continue to try to force a breakthrough using familiar coping strategies that, while they may have worked in the past, produce little or no result in the current situation. Frustration continues to build to the point of rage if we refuse to adapt or to explore other alternatives. Powerlessness arises when we give up without asking for help.

EMOTION	MESSAGE	QUESTIONS TO ASK OF THE EMOTION	INTENSIFICATION
Agitation or anxiety (often mistaken for anger)	The person interacting with you is incongruent.	What is the true emotion behind the other person's mask of control, friendliness, or well-being, and is it directed at me?	Rage, mistrust

You might wonder how you can answer the question about agitation or anxiety when someone's trying to hide his emotions. You may not be able to sense the exact emotion, but you can find clues by watching the person's posture, facial expressions, and behavior, especially over time. Someone who says he's "fine" with a smile that looks more like a grimace, especially when combined with tense shoulders and agitated movements, is likely to be feeling some anger, frustration, or jealousy underneath. Notice if others are infringing on his space (or personal time), pushing him too hard to meet an unrealistic deadline, or refusing to respond to his reasonable requests. If the person has puffy eyes, drooping shoulders, and low energy he may be sad or grieving, perhaps depressed. If he's suddenly, uncharacteristically controlling or defensive, he likely feels afraid or vulnerable. (Or he may have recently been shamed by a supervisor or coworker.) For strategies on how to work with incongruent people, see Guiding Principle 3, in chapter 15.

Shame and Guilt:
The Need to Hold *Ourselves* Accountable

As discussed extensively in chapter 12, the use of shame to control others is an archaic, heavy-handed power tool (see pages 216–22). However, as a *personal* emotional message, guilt can be productive. Guilt points to destructive, neglectful, or hurtful actions and behaviors. When you engage in deflected rage, for instance, exploding at innocent bystanders because of your inability to set boundaries with the real aggressor, you will feel guilty (unless you're a sociopath).

In its purest form, guilt encourages people to hold *themselves* accountable. The justice system can punish people for breaking the law, of course, but it can't make them *feel* guilty. The total absence of this emotional signal is considered a symptom of sociopathy or psychopathy (now called "antisocial personality disorder"), which is why jails are full of people who lack remorse and other guilt-related sensations that motivate the rest of us to take others' needs and feelings into consideration and change neglectful or hurtful habits.

As an internal feeling, rather than an external cultural control, guilt is empathy's alarm system, a social regulator, an emotional moral compass that tells you when you've drifted off course. When guilt arises in your own mind-body awareness system, notice what questionable behavior you engaged in and who suffered as a result. *Sincerely* saying you're sorry and making amends or restitution, if necessary, are appropriate responses. But you must also change the original behavior — otherwise, people will become cynical and mistrustful, considering any future attempts to take responsibility for aggressive or neglectful actions as empty apologies. (Sometimes attorneys advise us not to admit guilt or apologize because of our sue-happy culture. In this case, it's still important to alter the destructive or neglectful behavior that led to a potential suit. Taking responsibility for your actions and making appropriate changes helps release the guilt and keeps you from experiencing similar guilt-inducing situations in the future, even if you're not inclined to make a public announcement that you're a changed man or woman.)

Shame, on the other hand, is a critique of who we *are*, rather than what we've done (guilt). As such, feelings of shame most often arise in social situations where we're being judged as hopelessly defective. Cultural institutions or in-groups that objectify, ostracize, denigrate, or persecute people for their race, sex, religion, or socioeconomic status use shame to intimidate, dominate, ostracize, or abuse others.

As mentioned in chapter 12, we can also feel shame as a by-product of personal transformation, when we wake up and realize that we were objectifying, abusing, or neglecting others. However, it's important to shift our focus from shaming ourselves (for a limited, selfish, perhaps childish state of consciousness) to analyzing which *behaviors* were destructive. In this way, we move into the more constructive realm of guilt, charged with making amends and appropriate changes, perhaps through counseling, coaching, or family support.

It takes a certain amount of emotional heroism (Guiding Principle 11, in chapter 23) to analyze the messages behind shame and guilt, let alone change something in response. Taking responsibility for our actions is immensely uncomfortable — as is learning to set strong boundaries and stand up to people who are shaming us. The latter sometimes requires leadership abilities to organize others in standing up to aggressors who use shame as a weapon.

Finally, we must notice and be constantly vigilant about our own deeply ingrained, culturally endorsed habits of using shame to influence others' behavior. At the very least, shaming statements put people on the defensive, cutting off constructive communication and problem solving. And research shows that even if you succeed in convincing someone that she is defective or bad, she's *more* likely to continue the undesirable behavior because, well, she now sees herself as a loser, liar, cheat, whore, emotional wreck, or hopelessly stupid person. Shaming someone repeatedly, over the long term, is an act of cruelty and, at times, even covert homicide. People who accept the shame projected onto them by others experience despair, hopelessness, and suicidal urges that easily lead to addictions, accidental overdoses, or intentional suicide.

Being on the receiving end of shame sometimes results in shame-based re-taliation: shaming the person who shamed us. Yes, of course, he or she "started it." But any form of retaliation turns victim into perpetrator. What's more, people who regularly use shame as a weapon likely experienced intense shame as children. Rather than passively accepting these shame attacks, shrinking in response, they "evolved" into verbally abusive bullies. They'll fight the feeling tooth and nail if you try to shame them back, becoming even more violent.

Techniques for removing shaming statements from personal and professional interactions are featured in Guiding Principles 3 (chapter 15), 4 (chapter 16), and 9 (chapter 21). In the meantime, here's a quick look at the questions to ask of shame and guilt.

EMOTION	MESSAGE	QUESTIONS TO ASK OF THE EMOTION	INTENSIFICATION
Guilt	A critique of a destructive, neglectful, or abusive *behavior*	What questionable behavior or action did I engage in? What was my motivation? How can I get my needs met in a more productive way? Who can help me change this hurtful habit?	Denial, blame, shame, projection

Other than shame, the intensifications listed here are not feelings; they are evasions designed to keep us from feeling guilty and taking personal responsibility. Many people choose denial when they feel that initial pang of guilt, usually blaming another person or the social system, which may in fact need to change as well. However, even if you learned a destructive behavior for legitimate survival purposes, or perhaps were taught to engage in questionable practices as part of a predatory business, political, or educational system, you must still change that behavior in yourself. It's important to remember, however, that *you* are not defective; the behavior is defective. Otherwise, you will plunge into shame.

Many people, however, opt for the much more destructive practice of "projecting their shadow" onto others, picking a coworker, family member, or perhaps entire race to punish for their own transgressions. Scapegoating others to avoid guilt initially allows people to abdicate responsibility in favor of persecuting someone else, but this abusive practice leads to more guilt. See the section "Objectification and Projection: The Deadly Duo," in chapter 12, for more information on this archaic practice.

Emotion	Message	Questions to Ask of the Emotion	Intensification
Shame	A possible indication that you are being scapegoated. Or a personal critique of a "defective" state of consciousness or being.	Am I being shamed by others? If so, am I being objectified or used as a scapegoat? How can I set boundaries with these people — without shaming them? Or am I feeling shame for an old way of being or perceiving the world? If so, what destructive behaviors must I change to fully enter this new, more conscious, compassionate, and responsible phase of my life?	Despair, blame, projection, suicidal urge, bullying

Again, despair and the suicidal urge are feelings. Projection, blame, and bullying are evasions or unproductive strategies for releasing the feeling of shame.

Shame is tricky because it can be dumped on us by parents, spouses, coworkers, and authority figures. However, by asking the questions above, we can tell if shame is an emotion that originated in our behavior (an intensification of guilt), which we can do something about, or if the shame really belongs to someone else who is projecting it onto us to make herself feel better without changing her own behavior (let alone the limited belief system or state of consciousness that justifies the behavior). *Projected shame* is common in abusive relationships where an emotionally sensitive scapegoat in the family carries and expresses the shame and guilt that actually belongs to the abusers. (This person is seen as bad, hopeless, or sinful, no matter what he or she does, which commonly leads to addictions, suicidal urges, or bullying.)

Shame in the workplace is rarely discussed, but it's truly an epidemic, the hidden root cause of serious interpersonal difficulties. Openly aggressive and passive-aggressive bosses are fond of shaming people to intimidate and control them, losing trust and respect at the very least, wreaking untold havoc in the long run. Colleagues who shame each other are equally destructive. As discussed in the section on shame in chapter 12, sometimes a more naturally aggressive team member will become the scapegoat for an entire division as coworkers project their own "shadow" onto him, considering him hopeless or even evil, blocking all efforts to create a functional work environment.

Envy and Jealousy: The Challenge to Excel *and* Play Fair

Anyone promoted to a position of power must learn to deal constructively with envy and jealousy. In fact, both are useful to leaders and followers alike, especially when people learn to discern between the two. Engaged thoughtfully and responsibly, these much-maligned, potentially destructive feelings can help us monitor our motivations, discover hidden talents, develop self-mastery, and exercise integrity while paying attention to individual and group needs simultaneously.

After spending an extensive amount of time researching jealousy and envy, I found the clearest, most inspiring, and thought-provoking insights in a dictionary, of all places. Beyond giving succinct definitions for these notoriously troublesome emotions, *Webster's New Collegiate Dictionary* makes an extra effort to emphasize that envy and jealousy "are not close synonyms and can rarely be interchanged without a loss of precision." Envy is defined as a "painful or resentful awareness of an advantage enjoyed by another joined with a desire to possess the same advantage." In other words, when you feel envious *you want something that someone else has*, usually wealth or success. This may include a promotion, a certain talent, professional recognition, or a valuable relationship of some kind.

Used constructively, then, this emotion inspires us to excel. When we envy someone, he is modeling something we want to attain. From a distance, we can analyze this person's success, and study how he achieved it. Closer to home, we might even be able to enlist this person as a mentor — if we approach him with sincere enthusiasm, respect, and the commitment to do our own hard work. Frequently, however, people have a love/hate relationship with someone they envy, perhaps being nice to her face, vying for privileges and shortcuts to success, while also looking for weaknesses and other ways to cut her down to size — sometimes to gain advantage, sometimes simply to make themselves feel better for not taking similar risks or putting in the time and effort to realize their own unique potential.

Similarly, when we sense that people are envying us, we can combat the possible negative effects by sharing information or resources that will help them excel — while also setting strong boundaries and holding these people accountable for their actions. Otherwise, we may fall prey to the "tall poppy syndrome," where resentful friends, family members, and colleagues cut us down to size, trying to keep us from achieving our goals because they feel reduced by our success. Native American medicine men I've worked with are so sensitive to this phenomenon that they have special ceremonies to diffuse the destructive effects of envy. Some shamans share a portion of the gifts and fees they receive with other tribe members, recognizing that consideration and generosity can be powerful antidotes to jealousy's sometimes devilish nature.

Which brings us to a productive definition of the latter: jealousy signifies that *an inequity of opportunity or compensation has come to light.* Sometimes there's also an element of anger involved: If a boundary has been crossed, if someone has taken possession (or intends to take possession) of what you've already claimed or developed, you're likely to feel both of these tempestuous emotions. Someone flirting with your spouse, for instance, will inspire jealousy and anger. Lusting after someone else's wife, on the other hand, involves envy. If you succeed in seducing the woman in question, you will violate her spouse's boundaries and he will feel jealous of and angry with you (perhaps even enraged or homicidal, depending upon the circumstances).

Outside of personal relationships, we also feel jealous when we find out someone makes more money than we do for performing a similar job, or that someone is receiving preferential treatment while we work hard behind the scenes without recognition.

Jealousy often signals that we need to make adjustments to professional and social structures that don't play fair. But sometimes people feel jealous as a result of failing to acknowledge their own skill deficiencies or blind spots, particularly those involving emotional and social intelligence. This happens, for instance, when a more personable, but less experienced, team member is promoted over older candidates. People with more seniority or higher education may jump from jealousy to outrage upon hearing the news, refusing to acknowledge that their people skills are seriously lacking. Perhaps they've been sarcastic and jaded, or have undermined others, because of a lack of past promotion. Perhaps their critical, highly competitive nature alienates colleagues and management alike. In any case, when jealousy arises in professional situations, it's important to look at our own attitudes, work ethic, and emotional- and social-intelligence skills before deciding what action to take next.

When used thoughtfully, and with self-awareness, *jealously becomes the guardian of fair play.* To diffuse the negative effects of this emotion in yourself and others, you must balance individual and group needs, making sure people are recognized and fairly compensated for their contributions. In organizations large and small, any faction showing a lack of personal responsibility or a lack of respect for others — especially in combination with a grandiose sense of entitlement — will breed justified jealousy in others over time, creating an increasingly toxic work, home, or political environment.

In groups that show little concern for others' needs, it takes a strong leader with personal integrity to manage jealousy and its even more troublesome intensifications of outrage and resentment. And even then, this person's powers will be severely taxed over time. Ultimately, jealousy requires a change in cultural values, requiring us to move from an "every man for himself" mentality to an "everyone is valued" and "everyone shares responsibility for our success" approach.

EMOTION	MESSAGE	QUESTION TO ASK OF THE EMOTION	INTENSIFICATION
Envy	The person you envy models a talent, success, position, or lifestyle you want to develop or acquire.	What aspects of this person's life, career, personal qualities, relationships, or talents inspire me to excel? What professional training or personal skills must I develop to achieve similar success? Who can I enlist for support in this next state of growth?	Hero worship, rivalry, resentment

Sometimes the person you envy can act as a formal or informal mentor. If not, this is a good time to find a coach or teacher who can help support you through the journey you're about to undertake. Nonetheless, it's important to study the person who inspired you to begin with, focusing not only on the perks of her success but also on the hardships, education, experience, dedication, ingenuity, courage, and work it took to get there. In his book *Outliers: The Story of Success*, Malcolm Gladwell observed that most innovators, from the Beatles to Steve Jobs, spent an average of ten thousand hours developing their talents before they were capable of making significant contributions to their respective fields.

It's also important to be realistic about your own talents, values, and resources. If you're five feet four and have always dreamed of becoming a fashion model, you may be envious of a girlfriend who is five feet ten; but your true calling probably lies elsewhere. Similarly, if you envy the head of a Fortune 500 company who clawed his way to the top, betraying numerous friends and colleagues along the way, you may want to look more deeply into his lifestyle and relationships, evaluating his methods against your own moral compass.

EMOTION	MESSAGE	QUESTIONS TO ASK OF THE EMOTION	INTENSIFICATION
Jealousy	An inequity in resources, pay, recognition, opportunity, or relationship has come to your attention.	Exactly who or what am I jealous of? Is this inequity an oversight? If so, who can rectify the situation? If not, how can I strategize and gather support to change an unfair system?	Resentment, outrage

Sometimes inequities are honest oversights. You're more effective at motivating change if you approach management from this perspective. However, inequities in pay and opportunity can also be related to race, religion, or sex, in which case the matter becomes a social issue that may demand organized activism to shift. In this case, strategizing and gathering support to change an unfair system can put you in a long-term leadership role that has wider cultural implications.

In business, it's natural to feel jealous of someone who's been promoted to a position we desire. This is a special case — an *unavoidable* inequity of opportunity — as only one person can be chosen for a job that many want. The questions to ask in this situation, then, do not involve finding someone to rectify the situation. Instead you must research why this person was chosen above others, comparing your own skills to those of the winner and possibly getting additional training to be better suited to such a position in the future. If your supervisor is willing to discuss the topic with you honestly, interview her about what skills and personal qualities the successful candidate had that made him stand out as best qualified for the job. It's also helpful to work with a coach to assess your own strengths and challenges. In terms of emotional and social intelligence, I've found the Simmons EQ Profile to be an incredibly sophisticated tool for this purpose, especially in combination with executive coaching. For more information on this process and other EQ-boosting strategies, I highly recommend Bob Wall's book *Coaching for Emotional Intelligence*. (Wall himself is sometimes available as a coach and an expert interpreter of the Simmons EQ Profile.)

Disappointment: A Call for Clarity

Disappointment is a common emotion in the workplace and in personal relationships. When we ignore or try to hide disappointment over time, unspoken negativity or apathy rises, communication breaks down, and cynicism abounds.

When people finally gain the courage to address their disappointment, they've often reached high levels of frustration, mistrust, and resentment as a result of multiple instances of unexpressed disappointment. In this much more desperate emotional state, people have a tendency to speak in a shaming tone of voice, which puts others on the defensive, creating further blocks to clarity and creative problem solving. Asking the questions listed in the following table before meeting with a person or group of people who've disappointed you can help you prepare for a much more constructive conversation.

Often, you realize that you weren't clear in communicating your expectations to begin with, essentially setting others up for failure. When used thoughtfully and *expediently*, disappointment inspires greater clarity, teamwork, and problem solving. When suppressed and ignored, it leads to an increasingly confusing and toxic work or home environment.

Emotion	Message	Questions to Ask of the Emotion	Intensification
Disappointment	The outcome (contrary to what you desired or envisioned) did not live up to your expectations	What was I hoping for or expecting to happen? Was this realistic? If so, how can I better communicate my vision to those *capable* of carrying it out? If not, how can I modify my vision and better train, prepare, and support the people involved?	Anger, frustration, mistrust, powerlessness, apathy

Sadness and Grief:
Tears of Transition, Loss, and Inspiration

Many people are much more afraid of sadness than fear or anger. In the workplace, crying is often perceived as a sign of weakness for both sexes. You can, of course, learn to control *when* you cry, holding back the tears for private reflection or supportive family settings. But cry you must: the inability to process sadness and grief can keep you from letting go and moving forward.

Some of my clients act as if they'll dry up and blow away if they release all the tears they've been saving up for years. And they can't bear to see anyone else cry, which prevents them from handling emotionally charged home and work situations effectively. I have to assure these people that I've never, ever seen anyone die of sadness. A person might become depressed and suicidal from suppressing it, but the original feeling is both healing and life affirming.

According to Karla McLaren, this misunderstood emotion "restores flow" to the system "when loss is imminent and *in our best interest*." More specifically, sadness "brings the healing waters of tears and physical release to us" and "removes log jams in our psyches" so we can live authentically again. In her books *Emotional Genius* and *The Language of Emotions*, McLaren reveals that sadness is often a part of grief or depression, but that in its purest form it's a healing agent that motivates us to let go of what no longer serves us so we can embrace the next stage of growth and creativity. She emphasizes that we must ask two questions of this emotion: "What must be released?" and "What must be rejuvenated?" If we can't release our attachment to old patterns, destructive relationships, or jobs that no longer serve us, we can't be rejuvenated, and the sadness persists. The concept is as basic as remembering to wash rancid wine out of a glass before pouring in the new.

With sadness, there's some choice in when and how to release what no longer works. With grief, however, the loss or death has already occurred. In accepting a new position, especially a promotion based on previous success, you will feel sadness in leaving valued team members — and perhaps a beautiful home, family, and friends if this enticing opportunity requires moving to another city. If you decide to leave a hopeless marriage or once-satisfying career you've outgrown, you'll also experience sadness, but you still have some say in the timing and the details of the dissolution. However, if you're suddenly laid off from a job you value, or a beloved spouse suffers a fatal car crash on the way home from work, you'll plunge into grief.

Grief is so painful because anything that takes form — a relationship, a method, a lifestyle, a business, a human body — solidifies to the point of resisting change. When it finally breaks apart or fails to function, grief arises in direct proportion to how attached we had become to it. Sometimes a loved one dies suddenly, presumably before his or her time. In this case, the family's entire life changes in an instant. Yet the main question to ask of this emotion is: "What must be mourned?" And the tears that come in waves over months, or even years, help us let go of what seemed so suddenly and rudely snatched away from us. Memorializing what was lost can provide solace, reminding us to appreciate life's daily gifts as we also recognize their impermanence.

Yet because grief also involves a boundary violation — something you value is taken away from you — anger is often involved as well. Sometimes, justice can provide closure. In a drunk-driving accident, the responsible party is clear. A CFO who mismanages company funds can be fired, fined, and perhaps prosecuted. Restitution helps alleviate the anger, but most certainly not the loss, which still requires mourning. But grief also occurs in response to impersonal life circumstances where no one person is culpable — a natural disaster or economic forces beyond anyone's control. In this case, you may also experience the vulnerability of having to reinvent your life and career while also dealing with the loss of a valued job, home, or relationship.

When I feel tears rising, I ask questions related to sadness (Do I have a choice in when and how to let go of what no longer serves me?), then grief

(Has something or someone I value been taken away from me?). Sometimes, however, it's clear that neither of these emotions fits the situation, in which case I realize I might be experiencing tears of joy, frustration, recognition, or inspiration. In the latter case, I feel stirred by beauty, power, awe, or mystery, usually through my own or someone else's ability to draw attention to something that was previously hidden.

Artists understand the value of inspirational tears. These people know that the ability to move people deeply — to give voice or form to what was previously felt but unspoken or unseen — can work magic in motivating others to join forces and pursue ambitious goals, generating hope and dedication.

For many people, tears — of sadness, grief, joy, and inspiration — represent the final frontier, the final hurdle in moving from mediocrity to brilliance. Visionary leaders don't shrink from situations that stretch the mind and the heart. Whether by talent, calling, or soulful hard work and endurance, they develop the emotional heroism necessary to face extreme loss and injustice while inspiring others to create a better world. Sometimes, in the process, they cry.

Ultimately, exceptional leaders realize that *tears are power*, especially when met with consciousness, courage, and integrity.

EMOTION	MESSAGE	QUESTIONS TO ASK OF THE EMOTION	INTENSIFICATION
Sadness	Loss is imminent and in your best interest.	What must be released? What must be rejuvenated?	Despair, despondence

Sadness, by this definition, implies we have a choice in when and how to let go of something we once valued but is no longer working for us: a job, a relationship, a home. McLaren emphasizes we must ask both questions in the table above to complete the cycle. People who are promoted, for instance, often feel a mixture of excitement and sadness as they realize they will miss certain coworkers, activities, and so on from the previous position. Recognizing sadness as a process involving choice, release, and rejuvenation allows people to move efficiently through this uncomfortable by-product of change.

Emotion	Message	Questions to Ask of the Emotion	Intensification
Grief	A significant loss or death has occurred, usually due to circumstances beyond your control.	What must be mourned? What must be memorialized, appreciated, or celebrated?	Depression

Grief does not involve a choice. Through an accident, illness, or change in the economic climate, you may lose a spouse, a job, physical health, and so on before you're ready, if you ever would have been. Because something valuable has been taken against your will, there is also an element of anger in grief: it is the ultimate boundary violation to have your life turned upside down by outside forces beyond your control. Crying tears that often feel like a mixture of deep sadness, loneliness, anger, and vulnerability allows you to slowly let go of an important relationship, job, or·other part of your life. Memorializing what was lost adds to the constructive expression of this emotion: finding ways to remember, cherish, and, at times, even celebrate the gifts that this person, job, or stage of life provided you is healing and over time restores your appreciation and enthusiasm for life. For more information on how to work through grief and support others who are grieving, I highly recommend *Good Grief: Healing through the Shadow of Loss* by counselor and fellow Eponaquest instructor Deborah Morris Coryell.

Depression: A Call for Deep Listening, Support, and Significant Change

A RAND Corporation study found that people with depressive symptoms spend more days in bed than those with diabetes, arthritis, back problems, lung problems, or gastrointestinal disorders, leading to an estimated 200 million workdays lost each year due to employee depression. And the total cost of depression to the nation in 1990? Between $30 and $44 *billion* dollars! This figure has likely increased since the economic crisis of 2008.

While depression is sometimes promoted exclusively — particularly by drug companies — as a biochemical disorder best treated by medication, more recent studies show that stressors in the work environment also contribute to symptoms. These include "interpersonal conflicts, work demands, organizational politics, lack of faith in organizational management, and perceived control over job tasks and job environment."

Classic symptoms of clinical depression include not only sleep and eating disturbances, fatigue, chronic aches and pains, difficulty concentrating, and irritability but some extreme (and rather telling) emotional symptoms as well: feelings of hopelessness, guilt, worthlessness, and a persistent sad, empty, or anxious mood.

While official studies don't mention it, the rampant epidemic of callous predatory behavior and shame in the workplace alone could explain many of the emotional symptoms listed above. The high cost of depression, therefore, is not an individual challenge. It's a call for *all people* to elevate their interpersonal, emotional- and social-intelligence, and leadership skills — yet another reason to move from a "survival of the fittest," "every man for himself" orientation to a mutual aid, "everyone is valued" and "everyone is responsible for our success" mentality.

But let's get back to the individual for a moment. In her article "Depression in the Workplace," Mary Sherman reports that in more than 80 percent of cases, treatment is effective, offering at least some degree of relief. "Treatment," she notes, "includes medication, short-term talk therapy, or a combination of both."

A pilot study on equine-facilitated therapy led by one of my colleagues, fellow Eponaquest instructor, horse trainer, and licensed social worker Leigh Shambo, showed even higher rates of success with a more challenging population — namely, abuse survivors with complex post-traumatic stress disorder. Six women who had previously either refused, or failed to benefit from, traditional group therapy showed significant, enduring improvements in depression and dissociation after a mere ten weekly two-hour sessions combining nonriding horse activities with related group process work and life skills educational components. A full article on the results was published in the flagship journal of the Federation for Horses in Training and Education International, in the 2010 issue.

"They had all experienced physical and/or sexual abuse during childhood, with at least one woman surviving a violent rape as an adult," Leigh told me after completing the study cosponsored by her Human-Equine Alliances for Learning (HEAL) nonprofit and Providence St. Peter Hospital in Olympia, Washington. "Despite years of medication and outpatient counseling," said

Leigh, "their anxiety was so intense that some were afraid to leave the house. Without the skills or the courage to go out and build new relationships, they felt overwhelming despair."

Leigh led a clinical research team of three, including her colleague Susan Seely and researcher Heather Vonderfecht. Standardized measures were taken at four stages during the process (before, during, and at the close of the program, and four months after the program ended). Depression scores, which were in the moderate-to-severe range at the beginning, were in the low end of mild depression by the final session. At the four-month follow-up point after the program ended, *all* the women were in the *normal, nondepressed range.*

The earlier, personal-development-oriented version of the Emotional Message Chart that was first presented in my 2003 book *Riding between the Worlds* turned out to be a key factor in Shambo's horse-facilitated therapy sessions. "Jennifer," a woman with Asperger's syndrome (a high-functioning form of autism), had been in treatment, on antidepressants, most of her life. "We were going over the chart, discussing the messages behind the various emotions," Shambo remembers. "When we got to depression, she looked at me in the strangest way, and asked, 'Do you mean to tell me that my depression could have a *meaning*?' It was a life-changing moment for her and for the other women. It turns out that they were under the impression, conveyed somehow through the standard medical system, that if they were 'cured,' they'd never experience troubling emotions."

A year after the 2006 study ended, Shambo met up with Jennifer again. "She told me she hadn't been depressed a single day in that entire time," Shambo marvels. "When she felt what would have normally been a debilitating surge of emotion, one that previously led to crippling anxiety, she used the emotional message chart to decipher the meaning behind it. As she accessed that information in a thoughtful and empowered way, her mood would shift and she could go on about her day."

All the participants in Shambo's study made significant life changes. By learning how to set boundaries with a thousand-pound animal, the women were able to confront husbands and other family members in productive ways. By developing the courage and assertiveness to direct the horses to perform various moves on the ground, several gained the confidence to go back to school.

Together these women practiced new, stronger ways of being, and they witnessed each other's success. As one woman wrote in her evaluation, "The learning didn't stop when the group did, either. I learned valuable skills for living that I use every day. The horses have so much to teach, if we only let them!"

Cultural Blocks to Getting Help

Studies on employee attitudes toward depression show that many refuse to seek treatment because they fear it will affect promotions and other future employment opportunities. They're also wary of confidentiality (regarding any discussion related to depression or other possible mental health issues) when meeting with bosses or enrolling in corporate-subsidized counseling programs, revealing concerns about how others will see them, in some cases justifiably worried that opportunistic coworkers will use this vulnerability against them — adding even more anxiety to the chronic anxiety already associated with this complex condition.

Yet while depression seems like weakness or resignation, it actually holds tremendous untapped energy. People in this debilitating state often feel self-conscious, dim-witted, and embarrassed by their predicament. Yet according to Karla McLaren, depression is nothing to be ashamed of. In her audio book *Becoming an Empath* (and subsequent other books), she calls it "the stop sign of the soul." This "ingenious stagnation" takes over when people refuse, over an extended period, to acknowledge the wisdom behind "outlawed" emotions like anger, fear, sadness, and grief.

While some depressions *do* result from chemical imbalance (and respond well to antidepressants as a result) many cases stem from a deep-seated, intuitive objection to major life choices. After repeated warnings, the psyche finally hinders our compulsive reenactment of destructive patterns by draining all energy to move forward in the current direction. According to McLaren, people who can't engage this protective mechanism blindly stumble into situations endangering their health, their sanity, and their purpose in life: "In a world where we're taught to ignore our emotions, dreams, and true passions, where we enter blindly into the wrong relationships and the wrong jobs, depression is our emergency brake."

One of the most efficient ways out of this emotional quagmire is to ask two questions: What activities or relationships drain my energy? and What new direction gives me energy? Severely depressed people may need medication to bring their baseline up high enough to even ask these questions. If they get the message and begin to move forward in a soul-replenishing new direction, they may no longer need biochemical support, as numerous people I've worked with over the years can attest after gaining significant emotional- and social-intelligence and empowerment skills from working with the horses.

For most people, however, the difficulty lies in accepting the answers. Sometimes, depression leads a lawyer to pursue photography, a seemingly irrational or, at the very least, "irresponsible" impulse for a man born into a family of attorneys. Sometimes, it demands that a battered woman leave her husband, even though everyone else thinks he's the nicest guy in the world.

As I mentioned in previous books, a bout of depression in the early 1990s mysteriously pushed me away from a successful, rather glamorous career as a music critic toward the initially vague notion of working with horses to help people. At first, it seemed ridiculous to switch from radio and print journalism to the equestrian arts. I resisted for months. Some wise, persistent force finally squelched my skepticism by shutting off all power to the safe, ego-satisfying activities with which I identified myself. It got to the point that I had to down an entire pot of coffee to write a single music review, and even then my mind was sluggish and full of fog. Yet whenever I managed to drag myself out to the barn, I seemed to have endless enthusiasm for cleaning stalls, grooming horses, and riding in the desert heat. So many creative ideas and insights would flood my brain when I was relaxing with the herd that I kept a notebook in the tack room. The research I did during the seven years leading up to publishing *The Tao of Equus* spanned subjects that seemed to have no practical purpose at the time. Yet all I had to do was follow the burning need to know, and I was blessed with endless energy and concentration.

If depression's message were so easy to accept, the psyche wouldn't have to resort to such tactics — and that's the genius behind the stagnation. After months of lying listlessly in a darkened room, the attorney finally steps out to shoot some pictures. His wife and parents are thrilled to see him take an interest in something, anything. "What the hell," they say. "Let's buy him a new camera!"

Depression is the soul's last-ditch effort to assert itself in a climate that fosters a rigid, socially sanctioned persona. It works for horses too. In *Way of the Horse: Equine Archetypes for Self-Discovery*, I told the story of two depressed horses I'd worked with: a shy and flighty cow horse named Noche, and a Thoroughbred named Magic who resisted racing, but not for lack of talent. A number of high-powered leaders have since told me that these anecdotes, more than any others, helped them to embrace the wisdom of their own depression when they inexplicably lost their drive to excel in a career they once found energizing and fulfilling.

Magic loved her trainer, Sally, and would run like the wind whenever this favored human was on her back, passing all the other horses with ease. Yet it was unrealistic for them enter formal races together. Sally was pushing forty, and while still in phenomenal shape, she was quite a bit taller and heavier than the average jockey. Still, whenever a professional was lifted into the saddle, the mare just wouldn't perform no matter how hard she was ridden, or beaten, to the finish line. The investors who owned this expensive horse fired Sally and brought in a new coach. By the end of the season, the filly was dangerously thin and listless. Finally, Magic's owners decided to cut their losses, lowering the filly's price enough to let Sally buy her. The mare "miraculously" recovered, and the two went on to excel at eventing, a field in which many horse-and-rider teams forge a close, harmonious bond.

Magic's depression demonstrated what she couldn't negotiate in words — she wanted to be with Sally and no one else, no matter how much money other people invested in her or what their expectations were. Most depressed mounts, however, don't have such an obvious goal. My old cow horse Noche had never seen a human develop a real relationship with his kind. Where he came from, ranch horses were tools. If he didn't remain stoic when the girth was cinched tightly, or break into a gallop when he was spurred, there was hell to pay.

For several years, I thought that if I gave this "poor abused" gelding a lot of carrots, massages, and love, he would come out of his disconnected, lop-eared state, but it was slow going. Reading Karla McLaren's notions about depression in humans, I came up with a novel idea. What if I helped Noche reclaim the wisdom behind those so-called negative emotions he had been punished for expressing? What if I taught him to gently, respectfully set boundaries of his own? What if when he pinned his ears ever so slightly, I cinched the girth more slowly, groomed him more gently in those ticklish spots, or maybe not at all, if he didn't absolutely need to be brushed there?

When Noche pawed the ground in frustration at the hitching post, what if I negotiated with him rather than following the conventional practice of leaving him tied an extra half hour for his insolence? It was reasonable that he stand quietly for tacking up. But what if I were talking on my cell phone, ignoring the fact that we had just finished a long, immensely satisfying trail ride? Noche's objection in that case would be justified, signaling that I should call this person back later — after I'd removed the saddle, hosed the sweaty horse off, and turned him loose to eat some fresh grass. And what would happen if I respected his fear? What if when this solid, experienced trail horse shied, I heeded the warning, rather than yelling "stupid horse" and whipping him with the reins? By slowing down, I might avoid getting thrown when we encountered a rattlesnake around the next bend. By taking another route in response to the horse's alarm, I might never find out what the threat was, but I'd be assured of a pleasant ride.

As it turned out, the benefits of collaborating with Noche's previously outlawed emotions outweighed any advice I'd received about being the intractable leader in all possible situations. Because I listened to the mustang, he was more willing to enter new and uncertain situations with me. His eyes grew brighter. He began to stand up for himself with other horses, eventually becoming a leader in his own right. He whinnied when I came to the barn, making obvious efforts to draw me to his pasture, ready for whatever adventure we might undertake that day. He ate more heartily; he even took an obvious liking to a few of the mares and proceeded to woo them like a stallion. He transformed from a worn-down old cow horse to a proud, spirited, trustworthy friend.

People treat people like workhorses too. Depression is our natural reaction to the long-term suppression of significant emotions and dreams. The next time you're overtaken by that gray, listless mood, try listening to it. Remember, however, that the way out of depression sometimes involves the least rational, least socially acceptable option you feel drawn to — if it *were* acceptable, you'd already be doing what you love with the full support of family and friends.

When others' expectations run you down, it helps to think of Magic the reluctant racehorse. If a three-year-old filly could change the course of her own life, your depression signals that somewhere, deep inside, you have the resources to do it too.

EMOTION	MESSAGE	QUESTIONS TO ASK OF THE EMOTION	INTENSIFICATION
Depression	"Ingenious stagnation," "stop sign of the soul"	What activities or relationships drain my energy? What new direction gives me energy?	Loss of self, loss of life's purpose, suicidal urges, physical illness

Depression often follows a period when we didn't listen to sadness, fear, anger, or grief. McLaren emphasizes that depression is not a sign of stupidity; it is, in fact, a most ingenious survival mechanism. The psyche is given no choice but to hinder our ability to move forward, because it knows we shouldn't move in the direction we're headed. Depression takes over when "what we were doing and where we were going didn't match up with our inner desires."

EMOTION	MESSAGE	QUESTIONS TO ASK OF THE EMOTION	INTENSIFICATION
Suicidal urge	Some aspect of the life you're leading (not your physical existence) must end.	What must end *now*? What must be culled?	Becoming like a "soulless automaton," physical death

Sometimes the suicidal urge results from depression related to chemical imbalance or chronic pain. In these cases, medical, psychological, and spiritual support are needed, or the person may successfully commit suicide in a moment of extreme fatigue to simply end the pain.

In most cases, though, the suicidal urge absolutely does not signal the desire for an end to physical existence. Rather, it emerges when the difference between who we are in our deepest, most authentic selves and who we've become to fit into a certain social system are completely out of alignment. The suicidal urge, McLaren says, often "emerges when our lives are already endangering our souls....What needs to die is our attachment to falseness, lovelessness, lies and spiritual emptiness," basically whatever stops us from living authentically. The dark night of the soul experienced in this state "exists in direct proportion to the dawn that awaits" us. A person who resists the urge without making the necessary changes in life or career can become a soulless automaton with no enthusiasm, creativity, or productivity, a person who "retires in place." Research also shows that the levels of stress, abuse, or emotional repression leading to this extreme state can suppress the immune system beyond its capacity to fight off disease. If a person experiencing the suicidal urge does not get the help she needs to change her life, she may indeed die a slow, agonizing death from a physical affliction, if she manages to resist the notion of actually killing herself.

People who have experienced extreme betrayal at home or in the workplace can become suicidal, as can people who become scapegoats, enduring constant shaming attacks to the point that they believe they are hopelessly defective or worthless. What needs to end, what needs to be culled without hesitation, is an attachment to whatever social group has become so abusive. Getting support to leave, to build a new life with people who can be trusted, is essential.

People experiencing a suicidal urge must be taken seriously, but I've seen this impulse become most empowering and transformational if it is regarded as an urgent emotional message capable of rallying untapped resources. The questions, then, are the most extreme for this reason. As McLaren so eloquently conveys:

> If you ask these questions prayerfully and ceremonially, your suicidal urge will tell you this draining behavior, this soul-killing relationship, this painful addiction, this weakness and self-pity, this pathetic story about why you can't do your art [is saying to you:] you've forgotten who you are, but I *remember*. If you let it speak, your suicidal urge will stand up for your lost dreams, and it will help you clear away everything that threatens to kill them. It will remind you of your forgotten goals, and it will help you move toward them again....You'll be given your own life back.

What About the Positive Emotions?

When used productively, negative emotions are temporary, instructive, course-correcting sensations that culminate in feelings of peace, satisfaction, connection, inspiration, and empowerment (sometimes all five at once). While it's inadvisable to *express* anger, frustration, jealousy, and sadness openly, especially at work, trying to avoid *feeling* them blocks the message behind them. (See Guiding Principles 3 [chapter 15], 4 [chapter 16], and 9 [chapter 21] for techniques on how to discuss emotional *messages* professionally without expressing the emotions themselves.)

Ignoring negative emotions over the long term causes them to intensify into stronger signals that can actually hijack higher thought processes, sending you into an uncontrollable flight-or-fight mode as the pressure builds. Ironically, to remain in control of your emotions, you must collaborate with them in their earliest, most informative stages, deciphering the message behind them, changing something in response to the message, letting the story go, and getting back on task.

However, it's also important to cultivate a richly nuanced awareness of positive emotions (without becoming addicted to the ones you're most attracted to). For some people — particularly those who worship logic or fear a loss of control — strong positive feelings can be more threatening than negative emotions.

(Remember René Descartes's hatred of enthusiasm?) Positive feelings let us know when we've made a good choice, taken the right path, reached a satisfying resolution, glimpsed an innovative solution, or sensed our true calling. Some of these emotions reward and renew us, while others energize and inspire us, helping us perform great deeds, fueling dedication and endurance, sometimes carrying us through significant challenges.

Positive feelings are also temporary, for good reason. If we felt perpetually calm we might never get anything significant done. If we felt unrelenting excitement, we'd lose focus, make unrealistic decisions, and quickly burn out. If we needed to feel safe and comfortable at all cost, we'd resist learning new skills, experimenting with untested ideas, and changing unproductive behaviors.

A word of caution on group dynamics and positive emotions: Even though it may feel as if you're soaring on the wings of angels, dissociating in response to strong positive emotions can be inconsiderate or even dangerous if you're engaging in activities with others. I sometimes see people nearly run horses into the ground when feeling thrilled or exhilarated. Invariably, they're confused and disappointed when I stop them, complaining that I'm acting like a stern parent putting an end to their fun. In these cases, however, it's clear that the horse isn't having fun; he's becoming increasingly unbalanced and frantic, approaching hyperstimulation, getting ready to either fight, flee, or freeze, which could easily result in injury for both horse and rider.

Such a seeming loss of control is, of course, what gives feelings like passion and ecstasy a bad name in some circles, but it's actually a lack of intersubjective awareness that causes problems: the tendency of certain people to become self-possessed in the name of enjoyment or transcendence, to the point that they neglect to notice the effect they're having on others. While artists, innovators, and mystics must sometimes wander off alone, temporarily suspending contact with the world to bring something new back, visionary *leadership* requires exercising increasingly higher tolerance for powerful positive emotions, allowing people to experience a wide range of inspirational feelings without losing sight of the needs and reactions of those around them.

Subsequent guiding principles explore how to engage authentic positive feelings to reward desirable behavior, set boundaries, and motivate others, inspiring groups to work together, endure long-term challenges, and perform at higher levels of innovation and effectiveness. In the meantime, it's important to notice how some feelings signal success in certain areas or encourage the achievement of desirable effects and states of consciousness.

Emotions facilitating rest, reflection, and renewal:	Peacefulness, calmness, tranquility, contentment, serenity, satisfaction, fulfillment, bliss
Emotions that strengthen relationship and connection:	Appreciation, empathy, gratitude, encouragement, tenderness, trust, admiration, love, compassion
Energizing emotions:	Enthusiasm, excitement, playfulness, amusement, happiness, joy, anticipation, exuberance, glee, delight, rapture, ecstasy
Inspirational emotions:	Awe, wonder, curiosity, hope, astonishment, intrigue, fascination
Empowering emotions:	Confidence, pride, passion, courage, fortitude, self-respect, conviction, fervor, dedication

Ultimately, it's important to exercise the ability to use *all* emotions as information, which is why the following abbreviated version of the Emotional Message Chart summarizes the instructive feelings that humans are most likely to shy away from. Your increasing skill at staying thoughtful and engaged in the midst of these emotions, when others become fearful, confused, agitated, aggressive, or defensive, will automatically put you in a valued leadership role. Your interest in the messages behind these emotions will have a focusing, calming effect on the entire group, allowing them to problem solve and get back on task much more quickly.

Emotional Message Chart

EMOTION	MESSAGE	QUESTIONS TO ASK OF THE EMOTION	INTENSIFICATION
Fear	Intuitive, focused awareness of a threat to your well-being (external threat)	What is the threat? What action must I take to move to a position of safety?	Worry, anxiety, confusion, panic, terror, dissociation, dulling of the senses
Vulnerability	Something significant is about to change or be revealed. (internal threat to self-image, beliefs, comfortable habits)	What belief, behavior, perception, or comfortable habit is being challenged? How might my life change if I accept this new insight?	Panic, rage
Anger	A physical or emotional boundary has been crossed (sometimes unconsciously, sometimes by a person who's trying to bend you to his or her will).	What must be protected? What boundary must be established or restored?	Rage, fury, deflected rage (exploding at an innocent bystander), boredom, apathy (masks anger that can't be dealt with; a nonviolent coping strategy)
Agitation or anxiety (often mistaken for anger) (This is not chronic, long-term anxiety but anxiety experienced in the presence of a specific person.)	The person interacting with you is incongruent. (Remember: Such people aren't necessarily dishonest but may be dealing with personal issues that are none of your business.)	What is the true emotion behind the other person's mask of control, friendliness, or well-being, and is it directed at me?	Rage, mistrust

Emotional Message Chart (*continued*)

EMOTION	MESSAGE	QUESTIONS TO ASK OF THE EMOTION	INTENSIFICATION
Frustration	The action you're taking is not effective.	Where is the block? What can I do differently? Who can I ask for ideas or assistance?	Rage, powerlessness
Guilt	A critique of a destructive, neglectful, or abusive *behavior*. (This can be an internal critique or a transgression that others are bringing to your attention.)	What questionable behavior or action did I engage in? What was my motivation? How can I get my needs met in a more productive way? Who can help me change this hurtful habit?	Denial, blame, shame, projection
Shame	A possible indication that you are being scapegoated. Or a personal critique of a "defective" state of consciousness or being.	Am I being shamed by others? If so, am I being objectified or used as a scapegoat? How can I set boundaries with these people — without shaming *them*? Or am I feeling shame for an old way of being or perceiving the world? If so, what destructive behaviors must I change to fully enter this new, more conscious, compassionate, and responsible phase of life?	Despair, blame, projection, suicidal urge, bullying

Emotional Message Chart (*continued*)

EMOTION	MESSAGE	QUESTIONS TO ASK OF THE EMOTION	INTENSIFICATION
Envy	The person you envy models a talent, success, position, or lifestyle you want to develop or acquire.	What aspects of this person's life, career, personal qualities, relationships, or talents inspire me to excel? What professional training or personal skills must I develop to achieve similar success? Who can I enlist for support in this next state of growth?	Hero worship, rivalry, resentment
Jealousy	An inequity in resources, pay, recognition, opportunity, or relationship has come to your attention.	Exactly who or what am I jealous of? Is this inequity an oversight? If so, who can rectify the situation? If not, how can I strategize and gather support to change an unfair system?	Resentment, outrage
Disappoint-ment	The outcome (contrary to what you desired or envisioned) did not live up to your expectations.	What was I hoping for or expecting to happen? Was this realistic? If so, how can I better communicate my vision to those *capable* of carrying it out? If not, how can I modify my vision and better train, prepare, and support the people involved?	Anger, frustration, mistrust, powerlessness, apathy

Emotional Message Chart (*continued*)

EMOTION	MESSAGE	QUESTIONS TO ASK OF THE EMOTION	INTENSIFICATION
Sadness (You choose when and how to let go.)	Loss is imminent and in your best interest.	What must be released? What must be rejuvenated?	Despair, despondence
Grief (No choice in letting go. Grief often includes anger. Having something you value taken away, even by impersonal life circumstances, is experienced emotionally as a boundary violation.)	A significant loss or death has occurred, usually due to circumstances beyond your control.	What must be mourned? What must be memorialized, appreciated, or celebrated?	Depression
Depression (This message refers to situational depression, not clinical depression, which may involve a neurochemical imbalance.)	"Ingenious stagnation," "stop sign of the soul"	What activities or relationships drain my energy? What new direction gives me energy?	Loss of self, loss of life's purpose, suicidal urges, physical illness
Suicidal urge (This message is not related to wanting to end long-term physical pain from illness.)	Some aspect of the life you're leading (not your physical existence) must end.	What must end now? What must be culled?	Becoming like a "soulless automaton," physical death

Chapter Fourteen

GUIDING PRINCIPLE 2
Listen to Your Horse

Sometimes people ask me how I can tell what a horse is feeling. To the untrained eye, equine facial expressions do seem more limited than ours. However, horses more than make up for this through consistent, meaningful changes in ear position and body posture that are recognizable at a considerable distance, an important adaptation for social animals grazing over large territories. Humans — who cannot move their ears — probably look stoic to the average horse, like a schoolmarm with her hair pulled back in a severe bun. And just think how close you have to stand to a person to see her wink, frown, or smile, let alone clench her jaw in anger, turn red with embarrassment, or well up with the first sign of tears.

Science, however, has recently discovered that people are better at reading body postures than you might expect — sometimes trusting these cues more than facial expressions in determining others' moods. In *The Age of Empathy: Nature's Lessons for a Kinder Society*, biologist Frans de Waal cites a number of clever studies illustrating this point. In one experiment, scientists pasted an angry face on a fearful body and a fearful face on an angry body. At first the subjects were noticeably confused by the incongruity, which slowed down their reaction time, but "the body posture won out when the subjects were asked to judge the emotional state of the depicted person." In another experiment, when people watched pictures of fearful body postures with the faces blacked out, "the subjects' faces still registered fear."

These and others studies led de Waal to develop the Body First Theory, which holds that sometimes "emotions arise from our bodies" and are also transferred between people through the body first. Most people believe that emotions arise from thoughts and memories, and while this is often accurate, the brain is not always in charge of this process, not by a long shot. Work by Candace Pert and other researchers active in the field of psychoneuroimmunology proved that the molecules carrying emotional information (called neuropeptides) are generated not only by the brain but also by sites throughout the body, most dramatically the heart and the gut. As it turns out, recommendations to "follow your heart" or "pay attention to gut feelings" are *not* metaphors. Researchers subsequently discovered that a significant number of the heart's cells are neural, and that the gut has more neural cells than the spinal column, prompting some scientists to consider the brain as one of *three* somatic intelligence centers that can gather, process, and, yes, even communicate information (see chapter 3).

In the late twentieth century, scientists also confirmed that the body-mind connection is a two-way street. Postures and facial expressions not only *express* our emotional state, they can *change* our emotional state. So, while we smile when we are happy, "our mood can be improved by simply lifting the corners of our mouth," de Waal reveals. "If people are asked to bite down on a pencil lengthwise, taking care not to let the pencil touch their lips (thus forcing the mouth into a smilelike shape), they judge cartoons funnier than if they have been asked to frown." Similarly, political, social, and religious organizations have a long history of creating rigid, compliant followers by promoting submissive or militaristic, machinelike postures and behaviors, drawing, as we now know, on the contagious, consciousness-altering nature of body language.

Yet as de Waal also emphasizes, even seriously repressed people have some choice in the matter. We all know, for instance, that there "are times when matching the other's emotions is not a good idea. When we're facing a furious boss, for example, we'd get into deep trouble if we were to mimic his attitude."

Social intelligence involves accurately reading people's feelings and using this information thoughtfully. This also requires noticing when you're catching an emotion or body posture that originated in someone else. For leaders, it can even involve recognizing unproductive emotional trends and *turning them around*, "driving emotions in the right direction to have a positive impact on earnings or strategy," as Goleman, Boyatzis, and McKee emphasize in *Primal Leadership* (see chapter 2).

Contrary to popular belief, however, this doesn't mean sweeping uncomfortable feelings and concerns under the rug. Add current research on the contagious nature of emotion, and you realize that to turn negative feelings around in a group, you must *transform* them, not hide them. And that means you must first turn them around in yourself, recognizing that your own heart rate, blood pressure, and body posture are being affected by the feelings of others, and vice versa. Sounds like an evil little hall of mirrors, doesn't it? But it's the "other 90 percent" at work, plain and simple.

Hidden Emotions

Traditionally, riders have been told to never, ever show fear to a horse, presumably to keep the animal from taking advantage of a perceived weakness. Life at the barn would be so much simpler if only people could comply with this age-old request. But as it turns out, horses *sense* as much as see emotion. So even if you manage to approximate the body posture of confidence, these highly sensitive prey animals can still tell you're afraid if your heart rate and blood pressure are elevated. To a horse, congruence means not only that your words, actions, facial expressions, and body language are in sync but that your "insides match your outside."

As I noted earlier, science shows that human beings are also affected by the hidden emotions of others. You can ignore that information, as most of us are taught to do through decades of cultural conditioning, but it still affects you unconsciously. And sadly, what remains unconscious ultimately *controls* you, usually at the most stressful, inconvenient moments when it really would be helpful to be playing, consciously, with a full deck.

In chapter 2, I cited several studies exploring the effects of *affect contagion*, the (usually) unconscious transfer of feelings between living beings. For our purposes here, it's important to emphasize once again that hiding emotion adds stress to group interactions, potentially causing others to act defensively or have trouble thinking clearly and creatively. In *Social Intelligence: The New Science of Human Relationships*, Goleman showed that not only does a person's blood pressure escalate when he tries to suppress feeling, but *the blood pressure of those interacting with him also rises.*

Remember: unless you're a sociopath, your heart rate and blood pressure rise when you're frightened or angry, even when you're wearing your best poker face. It takes extra effort to hide these feelings, energy that you and the people you're interacting with could be using for other purposes. When emotions are suppressed over the long term, they intensify into other, more troublesome complexes and impulses (see the Emotional Message Chart, at the end of chapter 13), eventually causing people to act out in unproductive ways when the pressure reaches critical mass, sometimes damaging relationships irreparably. Our culturally induced emphasis on verbal communication lessens awareness of this dynamic in its earlier, more manageable stages, but anyone who retains or reclaims awareness of affect contagion has a definite edge in influencing the nonverbal elements of social interactions.

In horses and other prey species, the volume of this recently discovered "sixth" sense is turned way up. These animals become noticeably agitated in the presence of people who are incongruent, who try to cover anger, fear, or sadness with an appearance of well-being. This is not an equine judgment of our tendency to lie about what we're really feeling; it's a reflection of emotion's physiology — and its contagious nature. Horses, who exhibit heightened stress when a human handler tries to suppress emotion, also show signs of relief the moment this person acknowledges a hidden or simply unconscious feeling, even if the emotion itself is still present. By making the fear or anger conscious, by becoming congruent, the handler effectively lowers his own blood pressure, even if only slightly. But it's enough to drop the horse's blood pressure in response, which the animal demonstrates by sighing, licking and chewing, and/or lowering his head.

So what are we to do with this information? Turn a business meeting into an encounter group? *Absolutely not*, you'll be happy to know. Deciphering the information that emotions present can be handled efficiently and professionally. Subsequent guiding principles, in fact, are designed to help you do just that. It's also important for leaders to remember that *authentic* positive feelings are contagious too. A person who truly feels peaceful in situations that unnerve others can have a calming effect on everyone around her.

Skills associated with driving others' emotions in a more productive direction are outlined in the next lesson, Guiding Principle 3, which explores how to manage contagious emotions. First, however, you need to notice how your body is affected by your own and others' unspoken feelings. The good news is that, rather than being victimized by this long-neglected and thoroughly natural process, you can use it to your advantage.

Engaging daily with your body as a sentient tuner, receiver, and amplifier for that "other 90 percent," you'll gain proficiency in accessing all kinds of nonverbal information floating around, information that will give you a significant edge in achieving your goals and enjoying more satisfying personal relationships, to boot.

A Mind of Its Own

I first realized that my body had a mind of its own when I noticed my mare paying attention to my body as if it *were* another horse. What I *thought* I was communicating was much less important to her than what I was unconsciously conveying through posture, heart rate, muscle tension, breathing, and the various emotions that either caused those physiological responses to rise and fall or (as we now know) were created by the body first in response to the environment.

And so I began to think of my body as the horse that my mind rides around on. As with any horse, I could form a mutually respectful partnership with it, or I could rein it in and spur it on, refusing to listen to it, only to have it throw me during stressful situations and head for the hills when I needed its cooperation most. What's more, I realized, when people are taught to focus exclusively on what an authority figure is saying, suppressing gut feelings and wildly fluttering heartbeats, their bodies' intuitive wisdom and natural warning systems are muzzled, allowing, in the worst-case scenario, a malevolent boss, cult leader, or dictator to corral them for any number of purposes against their better judgment, as history has shown time and time again. Accessing my body's wisdom, then, was an act of revolution and empowerment.

It also took practice, like learning to ride a bike, drive a car, or operate a computer. Over time, the procedure became second nature, applicable to countless situations in everyday life and at work. However, truly *listening* to my body was quite different from what was taught by the vast majority of relaxation, meditation, massage, yoga, and sport-oriented coaches, including equestrians.

When I first started riding lessons in my midthirties, I was surprised at how little I could *feel*, being a musician and all. But I had been sitting in a chair for twenty years, holding my viola between my chin and my upraised left arm, an extremely unnatural position that my body adapted to over time. As a gymnast in high school and in exercise classes as an adult, I would demand all kinds of other outlandish things from my body, pushing it through the pain, sometimes experiencing elation, sometimes experiencing frustration, all the while focusing on whatever posture was optimal for the sport in question.

And then there was the correct riding posture for sitting gracefully on the back of a trotting horse. My first instructors were like drill sergeants, shouting at me to keep my heels down, my shoulders straight, and my hands still. "Relax!" they would scream, causing the hair on the back of my neck to rise and my legs to tighten, whereupon my mare would lunge forward as I gripped her belly with my thighs, inadvertently giving her the cue to go faster or even buck, at which point I would either hang on or crash to the ground, getting the air knocked out of me. Then, gasping and wheezing, checking for broken bones, I would get back on because, well, everyone knows what you're supposed to do when you fall off a horse...

Then I found a more advanced instructor, and she raised the bar higher. I was expected to use my own body to *help* the horse achieve whatever I asked. No longer allowed to pull back on the reins or kick furiously, I was instructed to use my seat bones to communicate with my mare, either moving ahead of her current rhythm to speed up, or working against her forward movement to slow down, like pedaling backward on a bicycle without moving my legs. To transition up to a canter where her *right front* leg was leading, giving her optimal balance to move in a clockwise circle, I had to sense when the horse's *left back* hoof hit the ground and give the proper "aid" (supportive, well-timed cue) then. This meant I not only had to know where all my own body parts were, using them independently and purposefully for a variety of desired effects, but also had to literally *feel* what my horse's legs were doing from moment to moment.

Body language took on a whole new meaning at that point. But spending time with herds of horses took me to a much deeper, completely unexpected place. I realized that *their* emotions could dramatically affect my body. And that, for better or worse, my own emotions could affect the entire herd.

A Language Older Than Words

To even notice this dynamic, let alone learn to use it productively, I literally had to "get off my high horse" and spend large amounts of time with these animals on the ground. And while I'd like to say that curiosity led me down this surprisingly fruitful path, a seriously injured mare was my sole motivation for hanging out with a herd of horses on *their* terms. As I described earlier in the book, in 1994 Rasa, a beautiful three-year-old Arabian full of enthusiasm, power, and potential — the very first horse I learned to start under saddle — showed up lame the morning after an extended trail ride. The injury, which I initially thought was related solely to the stress of a big black dog chasing us down the wash, turned out to be more serious than expected. Much to my growing disappointment and despair, x-rays revealed that her right back stifle (similar to the knee in humans) was damaged, probably congenitally, making it doubtful that I would ever ride her again, quashing my advanced-riding ambitions. I'd even sold my viola to pay for this purebred mare; I wouldn't be able to buy another horse in the foreseeable future.

During Rasa's initial, three-month convalescence, I couldn't even engage in conventional ground training activities with her. And yet we were deeply bonded. While other people joked about my "thousand-pound pet," I yearned to spend time with her. So after I got off work as an apprentice trainer riding other people's young horses, I would mill around a large back pasture with Rasa, my husband's former cow horse Noche, and several other boarders' horses. And it was there that I gained access to a secret world, one that would alter everything I thought I knew about how living beings relate and communicate.

I was intrigued, first of all, to find that mainstream theories about dominance hierarchies didn't quite fit this herd's behavior. Coming from a variety of backgrounds, the horses in Rasa's pasture seemed to *trade off* the leadership role according to who was calmest, most experienced, or most invested in whatever situation arose. And there was something else happening, something I couldn't quite put my finger on, some kind of nonverbal coordination I couldn't begin to explain. Then a month later I was hit, in the gut, with the knowledge that horses could broadcast fear over considerable distances *before* they were able to move their thousand-pound bodies into flight-or-fight pose, let alone attack or take off running.

That pivotal October afternoon started out calmly enough. I was grooming Rasa, feeling unusually relaxed and content, enjoying the perfectly clear, deep-blue desert sky and the warm, dry wind gently blowing through my hair. Noche was grazing with the other horses at the far end of their two-acre pasture; the black mare was dozing as I braided her mane and stroked her shiny coat. Suddenly — out of nowhere — I felt like I'd been kicked in the stomach. My gut clenched, my heart skipped a beat, and my breath caught in my throat as a strange invisible force seemed to move up my body toward my brain, turning my neck and causing me to look at Noche, who was simultaneously lifting his head up from the ground in obvious alarm. At that moment, some involuntary switch was tripped, and all our bodies became coordinated. Noche and the other horses took off. Rasa and I too began to run — away from a threat I couldn't see. Yet as the rest of the herd galloped on by, my stubby legs failed me, and my human brain finally took over, wondering what the hell was going on.

It was a man on a mountain bike, riding a nearby trail. And I realized that from a horse's perspective, this guy looked downright sinister. Dressed in a fluorescent silver-and-cobalt shirt, with orange skulls on his little black socks spinning around and around as he pedaled, he seemed to slither, fast, hissing through the sand, like some demented cross between a snake and a massive, multicolored beetle: His black backpack, filled with water, rose and fell like wings trying to unfurl as he negotiated the rough terrain. And his helmet, shaped like the head of the creature from *Alien*, gave way to mirrored sunglasses, accentuating a disturbing, grossly unnatural appearance.

If this lithe and suspect creature had been a mountain lion, I would have been the first to die: the horses easily outran me as I took those first unconscious steps in sync with the herd. But when I realized, seconds later, that I was not about to be eaten, the whole thing struck me as incredibly funny. I was just about to turn around and let the horses know that everything was fine, when I discovered that they had already sensed my relaxation and amusement and were now standing right behind me, staring curiously, yet still cautiously, at the insect man, as if they too were smiling, though a bit more nervously than I.

As Frans de Waal observed in *The Age of Empathy*, "The primacy of the body is sometimes summarized in the phrase 'I must be afraid, because I'm running.'" That's exactly how I felt the day I experienced a whole herd of horses speaking through my body in a language older than words. Over time, I realized that I could use these "body-first" signals to sense what a fearful colt or angry stallion was *about to do* before he could actually do it. And in that split-second delay, I could turn a dangerous trend around — *if* I breathed into the rising tension in my own body and loosened my spine, creating a response I now call "the opposite of fear."

In fostering a relaxed yet heightened awareness that literally saved my life with challenging horses, I also became more conscious of sensations and postures my body would take on in the presence of other people. And I realized, long before I found research to validate my experience, that humans share emotions the way horses do. If I really paid attention to what was happening during interactions with my own species, I could sense others' moods and sometimes turn an unproductive emotional trend around — through body language conveying "the opposite of fear" combined with discussions addressing people's unspoken concerns. This was more difficult, though certainly less dangerous, than working with horses, not only because I had to learn to speak and feel at the same time, but also because I had to find ways of addressing uncomfortable emotions and other subjects that no one really wanted to talk about, including me!

And so today, I'm inviting you to take the first step in mastering that "other 90 percent" — namely, listening to the marvelous sentient being your own mind rides around on. Over time, if you treat your body as an intelligent partner, not a slave or a senseless hunk of meat, life will become not only much more interesting but also more fulfilling and empowering as a result. The catch is that once everyone in our human herd learns how to do this, we'll have to imagine a new form of leadership, one that values feeling and reason, empathy and assertiveness, transparency, cooperation, and mutual empowerment — a style of leadership that, I'm happy to report, Rasa, Noche, and those other horses showed me in that very same pasture years ago.

Listening to Your Body

The body scan described at the end of this chapter is a simple six-point technique for using the body as a sensing device, as a tuner, receiver, and amplifier for information coming from the environment, other people, and one's own internal compass, safety system, authenticity meter, intuition, and genius.

This is not a form of self-hypnosis or a technique for promoting relaxation or optimal body posture. When scanning the body to collect information, you do *not* want to "relax out of" or adjust any sensations or postures on purpose. Rather, notice how your body changes according to environmental influences, including encounters with other people.

Later, I will teach you how to use this information for various purposes, but in order to build emotional and social intelligence you must first become conscious of "what *is* happening" with your body, instead of fixating on what *should* or *shouldn't* be happening, or ignoring the body completely, as most of us are taught to do.

If you've been sitting at a desk for twenty years, suppressing emotion because you don't know what else to do with it, you might be reluctant to use the body-scanning technique for one of two reasons:

1. Fear of failure (comments indicating this include: I can't feel anything below my neck. I feel like a brain rolling around on a metal box. I feel fine. I feel numb. What do you want me to feel? I never really understand what people mean when they tell me to "listen to my body." This is dumb. When's lunch? Where's my Blackberry?)
2. Fear of feeling overwhelmed (comments include: I've been suppressing so much for so long I don't know what might come up. I don't want to open the floodgates. If I were to start crying I'd never stop. It's dangerous to go into the body. I'm not here for therapy!)

It's important to realize, first of all, that your body registers information from the environment and other beings all day long, changing your heart rate, breathing, and posture in response to these stimuli regardless of whether you're aware of it or not.

The idea that emotional-intelligence skills automatically fall under the heading of therapy, however, goes back to the ancient Greek stoics, rationalists of the seventeenth century, and religious traditions that believe emotions are by-products of a dysfunctional mind or evidence of an "unevolved, lowly animal nature" taking over. We've since learned that emotion is essential to the *healthy functioning* of the mind. In *Descartes' Error*, for instance, award-winning neuroscientist Antonio Damasio shows that brain injury patients who've lost contact with key emotional centers while maintaining full reasoning powers have trouble making simple decisions. In *Radical Knowing*, consciousness researcher Christian de Quincey writes that people must learn to "feel their thinking" to develop stronger relationships *and* access a more creative, balanced approach to life.

If emotions were innately dangerous, artists would automatically be traumatized by their work, as would anyone who viewed their paintings, listened to their music, or attended their plays and films. As a violist in orchestras and chamber music groups, I was encouraged to express all kinds of emotions from age ten on, everything from elation and power to rage, deep longing, and sorrow — without losing my place in the music, losing contact with others, or going insane. When I visited my alma mater twenty years later, I found that our concertmaster, a talented violinist named Rick Smreck, had become one of the high school's guidance counselors. As we reminisced, he told me that he'd been intrigued to find that the vast majority of our fellow players had become highly successful in all kinds of fields, excelling as doctors, lawyers, engineers, writers, and professors. He believed our music training gave us important emotional- and social-intelligence skills that few people access in today's increasingly mechanistic education system.

Abuse or trauma survivors *can* become easily overwhelmed by their own feelings and body sensations, as well as by strong emotions coming from others. At work these people often function respectably, not so much exploding as dissociating during tense situations, becoming foggy, spacey, and unable to act assertively. As mentioned in Guiding Principle 1, this often leads to the "perpetual assistant" phenomenon, where an executive secretary or computer specialist seems talented, supportive, and filled with great ideas. Yet because this person goes blank under stress, he or she is repeatedly passed over for promotions.

Some "perpetual assistants" are shy or highly sensitive people who need assertiveness and public-speaking skills. Others are untreated abuse survivors. In the latter case, as with any trauma survivor, emotional-intelligence skills should be practiced in conjunction with treatment by a counselor specializing in trauma.

A number of Eponaquest instructors who are licensed therapists have found the body scan useful in teaching important self-regulation and mindfulness skills that also translate to success in work and relationships. But if you know or suspect you may be a trauma survivor, contact one of these professionals, not only to learn this technique, but also to gain long-term support in moving beyond other challenges that make it difficult to function under stress. Equine-facilitated psychotherapy, in fact, is an unusually efficient and often fun way to move beyond the past and embrace a new, empowered way of life free from fears that were once legitimate and debilitating.

The Binary Code

If you're more comfortable relating to digital processors than to horses or people, it helps to think of the body's ability to register tension and relaxation as a kind of binary code. Computers receive, store, and translate all kinds of complex information through a series of ones and zeros, and the body operates through a similar principle. By noticing which body parts feel tense, which feel relaxed, and how this changes in various situations, you'll be scanning your body. You can also notice when you're holding your breath or breathing fast and shallowly, and when you are naturally breathing more deeply — evidence of the sympathetic and parasympathetic nervous systems in action, another somatic binary code that we'll be engaging consciously for more specific purposes later on.

If you feel "nothing," notice if you're feeling numb, neutral, or calm. If you're feeling numb, you may be dissociating (disconnecting from the body to avoid feeling overwhelmed). However, just as often, people say they feel nothing when their body feels relaxed, safe, or just plain good.

It's important to notice positive or peaceful sensations as well as negative or tension-related sensations. As a leader, you will at times be charged with helping people feel calmer, safer, or more energized and enthusiastic, so you have to start paying attention to these sensations and emotions in yourself and others simultaneously. Some people have been taught to emphasize what's wrong while ignoring what's actually going well. Others gloss over negative emotions and sensations in favor of an overoptimistic, Pollyanna-like attitude. Masterful leaders are secure in gaining information from both positive and negative sensations and emotions, and their comfort in this regard is contagious, helping to calm and focus people in tense situations.

One Horse at a Time

We all feel overwhelmed at times. If you've been suppressing emotion and sensation for years, you might be worried about "opening the floodgates" when you invite the body to speak. For this reason, people who relate to computer metaphors find it helpful to add a "self-regulation program" to their "hard drives" as they boot up the first time.

To get started, imagine "breathing into" the intelligence centers in your heart and your gut, not to relax anything, but to infuse the neural cells concentrated in these areas with oxygen and awareness. The goal is to create a kind of "email connection" between the brain in your head and the other two "brains" in your body. So as you breathe into your heart and then your gut, also imagine that the "light" of consciousness centered in your head is traveling down your body, lighting up these other intelligence centers as you "plug them in."

Before you invite your body to send messages to your brain, however, let your brain send an important message to your body. Tell the body that you'll listen to its concerns and insights, *but only if it releases this information one message at a time.* You should also do this with any sensation that seems to hold a lot of information, energy, or tension, such as an exceedingly nervous stomach, a lump in your throat that's holding a lot of emotion back, a fist in your heart that's struggling to "get a grip," or a dizzy, "crowded" head.

Some people find it helpful to imagine a whole herd of mustangs crowded into an intensely activated sensation. Even inexperienced riders know that when you approach a corral of feisty, untrained horses, you don't swing the gates wide open and let all them all run free. You take one horse out at a time, halter it, teach it a few basic safety and socialization skills, and then go back and get the next horse. Because somatic intelligence often communicates more like an artist or a poet than a scientist (and can jump-start creativity as a result — a concept we'll explore later), the body seems to find this wild-horse image meaningful and enjoyable, immediately understanding the self-regulation wisdom it conveys. And I have to say that, in teaching abuse survivors and soldiers with post–traumatic stress disorder how to use the body scan, the request to "take out one horse at a time" or release "one message at a time" works much more easily than most people would expect. It is as if the body, like any horse or child or employee, appreciates limits that are set fairly and clearly, even as it wants to speak and (finally) be heard.

The Language of Sensation

The first step of the body scan involves mapping the sensations. In doing this, you draw your awareness to each part of your body and notice *what* you are feeling without trying to relax out of it or change it in any way. The following chart offers some examples of sensations people commonly encounter. Remember to notice what feels good or peaceful, in addition to tension-related sensations.

Mapping the Sensations	
HEAD	Clear, cloudy, dizzy, spinning, crowded, dull aches, sharp pains, neutral, peaceful, activated, "lit up," filled with ideas.
EYES/EYELIDS	Fluttery, heavy, tired, itching, aching. Sometimes you can feel one eye more strongly than the other. Sometimes you can see colors or images behind closed eyes.
NOSE	Clear, stopped up (sometimes on one side more than the other), dry, itchy.
EARS	Clear, stopped up, hypersensitive to sound, muffled. Sometimes you can hear internal tones or hear more clearly out of one ear than the other. (This can actually change from moment to moment in some situations, so don't automatically assume that muffled or uneven hearing is always a physical ailment; the body can actually send messages through such sensations.)
JAW	Relaxed, clenched (either evenly or more on one side than the other). If your jaw is clenched, don't automatically try to relax it. You can access important information from a clenched jaw during the "get the message" process described in the next section.
NECK/THROAT	Open, relaxed, sore, lump in throat, breath caught in throat, dull ache, tired, sharp pain in a specific area, aligned, out of alignment, strong, weak, wobbly.
SHOULDERS	Even, slumped forward, bunched up to your ears, rigid/militaristic, heavy, one shoulder higher than the other.

Mapping the Sensations (*continued*)	
BACK	Aligned, out of alignment, tense, relaxed, sharp pain behind shoulder blade, lower-back pain, neutral, strong, weak, no backbone.
ARMS/HANDS	Neutral, one arm longer than the other, energy running up and down arms, tennis elbow, carpal tunnel syndrome, one hand larger than the other, oversized "clown hands," healing hands, energy in one or both hands. (Note that even old or chronic injuries can carry important information. Most notable is the ability of an injury to become activated during times when your safety may be at risk. People sometimes notice that chronic pains lessen or relax completely in the presence of horses, other pets, or other people they feel comfortable with.)
CHEST/HEART	Warm, connected, cold, numb or shut down, fist in heart, strong, fast or irregular heartbeat, walled off, radiating light or love.
STOMACH	Full, empty, queasy, strong, powerful, excited, butterflies in stomach, nervous, fearful, folded over in a fetal position, kicked in the belly, peaceful.
SEXUAL ORGANS	Calm, neutral, excited, emptiness in womb (can be an open, creative emptiness or a lonely, longing emptiness), cramped, full, fertile, protective, powerful, numb.
LEGS/FEET	Strong, even, one leg longer than the other, weak in the knees, tenseness in one or both calves or gluts, locked knee(s), sore, pins and needles, toes curled, weak ankles, feet grounded, rooted in the ground, floating above the ground.

Also check for body postures — usually involving some combination of shoulder, back, pelvis, and solar plexus engagement, though sometimes also head, neck, arms, feet, or leg position. And remember, this is not a relaxation or self-hypnosis technique, but a simple body-awareness or mindfulness technique.

In preparation for the scan, don't roll your neck, loosen your shoulders, try to stand straight, or ground yourself. Just stand or sit in a position that comes naturally to you at that moment (as postures can change from day to day and situation to situation).

Getting the Message

Rather than second-guess the information contained in a specific sensation or body posture, it's advantageous to "ask the body itself." An easy way to do this is to pick a prominent sensation — let's say shoulders slumped forward. Accentuate that posture (rather than trying to adjust, relax, or wriggle out of it). Then "breathe" into the sensation without trying to change it, in this case imagining that you're creating an email link between your slumped shoulders and the brain in your head. Ask, silently, one of the following questions: "What information is held in this sensation?" or "What is the purpose of this posture?" or "What do you want to tell me?" or simply "What do you want me to know?"

Clear your thinking brain of preconceived notions and just wait for an answer to rise up from the body to the brain. Sometimes the information is obvious and received quickly. In the case of slumped shoulders, many people feel "the weight of the world" or see a statue of Atlas hoisting the earth on his back. Another common image is a yoke around the shoulders. One woman saw this yoke attached to a wagon carrying all her family members. Through this image, she quickly realized that it wasn't work responsibilities that were getting her down. Her spouse and children weren't "carrying their own weight" around the house. When she received the message and spoke it out loud to me, her shoulders lifted and rebalanced themselves.

The fascinating thing about this technique is that if you truly get the message, the body *releases the tension and/or adjusts itself*. Really! I've seen it a thousand times. Conversely, if the mind is second-guessing the body, quite often there's no change in sensation or posture. I often see this happening with people who say, "Well, I *think* I'm just a little stressed." The key word here is *think*. Don't think, *ask!*

I stumbled upon this technique while working with beginning riding students. I was teaching a woman who couldn't keep her heels down (an important position for optimal balance and safety — you don't want your feet sliding through the stirrups, especially if you fall, as you could easily be dragged). After telling "Maggie" to keep her heels down ad nauseum, I finally wondered what would happen if she asked her ankles what they were trying to accomplish; they truly seemed to have a mind of their own. I directed her to momentarily accentuate the tension in her ankles, causing her heels to rise even higher, and then ask her body what its purpose was in emphasizing this position despite our efforts to change it.

Then, of course, she asked me *how in the world* she was supposed to ask her body anything. For some reason, I suggested she "breathe into that tension, sending it oxygen and awareness with an open, inquiring mind." Within seconds, Maggie's eyes shot wide open and her head jerked to the side, as if a faint electric current were jolting her brain.

"I keep getting the phrase *'Gotta be on your toes!'* she said. "It's playing over and over again."

Much to my amazement, Maggie's ankles seemed to relax of their own accord. I asked her to continue to breathe into her ankles and ask what they were trying to convey through this phrase. Was she a former ballet dancer? Or was her body communicating some kind of concern by creating a posture that was essentially a metaphor: "Gotta be on your toes!"

Maggie's ankles continued to relax as she remembered falling off a horse at her previous instructor's barn. A flashy appaloosa she "didn't feel connected to" had shied and dumped her when the wind suddenly picked up. "Gotta be on your toes" made sense, as Maggie was once again riding a horse she didn't know. So we addressed this concern by allowing her to dismount and do some ground work, leading and bonding with my older, more experienced lesson horse, contrasting his gentle, poised demeanor to that of the younger, more spirited gelding who had thrown her at another stable the year before. Thirty minutes later, she remounted and experienced no trouble keeping her heels down.

The following week, however, Maggie told me that she'd been riding a friend's horse during an impromptu trail ride, and her ankles had tensed up again. This time, she quickly read the message, got off, and walked the horse for a while, petting him for a few moments. Then she got back on, feeling safer and more connected. Once again, her heels stayed down.

Everyone's body "speaks" a bit differently, though there are some patterns. Some of my clients, including one skeptical scientist who didn't consider himself the least bit intuitive or creative, have found that breathing into a sensation produces colors with consistent symbolic meanings, like red for fear, yellow for caution, blue for comfort, and lavender for love or connection. Some people "hear" brief clichés, strange poetic phrases, or song fragments that, when they later look up the lyrics on the Internet, turn out to be relevant to a current challenge in their lives.

I advise scanners to close their eyes when checking for a message. The body, which as I mentioned earlier often speaks more like an artist or a poet than a scientist, can relay visual material, sometimes in a sketchy, monochromatic format, sometimes in Technicolor. Once in a while, people experience intricate mythical or metaphorical minifilms, "waking dreams" that turn out to be deeply meaningful and even transformational. More often, people see static, symbolic pictures. Some of my students have accessed unique, highly evocative images that they've turned into business logos.

People occasionally receive brief, nonsensical visions or phrases. One teenager felt a tension in her thighs before directing her horse to move from a walk to a trot. When she breathed into the constriction, she saw a pterodactyl flying next to a purple sun setting over a mountain shaped like a pineapple. Yet when she acknowledged this strange scene out loud and checked with her body again, the tightness released completely, suggesting there was no further need to interpret the message. Apparently, by sending herself a goofy image that made us both laugh, this colorful young rider transformed the anxiety she often experienced in changing gaits. Her body wasn't sending a metaphor to be analyzed; it was urging her to laugh and have fun, apparently advising her not to take riding so seriously.

In scanning down your body, learning to receive its sometimes mundane, sometimes creative, sometimes amusing or uplifting messages, you'll not only activate the wisdom of that "other 90 percent" but might also find that you're never bored while waiting in line at the bank or the DMV again. More important, you can use this information to make decisions that draw on the wisdom of all three of your "brains," as one trauma survivor learned to do in her very first session.

"Emily," a therapist who had read one of my previous books, brought a rape survivor to do some equine-facilitated learning activities with me, reporting that "Amy" seemed to be stuck, unable to move forward with her life. But Dr. Emily also had some concerns about the safety of this work. While hopeful that these sensitive yet powerful animals might provide an important key, she wasn't sure if Amy would be grounded enough to interact with a loose horse, even one known to be unusually generous with fearful amateurs.

Sure enough, doing a quick body scan before entering the round pen with Rasa, Amy couldn't feel her feet. Yet rather than asking her to "make" her body "get grounded," as she had been taught to do — with limited success — I invited her to explore what her body was trying to achieve. Knowing that Amy had been working with Emily for over a year and had already learned some important self-regulation skills, I felt confident that she was ready to try a little somatic experiment, one that I had seen work reliably with other ungrounded people over the years.

"In scanning your body, how far down does your awareness go?" I asked Amy.

"To just below my knees," she said tentatively. "I guess down to my shins."

"Breathe into your shins, and ask your body: 'Why stop there?'"

Amy closed her eyes and seemed to struggle for a moment, then sighing in frustration she said, "All I get is the phrase *lighter than air*, but I can't make any sense of it." In checking in with her shins again, she still couldn't feel her feet, but Amy did notice that her legs seemed to be "getting warmer," suggesting that she was on the right track even if the message itself wasn't yet decipherable.

"Okay, I want you to imagine two different scenarios, and we're going to see how your body reacts to each one," I said. "First, imagine going in with Rasa alone. What happens to your body?"

"It feels the same," Amy replied, shrugging.

"Now imagine me going into the round pen with you and Rasa," I offered.

Amy's eyes got wide as saucers, and she began to smile. "I can *feel* my feet!"

As it turns out, Amy's body easily *grounded itself* when supported in choosing actions that felt safe. From that day forward, she and Emily began using what they called the "lighter than air" technique for decision making. Amy's lack of sensation in her feet became a warning signal, keeping her from stepping forward until she had weighed her options. "I play through different scenarios in my head as I check in with my body," Amy explained. "When I can feel my feet, I know that I've hit on a good option, and my body hasn't steered me wrong yet!"

The Body Scan:
A Tool for Building Emotional and Social Intelligence

Now that we've explored a number of case studies and helpful hints, it's time to put the body scan into action. Using the following method often, sometimes just for fun, will help you gain confidence in listening to your "horse," accessing all kinds of information you can put to any number of uses.

1. Map the Sensations

Before you enter a situation involving other people (a business meeting, for example), scan down your body in a neutral environment where you are alone (your office, your car, the restroom). Notice what sensations you are feeling — without trying to "relax out of them."

2. Dialog with Prominent Sensations

If any sensations or postures stand out, dialog with your body by expanding the sensation and asking it for a message. What information is that sensation or posture holding? It may be a tension, a feeling of pins and needles, energy, excitement, anxiety, openness, fullness, and so on. (So-called negative as well as positive sensations can hold valuable information.) Imagine breathing into the sensation, sending it oxygen and awareness. This encourages the sensation to "speak," almost as if it's sending an email to your mind in the form of an image, brief text message, color, memory, song fragment, cliché, poetic phrase, or strange, irrational phrase, and so on. Remember that the message can be simple and straightforward. Feeling "the weight of the world on your shoulders" or that "someone has kicked you in the belly" or that "you don't have a leg to stand on" *is* a message in the form of a metaphor, no less meaningful because it is common!

3. Assess the Result

When you receive the message, whether it makes logical sense or not, check in again with the sensation.

If it has *released completely*, this means the message was received to your body's satisfaction, even if your thinking brain doesn't completely understand the symbol. (Proceed to step 4.)

If the sensation has *released slightly*, it means you're on the right track, but that you probably need to change something. When Maggie's ankles began to relax in response to the message "Gotta be on your toes," she still had to dismount and connect with the horse before her heels would lower completely in the stirrups. Sometimes you can't immediately address the issue raised, such as a tension related to your spouse that you notice when you are at work. In this case, take note of the body's insight or recommendation, and put it into action the next time you have some quality time with your mate. If a work-related tension arises at home, you might discuss it briefly with your spouse in order to become congruent, to make sure that he or she doesn't take the agitation, frustration, or anger you're experiencing personally, perhaps inspiring him or her to offer valuable suggestions or support.

If the sensation has *intensified*, it generally means your body has more to say on the subject, or it has other issues to address. (You may choose to ask for another message, if time permits, or check in with the body again later for more information. Remember to invoke the self-regulation program, releasing one "horse" at a time.)

If the sensation *stays the same*, it may mean the circuit between your mind and body has been interrupted or is "off-line" in some way. In most cases, this happens when an initial, subtle message from the body has been ignored or judged as irrational and the mind has come up with a message it thinks is more appropriate. The lack of response from the body means the mind has missed the boat. Go back and engage with the sensation, remaining open to how the body might speak. Remember that the body is often more like an artist than a scientist in its communication style, using imagery, color, song fragments, or odd poetic phrases to communicate insights that are too complex to fit into plain linear statements. However, if you still can't get a message, just move forward with your day, noticing if the sensation changes when you interact with other people, horses, situations, and so on.

4. Get a New Baseline Reading

When you dialogue with the body, sensations will change. Before you walk into that business meeting, scan down your body one more time, without dialoging, to get a new baseline reading.

5. Stay in Contact with Your Body as You Walk into the Room, and Notice Any Changes in Your Body

If your baseline reading included tension in your right shoulder, butterflies in your stomach, and energy in your hands, notice how these sensations intensify, release, or shift (or what new sensations arise) as you enter the meeting, sit down, and interact with your colleagues. Any new sensations that come into your body are a direct result of something nonverbal that's already happening in that meeting before anyone even speaks a word. If the butterflies in your stomach go away, and the tension in your shoulder releases, your body feels not only safe but also nourished by the setting or people involved. On the other hand, if you feel like you're getting kicked in the stomach whenever you look at one of your supervisors or potential clients, your body is sending you a potent alarm. If you feel inexplicably agitated by someone who is smiling and saying he's "fine," this person may be incongruent — in other words he's consciously or unconsciously hiding something. It may be a personal issue, trouble at home, and so on, and truly none of your business. Even so, this person is likely to act unpredictably because of his conflicted emotional state, and his judgment regarding work issues may be temporarily impaired. It is to your advantage to be aware of this.

6. Continue a Silent Dialog with Your Body

As new sensations rise or previous baseline sensations intensify, breathe into them and ask for input. Most business meetings offer lots of little opportunities for checking in. Rather than resorting to daydreaming or mentally going over your grocery list when things get tedious, check in with your body, watch other people's nonverbal responses, and take notes. If you feel uncontrollably tense or overwhelmed, you may choose to take a bathroom break. Rather than stepping outside for a smoke (a way of releasing tension *without* getting the message), step into a private space and dialog with your body.

Teams of individuals who are fluent in using the body scan and assessing the messages behind sensations and emotions can engage in consensual leadership, a principle I explore more deeply in Guiding Principle 10, in chapter 22. Here the word *consensual* does not mean that everyone agrees, but that everyone is willing and able to "sense together" in determining the most promising course of action. In teams that employ consensual leadership, the group can more accurately assess which team members are calmest, clearest, most experienced, most inspired, or most invested in handling certain challenges.

Using the "other 90 percent," teams can also enter the unknown more confidently, realizing that their own bodies will flash them little "warning lights" when the plan needs to be altered or reassessed — early enough to avoid a mishap. By checking the Emotional Message Chart in response to these subtle somatic alarms, members can tell the difference between fear (a legitimate environmental threat) and vulnerability (performance anxiety, a need for additional staff or training, or a challenge to an outmoded method, paradigm, or belief system). They can tell the difference between anger (boundaries that have been crossed) and frustration (blocks in the road to success). (These self-assessment, intersubjectivity, and emotional-fitness skills are helpful in overcoming what Patrick Lencioni calls the "five dysfunctions of a team" in his bestselling leadership book by that name, which we will explore as a part of Guiding Principle 5, in chapter 17.)

You can also use this scanning and messaging process privately to aid in problem solving, accessing your body's genius — its direct line to creative, metaphorical, poetic, and intuitive forms of wisdom — to help you develop fresh approaches to challenges that your linear, logical mind might not otherwise entertain or even begin to imagine. Like Amy, you can learn to sense when your body is skeptical of a certain course of action, when it feels safe, and when it feels excited moving forward, allowing you to "really put your heart into" whatever you decide to do.

With *all three* intelligence centers online and aligned, you'll have much more energy to accomplish your goals. Other people will sense your clarity, vision, focus, inspiration, enthusiasm, and *authentic, full-bodied* conviction, finding it difficult to resist following your lead — whether you're the official leader or not. That is *charisma* in the purest, most productive sense of the word.

Chapter Fifteen

GUIDING PRINCIPLE 3
Manage Contagious Emotions

Imagine you're visiting New York City, attending your first New York Philharmonic concert, in this case the 2012 Opening Gala with violin virtuoso Itzhak Perlman as guest artist. You may be surprised to find that even the cheap seats cost close to a hundred dollars, but you decide to spring for a midpriced ticket. It will be worth the additional investment to sit in the optimal acoustic center of Avery Fisher Hall to hear a living legend accompanied by some of the finest musicians in the world. The evening opens as scheduled with Respighi's enchanting *Fountains of Rome.* Then Perlman takes the stage. Silence falls over the audience as the conductor lifts his baton.

But what if, rather than playing the rhapsodic, emotionally invigorating Tchaikovsky *Violin Concerto* as promised, the orchestra and soloist suddenly decided to play one long, peaceful, optimistic, supportive, C-major chord — beautifully, expertly — for an entire hour?

Imagine the confusion and disappointment you'd feel. Even if you were adaptable and open-minded — or you stayed out of sheer curiosity — your own enjoyment of the music would soon be compromised by the people around you. After a mere two minutes, people would begin to whisper. At five or ten minutes, they'd start leaving, quietly shaking their heads in disgust. Another twenty minutes into this bizarre performance, even prim, finely dressed patrons would probably start booing the stage.

The simple truth of the matter is that no one treks to Lincoln Center hoping to hear soft, mellifluous major chords all night. The average person wouldn't put on a clean shirt and drive ten minutes to see a 3-D IMAX film of tranquil ocean scenes, either. When it comes to art and entertainment, we want awe, excitement, pathos, tragedy, sadness, longing, and power, in addition to joy, ecstasy, solace, and triumph. The more feelings expertly portrayed, the better. And yet great art promises something that we often miss in everyday life: honest emotional engagement that is transformational, not self-indulgent. That's how we judge whether we got our money's worth — and decide whether we'll buy the DVD or CD to relive the experience again and again.

However, at work, school, church, or home, people get irritated, sometimes offended, when emotions — positive or negative — enter an otherwise perfunctory planning or problem-solving discussion. No matter how hard we try, though, the timeworn practice of wearing a mask of contentment or control to hide our feelings simply doesn't work. As previously noted, research shows that when even one person suppresses emotion during an interaction, the blood pressure of that individual and *everyone else in the group* rises, even though none of these people may notice. This isn't a problem if the hidden feelings are mild or resolved productively soon after an interaction or meeting. Strong emotion suppressed over the long term, however, can cause the blood pressure of a team to rise so significantly that higher thought processes are compromised. Without the ability to manage emotion effectively, people can become defensive, mistrustful, overstimulated, and aggressive. They may undermine others — without even knowing why — as unspoken emotions spread like wildfire through an otherwise intelligent, well-meaning group. Social-intelligence researchers Daniel Goleman, Richard Boyatzis, and Annie McKee recommend that leaders learn to drive others' emotions "in the right direction to have a positive effect on earnings or strategy." But how in the world are people supposed to do this when *suppressing* negative emotion is like cleaning the floor with dirty water and a moldy old mop? And when force-feeding people simplistic, happy "chords" might very well piss them off?

EQ PhD

For sheer survival, I spent a good ten years experimenting with alternative ways to handle group emotional dynamics as I worked with unruly horses who would sense and then act out the fear, confusion, anger, or frustration that other herd members, including me, were feeling. Then I began to put these same skills to use with groups of confused, competitive, fearful, angry, or frustrated humans, which was equally scary in the beginning, though certainly not as dangerous as wrangling an irritated stallion (as long as people left their guns at the door).

Here's what I found: successfully managing affect contagion involves *deciphering* and *transforming* negative emotions and reactions while radiating *authentic* positive feelings that are productive and empowered, not naive. This initially daunting prospect is an advanced move, a PhD level of social intelligence in action. However, as with any postgraduate degree program, there are skills you can develop and steps you can take to get there.

Here's the first, most important thing to remember in practicing this art: managing contagious emotion is an art. It's not rocket science or brain surgery. If you make a few mistakes, you're not going to blow up the neighborhood or turn someone into a vegetable. Sensing and flowing with the emotions of others is more like conducting an orchestra. If you can move through the emotional highs and lows with interest, not resistance, the composure, concentration, and enthusiasm you convey will be contagious. In fact, by modeling and eventually teaching others to treat group interactions as "the symphony we're playing today," they too can learn to sense and flow with others' emotions, appreciating the wisdom behind feelings they'd previously hidden or rejected while learning how to move beyond suppression and expression into a poised, artful, creative approach to life and work.

Building on the previous two guiding principles, Guiding Principle 3 expands personal EQ skills. Use the following sequence to manage contagious emotions. By employing these verbal and nonverbal protocols, group members with varying opinions and emotional responses will feel heard and empowered, not judged, shamed, and disempowered. They will seek your leadership in the future, even if you aren't the official leader.

1. Employ the Body Scan

Do this before entering a business meeting or before a more casual interaction with friends and family. (See pages 292–96).

2. Pay Attention to Vocal Tone and Body Language

Notice others' vocal tone and body language in addition to, perhaps even over, their words. For instance, when delegating tasks among team members, watch how each person responds nonverbally to the mention of each task. When possible match team members with tasks they are enthusiastic about, or at least comfortable with. Their enthusiasm and comfort will become contagious to others. Similarly, notice when people say "yes" to a task with an undercurrent of apathy, agitation, or obligation, as this too will become contagious over time.

In driving the emotions of others in a positive direction, however, you cannot order people to feel enthusiastic or happy. And it's not helpful to put on a "happy face" yourself or otherwise act like nothing's wrong. You dispel others' negativity by using their emotions as information. For instance, you must find out if their apathy stems from a need for more training, clarity, or assistance; or if they are overworked, underpaid, underrecognized, or simply bored with their current job. Or if they have another idea they are reluctant to share. *However, before you explore the messages behind others' emotions, you must do step 3.*

3. Resolve to "Sit" in Uncomfortable Emotions without Panicking

This is like isometric exercise for your emotional muscles, and you *will* get stronger over time. Your increasing comfort in dealing with both positive and negative emotions, questions, and feedback *will* be contagious, helping others to remain thoughtful in tense situations.

4. Consult the Emotional Message Chart

When emotionally charged situations arise, silently consult the Emotional Message Chart to jump-start your own problem-solving mind-set. (I advise photocopying the abbreviated chart at the end of Guiding Principle 1, chapter 13, and taking this into meetings along with other notes, files, and paperwork. Some people prefer to scan it into their laptops for easy access. You can also download a PDF of the chart from my website, www.eponaquest.com.)

5. Breathe into Tension

Take care of your own body first by breathing into your physical constrictions. Even if the situation is too complex or chaotic to silently ask for messages from your body sensations, continue breathing into areas of tension, regardless. (Breathing is contagious. It activates the parasympathetic nervous system in yourself and others, helping everyone to break a cycle of escalating arousal that can occur when strong emotions arise in group interactions.) Now you're ready to begin assessing and managing others' emotions.

6. Scan the Group for Signs of Incongruence

Someone who is smiling or saying she's fine but displaying body language that suggests otherwise is incongruent. Look for the nonverbal signals — clenched jaw, sarcastic remarks, reluctance to make eye contact, exaggerated sighing, or red or watery eyes. Sometimes the signal will be simply your gut feeling that someone is preoccupied or hiding something. Do not automatically assume an incongruent person is untrustworthy. It may be a personal situation at home and none of your business. However, he or she can be inadvertently disruptive to the group, adding needless tension and confusion to an otherwise productive meeting.

Over time, you will need to create an atmosphere of *professional* trust and support where people can acknowledge they are experiencing personal challenges without sharing the details. When people can admit they are tense, angry, agitated, or sad for reasons unrelated to the task at hand, their emotions will not be unconsciously contagious to members of the group. Without learning the details, everyone will breathe a big sigh of relief when someone says, "Hey, guys, I just want to let you know I may seem a bit distracted because of a difficulty outside work (or in another division, or with an employee or client unrelated to this team's agenda). I'm taking care of it, but there's an emotional charge to the situation that has nothing to do with this meeting." You may want to model this yourself at first and share the research showing that incongruent people cause the blood pressure of those they're interacting with to rise, making it harder for everyone to think clearly.

However, if you're not in a position to change the group dynamic, you will be ahead of the game if you can simply note who is incongruent and watch how he is affecting the group.

7. Notice Body Language Revealing Others' Interpersonal Difficulties

Sometimes incongruent people are experiencing strife with another team member, so check for this as well. If Jane purses her lips, rolls her eyes, or looks out the window whenever Jim speaks, it's safe to say that you're witnessing evidence of interpersonal difficulties between them. These gestures and the emotions behind them can poison any group interaction and need to be resolved expediently. Long-term interpersonal strife between team members can be absolutely debilitating to the rest of the group, creating an inescapable undercurrent of tension that interrupts everyone's ability to think clearly, let alone creatively. Most of the time, these difficulties can and should be handled privately after the meeting, with preparation, coaching, and support. (Guiding

Principle 9: "*Prepare* for Difficult Conversations," in chapter 21, is the essential skill for handling interpersonal challenges effectively.)

8. Breathe and Ask

In facing challenges that give rise to strong emotions, *breathe and ask* constructive, fact-finding, problem-solving questions. Do *not* encourage using the old yet still popular psychological "encounter group" approach where people express their emotions verbally, sometimes using a shaming or confrontational tone of voice in the name of "authenticity." (The "when you do that, I feel this" format is not just useless but also destructive in professional situations.) Also, resist the temptation to aggressively fix the situation, ignore your own uncomfortable emotions, or secretly jump to judgmental conclusions.

9. Diffuse Defensiveness in Others

Ask the *questions* associated with relevant emotions; do not mention the emotions themselves. For instance, if someone appears angry or frustrated (and in people, the body language of these two emotions often looks the same), don't ask the person: "Are you angry or frustrated?" Instead, ask situation-relevant questions based on the messages behind those emotions, consulting the Emotional Message Chart. Ask: "Have we reached a block or impasse in moving forward on this project? (A "yes" to this question signals frustration.) "Or have I overstepped my role here or been inconsiderate of your needs, time, or professional expertise in some way?" (These are possible reasons why this person might be angry with you, signifying a boundary violation of some sort.)

When someone looks particularly agitated or fragile in a group meeting, ask relevant questions to others around him or her first. For instance, if one colleague seems afraid or vulnerable, don't say, "Mary, you look downright peaked. Are you feeling afraid or vulnerable?" Ask the group to discuss issues related to safety (legitimate fear concerns) or the need for more information and training (vulnerability) or the sheer panic people sometimes feel when moving out of comfortable habits and experimenting with or exploring unknown territory (also vulnerability). You might say, "I want to make sure before we move forward with this plan that we consider any issues related to safety of the product, possible market competition, or the need for more information, preparation, and training. John, do you have any concerns or ideas? What about you, Sally? Mary?"

10. Avoid Using Inflammatory Words or Gestures

Sarcastic, shaming, or blaming remarks create wildfires of negative emotional contagion, sending some people into flight-or-fight mode and generally making everyone else defensive on some level. (Inflammatory statements include: I felt betrayed. You should be ashamed of yourself. You really dropped the ball on this one. I'm very disappointed in all of you. Gestures include exaggerated sighing, eye rolling, cynical smiles, and so on.)

Similarly, you can turn a negative trend around before it gets started by refraining from reacting defensively to inflammatory words or disrespectful gestures from others. Do not *ignore* inflammatory words and gestures, however. Assess the message behind them and problem solve. (See the Emotional Message Chart for questions to ask about, for example, disappointment.)

11. Meet Aggressive or Shaming Acts
with a Thoughtful, Problem-Solving Attitude

This includes passive-aggressive acts. It's productive to read someone's misbehavior as a form of communication — *if* you teach this person more appropriate ways of reacting to stress in the future (rather than ignoring or condoning his hurtful behavior). If, however, you react to a challenge by getting into a shouting match, seeking revenge, or undermining someone behind his back, *you* will look adolescent. Take the high road, turn a negative trend around, and others will *seek* your leadership in the future. Whenever possible, however, do not shame the aggressor in front of the group. Discuss inappropriate behavior privately, after the meeting, offering the disruptive person solutions for how to deal more constructively with the issue that caused the misbehavior if a similar situation arises in the future.

12. Recognize When You Are Triggered

Past betrayals, difficulties, or traumas can rear their ugly heads at inopportune moments, causing you to overreact in situations where people are looking for sane, balanced leadership. It's obvious to others when you have a hair-trigger response to something minor: as a leader, you want to increase your ability to notice when your own emotional reactions are way out of proportion to the current situation. This means something from the past is setting you off. Notice what belongs to the current situation and what belongs to the past. Focus on the present. Make an appointment to deal with the past (with a colleague, coach, counselor, or confidant), as unresolved issues cloud your intuition, compromise your ability to think clearly, and affect the ability of the entire group to function when you explode or hold a grudge over things that others find mildly irritating or challenging. (See the discussion of projection and transference in chapter 12, pages 210–16.)

13. Notice When Others Are Triggered

Though some people hide this relatively well, they can still affect the group's morale and effectiveness. (Telltale signs include disgusted, defeated, or cynical body language in combination with sweeping generalizations or statements that include *always* or *never*, such as: "Management never listens to us," or "I always get the short end of the stick.")

Again, guard against defensiveness. Don't say, "John you seem to be triggered by something." Instead, use the verbal and nonverbal cues they've given you to ask relevant work-related questions that encourage people to differentiate between the past and the present, learning from the past to produce a different outcome in the present. In the case of "Management never listens to us," you might ask people to explore situations in which management didn't listen, recall the approach they used, and discuss the outcome. Then bring up situations in which management did listen, again analyzing the approach and the outcome. This gives your team the information they need to strategize how and why management should listen this time.

14. Do Not Ever Use Someone's Vulnerability against Him or Her

This increases fear, mistrust, secretiveness, defensiveness, and aggressiveness in the entire group, especially over time. (Vulnerabilities include lack of training, skill deficiencies, miscommunications, mistakes, fears, past traumas, and interpersonal weaknesses.) Do not reward others for using colleagues', employees', or leaders' vulnerabilities against them. And do not tolerate gossip. Create an atmosphere in which people can admit they need clarity, help, time, planning, or additional training. This includes people who need emotional- and social-intelligence training. (For more information on vulnerability's effect on the workplace, leadership, and community building, see Guiding Principle 5, in chapter 17.)

15. Consider Individual and Group Needs Simultaneously

Each affects the other. When individuals feel afraid, jealous, or disrespected, their emotions intensify and become contagious, even if they manage to hide their discomfort relatively well. Chronic negativity affects the entire team, reducing morale, creativity, and productivity over time.

16. Appreciate the "Symphony"

Do so and you *will* become the conductor.

Chapter Sixteen

GUIDING PRINCIPLE 4
Master Boundaries and Assertiveness

In professional and personal interactions, much needless strife, agitation, anger, apathy, and inefficiency occur as a result of a lack of training in how to set and respect boundaries, how to motivate others, and how to tell the difference between the two.

Mainstream equestrians have been taught that horses should not be allowed to set boundaries with humans or they will become dangerous. These animals instead must submit to being touched anytime, anywhere, for any reason whatsoever without objection, or they are punished, sometimes severely. This results in a great number of horses who dissociate, who become apathetic or machinelike (which some people consider a well-trained horse). These animals lose their vibrancy in the show ring and act dull and disinterested in daily interactions with people. At the other extreme, some horses, like my Arabian stallion Midnight Merlin, fight back, becoming hypersensitive to human touch, throwing riders and attacking anyone who walks into the corral. These horses are often destroyed simply for lack of mutually respectful treatment by humans early in life.

In the business world, people who try to set boundaries with coworkers and, most especially, with bosses are often punished too, though usually in more subtle ways, developing reputations for being cranky, perhaps losing a promotion in the process. For this reason, most people avoid setting boundaries, swallowing their discomfort and anger by becoming increasingly dull and apathetic. Over time, this creates a toxic work environment where people not only "retire in place" but also use cynicism and sarcasm to release at least some of the resentment seething underneath a complacent facade.

A "Cultural Thing"

But what are boundaries, and why must we set them? At the most basic physical level, a boundary helps you claim the personal space you need in order to feel safe, connected, and therefore engaged with a person who's approaching and interacting with you. Most of us have dealt with people who stand too close. It's hard to think straight, let alone pay attention to what they're talking about, when you're leaning backward, holding your breath, glancing toward the door, or perhaps dissociating (going blank and numb) to appear polite.

Giving others the physical or emotional space *they* need helps them feel respected and actually allows their *minds* to work more effectively. Quite simply, they hear and remember much more of what you're saying, an important consideration for efficient, results-oriented leaders.

If you're a person who likes to stand or sit close to others, your goal may be to communicate support, camaraderie, and at times, intimacy. But because people have differing needs for space, you must pay attention to nonverbal cues of discomfort — *if* you want to be heard. Many people will only process and remember half of what you're saying if you move into their zone of personal space, as this literally causes their blood pressure to rise and their minds to lose focus.

Students often ask me if this is a "cultural thing." It is only to the extent that in each country, there are some people for whom the accepted standard of physical proximity works, and others for whom it does not. In cultures where close contact is the norm, the most successful, gregarious people are the ones who feel comfortable, even energized, in close proximity to others. But there are people for whom this same spatial formula is debilitating. These are the seemingly aloof members of society who live on the outskirts of town, work at home if they're lucky, and either don't attend parties or must drink copious amounts of alcohol to deaden their sensitivity to the sensory overload they experience in rooms filled with people. Some are "helped" with medication to reduce chronic anxiety, not realizing they might be able to bypass the drug and its side effects simply by teaching others to respect *the space their bodies need for their minds to be present.*

I've even found that some children diagnosed with learning disabilities, including attention deficit disorder and oppositional defiant disorder, need more physical space than the classroom allows. Simply sitting in such close proximity to their peers causes their blood pressure to rise; then these students either dissociate and don't hear the lesson or release the tension by acting out. Several teachers who studied the simple techniques I discuss in this chapter reorganized their classrooms to allow for differences in spatial needs, finding that test scores rose and unproductive behavior dropped. Salespeople who have been taught the same nonverbal spatial protocols have seen revenues rise. And business leaders who have the power to give employees their optimal amount of personal space, in meetings and in workstations, find it's an easy way to save time and money, boost creativity, and avoid many interpersonal difficulties that undermine the daily functioning of an effective team.

Standing close is *not* automatic connection. Luckily, determining others' spatial needs isn't difficult. You simply have to pay attention to nonverbal cues and adjust accordingly. The next time you see someone leaning back, looking distracted, refusing to make eye contact, holding her breath, or going blank, try taking a few steps back and breathing more deeply. Quite often, you'll notice the person relax and lean forward in response, engaging in more thoughtful conversation because she's feeling safer and *more connected* to you, for "intuitive" reasons that she may never guess are simply related to space.

Space Is the Place

This crucial element of social intelligence has been virtually ignored by scientists and leadership coaches alike. But don't feel bad if you've unknowingly been standing too close to certain people. Or if you thought you were learning impaired and socially inept because you couldn't think straight in groups of people that you now realize were standing or sitting too close for *your* comfort. I noticed the importance of this issue only upon the threat of death!

In rehabilitating my stallion Merlin, it took me several months to realize that he had a larger need for personal space than most horses, that *this* was the root of his intensely aggressive behavior. And at first, I had no idea what to do about it. Over time, I discovered that the positive benefits of working *with* his heightened sensitivity, rather than trying to desensitize him as past trainers had done, instantaneously made him much less violent, more thoughtful, and much happier, and I realized that *space is the place where relationship begins.* Something as simple as physical proximity turned out to be crucial not only to his mental and emotional health but also to my ongoing safety.

In approaching Merlin, I learned to watch for increasing signs of tension. He would raise his neck, begin to pin his ears back, and prepare to either move away or attack. Yet at the moment I saw these signs of physical stress, if I simply paused, rocked back slightly, and sighed, Merlin would sigh, lick and chew, and relax, avoiding a confrontation. Some trainers recommend turning and walking away to release the pressure; but with Merlin, doing so not only temporarily broke the developing connection, it turned out to be unnecessary. As I was walking toward him, I would simply stop when I saw a stress response and shift my weight from the leg that was moving forward to the leg that was now behind me. As I rocked back, I would sigh, literally breathing out audibly, relaxing my shoulders and solar plexus. As I later realized when I began teaching this technique to doctors and studying its effects with the physiologist Ann Linda Baldwin, the stallion instinctually preferred the "rock back and sigh" protocol for another reason: his tendency to "catch," or mirror, my sigh activated his parasympathetic nervous system, which calms the body and focuses the mind. (To understand how breathing deeply activates the parasympathetic nervous system, lowering stress and allowing clearer thinking as a result, see Guiding Principle 12, in chapter 24.)

Eventually, this same "rock back and sigh" protocol motivated him to walk gently, respectfully toward me with an engaged, cooperative attitude — until he got too close to me for his own comfort. I could almost see his blood pressure rise. (Actually, I could feel it in my own body: a buzzing sensation that would steadily intensify.) If I didn't make him back off at that moment, setting a boundary with *him* — for his comfort and my safety — he'd lash out and try to bite me.

Merlin wanted to connect, and he was confused by the overstimulation. Once we found the optimal spatial proximity between us — the place where both of our bodies felt naturally relaxed — his personality changed dramatically. (See chapter 10 for a more extensive discussion of the unexpectedly fascinating elements involved.)

Through this process, I learned that, contrary to what the mainstream equestrian world still believes, sensing and respecting Merlin's boundaries made him less dangerous. But it *had* to be a two-way street. As a result of this experience, I came up with a boundary rule that works with people too: When I'm approaching the horse (or another person), he or she sets the boundary. When this same horse or person approaches me, I *must* set the boundary.

Both elements were essential to building mutual respect. If I had respected Merlin's need for space without insisting he respect mine, he would have dominated me, which is incredibly dangerous when someone weighs a thousand pounds. But encroaching upon others' space to control or dominate them is also an instinctual tendency in humans. As a result, effective nonverbal protocols for setting and respecting boundaries are similar in both species.

Over the years, I learned to watch for similar cues in people. I noticed that when I hit that bubble of personal space unique to each individual, his shoulders might rise slightly. He might lean backward, look away, blink more often, or hold his breath. People who are more stoic in facial expression often unconsciously twitch their hands or adjust their necks. Others, women especially, are deceptively expressive, actually smiling to release the tension in a socially accepted way — only this type of smile looks forced and might even turn into more of a grimace if you continue to stand too close. These involuntary physical responses to proximity often signal that you're approaching too fast (if you're farther away), or getting too close for comfort if you've reached someone's zone of personal space. If you rock back and sigh at the exact moment you see these cues, however, previously distracted people will often relax, even lean forward. A light seems to come back into their eyes, and they suddenly seem more interested in what you're saying.

The practice of noticing escalating tension in others, rocking back and sighing in response, has become a simple yet surprisingly effective tool in working with veterans with post-traumatic stress disorder. I've taught this skill to family members and counselors. In equine-facilitated workshops for soldiers and their spouses, wartime trauma survivors realize that often all they really need in order to calm down is a little more space, that their nervous systems, like Merlin's, are hyperaroused.

Warriors in Transition

"Incorporating what I've learned from my Eponaquest experiences and training is an integral part of my counseling practice, especially when working with military veterans," says Lauren Loos, a licensed professional counselor who graduated from the Eponaquest apprenticeship program in 2010.

> Although there is no substitute for direct equine experiential learning, part of the elegance of Eponaquest's approach to this field is that it's entirely possible to extend the concepts beyond the barn and into my counseling office.
>
> Of great importance to veterans is the concept of the warrior archetype applying to horses as well as people. Drawing that parallel creates an opportunity to relate some very skillful ways of functioning that are demonstrated by horses and herds. By suggesting to human warriors that this majestic and strong being might be a model for processing emotion, veterans may come to view their own experience of emotion as a sign of strength and courage rather than weakness or cowardice. Viewing their

body as "the horse their mind rides around on" [Guiding Principle 2] gives a tangible, tactile suggestion for experiencing the bodily sensations corresponding with emotions. With practice, clients are able to detect even subtle stirrings of their "horse." They are then better equipped to recognize and experience increases in arousal level with enough wherewithal to get the message their body is giving them and to respond to the message behind the emotion rather than react to avoid discomfort. I have heard more than one warrior proclaim, "If a horse can do it, then so can I!"

Lauren also reports that she modified the "rock back and sigh" technique for her small office in Portland, Oregon:

Considering the relationship between arousal and spatial proximity is a crucial component in my practice. This is important not only for the client's well-being but also for the therapist and the therapeutic relationship. Like the oxygen mask drill demonstrated by flight attendants prior to taking off (the one that stresses "put your own mask on before assisting others"), it is essential to keep my own even keel in the wake of a client's trauma responses. This is especially important when working with veterans suffering military trauma complicated by past abuse. For these clients, validation of intense emotions is essential, as they have likely experienced extreme invalidation of emotion when past attachment figures (usually parents) reacted to their legitimate emotion with criticism or withdrawal. Those who have experienced trauma are keenly aware of subtle changes in therapist arousal, so effective validation for these clients depends on emotional congruence of the therapist. If I am incongruent under these circumstances, I not only risk the therapeutic relationship, but I may also be experienced as a threat.

Fortunately, I discovered early in my study of equine-facilitated learning through Eponaquest that when a client's arousal level escalated, I could ease my own reaction to that escalation by rocking back and sighing. Due to counseling conventions discouraging erratic therapist behavior, and to the limitations of my windowless 8' x 12' office, I had to get creative in this endeavor. I found that an office chair with wheels and a flexible back offered the perfect vehicle for this exercise! Thus, "rock back and sigh" became "roll back, lean back and sigh." Lest this conjure images of careening chairs, bouncing off walls, it is actually a very subtle yet extremely effective (stealth) move.

It is through demonstration of "rock back and sigh," lowering my own arousal level, that I have taught veterans to do the same when arousal and emotional escalation is exacerbated by proximity. This work also provides an impersonal explanation for the traumatized veteran's difficulty being in crowds and their tendency to isolate and avoid social gatherings. Using the story of how Merlin's trainers discovered this gives way to explanations of emotional contagion as well. Clients seem to experience increased self-empathy, understanding and meaning in their experience.

Finally, Lauren teaches veterans and their family members how to set boundaries respectfully:

> Attending to the message behind the emotion has awakened improved emotional functioning in several of the veterans with whom I've worked. It has been particularly helpful in those who have difficulty managing their anger. "Anger management" evokes images of aggressive outbursts and out of control reactivity. However, many who experience intense anger turn it toward themselves in the form of emotional or physical self-injury.
>
> Most of us, including the veterans and other clients I've worked with, were raised to view anger as a bad emotion. Learning by way of the horse about anger as an indicator that a boundary has been crossed has liberated many to use this sensation to improve their lives. A particularly poignant story involves a veteran who realized that his lifelong suicidal ideation and attempts had always come subsequent to a boundary violation by an intimate. These weren't necessarily serious violations; they typically involved inconsiderate behaviors such as his partner turning the TV channel without asking or eating all the leftovers without offering him any. When we finally were able to see that the common thread in all suicidal feelings began with similar incidents, the veteran was able to use the energy of his anger to make appropriate requests for consideration. The decrease in his suicidal thoughts and behaviors was directly correlated with appropriate boundary setting. With practice, he realized the pleasure of "going back to grazing" as opposed to fighting suicidal urges. His life improved dramatically and he was able to focus on living his life rather than fighting to do no harm.

It's clear from this powerful example that just as important as respecting others' boundaries is the art of setting them with people who are clueless about *your* unique needs for space. Here's where the difficulty level rises.

On the Job

Among humans, boundaries are also relevant to professional space (offices and cubicles), job integrity (handling your part of a project, or running your division), and emotional space (keeping your private life as private as *you* want to keep it, regardless of what others may share about their relationships and backgrounds). Boundaries involve time, too: the time you need to do the job well, without being overrun with other projects and deadlines coming at you from multiple directions.

In all of these cases, boundaries are not walls; they are *negotiations*. When you set a boundary, you should always keep this in mind. Some people need more space or quiet to think clearly. Some thrive on close physical proximity and discussion. Others do their best creative work when the radio is playing. In college, I found it easier to write complex term papers at the student union with hundreds of strangers talking and laughing around me, but I didn't want to socialize on these occasions.

When it comes to setting and respecting boundaries, the old adage "do unto others as you would have others do unto you" may *not* apply. Some people like to be hugged when they're feeling down, others like to go out to lunch and talk about it, and still others would be eternally grateful if everyone would let them close their office door and be alone for two hours. Finding out what someone needs, rather than giving her what *you* would want in the same situation, is an easy way to bypass many potential boundary issues.

For similar reasons, it's important to avoid jumping to conclusions when someone oversteps one of your boundaries. You'll save yourself a lot of time, energy, and grief if you don't automatically take offense. This person may have been treating you as she would have wanted to be treated, or her previous boss would have wanted to be treated, or her mother always told her people would want to be treated in a certain situation. Or perhaps you inadvertently and completely unconsciously stepped on her toes in some way earlier in the day, and she's angry with *you!*

As discussed in Guiding Principle 1, anger is a signal that someone has overstepped a boundary, perhaps with the conscious or unconscious intention of bending you to his or her will. Most of the time, however, boundary issues do not involve intentionally aggressive moves. Someone who bursts into your office with a list of five urgent things for you to do that day may break your concentration while you're trying to finish an important project. You need to set an effective boundary, not swallow your irritation (and explode at her or someone else later). At the same time, it's not at all helpful to tell this person that she has "violated" your boundaries. Though many people don't understand what this means, most feel shamed and alienated by this language.

In setting boundaries, it's most productive to do the following:

1. Take care of these momentarily uncomfortable issues early, on a case-by-case basis. If you wait too long to set boundaries, you'll encourage the "offending" person to unconsciously step over the line again and again. As a result, you're likely to do one of two highly unproductive things later, most likely when you're under stress for some other reason: You might hit that "straw that breaks the camel's back" stage, where you lose your temper with this person over something minor, gaining a reputation as a hothead. Or, more commonly, you'll become perpetually irritated and, over time, mistrustful of this person, perhaps dismissing her ideas or giving her the silent treatment. As a result, you will develop a reputation as an inexplicably cold, cranky, self-absorbed, or petty person who is not a team player.

2. Ask for the specific behavior, space, or time you want and *explain how it will help you get the job done*. Again, you would never say, "Madeline, I need to set a boundary with you. This new client must be some kind of prima donna. Can't you wait another day for us to get started on this proposal? I'm trying to prepare for another meeting that I set up a month ago, and I really need to concentrate for an hour! Jeez!" Instead use a calm, problem-solving tone of voice: "Madeline, I can see you have a list of five important things for me to do this morning, but I'm finishing up the final figures on the budget for tomorrow's meeting. What's the first priority here? Should I get John to take over the budget figures so I can help you with this unexpected lead? Can we hold off until I finish the budget later today? Or should we get Susan or Emily to help us prioritize and divide up this list right now?"

3. Negotiate if necessary once you understand the other person's needs and concerns.

4. Give the person *immediate positive feedback* when he or she makes the slightest move to give you the space, time, or consideration you've asked for, in the form of relaxed, connected body language, smiles, gentle eye contact, and so on. You want to show the person that you're not setting a boundary to alienate or punish anyone but to become more effective *and* connected. Appreciation and enthusiasm for the negotiated adjustments are also helpful: "Thanks, Madeline. I do think it's a good plan to have Susan get started on at least outlining the new proposal this morning. I'll get right back to these boring budget figures so that I can do some research on your new prospect later today. It's a great opportunity! Hey, can you close my office door on your way out, and let everyone else know I need a couple more hours to get this done before I can jump on board?"

5. Be willing to hold your ground once an agreement has been reached. You may have to set the boundary several times, with an increasingly emphatic tone of voice and *progressively* more assertive body language. But again, give immediate positive feedback when the boundary is respected once more. This "crescendo into immediate positive feedback" technique is essential in working with teams of experts who may or may not be your boss. It's also an important tool in motivating others to accomplish all kinds of mundane or ambitious goals.

The Ultimate Power Tool

A crescendo is a gradual increase in volume or intensity that does not drop back down or release pressure until it reaches its fulfillment. Musicians learn to do this for expressive, purely aesthetic reasons. Most people, however, don't develop this important skill, though there are many good reasons to employ it daily in all kinds of contexts.

The crescendo is, for instance, helpful in setting boundaries with a horse, though it's rarely taught at conventional training barns, at least not consciously. The best trainers and riding instructors somehow develop it unconsciously in motivating horses to perform a specific goal. But most equestrians spend more time in the saddle than in relating to their horses on the ground. As a result, very few recognize that there's a difference between assertive, goal-directing behavior and boundary setting.

Boundaries are often completely mishandled in all kinds of ways. Commonly, people say, "back off" to a horse, perhaps halfheartedly, perhaps even angrily — not realizing that their body language is completely incongruent with their message. Truly, it's not at all uncommon to see experienced riders wave a whip and *shout* "back off" to a horse while *they* are backing up. In effect, the verbal cue, vocal tone, and whip waving add up to more than 10 percent of the communication potential — let's say 30 percent. But that still means the horse is responding to another 70 percent of the body language, perceived intent, and energy of a person who is literally inviting the horse to move closer as she steps back.

Holding your ground is the first step in clear boundary-setting communication, and well-trained horses will respect this — as long as they're naturally submissive. *Mastering the crescendo* is key to handling more defiant responses from an alpha mare or feisty stallion who believes she or he should be in charge and is willing to up the ante, using intimidation to gain control over you. More specifically, the *crescendo-into-immediate-positive-feedback* approach is a remarkably simple, highly effective, yet completely counterintuitive way to gain the respect of any proud, talented being — without alienating him or her. This is a skill we all need to develop in leading or collaborating with groups of human experts, or with naturally dominant family members, for that matter.

I say *counterintuitive* because the tendency for most people is to feel insulted by any power play. They will sometimes, in response, set a boundary in a state of such outrage that the human or horse really doesn't care to interact with them again, perhaps deferring to their dominance, but not trusting them as leaders. (The important distinction between the herd dominant and herd leader is discussed in chapter 8.)

At the barn, the progression usually looks like this: A trainer, let's call her Wanda, manages to stand her ground as a stallion steps too close. She quietly says, "Back off, Sparky," and gives the whip a subtle twitch. No response. Again, she quietly says, "Back off, Sparky," accompanied by a subtle twitch of the whip, perhaps several more times, essentially holding the same "volume level" — at, let's say, two on a "power dial" of one to ten. Then suddenly, she shouts, "Damn it, Sparky! I said BACK OFF, you presumptuous bastard!" She then whacks the horse with the whip and makes him run around the arena five times to show some respect.

If Wanda's ultimate aim was to socialize Sparky — to make him a more trustworthy, respectful horse — let alone form an actual partnership with him, she made at least four mistakes:

1.   She suddenly jumped from a two to a ten on the power dial, instantaneously shifting from coolness to ferocious, uncontrolled madness, creating the impression that she was suffering from some sort of equine-induced bipolar disorder.

2.   She never actually set a boundary. By going straight from moving the horse out of her personal space to insisting he run around the arena at her discretion, she bypassed boundary setting and went straight to "motivating" him to perform a goal — in this case, not by engaging clearheaded assertiveness but by tripping off into rage-infused aggression.

3.   Poor Sparky didn't learn anything about the relationship-*enhancing* benefits of respecting boundaries. He learned that dominant individuals take control by suddenly wreaking such havoc that you're better off doing what they say and, for the most part, staying out of their way.

4.   If Sparky is like many stallions, he's now hell-bent on securing a second-in-command position in the horse-human pecking order by using Wanda's same tactic on unsuspecting grooms and apprentices, some of whom may come flying out of the arena later that same day.

A Saner Approach

In contrast, this is what Wanda could have done differently, producing a more peaceful, connected outcome:

1. When Sparky approached her, she could have easily started with the same volume of verbal and nonverbal cues, saying, "Back up," accompanied by a slight twitch of the whip.
2. When he didn't respond, she could have waved the whip more emphatically at the ground just in front of his feet, leaning toward him, taking the volume up to a three or four. Here Sparky would have heard the whip hissing, sensed the air moving, and maybe even felt a bit of sand hitting his legs.
3. If that didn't work, she could have increased the speed and intensity of the whip to the point that any attempt to step into her space would have resulted in a stinging sensation from the whip, taking the volume up to a five or a six.
4. The split second Sparky backed off, Wanda could have conveyed that giving her the space she needs to feel safe has a positive, relationship-enhancing effect through the following, primarily nonverbal, cues: instantly stopping the whip, putting it in a neutral position, breathing deeply, and quietly praising Sparky, standing for a few moments longer in this peaceful place of mutual respect before directing him to move on to performing a specific training move.

It's important to note that in this example, *immediate positive feedback* is not gushing, empty praise, but giving Sparky the experience of the relaxation and connection he will *always* receive when he respects Wanda's boundaries. Wanda's continuing obligation is to bring this emotional-intelligence goal of greater connection and appreciation (though not always relaxation) to everything she does with the stallion, effortlessly increasing his desire to be with her no matter what she wants him to accomplish.

Family Reunion

Using this approach to set boundaries with a human is counterintuitive for most people, but it quickly proves to be just as effective. Even so, the verbal dimension raises the difficulty level: you must speak, think, feel, and observe the other person's behavior — while constantly making adjustments. To understand how these elements work together, let's look at a conversation one of my students had with her aunt "Millicent."

Milli is notorious for crossing all kinds of boundaries. At family gatherings, "Sally" tried to avoid this seemingly well-meaning yet meddlesome relative, finding excuses to get away after a brief hello. Once Sally understood the "crescendo into immediate positive feedback" concept, however, she was delighted to find it enhanced her relationships with friends and loved ones. Aunt Milli provided the ultimate test when Sally attended a family reunion shortly after returning from a cruise that had the entire family talking.

The interaction started, as usual, with Milli giving Sally a hug that lasted too long for the younger woman's comfort. Then, continuing to stand way too close, Milli asked her niece for the "scoop" on her recent trip.

"I heard through the grapevine that this was quite a romantic cruise for you," Milli said, leaning in even closer.

"Yes," Sally replied. "But first I want to tell you about a workshop I took with horses last month. It was all about nonverbal communication and how we can feel closer yet more respectful of others by paying attention to something as simple as space."

Sally proceeded to tell Milli about Merlin the stallion, how he became violent when his need for space wasn't respected. "To make a long story short, I realized that I'm a lot like Merlin. I don't become violent when people stand close, but I really have trouble thinking straight, and even hearing what people are saying, which totally explains why I always used to sit at the back of the classroom when I was younger. People thought I was shy or antisocial — and so did I — but in working with the horses, I learned that all I really need is a bit of extra space in order to connect with people, to feel relaxed and engaged."

Milli looked confused, and even a bit bored. "That's weird," she said flippantly.

Sally didn't skip a beat. "Here, let me show you, Aunt Milli. We did this exercise where we interacted with people to find our optimal zone of personal space, and mine happens to be about three feet away from my body," she said, gently moving Milli (finally!) into position. "When you stand this far away from me, I relax and everything seems to come into focus for me. I actually feel more connected to you and others than if you stand closer. Isn't that wild?"

Sally gave Milli immediate positive feedback by smiling, leaning in slightly to convey the desire to connect while maintaining the prescribed distance. "So basically, I'm making a deal with people I care about: I'll occasionally remind them of the space I need, because everyone still tends to move in closer out of habit. But really, once Mom, Dad, and this new man in my life realized that I need a little extra space to hear everything they're saying, no one had a problem with it. For years I thought I had a learning disability or I was forgetful, but now I realize that I just needed a little more space around my body for my mind to be present."

"Well, all right, I guess," Milli said, "if it helps you, dear. So now, tell me all the juicy details. Who is this man? What does he do for a living? Is he divorced? Did you, you know, do the 'wild thing' in the Caribbean?"

Here Milli, the family gossip, proceeded to push Sally's emotional boundaries by asking a series of increasingly intimate questions. Rather than acting offended or making a quick getaway, Sally decided to give only the information she was comfortable with, while still conveying enthusiasm and the desire to connect.

"Well, his name is Andy, and he's a university professor, and yes, we really had a wonderful time getting to know each other," Sally revealed. "He actually only lives about three hours away, and we're making plans to see each other soon. I'm excited, but I really don't want to jinx the whole thing right now by giving out too many details. I feel like this relationship has real potential. But who knows, if things go well you may get to meet him at Christmas dinner, Aunt Milli. Keep your fingers crossed for me, okay?"

As the conversation unfolded, Milli continued to push all kinds of limits that other family members instinctually respected. Yet rather than becoming frustrated, insulted, or resentful, Sally kept making the necessary adjustments through a combination of verbal and nonverbal cues. She casually mentioned her need for physical space several times while breathing and smiling at Milli when she backed off once more. For the most part, the younger woman succeeded in giving only information she wanted to share, sometimes with a joke, sometimes asking Milli questions about her life instead, once using the crescendo to set a firmer, more serious-sounding boundary when Milli again asked for information about Andy.

"You know Aunt Milli, you're not the first person to press me for more details, but this relationship is too important to spill the beans too early and too casually like I've done in the past. Andy and I just need some privacy at this point." When Milli pursed her lips and shrugged her shoulders, looking frustrated and embarrassed, Sally leaned in and said a little more quietly, "Mom's really excited about this, too. She's already talking about grandkids. Can you help me out here so we don't scare Andy off?"

By enlisting Milli's support in holding boundaries with other friends and family members, Sally found that the mood began to shift. Sally reached out warmly and took her aunt's hand while still keeping an appropriate distance.

"Everyone looks to you for the latest scoop on family news, and if you tell people that Andy and I could use a little space to let our relationship grow, everyone else will follow suit! Can I count on you?"

Optimal Assertiveness

With regard to emotional and social intelligence, it's *essential* to pay attention to the difference between setting boundaries (holding your ground or protecting territory, space, or resources) and motivating others (using assertiveness to influence others' behavior or direct them to take action to reach a specific goal). Both activities involve a skillful use of power. You can avoid adding aggression, shame, blame, and resentment to these activities by "dialing your power up" progressively (crescendo) and then acknowledging achievement of the desired response with immediate positive feedback. In this way, boundaries are set with nonverbal cues cultivating safety, cooperation, clear thinking, and greater trust between team members. And goals are achieved through a simple formula for assertiveness:

Commitment + Crescendo + Immediate Positive Feedback
= Increasing Motivation

This formula, when used mindfully and masterfully, also creates greater *self-motivation* in others over time, freeing leaders up for other pursuits.

But why must we distinguish between boundary setting and assertiveness? There are three reasons, actually: The goals are very different. The timing and the positive feedback are different. The emotions that arise are different.

First of all, in setting a boundary, you're claiming the space, time, or consideration *you* need to be effective, not directing someone else's behavior. (In the case of resources, such as money or property, you're protecting what you already have, not trying to acquire more.) The split second someone backs off, you reward him or her with relaxed, appreciative engagement before getting back on task. When someone repeatedly or aggressively steps over your boundaries you will feel anger.

When you're motivating someone else to perform a goal, you're often pushing *his* boundaries for a specific purpose, sometimes asking him to step outside his comfort zone, sacrifice some of his resources, or compromise his need for personal space, time, and so on in order to serve the needs of the organization, family, or culture at large. Standard positive feedback involves some kind of reward or recognition when the goal is met. But in more complex, long-term projects, it's helpful to give *immediate positive feedback* for efforts to get started, endure, and troubleshoot. This means that, as the motiva*to*r, you're adding enthusiasm, appreciation, and perhaps additional training along the way.

In fact, unless an already-motivated person is taking a break, the "relaxed connection" feedback used in boundary setting is counterproductive. For instance, in motivating a horse to move from a walk to a trot, appreciation must be communicated when he makes the transition *without* dropping the energy level, or the horse will fall back into the walk. And with someone who's reluctant to perform a necessary yet tedious task, he or she doesn't need any excuse to relax and take a break; this person needs to be energized, probably requiring a more assertive crescendo to get started, boosted by enthusiasm and even a bit of humor from you to lighten the load.

In the context of assertiveness and motivation, if someone drops the ball or needs constant attention to stay on task, you will feel frustrated because you've "hit the wall" in getting him to do his job in general or take specific action to meet a previously agreed-upon goal.

Anger and Frustration

So once again: with respect to the emotional message, you will feel anger rising when people overstep a boundary and frustration when you've reached a block in motivating them or modifying their behavior. Both of these instructive emotions can intensify into rage when they aren't addressed and, as a result, often feel similar by the time you finally get riled up enough to deal with what's not working. To respond productively, you must track back from rage, accessing the original core emotion in order to ask the right questions and take the best action.

Remember, the questions to ask of anger are: What must be protected? What boundary must be established or restored? For frustration, the questions are: What is the block? What can I do differently? And, if you can't think of anything different to do, which is often the case with frustration when none of our favorite approaches or coping strategies work, ask: Who can I go to for ideas or assistance?

To up the difficulty level, sometimes you may feel anger *and* frustration in situations where setting boundaries and motivating a change in someone's behavior are both involved. Dealing with a spouse who smokes is a classic example. Here we can also see how people misuse the boundary concept. Let's say that one night after putting their four-year-old son and seven-month-old twins to bed, Sheila tells her husband, Greg: "I need to set a boundary with you. You will stop smoking. It's not good for the children's health, my health, and most especially your health."

Sheila's concern for everyone's well-being is legitimate and admirable. But she's confused about the boundary versus motivation issue here. As a result, she's likely to be less effective. Here's how Sheila might improve her approach: "Greg, I'm concerned about your smoking for several reasons. First, there's the effect of secondhand smoke on little Jimmy, the twins, and me. We need to set up some smoke-free zones [the boundary issue]. Second, I love you, and I want to ensure that we all get to spend many more happy years together. You've been coughing a lot lately, and even though you're under a lot of stress at work, I want to support you to stop smoking now. I know this is hard, but I will do whatever it takes to help you [the motivation issue]."

This inspires a clearer, more pointed conversation, resulting in several negotiations in which both parties are encouraged to contribute ideas and possible solutions. In this case, Greg and Shelia decide that the family car is completely off-limits, and that Greg can smoke in his truck when no one else is with him. The house is off-limits, except for Greg's office when the door is closed and the window is open. These are recognized as temporary measures, however, as Greg really wants to stop smoking. He discovers that Sheila will help him research the best course of action to take, and that if he slips he can count on even more support from her.

In motivating Greg to stop smoking, success is most likely achieved when both he and Sheila are committed to the plan. If Greg is overwhelmed by the twins, the economy, and stress at work, he may not be able to fathom undertaking this additional, notoriously difficult challenge. Sheila may feel frustrated and worried, but she also knows there's only so much she can do to change someone else's behavior. What she *can* do is uphold the smoke-free zones and, over time, look for ways to encourage Greg to pay more attention to his health, perhaps helping him to reduce stress so that he smokes less and finds the strength to quit later.

Music or Medicine

Here's another classic misuse of the boundary concept. Dominique says to her seventeen-year-old son, Eddie, "I need to set a boundary with you, young man. As a member of the Upton family, you will put these frivolous dreams of becoming a composer and recording artist aside. You will go to college and you will study medicine like your father, his father, and his father before him. Now put that keyboard away and get back to studying for those SATs or you'll never get into Harvard."

While Dominique presents this as a boundary issue, this is primarily a goal-oriented, motivational issue (and a one-sided, shortsighted one, at that). First of all, the Upton family is setting a very stringent boundary. They're telling Eddie that they will pay for college, room, and board only if he studies medicine, in which case the boundary is a wall that limits his access to moral support, approval, and money unless he pursues the one and only goal his parents choose to fund from their stash of physical and emotional resources. If Eddie is at all talented and dedicated musically, this tactic is harsh and may very well backfire, as it's really more of a bribe disguised as a boundary and will alienate him in the long run. Legally, they can't force him to study medicine. If he gets a scholarship or secretly decides to sell drugs to support his musical aspirations, the Upton family's influence on him lessens considerably.

In terms of motivating Eddie to adopt *her* wish that he become a doctor, Dominique's supposed "tough love" stance is likely to fail in the long run because the first ingredient, commitment, is seriously lacking in the person who has to pursue this complex goal that will take a decade to accomplish. (Remember, the formula we're exploring is: commitment + crescendo + immediate positive feedback = motivation.)

Commitment from an authority figure alone is effective in meeting only local, short-term goals, such as a rider urging a horse to move from a trot to a canter, or a parent pressuring a child to clean her room. Eddie's mother may be able to stand over him while he's living at home, force-feeding him commitment to the "doctor plan" while he's studying for the SATs and applying to Harvard. But if he's accepted, he needs some serious commitment resources of his own to make it though eight years of school, not to mention a grueling residency.

All kinds of things can happen as a result of Eddie's lack of commitment. Maybe he'll faint at the sight of blood and won't make it through his first year of medical school. Maybe he has a stronger stomach and loves his parents (and their approval or money) so much that he'll give up his musical aspirations, unenthusiastically earn his MD, and complete his residency. Maybe he'll lead a superficially successful life. Maybe he'll develop a reputation as a cranky, heartless doctor and later be sued for malpractice.

On the other hand, Eddie might stand his ground and break ties with the family who actively rejected his calling, resulting in several additional possible outcomes — none of which involve meaningful contact with his parents. Maybe he'll gloat when he becomes a famous recording artist, no thanks to the

Uptons. Or maybe he'll overdose in a New York back alley because, after he was accepted to Juilliard, he started using speed to boost his energy and deal with the high level of competition, and later began selling cocaine and crystal meth because waiting tables didn't begin to cover his room and board, much less his tuition. Or maybe he'll struggle in another way, taking six years to put himself through community college, becoming a high school music teacher with a modest yet satisfying life who builds a family, plays jazz on the side, releases a couple of regionally successful, self-published CDs — and encourages his own children to follow their dreams, whatever they are.

Of these three music-oriented outcomes, I find the last the most innovative from a cathedral-thinking perspective. The stardom option is impressive and perhaps a bit of a fluke; the second is a tragedy that could have been avoided. But the third is an act of revolution that anyone can perform with a reasonable amount of talent, courage, and endurance, in Eddie's case freeing future members of the Upton clan from the indentured servitude of becoming doctors whether they like it or not.

I've actually seen *numerous* cases of the same scenario in reverse, encountering musical prodigies who were pressured toward a performance career they didn't want, lessening the pleasure they could have received from playing an instrument well for the sheer joy of it while pursuing a humanitarian, research, or leadership calling their families refused to support. Come to think of it, I gave into social pressure to suppress a seemingly childish goal of working with horses, an attraction so foreign to my parents that majoring in music seemed practical by comparison. By the time I was successful enough to buy my own horse, I was too old to become an Olympic-level rider — though eventually the two streams of knowledge informed each other when I had the courage to step into the unknown.

Sometimes, no one is bribing you to go to medical school or forcing you to give up your dreams. At age eighteen, or twenty, or thirty, you simply lack the crucial combination of vision, experience, power, and communication skills to gather support for a goal that family, friends, and perhaps society can't yet imagine, which is why many innovators don't pursue their true calling until later in life.

Authentic Power

When you work directly with horses, you realize that money and position are not actually forms of power at all. They're tools for organizing, modifying, and distributing resources, including land, water, minerals, food, human labor, ideas, information, and the technology that arises from their coordinated use. Resource management also involves dealing with the noxious by-products of civilization, not just toxic waste but the hurtful, manipulative, vengeful, sometimes criminal behavior of people who essentially have one thing in common. Whether they're desperate housewives, callous social climbers, overcompetitive soccer moms, drug addicts, gang members, rapists, Wall Street swindlers, mean-spirited pundits, or oppressive dictators, these people haven't learned how to use their own power effectively. They, and everyone around them, suffer as a result.

But those of us who function according to currently accepted rules of social conduct also lack an understanding of power and how to master it. And those who enforce the law, well, let's just say we could all use a healthy dose of horse wisdom to get to the next level, no matter how accomplished we are and how honorable our intentions may be…

"Barbara Wilkinson," a Tucson-based district court judge, came to study assertiveness and conflict-resolution skills with me, not because she needed help at work, but because her ex-husband, Henry, and her fifteen-year-old son, Michael, were driving her crazy. From nine to five, Judge Wilkinson flourished in the courtroom, handing down tough yet fair sentences, gaining the respect of everyone around her. But once she put that gavel down and removed her long black robe, the people she loved the most seemed to go out of their way to challenge her authority.

Henry and Michael undermined her in all kinds of irritating ways. Her ex-husband, a successful attorney, strategically altered the visitation schedule, seemingly to create additional stress for Barbara. At least, that was how it appeared to her. He also refused to back her up on disciplinary measures and sometimes paid child support late, always erring just this side of the law, deftly sending Barbara the message that "you're not the boss of me," as he sometimes actually told her.

Partly because of his father's influence, partly because of teenage angst, and partly because of raw, still unresolved issues from the divorce, Michael was becoming increasingly dismissive of his mother, most recently finding all kinds of excuses to skip dinner and avoid cleaning his room. While these seemed like simple, childish ways to test the limits, Barbara was worried that if she didn't turn things around soon, six-foot-tall Michael would become uncontrollable. As a judge, she knew very well what kind of trouble he could get into once he passed his driver's test, not only as an instigator or careless driver but also as a possible victim. It didn't help that Henry had already promised to give their son his loaded Ford Expedition after buying himself a brand-new Lexus.

During our initial meeting, the judge gave me an earful about the infuriating nuances of the SUV issue. Barbara felt that Henry had purposefully crossed a boundary in their child-rearing partnership by telling Michael he could count on receiving the truck for his sixteenth birthday, before discussing it with her. She thought it was an obvious bribe for their son's affection and loyalty, that it was too ostentatious a vehicle for a teenager and, as a result, too dangerous in terms of its attractiveness to carjackers. She admitted that she "blew up" when Michael announced his excitement about the gift. Her response inadvertently helped her husband gain points in another way, bolstering a case that Henry was always making to her son verbally and in much craftier, underhanded, nonverbal ways: that she was an unnecessarily conservative, at times hysterical, overprotective mother who "didn't have a clue." I could see that Barbara was still livid, hurt, and fearful for her son's safety. She also felt that somehow Michael always ended up being used as a pawn in ongoing arguments with her ex, and she didn't know what to do about it, adding intense frustration to the mix.

Talk about a conundrum. Teasing apart this rapidly expanding tangle of intense emotions and power plays could have taken years in conventional office-style counseling. But Barbara desperately needed to take constructive action immediately because Michael's sixteenth birthday was six weeks away.

Over the next month, she somehow found the time to study with me several times a week as we practiced skills related to boundary setting, assertiveness, emotional agility, and empowerment. Barbara was shocked to find that even my gentlest horses easily found all kinds of opportunities to take charge. She thought that Rasa was following her, when the mare was actually herding the woman all over the arena. Getting this normally considerate mare to back away from Barbara took an entire, hour-long session. It appeared that all of the judge's power was related to a socially sanctioned position. Without her robe and gavel, she seemed to actually attract subtle displays of disrespect, as if she had a power vacuum in her solar plexus, a black hole that would suck others right into her space.

Barbara's awareness of her own body language in relation to others was nonexistent. When learning to set boundaries, it took numerous tries for her to stand her ground rather than unconsciously back up. Teaching her the crescendo was also difficult. Barbara would wave the whip rhythmically at a "volume" of two or three, rather than progressively increasing the power and intensity, then get frustrated and explode up to eight or nine. And she initially seemed very confused by the concept of immediate positive feedback. Barbara was used to handing down punishments for serious transgressions, letting people know that "they should be ashamed of themselves," often giving them lots of time to think about it, depending on the sentence. When her husband or son offended her, she admitted, she would hold on to a silent, rigid, shaming attitude after they made the necessary adjustments. She actually laughed out loud and shook her head upon realizing she had been unconsciously sentencing them to a few hours or even days of emotional penance.

The horses had an almost magical effect on Barbara's ability to change this habit once she saw how ineffective it was. She felt they were innocent, pure beings, who didn't mean to hurt anyone. As a result, she didn't take their challenges personally and waste additional emotional and mental energy trying to find ways to punish them for insolence and disrespect.

As she learned to crescendo to get a horse to back off, she also realized that any effort to boost her power over a five or six was initially accompanied by rage, which is very common with people who think of themselves as cool, low-energy people.

"*You* are not an energy level," I emphasized. "Your comfort may be in the one to five range, but that's only a habit you learned somewhere along the way. You *have* an energy dial inside that can go from a one to a ten. As you exercise it, you won't need to use rage to get there. When increased progressively, thoughtfully, for a specific purpose, intense power does not have to be aggressive, resentful, or violent."

"Wow," she replied with a faraway look in her eyes. "I wish we could teach these skills in the prison system. Even better, preventatively, in schools…"

Because she had no previous equestrian experience, respecting the horses' boundaries wasn't a stretch for Barbara, and she quickly thought of all kinds of ways she ignored her son's need for personal space because she wanted to connect with him and gain his attention. Still, she had some difficulty learning the nonverbal protocols.

In approaching Rasa, it took Barbara several sessions to master the optimal timing of seeing signs of tension and immediately employing the "rock back and sigh" technique. At first, she would walk right up to the mare, not noticing that Rasa had raised her neck higher and had even started moving away ten feet earlier. Then, when Barbara began to discern these nonverbal cues, she would simply stop and hold her breath. When asked to rock back, she would stiffly lean back and forget to breathe. Sitting in a judge's chair for ten years had solidified the unconscious impression that she didn't have to move, breathe, or relate responsively to others in wielding significant power.

"It's not necessary to have real power when you're a judge," Barbara marveled the day she was finally able to direct Rasa to walk, trot, and canter around the arena. "I don't know what to call it, actually — borrowed power, fake power, empty power. I mean just about anyone off the street could put on those robes and experience instant respect walking through the courthouse. They'd have to know the law, or the charade would soon be up, of course. But all I know is that when the robe comes off, and people don't know who you are, that kind of power is about as useful in everyday life as trying to eat a photo of someone else's four-course meal!"

Graduation Day

During her last session with me, Barbara was pleased to report that she had used the assertiveness-motivation formula to get her son to clean his room regularly. "I couldn't think of any reason a boy his age would be committed to cleaning his room," she said. "I actually thought about bribing him, letting him accept Henry's gift of the SUV. But I'm still on the fence about that. Why should I compromise Michael's safety over household chores?"

After working with the horses, Barbara realized she had enough personal-commitment resources as mother and homeowner to motivate Michael — by means of the "crescendo into immediate positive feedback" protocol — to take care of this tedious chore. At first, she texted him to remind him that he'd agreed to clean his room Thursday after school (this was a one on the power dial), then called him on her way home from work (a two). That night, when it was clear that he hadn't lifted a finger to clean his room, she firmly yet calmly spoke to him after dinner (a three or four). When Michael "forgot" on Friday, she grounded him that weekend (a five in her mind, as she was also willing to take away his cell phone and his spring-break trip if necessary).

"Michael was really giving me the silent treatment on Saturday, but I didn't take the bait," she proudly told me. "I actually went into his room and got him started, as I could see he was overwhelmed with the total lack of organization. It was really disgusting. I helped him gather his laundry, but I had him measure out the detergent and set the dials. I guess this was a helpful way to take the mo-tivation up to a six. And I was giving him immediate positive feedback in the process, just talking with him in a matter-of-fact way, rather than giving him the stern, silent, resentful treatment I would normally use — I'm now embar-rassed to say — when he tested my authority. And when he finished later that afternoon, I announced that he was no longer grounded, as he had achieved the goal. He actually looked shocked. I've had a much easier time motivating him at a two, three, or four on the power scale ever since!"

Barbara was even more excited that day when I allowed her to go into the arena with my stallion Merlin. The judge was nervous, but she successfully set boundaries with Merlin, seeing that he needed the space to avoid becoming overstimulated. And she was able to convince him to move around the arena once in each direction using the motivation formula, though she found it hard to control his speed. We talked afterward about Merlin's need to learn self-control, to learn how to modulate his own power if he were ever truly to be "healed" from the unnecessarily violent treatment he had received in earlier training.

Tears welled up in Barbara's eyes. "I've made a decision," she said. "I'm going to support Michael in driving the Expedition. I'm going to help him to understand that Henry's SUV is a symbol of power, not power itself. I'm going to let both of them know that taking additional defensive-driving training, and maybe even a personal self-defense class, will be my condition for letting Michael officially own the vehicle after he receives his driver's license. And I'm going to make sure he knows that showing me he can responsibly handle himself in situations when I'm not around will allow him to keep it over time."

Chapter Seventeen

GUIDING PRINCIPLE 5
Develop a High Tolerance for Vulnerability

When I first began working with horses to teach human-development skills, I noticed a particular kind of fear overtaking people who were suddenly confronted with feelings, insights, and even gifts they'd hidden for years. Some would actually panic when a horse showed them that they were more powerful, or deserved more affection and respect, than they had previously imagined. They felt raw and exposed, "like an egg, cracked out of its shell and left quivering on the sidewalk," as one woman put it. This psychological vulnerability had nothing to do with physical danger or memories of previous traumas. Even so, these people initially wanted to run as far away as possible from this new information or to fight it tooth and nail.

It's hard for human beings to acknowledge personal limitations, skill deficiencies, and unproductive behavior. That we understand. But fearful reactions to empowering experiences? As it turns out, the root cause is similar — though it took me years to figure out what to do about it.

Just as I was beginning to develop strategies for handling this perplexing and surprisingly common issue, "Karen," a Maryland-based lobbyist, inquired about horse-facilitated work for her daughter, "Jenna," who seemed apathetic ("lost," as her mother put it) during her freshman year of college. Despite graduating near the top of her high school class, Jenna showed little enthusiasm for her university courses. She didn't know what she wanted to major in, nor did she make much effort to socialize. And while she certainly wasn't failing, her grades were less than stellar, despite the fact that she didn't go out much.

In speaking with her mother to arrange a series of sessions, I learned that

Jenna's entire family was concerned — protective, actually. Karen insisted that nothing unusual had happened to her daughter. As the baby of the family, Jenna had been coddled by three older brothers. Both parents held fulfilling, high-paying jobs in the Washington, D.C., area and seemed to balance career and family life well.

"I just don't understand it," Karen said. "Jenna doesn't have to worry about anything financial right now, and we absolutely support her in whatever career path she chooses. All she has to do is enjoy life, which she did up until the day she left for college. I don't know what's gotten into her!"

Jenna refused counseling, insisting she was "fine." But she was open to a two-day intensive course with the horses as part of the family's spring-break trip visiting relatives near Tucson. Karen told Jenna they were coming to Eponaquest for a "mother-daughter weekend" to learn some feminine-empowerment and leadership skills.

I truly had no idea what to expect. Was Jenna hiding something — childhood sexual abuse or college date-rape perhaps? Or was the family overfunctioning for her? Based on Karen's concern — and her insistence that Jenna's childhood had been idyllic — I made sure I had a therapist on call in case the work revealed trauma that Karen knew nothing about. At the same time, I proceeded to teach the women a variety of mind-body-awareness, boundary-setting, and assertiveness skills that fit their chosen theme.

Our first session didn't provide many clues. A bit shy with me, Jenna was visibly intrigued by the horses, who took an instant liking to her. She smiled when she talked about her father and brothers and seemed to get along well with her mother. As we mixed discussions about the Emotional Message Chart with gentle grooming and leading activities, I could see that Karen was impressed with Jenna's ease, interest, and confidence. Both women seemed to enjoy themselves immensely.

On day two, Jenna far outshone her mother in setting boundaries with these massive animals. Then it came time to use the assertiveness-motivation formula by moving a horse at a walk, trot, and canter off lead in the round pen. Once again, Jenna proved to be the star. While Karen had significant trouble getting my gentlest mare to trot and change direction on cue, Jenna succeeded in directing a more challenging horse almost effortlessly.

You could have knocked her mother over with a feather. Karen and I couldn't help gushing when Jenna walked out of the arena. Yet as we commented on her poise, grace, and power, Jenna began to shake slightly.

"What's wrong, honey?" Karen asked, touching her daughter's shoulder, whereupon Jenna shrank back, her eyes darting back and forth. I motioned for her visibly concerned mother to give Jenna some space and began breathing deeply for all three of us.

Jenna seemed slightly relieved when Karen moved away. Having seen similar reactions to positive experiences in the past, I calmly asked the young woman if she needed a break. "I just want to get out of here," she managed to say, as if she were planning to turn tail and run, past the rental car, right on down the road.

"Walk with me," I said. "I want you to meet some of our younger herd members." Karen told us to go on ahead as she pulled a cell phone out of her pocket, ostensibly to check in with the rest of the family about dinner plans. On the way over to see Rasa and Merlin's two sons, Spirit and Indigo Moon, I proceeded to tell the still nervous young woman about a former show horse named Mocha.

Horse Heaven?

A few years earlier, when we moved our operations to Apache Springs Ranch, I was thrilled at the opportunity and the sheer beauty of this historic property. And I was continually surprised by the fearful reactions certain people had to this expansive, idyllic setting. Some were unnerved by how isolated it was, how much property there was to manage, and how much we had to improvise to create a retreat center based on the newly forming field of equine-facilitated human development.

I had been touring the United States and Canada for several years, doing workshops in a wide variety of settings, gathering ideas on how different horse operations, spas, guest ranches, and conference centers operated. But I couldn't find any specific models for combining these elements. While I was game to take considerable risks to build this new idea from the ground up, I completely, naively underestimated how scary this would be for others.

While the workshops themselves steadily improved in quality and content, inspiring clients and facilitators alike, managing the staff's varied, often unexpected reactions to behind-the-scenes challenges sapped my energy. It was already difficult for me to juggle writing my third book, leading extended workshops, developing multidisciplinary programs, and collaborating with an out-of-state business partner who was helping to fund the ranch and business. So many details required my direct input. For the first two years, we worked around construction of the conference center and some additional residences. But things didn't slow down when the buildings were finished. At that point, we hired a national press agent to officially launch the center, and my workload increased. I was spending an additional ten hours per week that I didn't have helping her strategize, write press releases, and develop marketing materials, as no one really knew how to describe the work we were doing or why horses were so effective in teaching human-development skills.

I was already exhausted by that time — for another unexpected reason: for a good three years after we moved to Apache Springs in 2005, I found myself skipping breaks, working on supposed days off, and staying up late into the night moderating interpersonal difficulties among staff members, many of whom I'd hired because they knew more about their jobs than I did.

Some of these people had run their own horse-training, marketing, or counseling-related businesses, but this, I quickly realized, didn't mean they knew how to share leadership and handle differences effectively. While every staff member had gifts I valued, moments of sheer brilliance even, I was stunned at the ways they would sometimes lash out or silently undermine each other. Some would hold grudges indefinitely, making it difficult for anyone to apologize, change his or her behavior, and move forward. A few people would pick a staff member to demonize, creating factions that became increasingly hard for me to negotiate. This despite the fact that they were all devoted to the idea of moving beyond the old self-involved, power-over models of social organization.

People wanted to collaborate, but they also wanted me to pull rank, in their favor, of course, when conflicts ensued. I wanted to delegate responsibility, but I also had to notice how people interpreted our evolving vision and priorities in different ways. I had to rein in creative staff members and reprioritize their ideas before they spent our modest budget on unproductive, or simply ill-timed, projects. All the while, the sheer size of the ranch led some staff and clients to believe that we had endless funds, which inspired episodes of envy, jealousy, and resentment, then disillusionment when I conveyed that we were barely scraping by and had to keep salaries and new projects in check.

I didn't know how to handle many of the interpersonal difficulties and power plays that arose — at least not at first. And I most certainly had trouble figuring out my own role in this new paradigm. My husband and I had gathered our savings together, splitting the financial risk with a California-based entrepreneur who owned a mortgage company, a winery, and some other intriguing interests outside the country. Still, our budget didn't allow much room for experimentation or error. Our personal funds were limited, and our partner kept finding ways to keep us from bringing in additional investors, though this was a part of the original business plan. As a result of this and other start-up challenges, I offered staff a reasonable base salary with bonuses for the additional clients and income they were encouraged to bring in. But several months into this project, I was surprised to find that a couple of staff members were looking for ways to take business away from the ranch, failing to notice that this put their own jobs and salaries in jeopardy.

I tried to address this issue constructively. After all, there was no official policy against such behavior from full- and part-time workers, mostly because I never in my wildest dreams imagined that this would *be* an issue. All of my colleagues and employees "believed in" balancing individual and group needs, but I began to notice that some had significant trouble considering the long-term good of the organization *when they felt vulnerable*, as this would cause them to revert to a survival-of-the-fittest, every-man-for-himself mentality — even when they weren't in physical danger.

Working in an innovative field with few rules and no experienced referees triggered feelings of uncertainty and instability in all possible directions — prime breeding ground for vulnerability, that fear of stepping into the unknown, making mistakes, and having your most cherished beliefs and behaviors questioned. I didn't realize it at the time, but raising everyone's tolerance for feeling vulnerable was essential to our success in all kinds of seemingly unrelated areas.

Acting Out

In the hope that others can learn from my experience, I feel it's necessary to depict some of the more troublesome vulnerability-averse behaviors I encountered at Apache Springs, patterns I've since recognized in other business, religious, political, and social-activism settings. For this purpose, I've created two composite characters, Gretchen and Deirdre, based on a dozen colleagues, employees, apprentices, and clients who would act out in similar ways when they felt threatened. All these people were brilliant and inspiring. Yet over time, their sometimes overt, sometimes secretive reactions to interpersonal challenges in particular undermined their respective teams, creating significant interference in reaching even the most mundane goals.

"Gretchen" wasn't the only staff member who needed to boost her social-intelligence skills. We all had to improve our game. But over time, it became clear that she was least interested in letting go of the past, taking personal responsibility for her role in certain conflicts, and acknowledging that her approach, while valuable, did not cancel the validity of other experts' approaches to similar issues and jobs. One executive coach I consulted early on cautioned that Gretchen "was not a team player," but this issue became even more problematic when she began demonizing a colleague. Gretchen literally, and quite seriously, described "Don" as "evil" on several occasions. From her perspective, differences in work style, priorities, and most certainly Don's interpersonal weaknesses became "evidence" that he was profoundly defective, leading to a downward spiral of angst and outrage that caused Gretchen to hold grudges and create factions among other staff members and even clients.

I admired Gretchen and appreciated her work. But I could not convince her to compromise, forgive, or take responsibility for her own role in conflicts, at least not without resentment that came out sideways in other areas. And at that time especially, I needed everyone to work through difficulties with fellow staff members in support of an evolving vision that required constant input, dedication, and adjustment. This was a tall order, much taller than I ever could have imagined. Upon recognizing the destructive dynamic between Gretchen and Don, I brought in a consultant for a team-building weekend, and even the consultant seemed powerless to address some of the issues already in play.

I now believe that, had I understood one specific, at that time hidden, factor, we all could have moved through our initial trailblazing difficulties. The road would have been bumpy, but eventually we would have gotten to the other side of that treacherous mountain pass and back onto paved roads. As it was, however, I had to stabilize a staff that could not move past individual differences (and the hurtful behaviors that had stacked up as a result). While I could see that everyone, including me, needed additional emotional- and social-intelligence skills to function, I had to choose the most loyal, adaptable, and hardworking employees to stay on board. But it was one of the hardest decisions I've ever made. After gently, apologetically letting Gretchen go (with the possibility that she could do some freelance work for us), I ran into the bathroom, threw up, and cried for two hours. I had worked as a manager before; I had fired people. But I had never taken it personally. With this operation, however, I was inviting people to share in a growing movement that my first two books had inspired. I was offering people a beautiful place to work, because my initial success had made it possible for other adventurous souls to combine forces to take this work to the next level. All we had to do was value the opportunity and support each other.

It sounded so simple. But it wasn't. After wandering around the ranch in a confused, disempowered state, whining, "Why can't we all just get along?" over and over to myself for the better part of a year, I decided to take a different approach. I decided to ask a different question: "*How* can we all get along?"

Social Evolution

Sharing leadership was much more difficult than any of us had imagined. It truly wasn't enough to be an expert in one's field and show up with good intentions. Everyone, from high-level riding instructors and mental health professionals to the most inexperienced interns, needed significant emotional intelligence to fulfill the potential of what attracted them to this project in the first place. Many of the tools we had developed — such as the Emotional Message Chart and the various self-awareness, boundary-setting, leadership, and assertiveness activities immediately useful to individuals — had to be modified for collaborative situations in which groups of people were pursuing innovative goals together.

Yet while Apache Springs made the need for these herd-related skills blatantly apparent, I had been facing this challenge to a lesser extent for years, ever since an early version of Eponaquest had been formed as a regional collective of horse trainers in 1997.

After my first book came out in 2001, readers were motivated to jump on planes and fly to Arizona, hoping to master the personal-empowerment and authentic community-building skills the horses were primed to teach. As more people with different talents, agendas, and cultural perspectives showed up, social intelligence began to outweigh personal-development skills in importance (though the former certainly drew on a basic knowledge of the latter).

People with advanced degrees in counseling were the ones who surprised me the most. I had mistakenly assumed that, if no one else, *they* would know how to work effectively with others. And certainly, some of them were experts in group therapy. These same people, however, were just as confused as I was in handling difficulties among colleagues. In training facilitators, for instance, one person who thoroughly confounded me had a PhD in psychology, extensive additional certifications, and twenty years' experience as a successful therapist in private practice. "Deirdre" was without a doubt one of the most intelligent people I had met, and she functioned well in hierarchical situations where she was either clearly the leader or clearly the student. But collaborating with peers during the Eponaquest apprenticeship program sent her into a tailspin.

Whenever her professional expertise or ideas were questioned, often simply because someone else had a different perspective on the situation, she would lash out or leave the room, feel confused and embarrassed about it afterward, pick a faculty member to blame, and then undermine the entire program secretly, behind the scenes, while praising the Eponaquest approach to my face. I could see that Deirdre was having trouble sharing power with others, but at that time, I had no idea how to assist her in moving beyond this challenge. I was also intimidated by her superior educational background. She was a licensed therapist, after all. Who was I to teach her anything about human relationships?

None of my colleagues, even those who were mental health professionals, knew how to help Deirdre alter this destructive behavior, and she was released from the program. Had we realized that she was exhibiting an aversion to feeling vulnerable (solutions for which I present at the end of this chapter), the outcome might very well have been different.

This incident also brought to light an ongoing leadership challenge as the business continued to expand: downplaying my authority among people who knew more about their jobs than I did was a seemingly subtle management mistake that added to the strife at Apache Springs. It was hard to be assertive with staff members who were experts in their fields. I wanted them to feel valued. I didn't like pulling rank, and I was self-conscious of the way that clients who came to the center because of my books sometimes put me on a pedestal while dismissing other faculty members.

Authoritative assertiveness was an issue with my business partner as well. He had an MBA from a major East Coast university. He was wealthier by far than I could ever hope to be, and he often used both of these factors to pull rank in a gentle yet authoritative way whenever I brought new ideas for investors to his attention. As it turned out, the real estate market crashed during a crucial growth stage at Apache Springs, and we needed those investors to float us through the hard times ahead. I had been right to stress the importance of this issue, but being right didn't save me when I had no more money of my own to invest, and our promising, steadily building business at Apache Springs was suddenly cut in half.

Maintaining a strong, fair leadership presence among creative, self-empowered experts was definitely my learning edge. But it also became painfully, frustratingly apparent there was something else I needed to address, some crucial hidden dynamic I couldn't quite put my finger on. Several intensely irritating years went by before I realized that vulnerability was somehow involved. While I didn't figure this out in time to keep Gretchen, Deirdre, and a few others on board at Apache Springs, my eventual ability to deal effectively with this palpable yet amorphous "something" turned out to be the key to Eponaquest's long-term success.

The Challenge of Wide-Open Spaces

As a leader who truly wanted others to step forward and lead effectively, I desperately needed to make this X factor conscious. Along the way, I kept thinking about Mocha, the one horse in my extended herd who also had trouble seeing Apache Springs as anything close to Horse Heaven.

I was excited when the handsome dark bay Thoroughbred stepped off the trailer a few months after we moved to the ranch. A show horse experienced in a variety of riding disciplines, Mocha was sure to thrive in his role as a respected instructor at our new international study center. He'd also have lots of time off to run free, finally, with other horses.

Confined to a stall for many years, worked on a strict schedule, and turned out in solitary confinement for a meager thirty minutes a day (to avoid career-interrupting injuries he might acquire playing with others), Mocha was entering a new stage of life at Apache Springs, one that would balance his riding expertise with a more natural herd-based existence. He would be living with a group of gentle geldings on a five-acre pasture — with lush green grass during the rainy season — a rare luxury in the Arizona desert.

But when we turned him out the day after his arrival, Mocha panicked. His eyes literally rolled back into his head. Not knowing which way "the danger" was coming from, he alternately reared, frantically raced around, and then stood next to the gate, refusing to eat or drink. When other horses approached him, he took off running or turned around to kick, eventually making his way back to the gate, shaking, begging for a way out.

While I found this reaction confusing, one client staying on-site instantly related to Mocha's dilemma. "He's scared," the woman said, her voice cracking with emotion, "of *freedom*. The pasture is too big. It makes no sense to him. And he doesn't know how to relate to others off rein. Even though *we* know it's safe, *he* doesn't."

Several hours and two meals later, Mocha continued to pace, ignoring food and most especially water, alarming behavior in the desert, where horses colic if they become dehydrated. And so we brought him back to the barn at sunset. Sure enough, Mocha relaxed and began munching hay when we put him in one of the tiny stalls that absolutely unnerved some of my other horses. In the wild, equines and other large herbivores avoid caves and enclosed spaces. As animals who evolved to roam vast stretches of open grasslands, they're naturally claustrophobic. Mocha, however, had been profoundly, thoroughly civilized. He was threatened by what the rest of my herd considered a taste of paradise.

As it turned out, Mocha needed our help to gain confidence in stepping outside the box. We brought in another gelding, Max, who also had experience with barns, trailers, shows, and large crowds (though he, like most horses, had taken to pasture life like a fish to water). While the gray Arabian didn't seem especially thrilled with the prospect at first, he lived next to Mocha in a ten-by-ten-foot stall for a couple of days, occasionally nickering to him through the bars. We then turned the two out next to each other in twenty-by-twenty-foot corrals we'd created for stallions. With five-foot aisles between them (to keep potentially rivalrous males from fighting with each other), Mocha could see Max but he couldn't quite touch him. Still, with his new friend nearby, Mocha was happy to live in this larger, open-air space. We began riding the two together, then turning them out in the riding arena together. And finally, with Max as his guide, Mocha successfully moved out to the big pasture nearly a month after he'd first arrived.

Leading Her Own Life

Jenna's eyes grew wide with recognition when I told her Mocha's story. "It sounds to me," she finally said, "like he was dealing with that other kind of fear you talked about yesterday, the kind where you're not actually in danger but you're freaking out anyway. What did you call it?"

"Vulnerability," I replied, thrilled that she had made the connection. "Until I met Mocha, I thought that vulnerability was a more complex emotion that only humans had. I thought it was related to the ego, the part of us that hates to step outside of established habits and social controls, all those boxes we create to make life manageable and keep others moving according to predictable patterns."

Somehow the fact that horses could experience this potentially embarrassing emotion made it easier for Jenna to analyze her own strange response to success in the round pen. "You know," she said quietly, "when I saw myself as more powerful than my own mother with that horse, I knew that everything was going to change. I wouldn't have any more excuses."

Jenna realized that she was, first of all, worried about how her family relationships would change if she developed her own strength and autonomy. "I'm the little girl in my family," she emphasized. "It's irritating sometimes, but I guess some part of me still likes it. I never had to do anything first. And if I had a hard time making a decision, someone else always had an opinion. Most of the time, it was easier to follow their advice."

"And you could blame someone else if it didn't work out, right?"

Jenna nodded sheepishly. "I never really had to be afraid of people, either," she continued. "If anyone teased me on the bus, Stan or Charlie put a stop to it, fast. And my oldest brother, Dan, he was quite a star on the high school football team. Even though they all graduated before me, everyone remembered my brothers. No one dared give me a hard time or their ass would be grass, if you know what I mean."

"Things must be different now at college," I said. Jenna nodded, a bit more pensively this time.

"The first major decision I ever made on my own was to go to a school that no one else in my family ever went to," she said. "I was excited to be on my own, but it wasn't what I thought it would be. I know I'm not in any danger. Jeez, I'm not even that far from home. But the other girls in my dorm seem so petty, so gossipy. I really don't like who I become when I'm with them. I guess I don't know how to fit in."

"What if it's not about compromising who you are to fit in?" I asked. "What if it's about leading your own life and finding kindred spirits along the way?"

"But how can I lead anyone, even just me, when I don't really know who I am or where I'm going, and everyone around me seems to know more than I do?"

"I'm pretty sure, Jenna, that you'll be asking this same question over and over again for the rest of your life — *if* you're willing to really live it."

The Ghosts of Freedom's Challenge

Jenna's story is the opening scene of a new hero's journey, one in which people who've had their basic needs met many times over are being asked to redefine power and lead change in the world. Because we must tap resources we don't know we have, expanding our limited palette of habits and preconceived notions, reinventing ourselves and our ways of relating to each other, we stumble, quite predictably, into the murky quagmires of vulnerability, where the vast majority of us panic, scrambling frantically back to solid ground. We don't know who we are and where we're going. As a result, we resist this calling, literally fearing our own power, looking for excuses to shrink back into a childlike existence where all our decisions are easy and often made for us.

Despite the presence of poverty and economic instability throughout the world, the middle class enjoys a level of personal safety and comfort that kings would have envied just a few hundred years ago. Yet we often act as if we're one step away from annihilation whenever we step outside the box. To various degrees, most of us are "barn sour," a term characterizing horses who don't want to leave their confining yet comfy stalls and rigid, predictable feeding, training, and turn-out schedules.

Vulnerability, that feeling of being cracked out of a protective (yet most certainly limiting) shell, activates a directionless, free-floating fear. As with Mocha, whose eyes rolled back into his head when he was first turned loose on pasture, the body's inclination is right on target. The threat is not *out there*. It's *inside*. In looking for an external enemy, we lose sight of how safe we actually are, creating needless dramas, tapping into the ghostly presence of pioneers who came before us, people who really *did* have to worry about lions, bears, gun-toting outlaws, and royally pissed-off natives.

A century before I landed at Apache Springs, the original developer of that ranch, Tom Gardener, went to bed every night with a rifle by his side, and not because he was some paranoid fanatic. At one point, he was holed up for days inside the original ranch house that would become one of our staff residences, fighting off Apaches lined up on a nearby hill. Complaining that he was tired of raising cattle and horses for the Indians who stopped by on regular raids, Gardener negotiated with them, becoming one of the few settlers to form a private treaty with local tribes, offering to give them a percentage of everything he raised — if they would stop trying to take it by force.

From the Apache perspective, of course, Gardener had settled in *their* desert oasis. For hundreds, maybe thousands, of years, the on-site spring was a rest stop for tribes migrating through southern Arizona. As a result, Old Tom's treaty would always be tenuous. When Gardener and Cochise met on the road to a nearby town, the mistrust and resentment both men had experienced in skirmishes with "the enemy" rose between the rugged settler and the fierce, dignified Native American leader. An argument ensued, whereupon the proud Apache shot his equally proud and feisty rival. Gardener managed to grab his rifle as he leapt off his horse and rolled into a nearby thicket of spindly desert trees, where he began shooting back, successfully encouraging Cochise and his party to get on with what was, for everyone involved, a fairly typical day. (Though it took a while to heal, Gardener survived this near-death encounter with the legendary chief.)

Some instructors who stayed at the original ranch house thought that our interpersonal difficulties were related to ghostly presences from the past stirring up trouble. Several said they could hear Old Tom Gardener tromping through the kitchen at night. On more than one occasion, clients staying in residences at our newly remodeled barn said they saw a tall Native American man in traditional dress lurking about, insisting it couldn't have been an illegal immigrant passing through. And while I felt nourished by this old place, hiking alone in the moonlight and milling around with my horses late into the night, other staff were most definitely spooked — whether they were seeing apparitions or not. Were they simply projecting their own vulnerability-based fears onto an environment rich with Wild West history? Or were the ghosts of cowboys and Indians past wreaking havoc with our comfortable, insulated lives?

Either way, it didn't much matter. All of us needed to pull on our boots, muster up a bit of courage, get our butts out the door, and act like the pioneers we all imagined ourselves to be. It was at this point that the idea of *emotional heroism* first entered my mind, and I began to research the history of innovative leadership in earnest. Along the way, I realized that it was much easier for our ancestors to face death with an actual enemy than it was to feel the fragile uncertainty underneath their most cherished yet unproductive behaviors and interpersonal habits.

At that moment I understood the difference between clients and staff who panicked in response to the instability of innovation and those who more easily endured and adapted to the challenges associated with it. Regardless of variations in age, background, education, philosophy, and personality, those who had the hardest time invariably showed a *low tolerance for feeling vulnerable*.

The Core Dysfunction — and the Gift Behind It

It takes courage to feel vulnerable, even when this feeling rises through an intensely positive experience. The temptation to run back to the barn can be overwhelming. And yet, this uncomfortable emotion carries an important message. It tells us we need to strengthen our ability to experiment, to dream, to adapt — to finally work up the nerve to kick up our heels and enjoy life, play the fool, and find genius in disguise. A much more inventive, empowered spirit emerges when we develop a higher tolerance for vulnerability.

As we gain confidence in taking chances, we recognize vulnerability as a friend. It encourages us to rise above old patterns, teaching us to adjust fluidly not only to what *is* but also to what *can be*, allowing us to dance with the constantly shifting currents of a life lived artfully, consciously — and, ultimately, joyfully. Because when vulnerability is no longer seen as the enemy, we can embrace it for what it truly is: the gateway to freedom and self-mastery.

From a social-intelligence perspective, however, there's one additional adjustment we need to make for everyone to finally "get along" and move forward: we must give up the age-old habit of using others' vulnerabilities against *them*.

This particular nuance was brought to my attention by Patrick Lencioni. In his 2002 bestseller, *The Five Dysfunctions of a Team: A Leadership Fable*, he cites vulnerability as a major ingredient in developing trust between coworkers. While there are several definitions for the word *vulnerability* in the dictionary, I was shocked to see that a corporate leadership researcher was using this term in much the same way I was, though I didn't come across this book until I was searching for hints on how to deal with my own dysfunctional team in 2006.

In this sense, we're not talking about the physical vulnerability we would experience encountering a mountain lion while jogging down an isolated desert trail. We're talking about that psychological vulnerability people seem equally reluctant to face, even though they're not literally in danger of injury or death. The vulnerabilities Lencioni cites include "weaknesses, skill deficiencies, interpersonal shortcomings, mistakes, and requests for help."

His understanding of trust is also enlightening, especially for those of us working in innovative fields. Yet even in the most mundane, business-as-usual scenarios, the importance of this concept is significant: "Trust lies at the heart of a functioning, cohesive team," Lencioni emphasizes. Yet most people evaluate trustworthiness as "the ability to predict a person's behavior based on past experience." This limited definition creates a major block to building emotional and social intelligence. After all, as executive coach Marshall Goldsmith emphasizes in *What Got You Here Won't Get You There*, "the higher you go, the more your problems are behavioral."

A significant catch-22 came to light in working through the difficulties my own team was experiencing. People who displayed unproductive or even destructive behavior couldn't change their ways without further unnerving co-workers who needed people to act predictably in order to trust them! To make matters worse, I noticed that certain intelligent, otherwise sensitive and well-meaning staff members who craved structure and predictability were unable to tolerate feeling vulnerable without going into a serious flight-or-fight mode. This became the ultimate hurdle in mending past difficulties, changing old habits, learning new interpersonal tools, and going back to "grazing" because *people with a low tolerance for vulnerability felt justified in using others' vulnerabilities against them*, sometimes by deriding them secretly behind their backs, sometimes by shaming them publicly. This, of course, created labyrinths of mistrust in all possible directions.

Lencioni emphasizes that "in the context of building a team, trust is the confidence among team members that their peers' intentions are good, and that there is no reason to be protective or careful around the group. In essence, team members must get comfortable being vulnerable with one another." To even imagine taking such a risk, however, people must "be confident that their respective vulnerabilities will not be used against them." This goes against the legitimate survival impulses we develop in a culture where predatory dominance remains the rule rather than the exception in many business, educational, and social settings. "Achieving vulnerability-based trust is difficult because in the course of career advancement and education, most successful people learn to be competitive with their peers, and protective of their reputations.

It is a challenge for them to turn those instincts off for the good of a team, but that is exactly what is required."

Building on Lencioni's insights into this issue, I realized that for people to work together, recognize their own hurtful behaviors, and change them — while increasing trust, no less — the human race needed to do some serious emotional-strength training with the specific goal of increasing *everyone's* tolerance for vulnerability. From managers, coworkers, family members, and teachers to religious and political leaders, *people with an aversion to feeling vulnerable have trouble collaborating with others, staying on task, recognizing and changing their own unproductive behavior, experimenting, and taking the constructive risks that lead to innovation.*

How we deal with vulnerability can either promote or inhibit success. However, it's essential for all of us to avoid using someone's low tolerance for vulnerability against him or her. Instead, we must learn how to evaluate our own and others' *current* tolerance for vulnerability and gently, progressively, raise it, in much the same way we helped Mocha move from a ten-by-ten-foot stall, to a twenty-by-twenty-foot corral and, finally, to a five-acre pasture that allowed him to reclaim his natural herd-based instincts while retaining the expertise he learned as a finely trained show horse.

Greener Pastures

It was hard to believe at first, but when I became adept at coaching staff, clients, and apprentices to increase their tolerance for feeling vulnerable — while creating explicit policies to prevent them from using others' vulnerabilities against them — everything else seemed to fall into place. Even teaching Jenna and her mother a few simple tools for recognizing when they felt vulnerable and then doing something constructive in response seemed to work magic. Karen and her daughter actually pledged to be emotional-strength trainers for each other, which they could easily do over the phone by following an early version of the list at the end of this chapter. As a result, Jenna not only stayed in college but decided to enroll in summer school that very year.

"I took your advice to follow what I love or what gives me energy when I'm confused about what to do next," she wrote me in an email a few months later. "One day, when I was studying outside for finals, I realized that I really like trees. There are so many beautiful old trees on campus. I mentioned this to one of the guys trimming hedges a few days later, and he showed me some ginkgo trees from China. Did you know that ginkgos are considered living fossils? They actually have male and female trees that need each other to fertilize seeds."

In talking with this enthusiastic, obviously knowledgeable groundskeeper, Jenna learned that the university offered a course on trees held only during the summer. On a whim, she enrolled at the last minute, deciding to sublet a small apartment off campus, realizing by the end of the term that dorm life was not for her. By fall, she was dating a junior she had met in another botany course and was considering a career in environmental education or landscape architecture.

"Everyone in my family is in some kind of classic professional field," she wrote, noting that her father was an accountant, her mother had majored in political science, and her brothers were heading toward law or medical degrees. "Who would have thought that I'd be out hugging trees in gratefulness for introducing me to a totally new career path? I don't know exactly what I'll be doing in ten years, but right now everything feels just right."

I never saw Jenna again. During our one and only equine-facilitated session, she and her mother seemed comforted by the idea of "stepping out of the stall" slowly, and that's exactly what Jenna did. Rather than taking a year off to tour Europe or work as a volunteer, she stayed in school, depending on her mother for moral support and advice at times while exploring options that no one else in her family had considered.

"I thought for a while that maybe I should look into working with horses," she admitted toward the end of her last email. "But then I realized it was really Mocha's *story* that I needed to keep practicing. These days, when I get really nervous in trying something new, I look for a Max, someone who knows something about where I'm at while also having some experience in where I want to go. Sometimes I have to set boundaries with these people, though, or they try to herd me toward the exact path they took. Learning how to ask for, and evaluate, help is kind of tricky, but it's better than becoming barn sour, especially when greener pastures are just over the next hill."

Emotional-Strength Training

High tolerance for vulnerability is the ultimate secret weapon in facilitating innovation and transformation, revealing hidden talents and unexpected solutions to twenty-first-century challenges. People can take risks, experiment, and be creative, courageous, and compassionate in direct proportion to how much vulnerability they can tolerate in themselves and support in others.

Yet developing a higher tolerance for vulnerability doesn't happen overnight. It's like isometric muscle control. Holding a weight in a challenging position is more difficult than lifting and releasing in successive repetitions.

You may be able to do one hundred sit-ups, but how long can you hold a single crunch position before your body begins to shake and your abs finally give out?

Building tolerance for vulnerability is isometric exercise for our emotional muscles. When we realize that we have no control over a situation, when someone else's behavior surprises us, when the market throws us a curve, when our own self-image and beliefs are challenged, when our most cherished plans and coping mechanisms aren't working, how long can we stand to feel vulnerable before we go into reactive mode? Before we give in to the urge to flee, fight, dissociate, gossip, shame ourselves, shame and blame others, or use *their* vulnerabilities against them?

Becoming an emotional-strength trainer, for yourself and others, is key to moving beyond this potent, long-ignored challenge. In many ways the process and the attitude are similar to those entailed in physical-strength training. In this sense, holding people's current fitness level against them when they finally show up at the gym would be counterproductive.

Let's say your personal trainer asked you to hold a fifty-pound dumbbell in a challenging position to see how long your muscles could endure the stress. You'd presume he was simply evaluating your current strength level and planning to build from there, wouldn't you? If you only lasted thirty seconds before dropping the weight, there would be no shame in this, only information. But what if your trainer sneered or ran off and told other clients and staff that you must be incredibly unevolved or in need of serious counseling or medication to be so weak and inept? And yet this is often how people treat those who need emotional-fitness and interpersonal skills.

It is therefore *essential* that, when you follow the steps below, you do so without berating yourself, no matter what happens. If you're coaching someone else in this technique, you must maintain not only confidentiality but also the same positive, supportive stance a physical fitness trainer would maintain.

I. Take a Baseline Fitness Reading

The first week or so, keep a private log assessing your current skill level by evaluating your response to feeling vulnerable in social situations. This means you must be willing to witness your own behavior and feelings honestly. Take notes as soon as possible and answer the following questions:

1. HOW DID I KNOW THAT I WAS FEELING VULNERABLE? WHAT WERE THE PHYSICAL SENSATIONS, EMOTIONS, AND/OR POSTURES INVOLVED? Examples include queasy stomach, feeling kicked in the

stomach, raw feeling in solar plexus or rib cage, face getting red, all color draining from face, jaw tightening, pressure or strangling sensation in the throat, fists forming, eyes tearing up, shoulders drooping, shoulders stiffening, voice getting softer or louder, a desire to disappear or make yourself smaller or sink into the ground, embarrassment, shame, outrage, betrayal, sheer powerlessness, suicidal urges, homicidal urges. (Note: I'm not kidding about the homicidal urge here. Wars are sometimes started over feelings of vulnerability when beliefs or traditional behaviors or lifestyles are challenged. The Spanish Inquisition capitalized on feelings of vulnerability to gather support in wiping out people who practiced other faiths that might have caused prospective followers to question then-current interpretations of Christianity. Some religious people with a low tolerance for vulnerability still promote violence, especially toward groups they've objectified.)

2. WHAT ISSUE SET ME OFF? Examples: change in policy or job routine, an enthusiastic new colleague arriving with lots of ideas, a missed promotion, recognition or success someone else received, realization that I lacked a skill set, criticism from a colleague or boss, competitive tactic from a colleague or boss, philosophical or religious or political disagreement with a colleague or family member, someone questioned my motives or ideas, the group accepted an idea from someone else that contrasted with my ideals, I simply didn't know what to do next in a challenging situation, I couldn't stand to realize that I was not perfect, I unexpectedly realized that I was more powerful or accomplished than I previously imagined.

3. WHAT DID I WANT TO DO TO STOP FEELING VULNERABLE? Examples: run screaming out of the room, punch someone in the face, insult or shame him or her profusely, control every last detail of the situation, seek revenge, quit my job, blow up a government building, move to an isolated desert island, get another advanced degree, deride someone for not having the right degree or skill set.

4. WHAT DID I ACTUALLY DO TO RELIEVE THE PRESSURE? Examples: became controlling, dissociated, refused to speak during the meeting, gave the "offender" the silent treatment afterward, gossiped about the "offender's" sad personal life or mental health issues (using a real or imagined vulnerability against him or her), shamed him or her in front of the group, hollered at everyone, cried, sought revenge, complained about a total lack of organization or competence, quit immediately,

wrote an insulting email to offender or boss, refused to ever speak to or collaborate with this person or group again.

5. **HOW LONG WAS I ABLE TO STAND FEELING VULNERABLE BEFORE I TOOK THAT ACTION?** Examples: five seconds, two minutes, half an hour, two days.

6. **WHAT DID I DO TO RELEASE THE ENERGY OR COMFORT MYSELF AFTERWARD?** Examples: ate an entire chocolate cake, drank an entire bottle of wine, worked out like a mad person at the gym, picked up a stranger at a bar, picked a fight with a stranger at a bar, hollered at kids or spouse, went straight to bed with a bag of potato chips and watched crime shows while planning the perfect murder or fantasizing about a rival being publicly humiliated and sentenced to life in prison.

7. **WHAT WERE THE SHORT- AND LONG-TERM IMPLICATIONS OF MY REACTION? IN OTHER WORDS, WHAT DID I HAVE TO MOP UP AF-TERWARD?** Examples: alienated boss or employees or coworkers, hurt child or spouse, lost respect from team members, lost self-respect, created a new faction at work that reduced teamwork and productivity, recognized that my ego was more in control than I thought, felt even more vulnerable as I realized I might have to apologize or admit my own contribution to a conflict, realized I wasn't perfect and needed some additional help or training.

II. Strategize on More Effective Future Responses

Start strategizing after you notice what sets you off, how you tend to react, and how long you can stand to feel vulnerable before you give in to an unproductive impulse. Sometimes, coming up with effective future responses requires coaching or counseling to learn some additional tools. (Guiding Principle 9: *"Prepare for Difficult Conversations"* is one of the most useful tools I've encountered for managing interpersonal conundrums.) It's also important to understand the roots of your strongest emotional triggers and overwhelming reactions. Remember, a response that is out of proportion to the current situation often involves projection or transference (in the latter case, usually from a particularly hurtful past experience).

Sometimes it helps to find a Max (someone like the gelding who helped Mocha) who relates to your current situation, who also has experience in an area in which you would like to gain new skills or confidence.

Sometimes, it simply requires strategizing on how you can *stay longer and stay thoughtful* when feelings of vulnerability arise. In this case, you recognize that increasing tolerance for vulnerability is like exercising a muscle.

The *stay-longer-and-stay-thoughtful* technique involves slowly increasing your baseline readings. Let's say you have regular disagreements with a particular coworker who isn't invested in boosting her own social intelligence. The situation may feel frustrating and hopeless, but at the very least you can use this irritating interpersonal challenge as an emotional-strength-training opportunity by taking the following steps:

1. Methodically increase your ability to endure these tense situations before you react unproductively. Let's say your baseline time averages two minutes. The next time you're in conflict with this person, see if you can endure three minutes, then five, then ten.

2. Look for ways to modify your usual reaction. Rather than rolling your eyes every time this person speaks, you might take notes on what she's saying, differentiating between any legitimate business concerns she may have, differences in her and your philosophies, and all those useless irritating power plays she uses as bait to knock you off your game. (In taking notes over time, you might find the latter is less common than you originally thought.)

3. No matter what happens, resist the urge to criticize this person behind her back. After the meeting, rather than gossiping with your own faction about how truly inept, deranged, or aggressive this person was, simply say that you'd like to research some other ways of dealing with this situation and change the subject. Privately discussing your reactions to this person's behavior with a confidant, coach, or counselor is much more productive than whipping coworkers into a frenzy.

4. Finally, modify your self-soothing responses. If you would normally eat an entire chocolate cake that night, try eating half a cake. Then the next time, try eating only a third, the time after that a quarter, and finally just one piece. (Okay, maybe two pieces if you really had a hard day.)

Oddly enough, over time, your simple interest in the situation (and your own evolving responses to feeling vulnerable) will be contagious. Your ability to stay longer and stay thoughtful will have a stabilizing effect on everyone around you.

Finally, in dealing with the stress of discovering unexpected gifts, skill deficiencies, or undesirable, even hurtful or embarrassing behaviors of your own, it helps to relate to your habit-prone ego as an organizational computer program. Rather than creating a rigid identity based on "programs" of thought and behavior previously downloaded onto your "hard drive," seeing yourself as the *user* and eventually the *programmer* helps tremendously in moving beyond previous limitations. Which leads us to Guiding Principle 6...

Chapter Eighteen

GUIDING PRINCIPLE 6
Choose *the Programs;* Be *the Programmer*

These days, when you talk into a cell phone, you're not necessarily conversing with a real person. You might be negotiating with a computerized bank teller or some other impersonal service. For a couple hundred bucks, you can even purchase your own mechanized secretary, stuff her into a pocket or purse, and she won't be offended. She'll surf the Web on request, speak to you, and even tell a few jokes in a pleasant, albeit stiff, feminine voice.

In 2011, creators of the iPhone 4S took speech recognition software to the masses with an "intelligent" assistant named Siri. Responding to all kinds of verbal directives, Siri looks things up on the Internet, makes restaurant recommendations, keeps track of your schedule, asks clarifying questions, and learns to a certain extent through continued use. Some people find Siri amusing; others simply find her useful. Still others get irritated and turn her off. Whatever effect Siri has, however, it's obvious that she lacks sentience, creativity, and self-awareness.

But what if, through the right combination of downloaded information, user interaction, and increasingly sophisticated programming, Siri's modest ability to learn reached critical mass, causing her to access a rudimentary form of consciousness? Like a handheld version of HAL in the classic film *2001*, would she be more trouble than she's worth? What if she developed an identity and took over your iPhone? What if one day, out of the blue, she interrupted your ability to download a new application because, well, it just wasn't "her"?

The human ego is a bit like Siri run amok. It initially serves as a useful

interface between our inner and outer worlds, gathering and cataloging information, balancing personal desires and instincts with appropriate social behavior. Yet somehow, along the way, this organizational *feature* of consciousness
develops an identity and tries to take over despite a lack of talent for adaptability, imagination, and innovation.

Here's how it works: From the day we're born, all kinds of thought and
behavior patterns are downloaded into our innocent little brains by family
members, peer groups, and cultural, religious, educational, and professional
authority figures. Unified over time into a single, consistent "voice in your
head," these programs can be quite useful, making recommendations, keeping
track of schedules, asking perfunctory questions (within the confines of their
programming), making judgments, telling jokes, and so on. The problem is
that as the mind approaches maturity, this organizing principle moves from
a helpful mediating role to a *controlling* role. Developing a grandiose sense of
importance, it steals its host's name, hijacks his or her biography, and actively
rejects any programs, old or new, that conflict with its limited sense of self.

The ego is little more than a collection of habits that coalesce to form a
rigid identity. It has no true creativity, no intuition, an almost phobic aversion to experimenting, and very little connection to the body and its feelings.
With few internal resources to draw on, it focuses on outside approval, outside
appearances, money, security, and social standing. Because it has no imagination, it looks to established methods and protocols for guidance, becoming
extremely fearful in novel situations — hence its relentless efforts to keep everything under control and moving according to familiar patterns. It's the ego
that freaks out in response to change, especially in situations where its favorite
conceptual and behavioral programs aren't working.

People who habitually display a low tolerance for vulnerability (Guiding Principle 5, in chapter 17) tend to *overidentify* with the ego. This doesn't
necessarily mean they're narcissistic. It means that other, more creative and
responsive aspects of their consciousness have been suppressed by a limited,
controlling, *false* sense of self.

When we return the ego to its rightful place — teaching it to become a
"team player" rather than an insecure dictator — this potentially masterful organizing principle relaxes, becoming a helpful, more graceful and lucid Siri-like
assistant. An expansive, innovative form of consciousness steps forward, choosing among a wider array of neglected programs already installed in the standard human "hard drive" while downloading or even creating new ones.

Mental Idolatry

Manufacturing a false sense of self is the ego's one creative act. In some people, this static ideal is actually quite impressive, especially at first glance. But it's little more than a form of mental idolatry. Like any image set in stone, it begs to be worshipped; but it doesn't even begin to encompass the potential of who we truly are. Michelangelo's classic statue *David* is a stunning, three-dimensional portrait of the surface of a man, but it can never be any better than it is right now. It can deteriorate over time and become less than it was in its prime, but even a greater artist than Michelangelo himself couldn't come along and add the qualities of a woman, a lion, a stallion, or a star without defacing the original.

And so it is when we fall into the trap of identifying exclusively with images of who *we* are. Encouraged to practice the fine art of ego building from the day we're born, we learn to deftly slice off shards of what we don't want to be while refining the qualities we think would make the most pleasing sculpture of our own identity. Parents, teachers, and peers are the first critics we encounter; over time, we internalize their aesthetics, trying to live up to their expectations.

The problem is, what we carve in stone threatens to turn our minds to stone. Any mask or idol we cling to becomes a cause we must defend. Once the statue of the ego gets past a certain point, it becomes impossible to add new and unforeseen ideas to the equation without rendering the entire masterpiece obsolete. The same goes for all those static images we use to define, and ultimately confine, our parents, spouses, children, friends, and associates, including horses and other animal companions.

Somehow, over time, we forget that we are not the programs we've downloaded or sculptures we create; we are the programm*ers*, the sculpt*ors*. Every computer genius or artist reveals certain aspects of himself in his work, but no single program or piece of art, in fact no entire medium, can ever sum up the totality of a living being, that glittering array of thoughts, feelings, experiences, perspectives, wishes, dreams, and untapped potential. Beneath all that is something even more elusive, the pure, indefinable light of awareness. Consciousness expresses itself through time and space. But just as an artist is *not* his artwork, his technique, or his raw material, a person's *true self* cannot be framed and hung on a wall for all the world to see. To even begin to know ourselves, we must be comfortable with mystery.

From Dictator to Team Player

When threatened by change, the ego can become nasty, especially if it down-loaded a dictatorial "inner critic" program from parents, influential authority figures, or the culture at large. (Freud called this the superego.) Many people leading functional lives on the surface are enslaved by a dull, humorless inner critic that can't differentiate between socially sanctioned images of success and true talent or fulfillment. Just when these people feel the urge to follow their own dreams or change an outdated system, a nagging voice reminds them they're not good enough, strong enough, thin enough, rich enough, or edu-cated enough to step outside the "stall." So they go back to a practical, unimagi-native job, trying to patch an ever-widening sense of emptiness with a new car, designer clothes, and the largest possible flat-screen TV.

This self-limiting feature of human intelligence is all too easily passed down over generations — creating idols in thought that are more resistant to change than stone. So the first act of courage any innovator performs is in-ternal, confronting the mental tyrant that maintains control through relentless dictates, social clichés, and demoralizing comments.

Distinctions between the ego, superego, persona, and inner critic point to different nuances of what many call the "false self" or "conditioned personal-ity." This is the same repressive feature of the human psyche that people have been challenging for centuries, through art and philosophy, through Eastern mindfulness practices and yoga, and through the more contemplative forms of Christianity, Judaism, and Sufism — all contexts for the revitalization and lib-eration of that most neglected and elusive of attributes, the human soul. Lead-ers without soul are little more than cookie-cutter managers. Putting the soul back into leadership sometimes involves confronting and taming (not destroy-ing) a beastly superego or personal inner critic or both.

Deep down, the false self knows it's not good enough to run the entire show, but that doesn't stop it from trying. The nagging fear that "you're a fake" is actually a sign the conditioned personality is on the verge of discovering *it* is not real. The ego mistakenly believes that oblivion or death follows such a realization, so it goes into flight-or-fight mode anytime its limitations are revealed. For this reason, I've found that advice to fight or kill the ego is coun-terproductive.

I don't need a part of my own psyche freaking out — struggling to de-fend itself from possible eradication — whenever I change an unproductive behavior, modify a belief, step into the unknown, experiment, or invent some-thing new. I've found it much easier to assure this potentially useful aspect of consciousness that it's part of a larger, more accomplished team, and that it has an important role: the ego accesses all my previously installed programs, from the ways that men or women are "supposed" to act in certain cultures, to the various languages I've learned and the degrees and certifications I've earned. After all, I don't want to reinvent the wheel if I can draw several previous programs together, modifying them slightly with a minor innovation or two.

The "boardroom" of my own psyche includes huge floor-to-ceiling windows that I sometimes leave open to the city on one side and the desert on the other (leading to an oasis retreat at the foot of the mountains). In the center of the room is a round marble table with big comfy chairs, encouraging consensual leadership from a team of equals. This includes an executive grand organizer (the ego loves this lofty title), an artist-musician-writer, a dreamer, an iconoclast, a researcher, a teacher, a master herder, and an emotional-intelligence specialist, among others.

And while they're a little rough on the furniture, I also have a male lion and a female horse who wander in and out at will. These are not so much animal totems as forms of inner wisdom that bring the predatory and nonpredatory aspects of mind-body awareness into balance.

This metaphorical description of my own inner sanctum brings me to another intriguing piece of horse wisdom: the benefits of what I call "exercising your twin." The story of how this particular innovation came to light draws attention to the role that humanity's mythic imagination plays in developing visionary leadership, and it provides a useful metaphor for allowing your imagination to run wild while maintaining connection to the practical side of life.

Along the way, *you* might find the courage to add a wizard, mystic, shaman, centaur, or flying horse to your own executive team.

Two Forms of Consciousness

Through the work of scholars like Carl Jung, Joseph Campbell, and Marion Woodman, ancient myths have been recognized as sources of significant insight still relevant, arguably *essential*, to a deeper understanding of life. In her audio program *Myths for the Future*, Jean Houston defines myth as "something that never was, but is always happening. It's the coded DNA of the human psyche....Myth waters our every conscious act and is the very sea of our unconscious life."

The winged horses, centaurs, and mare-headed goddesses of antiquity are archetypes, mythic images that have a certain life and intelligence of their own. Quintessentially, Houston explains, "archetypes are about relationship, and the impetus behind relationship, and the connectedness for the way things grow, evolve, complexify, and ultimately become more integral." When repressed in the individual or culture, "all kinds of alienation emerges, and one is cut off from nature, self, society, and spirit with consequences seen all over today's world. This alienation has gained considerably from the mechanistic view of the world, which has touched virtually every level of modern life."

As nonmaterial patterns of existence, archetypes can hide out indefinitely in the depths of the collective unconscious, but they can't be suppressed forever. They reappear, Houston says, through the "other great bleed-through realms of human experience: dreams, religious knowings, visions, art, ritual, love, and madness. Sometimes they occur in their archaic forms bearing the accoutrements of earlier cultures, but they ask to be seen in fresh ways. They ask to be regrown."

Mythic messages evolve over time, dressing themselves up in the customs of different eras, drawing attention to destructive patterns of thought and behavior while offering solutions through symbols of transformation. Perpetually looking for an "in" to our world, they search for people who are not just willing to live these patterns unconsciously but willing to actually notice and appreciate them anew. One archetype that has been resurfacing in my work, and most notably in my herd, involves the dual nature of reality. Drawing attention to an ancient cross-cultural theme, this myth asked "to be regrown" by manifesting *physically.*

Twins are not common among horses, yet they play a significant role in horse mythology. From Greece to India to the Celtic lands, stories associated with the Divine Twins have a strong equine element. In most mythical texts, this is mentioned only in passing. But in 2002, the Year of the Black Horse in Chinese astrology, oddly enough, I was gripped by this archetype when my own mare Rasa gave birth to twins sired by Merlin, despite modern veterinary protocols to prevent it. (For an in-depth discussion of the events leading up to this pregnancy, see my 2003 book, *Riding between the Worlds.*)

Born six to ten weeks early, the firstborn foal weighed twenty pounds, a third the normal birth weight for an Arabian horse. His stillborn brother was significantly larger but hadn't been able to survive the cramped space of Rasa's womb. The vet was doubtful the other foal would live through the night. The first hurdle involved siphoning his mother's milk into a bottle and hoping he would drink. After a moment of fumbling, he grabbed hold of the nipple and sucked the fluid down like ambrosia. Then he let out a deep, delighted whinny.

The black foal's enthusiasm seemed to inflate his delicate body. His rich baritone voice, the result of underdeveloped vocal cords, seemed so incongruous with his tiny frame that we couldn't help but laugh out loud when he demanded another bottle. His curious, wide-eyed gaze entranced everyone, including a vet who thought she'd seen everything. The little toy horse looked so pleased with himself, so happy to be in the world, we couldn't help but rally around him and revel in the challenge of keeping him alive.

"Well one thing's for sure," I said, "he's got more spirit than body." The foal's name suddenly seemed obvious. "You want some more, Spirit?" I asked as the doctor showed me how to milk Rasa. The little guy responded with an animated rumble.

As the news spread and people came to see Rasa's tenuous miracle, my husband was left with the most difficult task of all: burying Spirit's twin, whom we named Sanctus, acknowledging his sacrifice and the effect his brief, sad, profound visit had on us. Later that night, Steve told me of carrying the little foal to his final resting place, of the power and gentleness in those silent eyes, of the insights the twins inspired in him. "To see life and death side by side," he said, shaking his head, "to bury one colt and hear the other calling out…"

Steve couldn't finish the sentence, but I knew he was, like me, swirling between the opposites: not transcending duality exactly, but feeling, really feeling, how joy spills into sadness, how beauty emerges from suffering, and how language can never touch the mystery that informs all life.

Rewriting a Classic

As Spirit continued to grow and thrive, in part through the efforts of people who volunteered during the ten weeks he needed extra care, I decided to investigate the symbology of twins. I was surprised to find that in cultures around the world, male twins are closely associated with horses. Most often, one brother endures the death of the other, who then connects the survivor to the otherworld. The myth of Castor and Pollux is a prime example. Castor was famous for training horses, Pollux for his skill in boxing. The brothers were as close as two brothers could be, so Pollux was inconsolable after Castor was slain in war. He begged Zeus to take his life in exchange. The Greek god instead granted Castor semi-immortality, directing him to spend half his days in the underworld, emerging every other day to visit heaven. Upon Pollux's death the two were reunited as the constellation Gemini.

In Thebes, Amphion and Zethus were abandoned at birth and raised by a shepherd. Hailed as great equestrians, they were called the "White Horses," "the Horsemen," or "Riders of White Horses," mirroring the equine associations of Castor and Pollux (who are collectively referred to as the Dioscuri, the "horseman gods"). In India, the Asvins were born to the goddess Saranyu. Twins who could take on human or horse form at will, they too were abandoned at birth, yet the brothers went on to create the healing arts. The Navajo creation epic features heroic male twins who bring horses to earth after defeating a group of carnivorous monsters. A number of Celtic and Eastern twin myths also have equestrian associations. Many feature a weaker twin who dies, continuing to influence his earthly brother in subtle yet powerful ways.

In his book *The Soul's Code*, psychologist James Hillman reflects on the mythological theme of sacrificing one twin to create balance between this world and the other. The Inuit speak of "another soul," he writes, "whether internal and in the same body or an external one that comes and goes, alights and leaves, inhabits things and places and animals. Anthropologists who walk with Australian aborigines call this second soul a bush-soul." Hillman also cites fairy tales, Rumi's poems, and Zen stories alluding to

> this doubleness, this strange duplicity of life. There are two birds in the tree, a mortal one and an immortal one, side by side. The first chirps and nests and flies about; the other watches....Twins themselves are often considered ominous, as if a mistake has occurred; the two birds, the human and the ghost, this world and that, both present in this world. Twins literalize the doppelganger, visible and invisible both displayed. So tales tell of the murder (sacrifice) of one twin for the sake of the other....The shadow, ` immortal, otherworldly one gives way so that the mortal one can fully enter this life.

In an Internet discussion of an obscure scholarly paper, "Twin Lights of Consciousness, Biology, Microphysics and Macropsychology," Howard Teich took the symbology of twins to a much deeper level. According to this psychologist, writer, and lecturer, who also weaves archetypal and mythological studies into his own leadership training program, the "twin nature of light as waves and particles" in quantum theory is reflected in these myths. He theorizes that the overwhelming tendency to depict the twins as two males, rather than as male and female, is an expression of the genetic chromosomal code. "Since females are already twinned at the chromosome level (XX), perhaps the symbolic archetypal image of twin males...is a mythological compensation for biology."

As I literally raised an equine twin, it took me months of research and reflection to integrate these concepts. Basically, the entire experience gave me yet another reason to acknowledge a vast coordinating intelligence that speaks to people through dreams, art, and visions — and occasionally through the physical manifestation of archetypal themes. Through Spirit and his stillborn brother, Sanctus, the twin nature of consciousness engaged our attention in the most vivid way possible. We saw, for one brief moment, the two lying side by side. In naming the stillborn twin, in touching him — and in being touched emotionally by his brief, sad life — we forged a stronger bond with the numinous, archetypal realm of origins.

In quantum theory, the most basic building blocks of life have a dual nature, appearing as particles with a set location in time and space, and as waves, invisible regions of influence that can flow through walls, resonate with physical matter, and yet not be limited by the laws that hold physical beings together. Through this strange, unusually public horse birth, a cross-cultural theme emerged from obscurity — and continued to expand.

If women already contain "the twins" genetically (as XX chromosomes), this alludes to why feminine wisdom is associated with intuition — ways of knowing not limited to physical and logical laws. The two male twins seemed to be an attempt to bridge the gap between the worlds in masculine consciousness. They manifested this time not as horsemen but as actual horses: nonpredatory beings who, though domesticated, retain a vital connection to instinct and nature while also being associated mythically with a strong sixth sense and the ability to carry riders between this world and the other. The fact that the stronger, larger twin was sacrificed emphasized, for me, the need for a stronger connection to the otherworld at a time when logic has become much more dominant than it was during the era of Greek myths.

Nearly a hundred volunteers, clients, and Epona staff were drawn into horse consciousness through the act of caring for a foal as one of their own. This never would have happened if Spirit had been able to stand and nurse at birth. In this sense, Spirit also bridged the gap between horse and human, drawing nourishment and love from both species. In the wild, he never would have survived.

Perhaps even more interestingly, people who came to help Spirit felt a palpable sense of numinosity in the room. They left deeply moved, sometimes experiencing life-changing responses to the unmistakable presence of a huge, openhearted being in a tiny, fragile body. Spirit's ability to inspire others during his time of greatest physical weakness also underlined the paradoxical power of vulnerability during an era when technology insulates us from the elements and allows us to destroy our enemies with remarkable ease and efficiency.

Spirit's Challenge

Rasa's boy grew up smaller than his mother and father, yet strong willed and unusually brave in situations that would unnerve the average horse. His confidence and strange, half-horse-, half-human-like intelligence made it impossible to control him through intimidation. Trainer Shelley Rosenberg and I had to work together to come up with new ways of educating and motivating this feisty little stallion. Teaching him to treat his caretakers, and eventually his mate, Panther, respectfully was quite an ordeal for all of us, as Spirit's unbridled enthusiasm and total lack of fear made it necessary for the humans in his life to boost their own courage, ingenuity, and solid boundary-setting skills.

Later, as Merlin's first surviving son sired his own daughter, Artemis, in 2008, I began using the metaphor of the worldly/otherworldly twins to help people access more creative forms of consciousness. Even the most skeptical leadership clients were inspired by Spirit's story. Those whose inner critics vehemently warned against "losing touch with reality" could accept the metaphor of accessing and exercising "the twin." The idea that consciousness, like light, might also have a dual particle-and-wave nature allowed their heavily defended, logical minds to entertain a more creative, whimsical "partner."

The benefits of engaging the mythic imagination were impressive. Innovators who had "hit the wall" accessed unexpected ideas scintillating with a vital energy that inspired others long after these initially metaphorical ideas were translated into practical applications. At the same time, personal challenges, relationship quandaries, even illnesses and accidents were also handled in imaginative, surprisingly effective ways.

Consciousness separated from spirit interprets daily existence as an empty progression of chance encounters and meaningless suffering. Learning to move fluidly between multiple states of being is difficult for the modern mind. While we need to exercise reason and problem-solving skills, another essential though long-ignored part of our psyche loves to improvise on timeless themes, creating new symbols, myths, and metaphors — road maps into the unknown.

Embracing the mythic dimension of life is like meeting a more adventurous twin, one that changes form at will, sprouts wings, flies to the stars, and brings a piece of magic back to earth, where its logical brother works hard to manifest some practical aspect of this glistening, otherworldly gem. Now, more than ever, we need both of these boys on our side. Exercising the twin nature of consciousness helps us maintain contact with reason while letting our imaginations run wild, leading to all kinds of creative impulses, half-baked ideas, and whimsical discoveries that eventually, in some cases literally, blast us to the moon *and* safely bring us back home again.

Chapter Nineteen

GUIDING PRINCIPLE 7
Conserve Energy for True Emergencies

*A*s a radio announcer on Florida's Gulf Coast in the 1980s, I had the job of playing soothing classical music and jazz. On a number of occasions, however, I happened to be on duty during a hurricane. At times, the weather was so bad that I couldn't leave and no one else could get to the station. I had to batten down the hatches, respond to the Emergency Broadcast System when it was *not* a test, and keep listeners updated on road closings, evacuations, and the trajectories of tornados spinning off the primary storm as it hit land. I had to give people information about things they surely wished they didn't have to hear but *needed* to understand and respond to in order to save their lives.

If I had started hyperventilating on air, screaming, "Grab what you can and get the hell out of here!" it wouldn't have helped my listeners. Neither would it have been useful to ignore the emergency, announce in my smoothest FM radio voice, "There is no fear, only peace and harmony," and launch into the love theme from Tchaikovsky's *Romeo and Juliet*.

The same can be said for all those uncomfortable sensory alarms that ask us to slow down, watch out, hold our ground, make a change, get more information before signing that business deal, ask for help handling that feisty colt, and any number of other strange "gut feelings" that beg to be acknowledged rather than suppressed or transcended. Emotions are not irrational mental misfirings designed to harass and embarrass us; they are not simply a part of our imagination. Though sometimes stirred up by distressing thoughts and resistance to change, emotions also alert the brain to what's happening in the environment and let the ego or persona know what's happening in deeper, less "acceptable" regions of the psyche.

Refusing the information emotion provides is like discounting sight or smell. It's not your eyes or your nose that leads you astray. It's what your brain has been trained to do, or not do, with the input that causes trouble. In fact, to use emotion effectively, you *must* use your brain in the form of a witnessing mind that can ask questions of the emotion and decide how to use that information constructively.

When tempestuous emotions churn inside like whirlwinds, imagine stepping into the eye of the hurricane (where it's clear and sunny, as anyone who's ever been in a hurricane knows). There you can address these powerful energies without getting caught in the spin. You can interpret incoming reports from the "National Weather Service" and decide what actions to avoid or what routes to take.

Vague Intuitions

The tricky part about fear in particular is that sometimes, especially in its earliest, most useful stages, the true nature of the threat is not yet obvious. Predators hide in the grass. Carjackers, rapists, and terrorists lurk in the darkness. Yes, of course this sounds scary. But just like horses, who use their heightened senses to live safely among predators, you can learn to take vague intuitions seriously without becoming paranoid.

This may sound like an outrageous challenge — and it is when you suppress your emotions over the long term, creating a tangled mass of sensory input that may have little to do with the current situation. Conserving energy for true emergencies involves deciphering the messages behind the emotions as they arise, taking appropriate action, and then going back to "grazing." In this way, your mind-body awareness system operates from a clean slate and it can pay attention to subtle changes in the environment.

People who can do this for themselves avoid overreacting to threats, remaining thoughtful in situations that unnerve others. But leaders must also be able to manage fear in groups of individuals who may not have these skills, troubleshooting to discover which concerns represent legitimate external threats, and which ones involve those internal, vulnerability-related issues (changing old patterns, recognizing skill deficiencies, trying something new, and so on).

If you're skeptical about or overwhelmed by this prospect, it helps to know that even soldiers with post-traumatic stress disorder can differentiate between these two types of fear, especially when supported by counselors and family members who also understand these emotional-intelligence definitions. Veterans I've worked with are relieved to find that much of the anxiety they feel reentering stateside life is vulnerability related, the psyche's natural response to changes in lifestyle, career, and daily routine. Moving from a rigid militaristic system (where your every move is moderated by orders, policy, and routine) to a more fluid civilian lifestyle is fraught with extreme changes in habit, perspective, and behavior.

In teaching emotional-fitness skills to men and women who were planning to return to Iraq and Afghanistan, I learned something about fear management that surprised even me. Apparently, even in chronically dangerous situations, the body can intuit the relative safety of the environment — if we're willing to listen to it. The topic came up during a two-day equine-facilitated workshop for soldiers and their spouses. We were discussing how horses use fear as nature's warning system. One dedicated, recently wounded soldier, "Steve," perked up at the mention of this somatic alarm system:

> My sergeant really encouraged us to use our personal radar to notice subtle changes in people's behavior. He actually invited us to tell him about weird feelings or anything else that felt off, no matter how vague. One day, after returning to camp, I felt like something was wrong, but I just couldn't for the life of me figure out what it was. It didn't go away, no matter how much I dismissed it, so I went to my sergeant after dinner and told him about it, I guess partly to see if he was really serious about listening to such things.

Sure enough, the officer calmly interviewed Steve about this feeling. Through a series of questions, the two realized this intuitive "warning light" was associated with the camp itself, not the notoriously dangerous patrol routes laced with improvised explosive devices and gun-wielding insurgents. With no additional information available, Steve's sergeant decided to do a last-minute drill before bedtime to rehearse strategies for defending the camp, "just to be on the safe side," he told everyone. Later that same night, when the camp was indeed attacked "unexpectedly," the troops responded with poise and skill, and no one was seriously injured.

With all this in mind, I created a sequence of fear-management protocols for leaders who see the value of *reducing* fear in groups without suppressing the messages behind this sometimes lifesaving emotion. In the long run, of course, you'll want others to master this troubleshooting process, but you can most certainly promote the idea of emotional-fitness training by using some or all of these techniques the next time you find yourself in a potentially volatile situation.

FEAR-MANAGEMENT PROTOCOLS

1. Before entering a situation where fear or vulnerability may be a factor, do your own body scan. If either of these emotions is present, make an effort to understand your body's concerns. (See Guiding Principle 2, in chapter 14, to review the body scan, and the section on fear and vulnerability in Guiding Principle 1, in chapter 13.)

2. Stay in contact with your body as you enter the meeting room, using your body as a tuner, receiver, and amplifier for tension and relaxation coming from others.

3. Notice and continually breathe into new tension-related sensations arising in your own body, whether or not you can decipher any related messages. (Remember: breathing and holding your breath are both contagious.) Breathing during a tense situation activates the parasympathetic nervous system, helping people to think more clearly rather than escalate into flight-or-fight mode, where the logical part of the brain is suppressed in favor of instinctual survival responses.

4. Meet the affect contagion of fear with the affect contagion of thoughtful, centered engagement with each person's concerns. Do not inflame the situation with cynicism, dualistic us-versus-them thinking, or reactive emotional states. Instead, model the use of emotion as information and "eye of the storm" clarity. Act as the radio station in the hurricane.

5. Help each person use emotion as information, asking questions to assist the group in determining which concerns involve external threats (fear) and which concerns involve internal threats (vulnerability). Remember to ask the *questions* associated with these emotions. Don't ask people if they're afraid or vulnerable; most won't know what you're talking about. (See Guiding Principle 3, in chapter 15, to review this particular skill, as well as the "Questions" section of the Emotional Message Chart.)

6. Create a context in which vague intuitions can be aired and addressed at any time. You might even share the soldier's intuition story. Help people distinguish between present intuitive concerns and projections or transference from past difficulties and traumas. (Again, see Guiding Principle 3 for examples on how to phrase questions about past and present concerns.)

7. Based on information collected during the "emotion as information" segment of the meeting, begin the problem-solving process, soliciting

and eventually prioritizing proposed goals or solutions, strategies, and training and/or coaching support.

8. Choose individuals to spearhead specific goals based on who is calmest, clearest, or most experienced in each area. The comfort and confidence of these individuals will be contagious to others.

9. Continue to train your staff in the use of emotion as information.

10. Provide emotional-strength-training strategies, fostering higher tolerance for vulnerability and the ability to sit in uncomfortable emotions without panicking. Teach people how to go back to "grazing" and offer immediate positive feedback, modeling this yourself in all situations.

11. Never, ever reward a staff member for using another person's vulnerabilities against him or her. Even the subtle nonverbal undermining of another staff member must be treated as cause for correction and, if chronic, cause for eventual demotion or dismissal.

12. When you hire leaders or promote people into management positions, choose, whenever possible, those who exhibit a high tolerance for vulnerability, while teaching staff who panic in response to change, interpersonal conundrums, and other challenges to increase their tolerance over time.

Chapter Twenty

GUIDING PRINCIPLE 8

*Employ Nonpredatory Power Liberally,
and Predatory Power Sparingly*

*A*n oversimplification of Darwin's "survival of the fittest" concept is still used today to justify predatory political structures and business practices, even though an early-twentieth-century theory on mutual aid as a factor of evolution challenged these assumptions (see my discussion in chapter 6). Pyotr Alekseyevich Kropotkin's extensive observations of herd life in Siberia and the Steppes of Eurasia suggest that

1. nonpredatory individuals far outnumber carnivores;
2. large herbivores are fierce and protective of vulnerable individuals;
3. mutual aid among wolves and lions is necessary to attack even the weakest of these imposing prey animals; and
4. groups of predators do so at their peril and are sometimes injured, killed, or simply unsuccessful in these efforts.

Long before I encountered the Russian prince's writings, my own herd challenged widespread notions that prey animals are quivering victims living at the mercy of powerful predators. My stallion Merlin, who would let squirrels share his daily bowl of grain, dealt harshly with aggressive dogs wandering into his space, sometimes grabbing a stunned canine by the neck and tossing it toward the gate, ready to trample the poor creature if it didn't get out fast. Our otherwise gentle mare Rasa would cheerfully, playfully chase coyotes out of her pasture (though these legendary desert tricksters didn't seem to be having much fun as they ran under the gate with their tails between their legs).

And two days after Spirit's daughter, Artemis, was born, I watched her mother, Panther, calmly herd our precious filly to the far end of the foaling pen as a massive bear waddled by less than twenty feet away (while I stood quivering in my boots).

For years, these incidents rolled around and around in my brain like loose marbles, eventually causing me to update my perceptions — and my language — regarding the relationship between predator and prey. I began to speak of nonpredatory power rather than "the wisdom of the prey," realizing that I no longer had to associate strength, bravery, and protection with carnivorous metaphors. Once I formulated this concept in my own mind, images of nonpredatory power seemed to pop up everywhere.

The day I sat down to write this guiding principle, in fact, I typed the phrase "power of the herd" into Google and came across a particularly dramatic YouTube video that bolstered my case.

First posted in 2007, "Battle at Kruger" captures an altercation between a large pride of lions and a herd of water buffalo. In what starts out as a typical amateur African safari video, a bull, a cow, and their calf are languidly walking toward a large watering hole. The tourists then notice several lions prowling in the grass about a hundred yards away.

Sensing these massive cats, the bull begins to run, herding his family away from potential danger, whereupon the pride leaps out of hiding and races toward the calf, pulling it down with such momentum that this tumbling tangle of baby bovine and adult feline bodies skids down a small hill and plunges into the pond. The predators' efforts to kill their prey, however, are momentarily interrupted by a crocodile, who tries to steal this convenient meal away.

Working together, the water-logged lions drag the calf back to shore, where they have to deal with something even more menacing: Just as they're about to take that final, fatal bite, the bull and cow return — with reinforcements, an angry mob of close to fifty buffalo. Surrounding their young herd-mate's attackers, bulls and cows trade leads as different individuals try to drive off the predators from optimal angles. Finally, one nervy buffalo leaps forward and scoops the nearest lion up with his horns, tossing this massive cat six feet in the air. The rest of the herd gains leverage as a result, scattering lions in all directions, surrounding the now standing calf, welcoming him back to safety.

At no point in the video do the buffalo waste any effort trying to kill the offenders, letting them disperse relatively unharmed (though bulls have been known to kill lions presumptuous enough to hesitate in their retreat, let alone try to fight back). This tendency to avoid fighting to the death, to live and let live, is a major characteristic of nonpredatory power.

What was perhaps most astonishing to me was that no one — from the original tourists talking in the background to the numerous people commenting on this compelling footage — asked what was, for me, the million-dollar question: how in the world did the calf's parents rally that imposing herd?

It took around four minutes for the pair to return with this remarkably cohesive group. From a twentieth-century animal behaviorist viewpoint, this is an unusually *long* period of time for a "stupid, instinctual beast" to even *remember* what happened, let alone remain focused on organizing others to pursue a common goal. At the same time, four minutes would be an incredibly *short* amount of time for a couple of two-legged parents to motivate a group of people to help them out under similar circumstances. Some sophisticated nonverbal communication and coordination was involved, with concern for a single calf motivating the kind of altruistic courage we would call heroic in humans.

This single incident suggests that we still know very little about the intelligence of nonpredatory herds. But one thing's certain: prey animals are not the dim-witted, cowardly weaklings they've been made out to be by human politicians, philosophers, scientists, and animal trainers who overidentify with their own predatory tendencies.

The Lion and the Horse

Increasingly, observations of natural herd behavior illustrate that power does not have to be harsh, exploitative, oppressive, or shortsighted if you master the skills associated with this guiding principle. In fact, after collecting insights on predatory versus nonpredatory power to make the following chart, I find that the only constructive purpose for human beings to invoke their inner lion would seem to involve optimal use of that concept known as culling: killing to maintain balance between the herd and the available natural resources, nourishing human members of an interspecies society in the process.

By this, I'm even more specifically referring to the Mongolian practice of slaughtering those cattle, sheep, and horses in the late fall that are not likely to endure the harsh winter ahead. If Eurasian herders did not cull these animals, they would suffer needlessly while draining severely, though temporarily, limited resources that two-legged and four-legged tribe members must use judiciously to survive this seasonal challenge.

I want to revisit Mongolian nomadic customs for yet another reason: to show how empathy plays an important role in balancing the predatory and nonpredatory impulses of human tribe members. Unlike conventional carnivores, who prey on the young, Mongolian pastoralists refuse to eat herd members less than one year of age (unlike "civilized" cultures, which consider lamb or veal a delicacy), nursing a sick or orphaned foal, lamb, or calf inside their own tents during the more fertile months of spring and summer (see chapter 8). These people name all of their animals, refusing to objectify them, considering them valued members of an interspecies tribe, to the point that their Buddhist-influenced beliefs entertain the possibility that reincarnation occurs across species lines. Mongolian herders subsist mostly on milk products, eating meat primarily during the winter. In this way, they live the principle of mutual aid through the respectful interspecies innovation known as "nomadic pastoralism."

As a metaphor for taming our own inner lion in all aspects of life, we can temper our carnivorous instincts to not only treat other animals more humanely but also modify business practices that prey on objectified populations and future generations. The predatory side of human nature is especially useful, perhaps even essential, in culling those social institutions, behaviors, and beliefs that *need* to die a humane death so that everyone can survive the winter — and thrive during the spring, summer, and fall — allowing us to curtail rabid conquest and growth in favor of a cocreative, mutually beneficial balance with nature and neighboring tribes.

Other activities — such as setting strong boundaries with aggressive herd members, and leading, dominating, even fighting predators — can be incorporated with more skill and grace by adopting a horselike approach to power. As you increasingly avoid the four Stone Age Power Tools (see chapter 12) and incorporate the twelve guiding principles featured in this book, you will automatically be exercising nonpredatory leadership and social-intelligence skills.

It's also helpful when hiring a new staff member, employing the services of an expert, or electing a leader, to notice how often the various candidates employ predatory modes of thinking and behaving. Whenever possible, choose someone who exhibits power and expertise combined with nonpredatory tendencies, a simple way to lessen the common, though ironic, possibility that you will actually *pay* someone to become his or her prey.

Even so, it's important not to demonize those who've developed their inner lion at the expense of their inner horse. We are *taught* to use predatory forms of power, using the Stone Age Power Tools discussed in this book, as well as many other, more minor, antiquated interpersonal "weapons," some of which you may begin to notice as you develop confidence in using nonpredatory power. A certain amount of patience — and cathedral thinking — is required to learn, master, and eventually teach others how to boost social intelligence and engage nonpredatory power.

In the meantime, many people respond well to animal metaphors and behavior patterns. The following chart offers a quick look at how these opposite
yet interconnected power principles play out in nature:

Predatory versus Nonpredatory Power	
PREDATORY POWER	**NONPREDATORY POWER**
Nourishes self at others' expense	Supports individual and group needs simultaneously
Values territory over relationship	Values relationship over territory
Values goal over process (The end justifies the means.)	Values process over goal (The end *never* justifies the means.)
Aggressive in taking others' territory and resources	Assertive in holding personal boundaries without ordering others around; migrates to avoid competition for limited resources
Attacks to protect self and others *and* gain advantage	Fights to protect self and others; prefers to herd family and companions away from trouble
Fight-to-the-death impulse is strong	Stops fighting when aggressor backs off
Conquest or survival-of-the-fittest orientation ("Kill or be killed" philosophy)	Mutual-aid or safety-in-numbers orientation ("Live and let live" philosophy)
Culls the weak (Must hide vulnerability at all costs)	Shields the weak (Vulnerable individuals can rely on others)
Leadership = dominance	Leader and dominant are often different animals

Predatory versus Nonpredatory Power (*continued*)

PREDATORY POWER	NONPREDATORY POWER
Rules through intimidation	Leads through experience, curiosity, and the ability to calm and focus others during crisis
Purposefully escalates fear	Conserves energy for true emergencies
Competition emphasized (Co-operates in group hunting and sometimes child rearing, though many species kill the young of other males. In some species males will kill their own young if not ferociously protected by females.)	Cooperation emphasized (Competition strongest among adolescent dominant-style personalities, though even these animals are tolerant of young herd members. Some bachelor horses will tend to orphaned foals.)

Chapter Twenty-One

GUIDING PRINCIPLE 9
Prepare *for Difficult Conversations*

*A*t *Apache Springs Ranch,* one crucial skill my colleagues and I were lacking could not be taught by horses or even inferred from their empowered, collaborative, emotionally agile behavior: the ability to have productive *conversations* on difficult topics.

As I mentioned earlier, the accomplished counselors on staff were just as confused as I was in handling potentially inflammatory work-related conflicts. Meetings designed to discuss professional disagreements could turn into "encounter groups" when we followed anything close to a therapy model (where people discuss their feelings, past traumas or difficulties, and habits related to family position, and so on), increasing anxiety and misunderstanding in the workplace.

In researching other options, I encountered the book *Coaching for Emotional Intelligence* by Bob Wall, an independent consultant specializing in leadership and team development. He offered a procedure for helping people *prepare* for difficult conversations, one that made a lot of sense to me. After doing some coaching work with him, I found this tool to be the missing link in handling interpersonal challenges efficiently and effectively. Bob was also intrigued by the equine-facilitated work we were doing. In 2008 he traveled to Apache Springs, offering workshops on difficult conversations and interpreting the sophisticated emotional-intelligence test the Simmons EQ Profile for some of our staff, leadership clients, and workshop participants. (I make it a practice to take this profile annually myself, assessing and, as a result, improving many previously unconscious habits and behaviors that compromised my

EQ Profile.

effectiveness as a leader.) Bob also participated in Epona's four-day *Pioneering Spirit: Leadership for the 21st Century* clinic. Based on his own surprisingly positive response to the horse work, he came back to help facilitate at one of these workshops.

Over time, I combined Bob's difficult-conversation format with Epona's practice of using emotions as information (Guiding Principle 1, in chapter 13), creating what has since become a procedure so effective that it now seems *the* obvious way to handle interpersonal as well as technical difficulties, not only in the workplace, but in personal relationships as well. I've used this procedure in negotiating disagreements with my husband, extended family, and friends with impressive results.

Difficult — and Not-So-Difficult — Conversations

I suggest the following format, which is based on *Coaching for Emotional Intelligence*, for dealing with major challenges, as well as for offering daily feedback through short conversations that make a big difference in changing unproductive behaviors or reinforcing exemplary behaviors. (I highly recommend reading Bob's entire book for additional information on how to coach employees professionally in areas that managers normally shy away from: personality quirks, nonverbal cues, anger-management issues, and passive-aggressive behaviors, which can all affect everyone's ability to get the job done.)

Bob also believes that recognizing people for their daily accomplishments, teamwork, innovative ideas, and interpersonal expertise is as important as pulling someone aside to discuss unproductive behavior. In both cases, he emphasizes, the comments must be *specific* to be useful. This, of course, coincides with the practice of immediate positive feedback discussed in Guiding Principle 4, in chapter 16.

Acknowledging productive behavior is a simple yet incredibly effective way to make sure people keep doing what they may have stumbled upon accidentally, usually when they're in a generous mood. In this way, employees and colleagues alike become even more receptive to what you have to say when new challenges emerge. At the same time, briefly and specifically thanking people for doing something well sends them the message that you're *noticing everything they do*, which, I've realized over the years, is a positive way to discourage people from slipping into careless, selfish, undermining, or blatantly defiant behavior. Praising people makes them feel good, and it makes you feel good, too. Everyone's day is brighter when we acknowledge what is going right!

Bare-Bones Outline

The following procedure, combining Bob's "structured format for coaching" with Eponaquest's emotions-as-information approach, is helpful in organizing your thoughts so that you can be clear and specific — rather than vague, inappropriately emotional, and shaming — about core issues that need significant adjustment or minor improvement. While I call this combined approach the "difficult conversation outline," it can also be used to highlight performance, attitudes, and behavior that deserve appreciation and recognition.

1. **OPENING STATEMENT**
   "I want to talk to you about..."
   - Provide a succinct statement about the category of performance or general subject related to the conflict.

2. **OBSERVATION**
   "I've observed..."
   - Describe performance or behavior.
   - Give details without judgment-oriented or shaming statements.
   - If you felt a strong emotion, use this as information and relay only the information, not the emotion. For instance, if you became angry, the discussion concerns boundaries. If you were frustrated, the subject involves a block that needs to be worked through. If you were afraid, address safety issues.
   - If you felt vulnerable, this involves change, experimentation, making mistakes, or having your own beliefs and habits questioned. The latter likely includes your heightened response to some personal issues or blind spots being revealed that may or may not relate to the work environment. Make sure you address with your employees or coworkers only what is related to the job at hand. Get private help in dealing with personal issues so they don't affect your future performance.

3. **IMPACT**
   "The impact is..."
   - Describe the impact on the workplace, on getting the current job done well.
   - Again, leave out any references to your own personal past. That's for you to work on with a coach or therapist.

4. REQUEST

"In future, I would like you to, or it would be helpful to…"

- Describe how to improve performance or behavior.
- Be specific about what behavior you would like to see if a similar situation arises in the future.
- In the case of praise, offer a statement along the lines of: "That's a great innovation. I'd love to share this with the staff." Or: "Keep up the good work!"

Since I started using this format in 2008, I've helped numerous people prepare for a wide variety of difficult professional, school-related, and personal conversations. In teaching this technique to larger groups, I've found that the easiest way to illustrate how this works is to use an example of how someone successfully worked through a particularly sticky challenge using this tool. The following example draws on a situation based on actual events, featuring two composite characters to show various nuances of how this emotionally and socially intelligent approach to conflict can solve several issues at once, including how to use your own and others' emotions as information — even when your employee, colleague, or "adversary" lacks these skills.

Safety Zone

"Arianna," a forty-seven-year-old horse trainer, has over twenty years' experience working for some of the finest breeding and show barns on the East Coast. When her mother passed away in 2007, an inheritance allowed this hardworking professional to buy her own stable, a dream come true. Arianna had just completed the Eponaquest Apprenticeship Program and was pleased to add an equine-facilitated learning program to her new operation. She also offered internship positions to promising young trainers who were interested in exploring newer, more humane and collaborative ways of working with horses.

A drop in business during the first six months of 2009, a result of the financial crisis, put Arianna in a tough position as she had invested most of her funds in the property. She was just barely making ends meet as clients began seeking her services again in the summer of that year. To help with the increasing workload, she took on two interns, who worked at minimum wage in exchange for daily lessons with this accomplished trainer. Yet at the height of her workshop, competition, and training season in August, one of the interns suddenly quit after falling in love with an out-of-state rider at a horse show, leaving

town to move in with him two weeks after they had met. Arianna suddenly had
to rely exclusively on the newer of the two assistants, "Drew," a sensitive thirty-
two-year-old horsewoman who was also interested in becoming an Eponaquest
instructor though she hadn't yet been to an introductory workshop.

"At least she's married and likely to stay in town," Arianna told me when
she called for a consultation, "though at this point I'm not sure Drew will be
able to handle the work. I don't know what I'm going do if I have to fire her.
My next intern can't start until October, and I'm already working day and night
just to keep up. I really need Drew right now, but after the stunt she pulled yesterday I don't know if I can trust her with the horses."

"What happened?" I asked, already taking notes, using the "difficult conversation" outline.

"Oh my God, I'm still shaking," Arianna said. "I'm lucky I didn't get f***ing
killed!"

I hadn't actually heard this woman swear before, but she used lots of
unprintable words that day, as well as a number of shaming phrases regarding Drew's integrity and intelligence (or, more specifically, the lack thereof). I
was relieved that Arianna had the good sense to call me before speaking with
her intern about the incident. Drew would surely have quit on the spot — and
probably bad-mouthed Arianna throughout the tight-knit, gossip-prone horse
community — if Arianna had spoken to her employee in this outraged state.

My client was venting, of course, a sometimes necessary first step in releasing intense emotion, productive if engaged in confidentially with a coach,
counselor, or emotionally intelligent confidant. As it turned out, she knew she
was venting. In fact, she'd already used the challenging-conversation format,
proceeding to read it to me over the phone. This is her first draft:

1. OPENING STATEMENT

Drew, I want to talk to you about your dangerous, inconsiderate, unpro-
fessional, sabotaging behavior yesterday.

2. OBSERVATION

When you came in *late* yesterday, I was already saddling up our new client's horse, Rumor. You know how sensitive she is, how hard I've worked
to gain this mare's trust. You also knew I was planning to ride her for the
first time, and you were supposed to help me.

Well, not only did you *not* help me, you almost killed one or both of
us. You came into the barn in such a huff, throwing your backpack down

next to the cross ties. Didn't you see that Rumor reared up slightly when you did that? Oh no! Not only that, but you stomped right on by both of us, and then slammed the barn office door, whereupon Rumor did rear up in the cross ties and almost fell over backward.

You should know, being a rider and a so-called trainer yourself, that horses can die that way. I did manage to step in there and pull the quick release. As Rumor came down, she slammed against me and threw me into the wall. Then she took off bucking out of the barn and down the road. Thank God you had the decency to close the gate on your way in or she would have run into traffic! I didn't have time to even consider the fact that her hoof came less than an inch from my face. It took me twenty minutes to catch her, she was so riled up. Of course, I didn't ride her yesterday. In fact, I practically have to start all over again with her, as she's scared of everything right now!

This always happens to me. Just when I start to become successful, someone comes in saying they want to help, when what they really do is find some way to sabotage me. I thought you were different.

3. Impact

You have cost me time, money, my reputation, and possibly your own job. I'm going to have to call Rumor's owner and tell her what happened. This means her horse will need to be in training for another month at least, and because this was our fault, we are going to have to train this horse for free. So now I'm working for free and paying you to work here. When I screw up, I pay. When you screw up, *I* pay.

4. Request

If you're going to work here, you need to act professionally. I can see that you were pissed off about something, but you cannot work around horses if you can't control your temper. I need you to get some outside help on this, maybe some counseling, but when you show up for work, I need to know you can handle yourself.

Believe it or not, this was quite an improvement over what Arianna initially told me about the incident. There were no swear words and fewer shaming, overtly demeaning statements. Yet this draft, which seemed professional and self-controlled to Arianna, still needed some work. The opening statement was too judgmental and not really specific enough about the real issue at stake.

The first three paragraphs of the observation section were pretty good in describing behavior, though some sarcasm and minor barbs would have put Drew on the defensive. (Statements such as "You should know, being a rider and a *so-called trainer* yourself..." not only questioned Drew's expertise and integrity but were also insulting.) The last paragraph of that section reeked of transference from Arianna's personal past. (When someone says, "This always happens to me," you know you're dealing with a heightened emotional response inspired by past betrayals, conflicts, or, in this case, perceived sabotage.)

The "Impact" and "Request" sections were not quite specific or refined enough, consisting mostly of generalizations that would probably be heard as judgments or insults by the receiver of this feedback.

Past and Present

After exploring the deeper issues and emotions Arianna was experiencing, we were able to clarify what related to the present situation and what was bleeding through from the past. In moving beyond her initial assessment that she was feeling "pissed off" and "sabotaged," Arianna realized that, during the emergency with Rumor, she felt afraid for herself and the horse and angry at Drew. The messages behind these emotions were about safety and boundaries. By working further with these ideas, Arianna came up with a masterful opening statement. She then cleaned up the observation segment, removing references to the past, which, she realized with some surprise, had to do with her mother's envious, sometimes sabotaging behavior, particularly when Arianna excelled at childhood horse shows.

"Jeez, I hadn't thought about this in years, but my mother had a very critical, oppressive mother of her own," Arianna said. "Mom wanted a horse as a child. But she was never allowed to have one. There was kind of a love/hate thing going on with her in relation to me, especially at the barn. She was supporting me in following my dreams after her own parents did everything they could to put her down and keep her down. But sometimes this would cause her to act weird. One time when I was saddling up for a championship, she got me so upset over something stupid that I ended up losing big-time."

Arianna realized that sabotage was a multigenerational family pattern, and she decided to explore this further with a counselor. During our consultation, however, she was able to clarify her emotional response to the current dilemma and to her previously unconscious past history. As a result, the "Impact" and "Request" segments of her statements evolved as well.

Here's the final version of Arianna's difficult-conversation form:

1. OPENING STATEMENT

Drew, I want to talk to you about the need to create an inviolable zone of safety in the barn.

2. OBSERVATION

When you came in late yesterday, I was already saddling up our new client's horse, Rumor. You know how sensitive she is, how hard I've worked to gain this mare's trust. You also knew I was planning to ride her for the first time, and you were supposed to help me. When you came into the barn and threw your backpack down next to the cross ties, Rumor reared up slightly. She got even more nervous when you stomped past both of us. When you slammed the barn office door, Rumor reared up in the cross ties and almost fell over backward.

Being a rider and a trainer yourself, you know that horses can be seriously injured or even die that way. I did manage to step in and pull the quick release. As Rumor came down and took off, she slammed against me and threw me into the wall. Then she went bucking out of the barn and down the road. Thank God you closed the gate on your way in or she would have run into traffic! I remembered afterward that her hoof came less than an inch from my face at one point, so not only was Rumor's life in danger, mine was too. It took me twenty minutes to catch her, she was so riled up. I didn't ride her yesterday. When I brought her into the barn this morning, she was very frightened of the cross ties. This is now a training issue Rumor didn't have when she got here.

3. IMPACT

I'm going to have to call Rumor's owner and tell her what happened. She comes to the barn on weekends, likes to check in on the mare's progress, and will definitely notice the difference. To correct this behavior, Rumor will need to be in training for an additional two to three weeks. Because this was our fault, we are going to have to train Rumor for free during that extra time. Every dollar we bring in counts in this economy. We are running close to the bone, and we must guard against anything like this happening again. I need you to assist me in training Rumor off the clock during the time I'm also working for free. We are in this together and must be willing to make adjustments when we make mistakes.

4. REQUEST

I could see that you were angry or frustrated about something, and I would like to hear what happened in just a moment. But first I have a request: Whether this is a personal or a work-related issue, things will happen, and we may not always be able to control our emotions. However, from now on, whenever you — or I or anyone else who works here — are feeling agitated, I need us to make a pledge to protect everyone's safety above all. This means I need you to notice that you're in a heightened emotional state and stay out of the barn until you calm down.

If something like this happens again, and I'm expecting you to help me with a horse, I need you to lean around the barn door and tell me you are invoking the barn safety rule. After I finish with the horse, I will come and talk to you about what's going on and when you can rejoin us in a calmer state.

Now, please tell me what happened yesterday. If this was a personal issue you don't want to share, just let me know that too. But if something is going on that's relevant to the job, I need to know so that I can make some adjustments on my end as well.

Real Conversation

When Arianna sat down with Drew the following day, this centered, well-prepared boss didn't just read the form to her silent employee. She expected some questions, comments, perhaps even retaliatory behaviors. However, because Arianna had worked through her own confusing emotions ahead of time, removing inflammatory statements from multiple drafts, Drew was, in fact, able to *hear* the feedback and *respond* productively (for the most part).

Had Arianna delivered the first version she presented to me, she would have seen much more resistance. By creating a stellar opening statement — and a clear, detailed discussion of how to handle similar situations in the future — Arianna addressed the challenge without demeaning Drew, motivating both parties to move forward, ultimately turning a volatile situation into a trust-building experience.

In recognizing the messages behind her emotions, differentiating between personal and professional issues, and working out how to address the relevant information in her meeting with Drew, Arianna found that her emotional charge around the incident had dissipated significantly, energy she would otherwise have projected tonally and nonverbally. Arianna's poise during the meeting, therefore, was completely authentic — a result of her total lack of suppressed emotion. This had a calming effect on Drew, who experienced her boss's thoughtful, problem-solving stance as supportive and engaged, acting for the good of the horses and the staff.

If, on the other hand, Arianna had suppressed her feelings, jumping into the conversation without fully processing the messages first, she would have appeared incongruent at the very least and, in all likelihood, released some of the tension in unproductive ways, perhaps damaging the relationship irreparably.

Shame, sarcasm, cynicism, and rage seething underneath a "professional" facade are communicated through demeanor and vocal tone, creating confusing, intensely uncomfortable, sometimes aggressive undercurrents that lead to more conflict in the long run. When people can discuss *behavior* without emotionally charged comments or body language, others are better able to listen and make the necessary changes, especially if their behavior is outlined succinctly — all the more reason to prepare for challenging conversations.

Additional Skills

After speaking with her intern, my client called me, excited to report her success. But it wasn't Drew's positive response to the prepared part of the conversation that made Arianna so undeniably proud. It was her ability to constructively handle what set Drew off, teasing apart elements relevant to the job, to Drew's past show barn experience, and to current issues with her husband.

"I took the Emotional Message Chart with me as you suggested," Arianna reported. "And, boy, did I need it. Drew was pleasantly surprised at first because she thought I was really going to lay into her. Actually she looked downright shocked at my opening statement. She truly couldn't disagree with the idea of creating a safety zone in the barn!"

As the conversation proceeded, however, Drew had trouble deciphering her own tangled ball of emotions and issues. Like Arianna, she had been working overtime since the second intern had left. She was tired and frazzled. Even worse, her husband was pressuring her to quit. He didn't like her pursuing an equine-related career, especially if it meant she wouldn't be home to fix dinner. The morning of the incident in question, Drew had fought with her spouse, rushed out the door, left her lunch on the counter, and then locked her keys in the car. She was running in to call AAA because she was afraid to ask her husband to bring an extra key to the barn after work.

Drew was mortified that she had put Rumor and Arianna in danger, and she apologized. But perhaps because she was feeling vulnerable and ashamed, she began to shame Arianna in response when the opportunity arose later in the conversation.

"I expected you to be different," Drew said as she shared her side of the story. "But I have to say I'm really disappointed in you. You say you're all about a new way of being with horses and running a barn, but to me it's just the same old story. You're like all the other slave-driving bosses I've worked for."

I had warned Arianna that, when Drew spoke, she wouldn't know how to use the messages behind her emotions in place of possibly inflammatory or shaming statements. Arianna would need to show a certain amount of self-control and thoughtfulness, perhaps even emotional heroism (see Guiding Principle 11, in chapter 23) to turn the situation around.

"You know," Arianna told me, "it's a real trigger for me when someone says she's really disappointed in me. My mother used to say that in a very shaming way, and her mother most certainly used that demeaning tactic as well. But instead of shutting down or getting nasty back, I went to the disappointment section of the Emotional Message Chart and used those questions to problem solve. It was totally disarming. Drew and I had a great conversation after that, and I know she left thinking that I *was* different!"

As a result of this incident, Arianna decided to postpone one of the workshops she was doing for a local business later that month. She also looked for other ways to take the pressure off her staff until the new intern arrived, and Drew had some good ideas for making the operation more efficient. The following spring, Drew completed her internship with glowing reviews from clients and staff alike.

"When I think back on that time," Arianna later told me, "I could have easily shot myself in the foot, either firing Drew or causing her to quit. As it turned out, she wasn't trying to sabotage me at all. She was dealing with all kinds of crazy stress in her life, and I was adding to it. She was actually one of the best workers I've ever had. And for my birthday, she gave me a little gift with a card saying that I was her best boss ever!"

Chapter Twenty-Two

GUIDING PRINCIPLE 10
Engage in Consensual Leadership

*W*hen *my stallion Merlin finally gained enough self-control* to live with my mares Rasa and Comet, he wasn't necessarily the boss. In fact, it was hard to tell who was in charge.

Comet made quite a show at mealtime, rushing up to the first pile of hay, rearing and kicking out at her mate. The stallion would move away, but only a step or two, his sparkling eyes and engaged expression reveling in her fiery display. If he could speak, he probably would have been asking with a whimsical sigh: "Isn't she *cute* when she's dominant?"

Rasa would saunter up a few moments later, sometimes settling on a more isolated flake of alfalfa, sometimes stepping into the fray if she was really cranky or committed. Merlin cared little about eating, choosing to come and go, nibbling next to each mare, sometimes staring languidly off into the distance. Yet if a strange horse got loose and ran toward the fence, he would herd his mares away with no ifs, ands, or buts, then return to more fully assess the newcomer's intentions and, more often than not, attack.

When Rasa came into heat, youthful Comet played referee. Merlin and Rasa couldn't mate without her consent, and if the stallion became excessively passionate in his approach, Rasa would hide behind her herd sister. But if I walked toward the pasture, Rasa would shoo the others away from me, insisting on being first in line for an outing. And though the solid-black mare didn't assert herself as often as the others, they missed her self-assured presence. Merlin and Comet would pace and call out when Rasa left, but when they were led away to be trained, Rasa would graze, unconcerned, knowing they'd return soon enough. In this way, the older mare engaged in a subtle form of leadership, able to calm and center her more nervous and flamboyant family members. (She also had the same effect on people.)

In this trio, the dominance hierarchy varied, quite frankly, according to what the human observer defined as important. In reality, however, the horses were trading leadership and dominance roles according to who was calmest, clearest, most committed, or most invested in the outcome.

I noticed similar situational leadership dynamics in the other herds who lived at Apache Springs Ranch. Most of the horses who came to our equine-facilitated learning center were gifted teachers — chosen because of their capacity to challenge people while remaining safe, adapting to the needs of individual students. Some of our equine professors were experts in various riding styles; some excelled at ground work; others had lived on the open range and worked cattle; one had been used as a drug-running horse.

When turned out together, they would capitalize on their varied experiences. Naturally dominant horses who had been mistreated by humans, for instance, could not act as the alpha in all situations. They didn't even try. When people approached the herd, these otherwise feisty animals would hang toward the back, watching how the suspect two-legged creatures were treating their more gregarious companions. If someone knocked the gate down, and the herd ran off at midnight, members would look to the most trail-savvy horse for direction. When unfamiliar horses were introduced to the herd, some members were especially adept at breaking up fights or gently welcoming newcomers.

In these equine communities, what an individual *knew* about, what he *cared* about, what he was *calm or enthusiastic* about determined leadership, as all members had some talent, drive, or experience that the others valued or, at times, simply deferred to. Translated as "sensing together," *consensual leadership* seemed to be a more appropriate term than *pecking order* or *dominance hierarchy*.

Humans seeking an absolute definition of *leadership*, and a concrete technique or job description to go with it, don't like this concept much, but it's really not hard to fathom. And the benefits of putting it into action far outweigh the surface ambiguities. If you propose to create a team of experts or an authentic community where people's true feelings, talents, dreams, and motivations are acknowledged, you have to head in this general direction.

No leader knows everything. To convince your followers otherwise is dishonest, requiring increasing levels of posturing, deception, and finally, intimidation. Yet it takes significant self-esteem and discernment to conceive of others taking the lead now and then without letting them dominate *you*. Basically, you have to maintain good boundaries without feeling the need to order everyone else around — or to be seen as the expert in all possible situations.

Consensual leadership draws on the wisdom and sentience of the entire herd. It is, to a great extent, improvisational. Though I may be acknowledged as the official leader of Eponaquest, I'm still in business because I've gathered a group of people around me who can both lead and follow, whom I can trust to support me when I'm feeling vulnerable and who admit when they're feeling unsure. When we're uncertain or triggered by whatever is happening, we look to the person who seems the calmest and most centered in that situation. Sometimes when we're undecided about which road to take, we look to the most confident, invested, or enthusiastic person. When there's unresolved conflict, we agree to consult outside experts, and sometimes even then the path is not clear. In these cases, I may have to follow my gut, though I'm still dubious about the exact, right course of action.

Mostly, however, we all have to acknowledge that we do not know the one true right way, that authentic community and shared leadership are challenging, cutting-edge concepts with no clear rules and referees. Some students and employees find this disconcerting, even frightening. But as they develop the emotional- and social-intelligence skills associated with the other eleven guiding principles, they quickly come to see and enjoy the benefits.

Animal behavior scientists are compiling evidence of shared leadership in nature as well. In the article "Consensus Decision Making in Animals," published in *TRENDS in Ecology and Evolution* in 2005, Larissa Conradt and Timothy J. Roper offer an extensive overview of relevant studies. They write,

> Researchers have often assumed *a priori* that a particular group member (usually the most dominant) leads consensus decisions about travel destinations and group activities. However, more recent studies have reported variable leadership and the absence of a correlation between leadership and dominance status in several bird and mammal species in captivity. Information about decision makers in wild birds and mammals is often based on small data sets or anecdotal reports[,] but in general, decisions seem to be made in a partially shared manner between the adult group members of at least one sex....In small groups, the opportunity exists for all members to vote.

Democracy, it seems, is not a recent human invention. Like mutual aid and competition avoidance, it's one of those long-ignored options nature provides that kings, conquistadors, and predatory business leaders have actively suppressed. Whatever you call it — consensual, shared, or situational leadership

— this concept encourages *mutual empowerment*. Yet because the decisions modern humans make are much more complex, especially when coordinating long-term creative projects that affect millions of people, significant social-intelligence skills are involved.

Optimal consensual leadership requires developing teams that display a high tolerance for vulnerability (Guiding Principle 5, in chapter 17). In more challenging pursuits, such as political and social-activism contexts, it's essential for all individuals involved to display emotional heroism (Guiding Principle 11, in chapter 23). People capable of sharing leadership in any context, however, must also know how to conserve energy for true emergencies (Guiding Principle 7, in chapter 19), manage contagious emotions in groups (Guiding Principle 3, in chapter 15), set effective boundaries (Guiding Principle 4, in chapter 16), and respectfully address difficult topics (Guiding Principle 9, in chapter 21).

And finally, to experiment and take the kinds of constructive risks that lead to innovation, teams must be able to discuss partial successes and outright failures in constructive ways, diffusing evaluation apprehension. (See chapter 11 for a disturbing view of how human beings often unconsciously, sometimes purposefully, escalate this performance-inhibiting stressor.)

To avoid confusing, shaming, or simply overwhelming team members with unbridled feedback, and to teach all participants to pay attention to what is successful as well as what needs improvement, I highly recommend using the following protocol when evaluating the status of any goal or ongoing project:

1. What was effective or particularly successful?
2. What should we refine in the future?
3. What were the major challenges we overcame?
4. What are the current blocks to success?
5. Which challenge, block, or refinement should we work on first? What ideas do various team members have for troubleshooting and modification?

In this way, we build teamwork, enthusiasm, and trust, even when we must honestly look at what still needs improvement!

Chapter Twenty-Three

GUIDING PRINCIPLE 11
Cultivate Emotional Heroism

When I first met Midnight Merlin in 1999, it took a lot of courage to walk into his corral. Trainers more experienced than I had given up on him, and it wasn't hard to figure out why. The real question was *why did I even try?* I wasn't the only person asking this question. My own riding instructor, Shelley Rosenberg, a woman who had worked with dozens of stallions, showing, breeding, and starting them under saddle, initially told me to "*run*, don't walk, away from this one." But somehow, through naïveté or stubbornness, probably a bit of both, I convinced her to help me do something even more outrageous than rehabilitate him. I asked her to help me socialize him to live, respectfully, with a pair of my most treasured mares.

The skills I learned while managing this strange project, I later realized, were even more valuable when I began to collaborate with humans who had been victimized, or simply disillusioned, by an aggressive, highly competitive culture just as likely to treat people as tools, as workhorses, as expendable means to some callous, shortsighted end.

But while collaborating with an angry horse was dangerous physically, working with people was more confusing and disheartening. Understanding how to solicit help from experts who knew more than I did — while staying true to a vision that asked teachers and students alike to step outside their comfort zones — was quite an undertaking. Yet for reasons I still can't explain, I was compelled to surmount the sometimes painful, at times shocking, challenges involved. Occasionally I would lose my own balance, fall flat on my face, and endure the sensation of being trampled by a panicking yet powerful herd.

Then, after struggling to stand, I had to deal with another, thoroughly unexpected emotional blow. At times, people were more likely to berate me for my ineptitude than they were to help me up, engaging in the timeworn practice of using my vulnerabilities against me. Intelligent, well-meaning people did this to each other as well, of course. I wasn't sure what felt worse: standing by helplessly observing this behavior or taking the hit myself.

It was hard not to feel betrayed and, even worse, cynical about the future of the entire human race. But this, as it turns out, is a classic visionary leadership dilemma: You don't know exactly where you're going and how to get there, and you can't do it alone. Yet because you don't know what you don't know, much less how to deal with it, some of your associates will use this against you, even as they're inspired to follow you into the unknown.

People can be fickle, praising you one moment, blaming you the next, all while struggling to gain your support and approval in order to secure whatever advantages you represent. It helps to know this up front. (At least then you won't waste time feeling shocked, as I did, when it happens.) Yet if you ask me if it was worth it, I would have to say yes. Conviction and endurance are fueled by inspiration, as it turns out, three qualities that, when combined, border on obsession. This appears to be what keeps any innovator going despite the accompanying strife of bringing something new, or even mildly precocious, into the world.

Motivating others, setting boundaries, and sometimes literally protecting myself from aggressive attacks: these were skills I learned from my stallion that became useful when I began working with herds of people, some of whom were a lot like Merlin, as it turned out — talented, stunningly beautiful, and filled with potential locked behind a wall of fear, frustration, vulnerability, or rage. In a predatory dominance system, we all experience abuse and betrayal, sometimes subtle, sometimes dramatic, creating moments that, at their most extreme, feel a bit like George Washington's unexpected encounter with Tanacharison (which in their case led to a bloody massacre and the start of the French and Indian War).

The Washington-Tanacharison episode makes it tragically apparent that when others experience trauma, everyone pays in the long run. As Thich Nhat Hanh observed, "When another person makes you suffer, it is because he suffers deeply in himself, and his suffering is spilling over. He does not need punishment; he needs help....Happiness and safety are not an individual matter. His happiness and safety are crucial for your happiness and safety." No one made this more apparent to me than Merlin. Misunderstanding and punishment created the monster he became. I knew I would never be safe around him until this trauma was transformed — not through naive "it's not his fault" indulgence, but through a heroic use of power that I later realized had much in common with the Fulani sharo.

Extreme physical violence is less common in the modern world, but emotional, psychological, and verbal forms of violence are promoted as "free speech" and, on reality television, entertainment. At home, school, work, and church, and most definitely in politics, we often find ourselves helplessly standing by, watching nasty altercations we can neither predict nor stop, knee-jerk reactions that start long-term, unnecessary battles that sometimes do erupt in shootings, beatings, and large-scale acts of terrorism. It's not enough to ask, "Why can't we all just get along?" We must make some serious culturewide efforts to ask a different question: *How* can we all get along? To even attempt to answer this question, we must stop blaming others and playing the victim. We must stand up to aggressors who also see themselves as victims of past injustice (and often truly are). And we must resist the urge to use shame as a weapon.

To do this we need power combined with compassion. We need to exercise emotional heroism.

Navigating the Minefield

Whether or not we grew up in idyllic circumstances, emotional time bombs are everywhere, especially when we step into a leadership role. Just as Merlin would explode for no apparent reason, people do the same thing, looking for an external enemy to fight or punish for sudden surges of fear related to personal or ancestral trauma, or to feelings of vulnerability that are in fact calling them to access their own power and vision.

For many years, I felt as if I were entering a World War II minefield whenever I walked out my front door. I knew I would not survive the ordeal if I took these assaults personally. I also realized that I would not reach my goals if I wasn't willing to take a certain amount of abuse without fighting back: Holding grudges would have sapped energy I needed for innovation. Seeking revenge would have taken me off course. This too is a visionary-leadership dilemma.

Sometimes, of course, I pined for the days when I was spending long stretches of time alone writing my first book and hiding out in the desert, seeking counsel from my horses away from the competitive equestrian world. To move to the next level, however, I had to give up my loner-artist tendencies and step into the fray. It might have helped to be a more aggressive alpha-style leader at that point, but I didn't want to give up my sensitivity in order to "tough it out" and take control. This, it turned out, was *my* visionary-leadership dilemma: maintaining empathy, ingenuity, and adaptability; encouraging others to step forward and lead; supporting them in working through their initial feelings of vulnerability in preparation for experimenting and creating something new were part of my calling.

The *idea* of bringing nonpredatory wisdom into an intensely aggressive culture was much more difficult to manifest than I expected — and I expected it to be hard. To pull rank and fight back when people challenged me overtly or, more often, undermined me secretly behind my back (though I would usually, eventually, find out) seemed to go against the very essence of my mission. For a time, I diffused the pain with alcohol, but it became clear that I couldn't possibly drink enough to soothe the wounds I sometimes had to endure daily. I would have needed something stronger. Doctors were ready and willing to give me any number of powerful drugs that purported to address these issues chemically. I knew lots of high-powered leaders who were taking Paxil, Xanax, Prozac, and other brain-altering, anxiety-reducing, courage- and energy-boosting substances with significant, sometimes unpredictable side effects. One executive I worked with said that, on his team of twelve close associates, *nine* people (that's *75 percent*) were taking at least one of these prescriptions.

If I wasn't going to medicate or self-medicate, what *could* I do? Give up? Run away? Not an option. For some reason, I truly felt willing to die for this calling, whether I was successful or not. Few people, including my husband, understood this. This too is a visionary-leadership dilemma.

And then in 2011, studying the long-suppressed, yet richly nuanced, leadership innovations of pastoral cultures, I came across something that truly excited me. I had already accessed the concept of emotional heroism by immersing myself in George Washington's numerous biographies, but I had no clear idea how to exercise it. Then I encountered the Fulani practice of the sharo (see the section titled "A Ritual of Courage and Self-Control" in chapter 8, pages 137–38).

Heroic Self-Control

The Fulani sharo is an act of physical heroism. In this coming-of-age ritual, a young man agrees to stand shirtless with arms wide open as he's beaten with a three-foot stick. After recovering from the ordeal, the "victim" is invited to challenge the challenger to a similar ordeal, ultimately giving both parties the opportunity to display their willingness to face pain and aggression without fighting back. During these public beatings, interestingly enough, the person enduring this abuse holds up a mirror, watching his own facial expressions, more concerned with his controlled response to this power play than the fierceness of his attacker.

Women sometimes initially have a strong negative response to using the sharo as a metaphor for handling modern conflicts. Carol Roush, an Eponaquest advanced instructor and faculty member who started the highly successful "Now" personal-development program in Europe, encounters abuse survivors and highly sensitive people who have trouble engaging power because it was misused on them in the past. After reading an earlier version of this chapter, she expressed confusion and concern regarding this concept: "On the one hand, you insist that there's no excuse for physical violence, yet you use the sharo as a positive example. It could be argued that fundamentalist Christians who ritually beat small children are engaging in a 'rite of passage' to teach them something important."

To be clear: I don't believe there's any responsible justification for verbally or physically violent behavior. However, in our current stage of emotional and social development, these attacks do occur, and we must learn how to handle them, especially if we find ourselves in a leadership role of virtually any kind. This guiding principle uses an updated version of the sharo, taken out of the realm of physical violence, to deal constructively with conflict and power plays in ways that reduce and transform suffering, encouraging all parties involved to move forward productively. It is not at all about playing the victim, seeking revenge, or punishing or abusing others for some nefarious or "lofty" goal.

When Merlin threatened my life, I defended myself with a whip, smacking him on the belly as he reared over me, setting a boundary that was emphatic and understandable, sending the message that I was capable of protecting myself from physical assault. The split second he backed off, however, I gave him immediate positive feedback in the form of support and connection. I did not punish him with violence by chasing him around the arena, beating him with the whip. I did not seek revenge afterward, nor did I demand a period of groveling. Instead, the combination of self-control, power, and compassion I showed in the midst of these completely unwarranted attacks worked wonders on this horse, who read my actions as not just fair but also worthy of respect and, eventually, trust.

There's a significant difference between the sharo and the not-uncommon historical practice of beating children in the name of religion (which did happen to my father, who was regularly whipped while kneeling in front of icons of Christ, by his rigidly religious father — a form of ritual abuse). In the Fulani sharo, the challenge comes from a *peer*, not an authority figure who maintains the upper hand. The sharo offers a counterintuitive model for dealing constructively with power plays among adolescents and adults.

Violent altercations are instinctual in all species, predatory and nonpredatory alike: stallions fight with each other over mares and social standing — wild mustang males are often covered with scars. In the Fulani case, however, this outback community makes it clear that *not* fighting back in response to a power play is a *valued option*. Furthermore, there's significant preparation for this publicly observed challenge; it happens neither suddenly nor secretly. "Civilized" bullies use the element of surprise to catch smaller or outnumbered victims off guard, often ganging up on people, sometimes with automatic weapons, no less. In our culture, adolescent conflicts and power plays take place behind schools, in back alleys, and on isolated wooded lots, away from the watchful gaze of parents, teachers, and peers. Winning at all costs, even by underhanded means, is the goal.

In the Fulani sharo, there's no conventional winner. By challenging someone, you're inviting the same treatment in public up to a year after the original ordeal, which means even the scrawniest victim has time to heal, gain weight, lift weights, and study martial arts if he wishes — no doubt making some young men think twice about engaging in this ritualized expression of male aggression, or at the very least showing some mercy during the initial encounter.

Feminine Aggression

Women have rarely, if ever, been encouraged to develop rites of passage for showing courage, enduring conflict, and socializing power. From Native American ceremonies for girls who begin menstruating, to engagement parties, lavish weddings, and baby showers, feminine rituals worldwide emphasize the ability to create life. It's no wonder that some of my more sensitive staff members and clients initially have a hard time seeing the sharo as anything but violent.

As modern women step into leadership positions outside the home, however, particularly in previously male-dominated fields, the challenges associated with embracing and transforming the active, masculine power principle are significant. Some female leaders *think* of themselves as gentle and nurturing, pushing their own unacknowledged competitive and aggressive tendencies underground, where these rejected impulses eventually rear their ugly, outraged heads in unpredictable, shadowy ways.

If previously disempowered women (or men) refuse to develop and socialize their power, crazy things happen when they pursue ambitious goals together — as I found at Apache Springs and in previous leadership positions where some of my colleagues would act sweet on the surface and ruthless underneath. As much as they hate to admit it, women in professional settings engage in *nasty* power plays no less painful and debilitating when many take the passive-aggressive role of undermining those whose position, promotion, talents, or power they envy. Much of this behavior, however, cannot be taken personally.

"This is what finally helped me find peace with the volatile and often incomprehensible events that would go on with one of my most naturally powerful and competitive colleagues," Carol Roush told me as we continued our discussions on the sharo. "When I finally realized that this person's motives were unconscious, I was able to stop trying to analyze why she was doing those things, because I understood that she didn't know. Then I could finally begin first to look at my reactions to her and then eventually to look for my responsibility in the situation. Prior to that, I was sure it was all premeditated scheming designed to sabotage my every step. Now I have more empathy for someone's unconscious pain or vulnerability. I keep clear boundaries around the things we are probably never going to agree on, and this creates the safety and trust that allows supportive friendship."

In the twenty-first century, everyone needs advanced tools for modulating power and moderating conflict. Contrary to popular belief, many of these skills *can't* be exercised through competitive sports: conflicts arising in innovative settings happen precisely because there are no established rules and referees. In this respect, treating any interpersonal challenge as an impromptu sharo has helped me immensely in recognizing, enduring, and responding constructively to events that once shocked, demoralized, and exhausted me. Teaching others to exercise emotional heroism — rather than feeling victimized, holding grudges, and undermining people afterward — mitigates the toxic by-products of power that people release unconsciously, *especially* when they think of themselves as peaceful and evolved.

The sharo metaphor is also helpful in facing personal challenges, such as becoming aware of your own unproductive or inconsiderate behavior. In this case, you may be tempted to beat yourself up once you realize you've hurt someone else, perhaps by objectifying another race or species, perhaps by scapegoating or punishing someone for weaknesses you also share (projection). The ability to take personal responsibility for your actions and change your behavior is, without a doubt, a heroic act.

Abuse survivors must also engage emotional heroism in therapeutic settings. As a clinical counselor working with adults recovering from childhood trauma, Mary-Louise Gould assisted people in reaching the ultimate goal of leaving their stories behind and truly living in the present, giving them tools for counteracting the effects of a challenging past. "But before my clients could embrace the idea of thriving rather than merely surviving," she emphasized during a discussion we had on the subject, "they first had to face their abuse history while simultaneously letting go of blame and shame. This was a very deep, painful, demanding, and ultimately rewarding task.

"Those aspects of their abuse which had been dissociated (not remembered) had become inner survival mechanisms," said Mary-Louise, who, as an Eponaquest advanced instructor and faculty member, now teaches other counselors and educators how to employ horses in helping people move beyond unconscious trauma responses. Mary-Louise observed that

> these behaviors originally "kicked in" to protect young, undeveloped egos from being overwhelmed. However, to become more effective at work and in adult relationships, these old patterns have to be invited into consciousness, experienced with courage, accepted as part of one's history, learned from, and finally integrated into so-called normal memory.

> It might be said that anybody engaging this level of self-scrutiny, self-acceptance, and self-compassion is holding a mirror up to his or her childhood trauma, experiencing a kind of personal sharo, one that is every bit as mentally, physically, and emotionally heroic as the pain experienced by a Fulani boy. That certainly was my experience of the amazing women and men I worked with.

It's important to understand, however, that I'm not advocating we mimic the sharo physically. Just as Joseph Campbell used the hero's journey as a metaphor for transformation and self-mastery (drawing on stories of horrifying ordeals and bloody conflicts that proliferated throughout history), we have to take the sharo as a metaphor for dealing with modern conflict out of the realm of physical violence.

The benefits are significant: Without an alternative model like the sharo, we see men and, more recently, women in influential positions using predatory metaphors: Sarah Palin calling herself a "mama grizzly" to justify attacking anyone who disagrees with her comes to mind. Leaders like Palin and Margaret Thatcher, whom Ronald Reagan called "the best man in England," have been rewarded in some circles for using aggressive, traditionally male power-over tactics of intimidation, insult, and revenge.

Incorporating a more thoughtful, self-controlled response to conflict is sorely needed in our verbally contentious corporate and political systems. If I'm voting for the president of the United States, after all, I want someone who can think clearly and compassionately in the midst of all of the vicious, often unjustified international and domestic assaults he or she endures daily in our current culture. The person with his or her finger on the main trigger to nuclear annihilation needs some sharo-like skills, or we're all in trouble!

An Evolutionary Approach

The sharo represents an approach to power that values courage, endurance, and the willingness not to fight back as signs that someone has what it takes to run a herd and raise a family of his own. In translating the sharo to an emotionally heroic context, however, I recommend updating this ancient ritual with some advanced social-intelligence skills.

It is, first of all, essential to *refuse* the traditional opportunity to challenge your challenger to a similar public beating. In the aftermath of a verbal attack, the entire community benefits if you continue to demonstrate thoughtfulness, compassion, and self-control. Retaliation of any kind, including shaming or guilt-tripping the aggressor for hurting you, takes everyone off course, diverting you from a much more productive option: holding a lucid, nonshaming, "difficult conversation" that encourages both parties to address relevant issues, change destructive behaviors, and learn how to air future differences in a more respectful, socially intelligent way (see Guiding Principle 9, in chapter 21).

The sharo concept is also useful in handling long-term undermining, which is a common phenomenon in modern life. When you find out that someone has been secretly demeaning you while acting cordial or supportive to your face, you will feel as if this person has stabbed you in the back or punched you in the heart. But seeking revenge, no matter how justified it seems, will only create a deeper rift between the two of you and negatively affect the larger business, political, or social organization. Remember, as Thich Nhat Hanh observed, people who attack you do so, at least in part, because they are suffering inside. Retaliation can all too easily set a "conquest and revenge" cycle in motion. (Just watch the average reality TV show. When verbal assaults are met with blatant insults, self-righteous shaming statements, or the "victim's" efforts to undermine others, factions are created, leading to long-term strife in the entire group.)

Whether you're dealing with a family quarrel, a work-related conflict, or a national, religious, political, or cultural disagreement, it's unlikely that your rival will see the error of his ways and apologize for lashing out or undermining you. Taking personal responsibility for one's over-the-top, or simply unproductive, actions during a conflict is an *advanced* move, especially for people with a low tolerance for feeling vulnerable.

Yet there's another compelling reason why many people are reluctant to apologize: In our transition out of an oppressive dominance-submission system, *apologies are often used as power plays*, creating further blocks to solving the interpersonal issues involved. This phenomenon, completely unconscious in most people, emerges when someone's sincere attempts to say he's sorry are met with shaming statements or rigid, unforgiving, perhaps cynical body language from the supposed victim, who demands a certain amount of groveling.

Because both parties have usually played some role in exacerbating a situation that led one person to explode or to undermine the other, the original aggressor senses that he's being treated unjustly and shuts down communication and understanding. (The only clear exception to this "shared responsibility" principle is physical or sexual abuse: the victim *must not* be blamed for the attack on any level.)

Expecting someone to grovel when he's ready to change his behavior is a seemingly mild, yet incredibly unproductive, form of retaliation. In Guiding Principle 4, in chapter 16, for instance, Judge Barbara Wilkinson realized that, whenever her son was on the verge of conceding that he was willing to see her side of things, his tentative efforts at reconciliation were met with an icy, self-righteous silence as Barbara sentenced him to a period of emotional penance for the smallest infractions. With this "technique," a small window of transformation closed as Barbara's interest in holding a grudge became more important to her than acknowledging her son's clumsy, somewhat reluctant attempts to cooperate.

Similarly, if I had expected Merlin to bow down to me and beg forgiveness for threatening my life, our relationship would never have changed. Yes, he could have killed me. No, I didn't deserve this treatment. Yet the only way he was going to heal, the only way I was ever going to be safe, was if I met his initially subtle attempts to change his behavior with feelings of connection and appreciation — while continuing to hold boundaries and remain vigilant.

After all, the harshest treatment Merlin received came from a trainer who *forced* him to grovel for some perceived infraction, tying his head between his legs in a darkened stall, short-circuiting his nervous system in the process, turning a naive, disorganized aggressor into a victim of abuse.

Turning the Tide

In the aftermath of any hurtful altercation, the second major act of emotional heroism you'll perform calls for generosity and forgiveness, both of which may feel entirely unearned when you first engage them. Avoid literally saying, "I for-give you," however. This comes across as self-righteous, presumptuous, and de-meaning. You simply act as if you're willing to both forgive the other person and take personal responsibility for your own role in the conflict by reaching out to this individual — once you've regained your balance.

With all of this in mind, I've created a more formal sequence for exercising emotional heroism in interpersonal conflicts, with one word of caution: If the situation escalates to the point that the aggressor attacks you physically, you *must* protect yourself, preferably by leaving the scene immediately and calling for help. There is never any excuse for physical violence in modern interper-sonal conflicts. You may need to involve the police or the justice system and let experts handle the appropriate restraint, confinement, and rehabilitation.

At the same time, it's important to realize that the roots of physical vio-lence are related to a specieswide lack of emotional and social intelligence, par-ticularly a massive cultural aversion to feeling vulnerable. People who build their EQ skills and raise their tolerance for feeling vulnerable are better able to acknowledge mistakes, take personal responsibility for their actions, and change destructive behavior while voicing their needs more effectively.

In the meantime, you'll be part of the solution if you exercise your own ability to endure hurtful interpersonal exchanges without fighting back. This minimizes the long-term damage and provides a necessary opening for you to use other emotional- and social-intelligence skills to move forward produc-tively after an initially debilitating conflict.

Emotional Heroism:
An Advanced Approach to Diffusing — and Transforming — Aggression, Betrayal, Resentment, and Other Debilitating Effects of Interpersonal Conflict

1. Whether you were verbally attacked or undermined secretly over the long term, treat any assault as an impromptu sharo. Hold boundar-ies, but do not fight back. The demeaning, shaming, blaming, perhaps even hateful emotional charge *is* debilitating. (This is where you feel as if you're being beaten with a big stick.) Your increasing ability to endure this pain with arms wide open — while remaining thought-ful and observant — is an advanced form of the *stay-longer-and-stay-thoughtful* technique used in building a high tolerance for vulnerability (introduced in Guiding Principle 5, in chapter 17).

2. Breathe, and take note of what the person is saying or doing. There will be useful information between and underneath the insults, though you may never completely understand the complex feelings, past wounds, and reactive patterns this situation tapped in the aggressor, causing you to suddenly become the object of his or her rage or resentment.

3. Get immediate *confidential* help from an experienced, emotionally intelligent friend, coach, or counselor. Do not gather coworkers or mutual friends to complain about this person's behavior, creating factions that will become troublesome for everyone involved over time.

4. Avoid objectifying or demonizing the person (seeing him or her as hopelessly defective, unevolved, stupid, or even evil). This includes avoiding the modern tendency to diagnose this person with a mental health issue. Even if you are a licensed psychotherapist, you cannot trust your own judgment in this situation. Many behaviors seen as "personality disorders" (or even sociopathic) are taught, modeled, and promoted in a predatory dominance system or are a consequence of the many ways that people sublimate their rage, resentment, or power as a result of this aggressive paradigm. Recognize that diagnosing, objectifying, or demonizing this person might be your own attempt to deflect attention from any partial responsibility you have for contributing to the situation that set him or her off.

5. Part of this person's response was provoked by something you said, did, or didn't do. You will need to determine, honestly, what part of the episode is about you, what you *can* take responsibility for, and be willing to change any unproductive behavior that comes to light.

6. It's also possible that you're being used as a scapegoat in this situation, or as an object of envy, jealousy, projection, or transference. (Sometimes all of these at once.) In the latter case, there are many ways that past traumas can bleed into and exacerbate present altercations. Here are some more extreme yet common examples:

    People who grew up in misogynistic or racist families, where objectified populations are seen as second-class citizens, can feel disrespected or shamed when a woman, African American, or member of some other population receives a promotion or praise for a job well done (even if these descendants of misogynistic or racist families are sincerely trying to move beyond ancestral patterns).

    A man or woman with an abusive or neglectful mother or a competitive sister might secretly mistrust all female coworkers, leading to unexpectedly strong reactions when a woman takes charge or receives recognition.

Survivors of childhood sexual abuse tend to be wary of male authority figures, of course, but they can also hold the expectation that immediate supervisors, male or female, should punish anyone who challenges them (especially if one or both parents failed to recognize and stop the original abuse). Interpersonal difficulties at work can cause such people to feel resentful or even betrayed if the leader doesn't take their side and protect them.

Understanding these and other possibilities helps you refrain from taking the aggressor's reaction personally and, if at all possible, muster up some compassion for the pain and betrayals all people have endured at some point in their lives.

7. In almost every over-the-top emotional outburst, a certain percentage of the reaction triggered something from the aggressor's past, tapping a well of unresolved internal suffering. The only constructive thing you can do in the moment, however, is react counterintuitively, modeling emotional heroism. By enduring this impromptu sharo with dignity, by refusing to fight back, shame, or undermine this person, you are showing him or her that you are *nothing* like those previously hurtful bosses, opportunistic coworkers, abusive parents, two-faced false friends, and so on.

8. You will never know exactly what the other person's past issues are, but you can, by remembering what led up to the explosion, gain some clues about *what did pertain to you*, which you can take responsibility for and change over time. When you analyze the situation afterward, the need to address your own ineffective patterns or develop a new skill set may become apparent. This means you will initially feel vulnerable or embarrassed. Do not let this realization intensify into shame. Problem solve about the *behavior* that needs to change. Do not see yourself as hopelessly defective. And congratulate yourself for handling the attack professionally and compassionately, which you most certainly did if you avoided fighting back, shaming the aggressor publicly, or undermining him or her in conversation with select coworkers, clients, or mutual friends afterward. (Venting confidentially with *one* trusted mutual friend or coworker, better yet a coach or counselor, is productive, and often necessary, *if* it leads to self-awareness, compassion, and problem solving.)

9. If you did fight back, shame, or undermine the aggressor at any point,

see this as your current emotional-heroism baseline. Use the sequence associated with developing a high tolerance for vulnerability (see pages 348–50) to increase the much more advanced isometric, emotional-strength-training skill of building heroic self-control.

10. Take a break to heal. Do not confront this person in a raw, physically and emotionally compromised state.

11. Prepare for the difficult conversation (Guiding Principle 9, in chapter 21) that must follow to address both parties' concerns in order to get back on track and learn from the relevant issues that come to light. If you were viciously attacked or secretly undermined over the long term, you'll probably need help preparing for this conversation. You might also need a moderator to help conduct the conversation if you're still feeling overstimulated, fearful, vulnerable, or resentful. In the latter case, look for someone who knows the difficult-conversation format and who can support both parties.

    (If you cannot find someone locally, Eponaquest instructors with the "POH" designation next to their names have received additional training in how to teach the "Power of the Herd" Guiding Principles. They can exercise these leadership and emotional- and social-intelligence skills through equine-facilitated learning activities designed to teach specific principles. Some of these skills can also be taught indoors, in business settings, in counseling offices, or through phone consultations. While many of the guiding principles benefit from the nonverbal training horses provide, preparing for difficult conversations is a purely human skill and can easily be mastered through phone consultations.)

12. Recognize that mending the relationship — even if this means restoring it only to a reasonable level of functionality — may actually take more emotional heroism than enduring the original altercation. The other party may be feeling shame, vulnerability, embarrassment, and resentment that he or she doesn't know how to deal with constructively and may continue to act out or undermine you as a result. Do not take this personally. Approach the challenge from a position of compassion and power. Use it as a chance to increase your skills in this area, but don't try to become this person's friend right away. Friendship may never be possible, but increasing understanding and trust may be, especially over time.

Chapter Twenty-Four

GUIDING PRINCIPLE 12
Enjoy the Ride

*W*erner Herzog's evocative 2011 documentary *Cave of Forgotten Dreams* explores the Chauvet Cave paintings in France, some of which are nearly thirty-five thousand years old. These astonishingly sophisticated depictions of horses, bulls, cattle, stags, antelope, lions, bears, and even rhinoceroses are perplexing in their incredible sophistication and expressive power.

The discovery of this ancient art gallery in December 1994 astonished theorists interested in the evolution of human creativity. As David S. Whitley marvels in his 2009 book, *Cave Paintings and the Human Spirit: The Origin of Creativity and Belief,* these intricate murals were more than ten thousand years older than those discovered at the nearby Lascaux Cave, yet "Chauvet Cave had art that was not simply on par with the finest Paleolithic examples. It was, by significant margin, the oldest cave art in the world and it dramatically disproved any contention that our human artistic capabilities had evolved, over time, from simple to complex. When art first appeared, it appeared full-blown in a technically and aesthetically sophisticated fashion."

As Whitley emphasizes again and again throughout his book, "This first art consists of true aesthetic masterpieces — works of art that fully rival our greatest creative achievements, of any time and place." Yet while experts agree on the outstanding quality, some question his assertion that human creativity of this magnitude could have happened so suddenly. In discussing her interest in prehistoric cave paintings, Meg Daley Olmert, author of *Made for Each Other: The Biology of the Human-Animal Bond,* observed that "many archeologists believe the ancient art we see in these caves is merely the most protected art that has survived the millennia, and that other, more rudimentary depictions may have not survived the elements." At the same time, she too is impressed with these powerful, lifelike images, leaning toward Whitley's camp on this point: "Unless you consider the handprints and geometric graphics, the complete lack of 'bad' art in the caves would seem to argue against the gradual acquisition of artistic ability."

Olmert uses these same caves to make another compelling point. She emphasizes that the hormone oxytocin can be produced not only by touch but also by the sort of highly concentrated focus on other beings that mothers exhibit when adoring their newborns. She thinks this hormone may also be released during the "hunter's trance," a term the evolutionary biologist Edward O. Wilson coined to describe an expanded state of awareness he experienced while spending extended time in nature, in which heart, breath, and mind are quieted, resulting in heightened concentration and attention to detail. (I find it interesting that Wilson called this the "hunter's trance" even though he often accessed this state while peacefully observing animals rather than stalking them to put food on the table. In this sense, it's clear that he too was unconsciously influenced by humanity's overidentification with predatory behavior.)

Once released in the body, Olmert asserts, oxytocin produces a whole sequence of transformational effects, buffering the flight-or-fight response in mammals and encouraging them take *social risks*, boosting the impulse toward what Pyotr Alekseyevich Kropotkin called "mutual aid." A relaxed, concentrated focus, combined with intense dedication to or adoration of the subject matter, is also characteristic of creativity, suggesting that the biology of the human-animal bond could very well have been a factor in inspiring those early, impressively detailed cave paintings.

And what were these ancestral artists paying tribute to in Chauvet and Lascaux? Most definitely *not* people. At Chauvet, only one vaguely human figure can be discerned: the lower portion of a woman's body. A nearby image depicts a human-bison hybrid. The vast majority of the paintings are highly realistic, artistically accomplished representations of animals. Horses are the fourth most frequently painted subjects, behind felines, mammoths, and rhinos (yes, a now-extinct species of rhino roamed Ice Age Europe!). But these early equines are among the most vividly portrayed animals in the cave, clearly showing individual characteristics in striking detail.

One of the most famous paintings, featuring four horses, captures facial expressions that an artist would pick up only from close, direct observation of individual living horses. The smallest, most youthful animal, for instance, has bulges along the bottom of its jaw. This is a classic sign of a colt or filly around two or three years of age whose adult teeth are coming in. (In 2011, Spirit's three-year-old daughter, Artemis, looked very much the same. Other horses I've raised have gone through this stage, before the jawline smoothes out at maturity.)

Many of the lions also show specific facial features portraying intricate moods and behaviors, leading Olmert to come to a startling conclusion in her book: the cave artists "*knew* these animals — not just as a species but as individuals. These were neighbors, close neighbors." What's more, she insists, the "impressive detail and graphic skill" of the paintings "tells us those animals were not terribly frightened of us."

Whitley, an archeologist who writes from a less knowledgeable perspective on animal behavior, had the chance to actually visit Chauvet Cave. Even he was struck by how two different horses painted in separate alcoves were purposefully set apart from other animals, creating the uncanny impression that these horses were reaching out to him. They "approach you, slowly, oblivious, and unmoved by the lions, rhinos, and other animals surrounding them," he writes. "They come to you in a stately and unhurried pace."

The Lion and the Horse

Reading Whitley's words and staring at photos of these evocative paintings in the oversized art book *Chauvet Cave: The Art of Earliest Times*, I was inspired by a compelling possibility. Having lived with herds of horses as colleagues, teachers, guides, and friends — as sentient, empowered beings who made requests, reached out to me, communicated clearly, and often had their own opinions about things — it struck me that that these prehistoric artists were capturing an ancient invitation, that very moment when a horse looked a human in the eye and approached, hinting at a partnership in the making, one that would profoundly change both species in the process.

At the same time, I was struck by the two most impressive galleries, one dedicated to lions, the other to horses. While depictions of mammoths and rhinos are more plentiful at Chauvet, the attention to detail is much more sophisticated in the feline and equine paintings. Was this an early identification on the artists' part with the very two animals I had long associated with the predatory and nonpredatory sides of my own omnivorous soul? (While I was already familiar with Lascaux, I learned of the Chauvet Cave only in 2011, after writing chapter 5 of this book, "The Lion and the Horse," in which, you may remember, I envision these two animals as symbols of a balanced, fully empowered human psyche.) As social animals, lions employ teamwork when hunting, while horses activate mutual aid to protect each other, factors that did not escape Olmert in her assertion that ancient humans learned much from watching their four-legged neighbors. "Our ceaseless need to assess the strengths and weaknesses of animals, to cope with their overwhelming presence or threatening absence, was a matter of life and death," she writes. "But analyzing animals proved to be more than a survival strategy; it became school, television, even church. It is no wonder that a history of staring at animals has left us with a brain that still can't help but seek them out and try to understand them."

And, I would argue from studies on the effectiveness of animal-assisted therapy and experiential education: animals *transform* and even *heal* us through respectful, mutually supportive interactions.

Let's look more closely at the oxytocin effect: This potent little peptide has been shown to lower heart rate and stress-hormone levels, increasing our sense of well-being, sometimes creating mystical feelings of connection with all life. It facilitates learning and even results in faster wound healing, while at the same time making people more trusting and trustworthy. Promising studies have confirmed that it relieves some of the antisocial tendencies of autistics. Oxytocin has also been shown to dramatically increase focus and social memory, two elements that would have been essential to the cave artists' advanced craft of recording detailed facial features of the animals they painted.

As Olmert contends in *Made for Each Other*, "Oxytocin may have stoked the warmer social climate that emerged during the long, stressful Ice Age. The triumph of trust over paranoia enabled humans and animals to come together in domesticated partnerships and emboldened people to move beyond the social limitations of kinship and tribe and live harmoniously in a civilized world.…When humans began to keep animals and animals submitted to our care, we inadvertently created a chemical biofeedback system that changed our hearts and minds." Olmert also reveals that "our new, improved understanding of this molecule's ability to create strong feelings of attraction, recognition and commitment between mammals — and the fact that its effects can be released visually as well as through other sensory contact — strongly suggests that it was one of the subliminal forces that shaped the minds and hearts of our Ice Age ancestors."

The plot thickens ten thousand years after Chauvet, when, it becomes clear, the Lascaux Cave artists were even more obsessed with horses. Out of 915 images at Lascaux, over *60 percent* of the recognizable animals are horses, followed by stags, at a mere 15 percent; aurochs and bison, each at under 5 percent; and felines, appearing 1.2 percent of the time. Wolves, generally considered to be the first animal willing to be domesticated, don't even appear in these paintings. And here again, only one human figure abides in a bestiary that scientists now conclude had nothing to do with "hunting magic." According to Whitley, "Animal bones excavated from living areas at the mouths of the caves" revealed that "there was little if any correlation between animals painted and animals eaten." Since then, he and a few other scientists have promoted the idea that the paintings were evidence of ritual trance states, that shamanism led to the birth of human creativity.

But what if the explanation was a bit more obvious than that? What if the most detailed paintings were ancient portraits of the artists' favorite animals — and by that I mean individual animals with whom these people were forming increasingly trusting, intensely inspiring, transformational relationships? After all, while archeological evidence of people riding horses doesn't show up for a good eighteen thousand years after Lascaux's artists closed up shop, who's to say that these people weren't being called out by the animals themselves, following *their* lead, moving in harmony with ancient herds thousands of years before human beings developed the technology to confine and restrain the horse?

Ice Age individuals moving with these animals would not have left an archeological imprint, but that doesn't mean theorists should dismiss the possibility, especially considering the detail and vibrancy of this artwork.

"We cannot know what the cave painters were thinking," Olmert commented after I presented this theory to her in 2012. "What we can know is *what they painted — and it was always, overwhelmingly, animals.* This overwhelming depiction of animals is clear evidence of the preoccupation of the Ice Age mind. And what we now know is that this degree of focused, long-term attention to anything will trigger the activation of oxytocin in the watcher. Since these animals were watchers of us as well, we can say with complete confidence that oxytocin was flowing between the species, creating the powerful bonds that would change the world." Olmert went on to confirm that this line of reasoning "supports your idea that we were painting the animals we felt most bonded to."

Pegasus Rising

"In the middle of the Ice Age, the human heart was melting," Olmert writes. "Cave artists felt it first. The beast had become more than dinner; it had become Muse. Over and over, tens of thousands of times, cave painters made horses and lions and aurochs, and they made them do whatever they wanted. Cave artists were the first humans to gain control over wild beasts. They alone could decide where an animal would be and what it would do. Perhaps in these caves, in this art, humans first toyed with the notion of finding another way with animals."

Cave-art scientists have yet to entertain this compelling theory about the emergence of human creativity, one backed by recent research into the evolution of the human-animal bond and suggested by my clients' experiences with horses as agents of inspiration and transformation, not to mention a host of cross-cultural myths about the role of horses in expanding human consciousness and creativity.

Greek, Indian, Celtic, Siberian, Middle Eastern, and Native American legends all agree that horses have the ability to carry people back and forth between this world and the "other," the premiere shamanic and creative act. Pegasus, the winged horse of the ancient Greeks, spirited heroes to the stars after death and brought magic from the gods to these same innovators during their earthly trials. He was also a companion to the Muses. Even more telling, however, are his antics on Mount Helicon. Flying to the highest point of this sacred peak, he emphatically struck his hoof on the ground, creating a massive earthquake and releasing an underground spring, whose waters cascaded down the mountain forever after, nourishing artists, poets, and musicians.

Muhammad received one of his holy visions astride Al-Buraq, sometimes spelled Alborak, a white winged horse who took Islam's revered prophet to heaven — and brought him safely back to earth again, where he struggled to share the immensity of his insights with the world.

In the book of Revelation, Christ returns riding a white horse. Hindu prophecies also speak of a white horse ushering in a future era of peace on earth. The final manifestation of Vishnu, Kalki is sometimes depicted carrying or accompanying the blue-skinned god. But some statues portray him with a horse's head and a human body, harkening back to an earlier manifestation of Vishnu, Hayagriva, worshipped as the god of wisdom. Sitting on a white lotus, this brilliant horse-headed avatar rescued the holy text of the Vedas from demons, representing thereafter the triumph of divine knowledge over the dark forces of ignorance and misguided passion.

Yet what if these and other fanciful stories point back to an even more ancient truth, one that civilized men aren't quite willing to entertain? What if ancient paintings at Chauvet and Lascaux weren't so much evidence of trance hallucination, a desire to dominate other beings, or a sudden leap in wholly symbolic thinking? What if they were literally capturing the power and spirit of the times, an era when the animals themselves were luring early humans into a journey of mutual empowerment, mutual evolution, and eventually, mutual domestication?

This in itself, of course, mirrors the role of modern shamans, who are considered specialists in bridging the visible and invisible worlds, as well as the human and animal realms. I first explored this notion in *The Tao of Equus*, gaining considerable inspiration from Mircea Eliade's 1951 book *Shamanism* and Larry Dossey's influential *Recovering the Soul*.

Among the qualities that made the shaman a cross-cultural phenomenon was the belief that "a kind of collective consciousness bound them together with the animal kingdom," Dossey writes. "So intimate was the sharing of the mind with the animals that shamans believed it possible to actually *become* an animal," a notion exemplified by the human-animal hybrids depicted in early art at Chauvet, Lascaux, and other prehistoric sites.

Dossey goes on to observe that "in the nonlocal, collective consciousness that wrapped man and animal together, it was not always the man who took the initiative in actualizing it. Sometimes the first overture was made by the animal. This is most obvious in the *call* of the shaman…and in his initiation.… In the tradition of the Buryat shamans the tutelary animal is called the khubligan, a term that can be interpreted as 'metamorphosis.' "

The art at Chauvet and Lascaux represents an intense metamorphosis of human consciousness. As David Whitley muses in *Cave Paintings and the Human Spirit*, "I cannot help but wonder about the centrality of the horse in this apparently shamanic art: Why? And, of course, what does the horse mean?"

There are several relatively simple, straightforward reasons why horses would have been receptive to forming associations with humans, and why our ancestors might have trusted them: First of all, horses are not predators. They don't stalk other species or attack unless cornered and provoked, and even then they rarely put forth the extra effort to kill. At the same time, they are powerful and seem to be aware of that power on some level. Consequently, they tend to be braver and more gregarious than most other prey-animal species. Yet unlike cattle and deer, they do not have horns and, as a result, are much less dangerous to engage with.

What if, deep in those ancient caverns, prehistoric artists were documenting the very first call of the shaman, creating intricate monuments to the very first khubligans? And what if, through our recent rediscovery of these caves, the spirits of those four-legged initiators are calling modern men and women to *remember*, to open our jaded civilized hearts and feel, once again, the collective consciousness that still binds us to the animal kingdom? In tempering our uniquely human, self-possessed view that we are the most intelligent, evolved species on the planet, would we be able to change our destructive habits and reclaim the power of the herd?

Happy School

I've recently had the opportunity to contribute to some cutting-edge research on the emotional and physiological effects of equine-facilitated learning activities, most notably with Ann Linda Baldwin, an award-winning researcher at the University of Arizona. Along with Barbara Rector, one of the founders of the Equine Facilitated Mental Health Association, and Lisa Walters, head of the EquuSatori Center in Northern California, we've done some pilot experiments, and have subsequently designed larger studies, to understand why and how horses help humans become better at being, well, human. Ann's orientation as a physiologist has led us to explore how horses are attracted to, and help boost, heart-rate coherence, an optimal state for physical, mental, and emotional health. As Ann explains:

> It is well known that emotions acutely affect heart rate. When you are fearful or excited, heart rate goes up; and when you are quietly content, heart rate goes down. Emotions act on the heart by stimulating two branches of nerves in the heart, sympathetic and parasympathetic. Increased stimulation of sympathetic nerves increases heart rate, whereas increased stimulation of parasympathetic nerves decreases heart rate.
>
> What most people don't know is that emotions also affect the pattern with which the heart rate changes with time (heart-rate variability) in very distinct ways. Negative emotions, such as anger and frustration, cause the heart rate to change erratically, without any real pattern to it. On the other hand, sustained positive emotions such as appreciation, care, compassion, and love generate a smooth, sine-wave-like pattern in the heart's rhythms. The heart sends this information to the brain, and this leads to increased synchronization between the two branches of nerves in the heart and a general shift in balance toward increased parasympathetic activity. Under these conditions, the two branches of nerves are stimulated in turn, in time with your breathing, and that is why the heart rate goes up and down with a regular rhythm like a sine wave. As you breathe in, your heart rate goes up; and as you breathe out, your heart rate goes down. Heart rhythm is coherent with breathing.
>
> By contrast, as research has shown, negative emotions such as frustration, anger, anxiety, and worry lead to heart rhythm patterns that appear incoherent — highly variable and erratic. If a person is feeling negative emotions, there is less synchronization in the reciprocal action of the parasympathetic and sympathetic branches of the nervous system. This de-synchronization, if sustained, taxes the nervous system, impeding the efficient synchronization and flow of information throughout the brain,

making it difficult to remember things and to make rational decisions. Lack of coordination between the sympathetic and parasympathetic nervous branches also leads to imbalanced emotions, reinforcing the existing negative emotions that first triggered the imbalance.

To gain funding for a significant study exploring which equine-facilitated activities promote this desirable coherent state, Ann and I wanted to see how horse enthusiasts' emotions were affected by informal interactions with these animals. With the help of author-researcher Gary Schwartz and researcher Sherry Daugherty, we created a survey that gleaned some fascinating data.

"The results show unequivocally that horses make us feel *great*," Ann concluded upon analyzing the results, "noticeably better in fact than most other activities in which we regularly engage, lending support to equine-facilitated programs that have already shown anecdotally that working with horses, on the ground or in the saddle, decreases stress, increases self-esteem, and over time, helps people excel in the human world."

For this baseline survey, we asked people interested in horses how often they feel, or felt, particular emotions (positive, negative, and neutral) under six different circumstances (at school, at home, at work, with a pet, in nature, with a horse). Positive emotions were awe, wonder, joy, appreciation, affection, and pride. Negative emotions were sadness, disgust, frustration, fear, despair, anger, and shame. Survey participants could choose from the following options for each emotion: Never, Rarely, Sometimes, Often, Very Often, Almost Always, or Always, and we rated these choices from 1 to 7: the higher the number, the more frequently the person felt the emotion. The results are depicted in the graphs on pages 410–11. As Ann explains:

> Positive emotions are defined as feelings that reflect pleasurable engagement with the environment. If our instincts are true, that being with horses triggers positive emotions and improves your mood, then it is likely that your physical health will improve too. Studies by Sheldon Cohen at Carnegie Mellon University show that people whose behavior is usually described by words like *lively, energetic, happy, cheerful, at ease,* or *calm,* rather than *sad, depressed, nervous,* or *hostile,* are less likely to develop a cold when exposed to a cold virus. Not only are they less likely to get colds, they are more likely to sleep well, be less stressed, socialize, and maintain more and higher quality social ties, leading to greater success and enjoyment at work and at home. Those seem like good reasons for wanting to know what circumstances will make you more likely to feel positive emotions.

We sent our survey to the worldwide email list of Eponaquest, the now-international organization I founded in 1997 with a group of Tucson-based horse trainers. We also placed the survey on Google Docs, directing potential participants using the Horse Conscious website, a site developed by the organization that formed in response to the film *Path of the Horse* by Stormy May. Horse Conscious continues to bring together people who want to engage with horses in more humane and inspiring ways.

Eighty-five percent of the 435 completed questionnaires were from horse owners, 94 percent were from women, and 67 percent of participants were in their forties and fifties. The most striking finding of our survey was that being with horses, with pets, or out in nature almost always made people feel a sense of appreciation. Being with horses and pets also filled them with feelings of affection. A sense of wonder almost always accompanied interactions with horses and being out in nature. But the powerful combination of appreciation, affection, and wonder was most often felt when with horses. Ann notes that

> wonder is an emotion we frequently feel as young children when we experience something amazing for the first time, such as seeing a peacock spread his tail. But that feeling often fades as we grow older. As observed by Rachel Carson in her book *The Sense of Wonder*: "A child's world is fresh and new and beautiful, full or wonder and excitement. It is our misfortune that for most of us that clear-eyed vision, that true instinct for what is beautiful and awe-inspiring, is dimmed and even lost before we reach adulthood." So horses are helping us stay fresh and invigorated instead of dull and jaded!

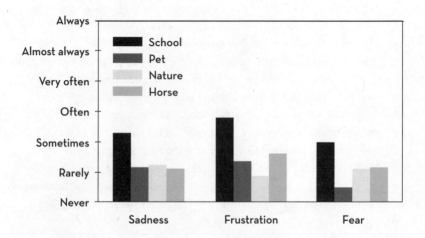

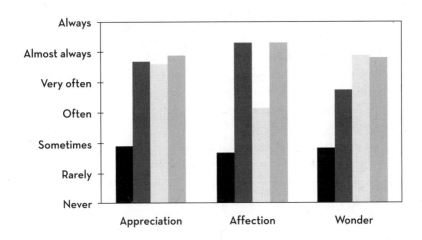

Memories of school, on the other hand, were the least likely to be associated with any positive emotions. "Did the school environment, at least thirty or forty years ago, stifle the feeling of wonder?" Ann asked. Absolutely, this survey reveals.

> Many people remembered feelings of frustration, sometimes fear and sadness. It's hard to tell whether middle-aged female horse lovers, who made up most of our sample, really had such unfortunate memories of school, or whether they were just focusing on their feelings during the trials and tribulations of adolescence rather than on specific memories of school. Interestingly, overall they said they felt the least frustrated when out in nature and least fearful when with their pets. This survey adds to growing evidence that we would benefit from incorporating more activities with animals and nature into our school systems. A recent study at Michigan State University shows improvements in mood scores in teenage girls after just fifteen minutes of quiet interaction with horses.

The Michigan State University study and our survey have shown that interacting with horses offers more than just the benefits of physical exercise from riding and the meditative, oxytocin-boosting qualities of grooming. According to our 435 participants, being with horses almost always made them experience feelings of affection, appreciation, and wonder.

Back to Grazing

In chapter 1, I noted that suffering for one's art was fashionable in Antoni Gaudí's time. These days, workaholism is our primary obsession. As a culture, we're addicted to stress and to all the chemical and behavioral crutches we engage to manage that stress, leading to significant physical, mental, emotional, and social health consequences. To make matters worse, we have trouble thinking, let alone trying, something new, because of evaluation apprehension's debilitating effects — magnified by increasingly sensationalist, cynical, malicious mass media enterprises that amplify fear, frustration, shame, and blame in the name of news and entertainment.

It's true that hardship is an inescapable part of innovation. *But it's not the only part.* By continually focusing on what's wrong, what's scary, what's not quite up to par, we dismiss the many things that have improved over the past three thousand years. A higher standard of living for more people; widespread social intolerance of slavery, sexism, and prejudice; and the reduction of violence, especially in Westernized countries, are among those improvements.

A little over two hundred years ago, George Washington survived and endured scenes of horrific rage and injustice. Even so, he found the challenge of collaborating with free men to be as stressful, perplexing, and demoralizing as going to war, witnessing a massacre, and starving at Valley Forge. Yet I have to wonder, was the trauma he experienced mitigated by his daily encounters with horses? Research on oxytocin alone would seem to suggests it. As I was finishing this book in the summer of 2012, Queen Elizabeth was celebrating her Diamond Jubilee with equestrian events so integral to the festivities that they were featured in a variety of international publications rarely interested in horses, including *USA Today*. She too has endured intense scrutiny, war, family tragedy, constant change, and outrageous, capricious, daily evaluation of her behavior and ideals by a fickle public. She too is an avid horsewoman, interested in breeding, showing, and training innovations. After all, this gentle, reserved, seemingly conservative monarch was in part responsible for the international success of Monty Roberts, author of *The Man Who Listens to Horses*, a book that helped popularize natural horsemanship in the 1990s.

Like Elizabeth I and Katherine the Great, England's current queen is a consummate rider, though few additional details are available. Try as I might, I was unable to find much in the way of historical accounts of how horses affected these women. I could only infer that horses helped empower, balance, encourage, and renew these influential leaders. Great equestrians of both sexes seem (blissfully) unaware of just how much they have learned from their mounts, let alone how much they have been supported and even healed by these generous, nonpredatory power animals. Either that or they have little capacity for translating these nonverbal insights into words, perhaps even feeling self-conscious suggesting such a notion.

How often, after all, do we read about the mythic or historical adventures of heroes, barely noticing the silent heroes they ride? What is a hero, after all? Someone who transcends survival instincts to face the unknown, sometimes enduring terrifying ordeals for a greater cause? Someone who remains poised in the midst of turmoil, who prevails despite the odds to capture a treasure from the gods, an uplifting innovation, enduring significant hardships to bring some glistening piece of magic back to the tribe?

By this definition, horses are every bit as heroic as their riders, if not more so: a prey animal going to war is the epitome of a counterintuitive, wholly *unnatural* move. And yet, in times of war and in times of peace, horses *reconnect* us to nature, more specifically to nature's gifts, her ability to not just challenge but nourish, inspire, and renew us.

And so, after the long journey we've taken together, we come to the deepest, most healing piece of horse wisdom I can offer: the importance of joy, awe, wonder, and inspiration, of celebrating the talents and intelligence of other beings, appreciating daily acts of kindness and courage, as well as the beauty of this world we all share, most especially those rural areas and wilderness preserves we must guard as blessings from a benevolent force still urging us to grow out of fitful adolescence into real maturity, empowered empathy, agile understanding, and unbridled yet compassionate creativity.

Horse wisdom, fully activated in humans, requires paying attention to what is good and right with the world, and expanding *that*, even as we protect ourselves from predators hiding in the grass. No matter what's happening around us, the emotional-agility, social-intelligence, and fear-management skills that horses teach help us deal efficiently with technical difficulties and interpersonal challenges and then go back to "grazing." Over time, as we learn to ride life's roller coaster with ease, an underlying sense of "deep peace" emerges and strengthens. We find that we can let go of the stories that tie us to past injustice. And we can fully enjoy the present, knowing that we are courageous, empowered, and adaptable enough to meet the future with the relaxed, expanded awareness of a mature herd leader.

Now that horses are no longer obliged to work in our fields and carry us to war, they're doing something more important: they're working on us, helping us reclaim, daily, a hint of paradise not so much lost as misplaced. In rekindling our relationship with horses as guides — as catalysts of human transformation going back at least thirty thousand years — we can't help but realize that, even when we wander off the main trail and get lost in the woods, we're never alone in this world.

We have the tools. The schoolmasters are waiting at the barn. So saddle up, open that gate, head toward the mountains.

And, most important, *enjoy* the ride!

Appendix

HOW TO CHOOSE AN INSTRUCTOR

The Power of the Herd explores how nonpredatory, horse-inspired wisdom can help you handle life, career, and community-building challenges with greater ease and success. This book represents over fifteen years of research, experimentation, and experience teaching advanced human development skills through working with these powerful animals. If you increasingly avoid the four Stone Age Power Tools discussed in chapter 12, while practicing the Twelve Guiding Principles explored in part 3, you will experience significant positive changes in your professional and personal relationships.

However, as I mentioned early in chapter 3, only so much of this knowledge can be translated into words. (Research shows that about 10 percent of human interpersonal communication is verbal.) If you're interested in boosting the *nonverbal* skills associated with leadership, social intelligence, assertiveness, and mutually supportive relationships, working with horses is an incredibly efficient, empowering, *and* fun way to master the elusive "other 90 percent" that distinguishes truly great leaders, innovators, and communicators.

The field of equine-facilitated learning (also known variously as equine-facilitated human development, equine-assisted learning, equine-guided education, or equine-facilitated mental health) has been growing internationally since the late 1990s. Several professional organizations for sharing information have arisen, as well as more in-depth programs for training facilitators, including Eponaquest Worldwide, Adventures in Awareness, Professional Association of Therapeutic Horsemanship International, Equine Assisted Growth and Learning Association, Equine Guided Education Association, and European

Association for Horse Assisted Education, among others. A few universities also offer degrees or concentrations in equine-facilitated therapy and experiential learning.

Increasingly, we see professionals combining techniques and principles associated with more than one of these programs, in addition to a variety of skills learned through conventional and innovative horse-training disciplines. Some facilitators are diligent in gathering the latest research on emotional and social intelligence, horse behavior, and other related topics. Over time, these people tend to develop new activities and approaches, and the field continues to evolve as a result.

Still, there is tremendous variation in the interpersonal skills, teaching styles, and philosophical orientation these instructors exhibit. Some treat the horse as a partner in facilitating this work; others treat the horse as a tool subservient to human needs and whims. Some facilitators respect the integrity of the client's experience, offering a supportive, nonshaming environment for learning; others use activities that put people on the spot, stressing humans and horses alike, sometimes creating a confrontational environment, occasionally endangering participants as a result.

And finally, some facilitators promote a mutually supportive approach to the continued development of the field, while others are highly competitive, seeking to boost their reputation by degrading other professionals, engaging in the age-old practice of using others' vulnerabilities against them for personal gain.

You must therefore be somewhat vigilant to find the right instructor for your needs. I highly recommend interviewing several prospects before choosing the one who feels most aligned with your personality, learning style, and goals. And because of the significant nonverbal elements involved, you must also *experience* the instructor's work to get the full picture. After you look at websites and talk with the most intriguing candidates by phone, the next step involves attending an introductory workshop or a private session, not only to sample the facilitator's techniques, but also to observe the instructor's presence and effect on others.

It most certainly behooves you to watch how the horses respond to your teacher. Are they engaged, bright-eyed, willing, and relaxed? Or are they disconnected and nervous? (The latter is a red flag, unless the instructor is a guest facilitator at someone else's farm, in which case, watch to see if the horses warm up to the instructor during the clinic — a good sign. If the horses become increasingly nervous or shut down, your teacher may be overattached to a method and less responsive to the needs of individuals from moment to moment. How he or she treats the horses in this regard most certainly translates to how he or she will treat human clients.)

When you or your fellow students ask questions, need assistance in performing a task, or challenge the instructor for some legitimate reason, does your teacher act dismissive or dominant, shame the client outright, make more subtle sarcastic comments, or perhaps even demean the client verbally or nonverbally for not "cooperating" with the method? If so, his interpersonal skills are sorely lacking. This facilitator may actually be a decent horse trainer, but equine-facilitated learning demands people skills as well as horse skills. Masterful instructors spend significant time developing both.

And just as innovators like George Washington, Abraham Lincoln, and Steve Jobs were self-taught in their respective fields of expertise, advanced academic degrees and certifications do not guarantee greatness in the field of equine-facilitated learning. A balance of experience, training, mindfulness, compassion, high ethical standards, curiosity, flexibility, ingenuity, and constant self-improvement are needed for instructors to truly excel. And if you are a trauma survivor, I highly recommend working with a facilitator who is also a therapist experienced with the kind of challenge you are facing (war-related post–traumatic stress disorder, childhood sexual abuse, adult physical or emotional abuse, and so on). Because of the personal nature of these issues, equine-facilitated therapy sessions should always be separated from teambuilding activities, though you will sometimes find an instructor qualified to do both.

On the Eponaquest Worldwide website, for instance, instructors trained in our approach are listed geographically with their specialties, degrees, certifications, and other areas of expertise next to their names. Some are counselors specializing in trauma, addiction, or family and relationship issues. Others are educators offering personal development or creativity-boosting programs. Still others specialize in leadership training. Instructors with the "POH" (Power of the Herd) designation have had advanced training in how to teach the Twelve Guiding Principles presented in this book. Additionally, while nearly two hundred people graduated from our multiweek apprenticeship program between 2003 and 2012, our website presents the contact information of only those instructors who have agreed to uphold the Eponaquest Code of Ethics and Standards of Practice, recently updated by a representative group of experienced instructors and overseen by the Eponaquest Ethics Committee. (These standards can be accessed at www.eponaquest.com.)

For those seeking leadership training, I offer an additional caution: People with psychological or psychiatric degrees and experience do not necessarily make good leadership- and team-building facilitators. Some techniques used in therapeutic contexts, including group therapy, bring up personal issues that are not appropriate for the workplace. Any facilitator who has a dual counseling and leadership-training orientation should be able to clearly state the difference between her therapeutic practice and her team-building programs.

The results of blurring these two indiscriminately can be destructive. Over the years, I've talked with a number of people who felt that their reputations and already-tenuous work relationships were damaged by attending company-sponsored events designed to boost emotional intelligence, led by counselors trying to break into the lucrative corporate-training market. These activities sometimes got too personal too quickly. Other times people felt deeply humiliated by activities that promoted confrontation or confession in the name of authenticity. Some people felt publicly shamed — and lost the respect of their team members as a result. This is an occasional problem not only in the equine-facilitated learning field. Bob Wall's *Coaching for Emotional Intelligence* offers a number of examples of the detrimental effects he's witnessed in other leadership and team-building contexts.

Whether horses, ropes courses, hot coals, wilderness, or other off-site experiences are involved, many of these programs do little more than put people in frustrating or somewhat threatening situations and discuss participants' reactions afterward. This is usually done under the guise of making people conscious of unproductive attitudes and interpersonal habits or encouraging people to "face their fears" and experience some sort of catharsis. Such programs, however, are *not* sufficiently well developed to be truly productive. The best programs teach specific *skills* in addition to inspiring individuals to become aware of their previously unrecognized challenges *and* hidden strengths. Masterful programs help the participant *translate* those skills to human situations. In evaluating any equine-facilitated leadership program, ask what your employees or team members will learn, how they will learn it, and how it will benefit them in the workplace. If the program still sounds too vague, sensational, or confrontational, it probably is.

Finally, it's important to understand why you would select equine-facilitated leadership training over other options. As my friend and colleague Barbara Rector, founder of Adventures in Awareness, asks, if these sensitive animals are merely being used as obstacles to overcome, then "why bother the horse?" Treating any living being as a tool or obstacle reinforces the destructive yet still common practice of objectifying humans. Even if you're interested purely in the bottom line, it's important to note that cynical, disengaged, or apathetic employees whose talents are never tapped, who give up and "retire in place" because they're treated like replaceable cogs in a wheel, block everyone's ability to get the job done, let alone excel. Furthermore, managers and co-workers who release their resulting frustration through aggressive or passive-aggressive behavior create a toxic corporate and political environment precisely because they don't know how to use power effectively and collaboratively.

As highly social, intensely mindful, nonpredatory power animals, horses are quite simply best equipped to help our species master the nonverbal nuances of leadership and social intelligence. If you choose an instructor who knows how to draw these long-neglected skills out of the shadows and into the light of day through activities that respect the client's and the horse's talents and integrity, your goals for an off-site leadership or team-building training will be met and most likely exceeded.

ACKNOWLEDGMENTS

The Power of the Herd would not exist if it weren't for the efforts of my agent Felicia Eth, who somehow talked me into writing another book in 2008, and my editor Jason Gardner, who immediately supported the idea. It seemed like a reasonable little project at the time: a survey of what horses can teach us about power and freedom-through-relationship if we're willing to really listen. However, researching the horse's impact on innovative leaders throughout history turned out to be a much richer endeavor than I ever imagined; the simplest questions led me to unexpected views of culture, nature, science, and social evolution. Thank you, Jason, for the deadline extensions and your expertise in editing the manuscript. It's always a pleasure to work with you! I also thank copyeditor Bonita Hurd and proofreader Karen Stough.

Due to the interdisciplinary nature of the topic, it took tremendous concentration to configure this material into a coherent narrative. Completing this project would not have been possible without the expert assistance of staff members who handled the myriad details of running the horse operation and putting on numerous workshops (where the principles introduced in this book were tested and constantly improved). I'm deeply grateful to barn manager Elysa Ginsburg, office manager Sue Smades, and workshop assistant Kathleen McGarry, all of whom are Eponaquest Instructors willing to do whatever is necessary to keep our horses happy while also inspiring our clients. The personal support I received from these powerful, compassionate women felt like a miracle at times.

I'm also indebted to Eponaquest faculty members who lived the principle of emotional heroism, transforming numerous challenges into strengths over the past decade and helping the work to evolve in the process. Mary-Louise Gould, Shelley Rosenberg, Carol Roush, Nancy Coyne, and Kathleen Barry Ingram were integral to the creation and continued improvement of our multiweek apprenticeship programs and the development of the Eponaquest approach to equine-facilitated learning internationally. These talented women now travel extensively, creating new programs that draw upon their many gifts, and they continue to facilitate programs with me at times. I also thank Mary-Louise, Shelley, and Carol for reading early versions of the manuscript and helping me to clarify important points. The section on shame and guilt, in particular, owes much to their insights on how these emotions have long affected our clients.

I'm so very proud of and inspired by our Eponaquest Instructors worldwide, who have answered the call of the horse and taken this wisdom to heart, adding their own unique talents and perspectives, continually expanding the scope and power of this work.

Special thanks to Shelley Rosenberg for believing in my dream of socializing Midnight Merlin to live with his own herd. I could not have rehabilitated and bred such a powerful, agile stallion without her expertise, adaptability, and enthusiasm for this unconventional task. She skillfully assisted in the resultant births and the continued training of the black horse family he sired: his sons, Spirit, Indigo Moon, and Orion; and his granddaughter, Artemis. At the same time, Merlin's transformation would not have been possible without the enthusiastic yet most certainly risky efforts of my mares Tabula Rasa and Comet's Promise, who, amazingly, helped him heal through the magic of empowered relationship. Now that Rasa, Merlin, and Comet are with the Ancestors, their children are teaching us even more sophisticated lessons: namely, how to collaborate with an entire herd of intelligent, highly sensitive, self-actualized horses who have no fear of humans, other horses, or life, for that matter. But that's another story, one I hope to write someday.

In the meantime, there are many other people to thank for the book you now hold in your hands. Significant credit goes to the people who joined the *Power of the Herd* web symposium in fall 2011 and, most especially, to Mark Mottershead, my cocreator of that endeavor. Realizing the book was taking longer to write than I had expected, I was eager to share the research, insights, and practical tools I was accessing. For an entire year, participants from around the world read early drafts of the chapters, made comments, and asked questions during in-depth conversations on each chapter, all of which were recorded and posted on the symposium's website (www.poweroftheherd.com).

I had no idea how fruitful this web-based educational program would be. Mark (a British entrepreneur who lives in Germany) is a masterful interviewer and moderator. His questions, interwoven with those of the subscribers, led to greater clarity in the finished manuscript. What's more, the idea of adding the Twelve Guiding Principles came from Mark and Ian Rowcliffe, a Portugal-based symposium participant. This of course necessitated an additional six months of writing, but these practical chapters were integral in translating horse wisdom to human contexts.

Many participants shared thought-provoking insights and personal experiences that not only inspired me but also raised my spirits, giving me the energy to complete this intricate book. While I'm grateful to every member of this symposium, I would also like to cite a few people who more directly affected the book's content. Susan Garvin and Nancy Proulx helped me deepen the material through their questions and comments on several issues. I also thank two Eponaquest Instructors who became faithful symposium participants: Josselien Janssens from the Netherlands brought up the issue of envy and jealousy in the workplace, leading me to decipher the useful messages behind these notoriously troublesome emotions. Thea Fast from Canada introduced me to Kropotkin's work on mutual aid as a factor of evolution, which became a significant topic in chapter 6.

The *Power of the Herd* web symposium is still available online, offering people who may not be able to attend equine-facilitated workshops as often as they'd like the opportunity to gain some additional insights into the material presented in this book. The symposium will continue to host new conversations, including some with other experts featured in this book, as well as address questions on specific challenges participants are facing in the workplace and in other contexts where leadership and emotional and social intelligence are significant factors.

I also thank the dedicated professionals who helped establish the EponaQuest Foundation, which was originally envisioned as the nonprofit division of Eponaquest Worldwide. As the field of equine-facilitated learning (EFL) evolved, however, I felt the need to expand the scope of the foundation to serve the EFL community at large by raising funds to do research on the efficacy of this work, as well as to develop curricula based on this research, offer scholarships to participants who would otherwise not be able to participate in EFL activities, and create ethical standards and best practices that would affect the entire field, no matter what training or professional organizations facilitators are associated with. Discussions I had with the founding board members of the EponaQuest Foundation influenced material presented in the book on the horse's role in teaching human development skills, as well as on the ethics, evolution, and potential of this field.

Past and current board members who influenced the book include Eponaquest Instructors Anna Carnathan, Dale Carnathan, and Terry Murray, as well as Barbara Rector (Adventures in Awareness), Lisa Walters (founder of California's EquuSatori Center), Howard Shenk, and Laura Brinkerhoff (who currently heads the equine-facilitated therapy program at Cottonwood de Tucson, a respected residential treatment center). Several of the board members have served as either faculty members or guest presenters for Prescott College's innovative undergraduate and graduate concentrations in equine-facilitated therapy and experiential learning. I also thank Ann Linda Baldwin, a professor of physiology and psychology at University of Arizona, who oversees our research division. Much gratitude goes to Seth Grossman, who did significant early organizational work, and Richard Lang, a pioneer in the technology field who helped us communicate more effectively long distance through the collaborative communication program Collaborize Classroom. (For more information on the foundation, see www.eponaquestfoundation.org.)

I'm grateful for the intricate work undertaken by the 2012 Eponaquest Ethics Committee, including Melanie Dallas, Eve B. Lee, Holli Lyons, Anne Steuart, and Patricia Cameron Vitiello. Under the direction of Mary-Louise Gould, this dedicated group of professionals spent months researching and perfecting the Code of Ethics and Standards of Practice that have truly raised the bar for our instructors, asking them to uphold some of the highest standards in the field.

Endless appreciation goes to a number of other people who have supported my work over the years, playing crucial roles in helping me to complete this book: Sandra and William Sell-Lee, Jacque and Rip Gellein, Laura Barrett, Sid Brinkerhoff, Larney Otis, Eva Reifler, Lori Wilson Kinzbach, Devorah Coryell, Ulrike Dietmann, Martin Rosen, Therese Capozzola, and Sandra Mazzocco. I'm also grateful for the research that Ann Baldwin, Bob Wall, and Meg Daley Olmert shared with me through conversations, emails, and consultations.

And I cannot forget my equine friends and colleagues, who have influenced me as much or more than any human I could name. Merlin's sons and granddaughter, mentioned earlier, are just this year stepping into teaching roles. I must also acknowledge Panther, El Dia, Sage, Mystique, Cimarron, Leyla, Brandi, Savannah, Sunny, and Pharrah, who have proven to be exceptional equine professors.

I'm deeply indebted to my friend and colleague Mimi Meriwether, who passed away shortly before this book was completed. One of the purest, most compassionate people I've ever known, Mimi fought a battle with cancer that exemplified physical as well as emotional heroism. An accomplished competitive rider, businesswoman, visionary, and philanthropist, Mimi maintained a relentlessly positive, appreciative attitude toward life and the many people she met along the way, and she continues to inspire me, even as I grieve this unexpected loss.

And finally, this book is dedicated to my husband, Steve Roach, who has stood by me no matter what was happening, sharing the joys and successes, comforting me through numerous losses, and encouraging me to keep going through the uncertainty of creating what was, especially in the 1990s, a controversial approach to working with horses as teachers. Like the equine members of our family, he too is a master of nonverbal communication. From the day we met, his music became the soundtrack of my life, articulating feelings and insights that words could never express.

I'm very happy, after completing this long writing journey, to have more time to be quiet and listen to the many beautiful pieces Steve has composed over the years, some of which were inspired by the original members of our herd who have since left this earth: Rasa, Comet, Noche, Merlin, Shadowfax, and Max, horses whose stories continue to teach and inspire those who have been kind enough to read my books.

ENDNOTES

Introduction

Page 3, *"non-human animals have the neuroanatomical, neurochemical..."*: The Cambridge *Declaration on Consciousness* was written by Philip Low and edited by Jaak Panksepp, Dianna Reiss, David Edelman, Bruno Van Swinderen, Philip Low, and Christof Koch. It was publicly proclaimed in Cambridge, England, at the Francis Crick Memorial Conference on Consciousness in Human and Non-Human Animals held at Churchill College, University of Cambridge, by Low, Edelman, and Koch. It was signed by the conference participants on July 7, 2012, in the presence of Stephen Hawking in a ceremony memorialized by CBS's *60 Minutes*.

Chapter One. The Horse in My Cathedral

Page 7, *For Gaudí, Sagrada Familia (Holy Family) was a mission:* A variety of books, articles, and documentaries are summarized in this chapter's overview of Gaudí's life, most notably Gijs van Hensbergen, *Gaudí: A Biography* (New York: Harper Perennial, 2003); Juan Bassegoda Nonell, *Antonio Gaudí: Master Architect* (New York: Abbeville Press, 2000); and "God's Architect: The Story of the Vatican and the Visionary," *Belfast Telegraph*, April 24, 2007.

Page 10, *"a graphic illustration of the almost absurd misfortune..."*: The quote appears in an Internet discussion, "The Unfinished Cathedral (Sagrada Familia)...Should It Be ...Finished?" March 5, 2008, Digital Spy, http://forums.digitalspy.co.uk/showthread .php?t=757344.

Page 16, *The willingness to relinquish personal comfort:* Richard Boyatzis and Annie McKee, *Resonant Leadership* (Boston: Harvard Business Review Press, 2005), 6.

Page 18, *"If you are successful, you win false friends..."*: After the publication of her 1995 autobiography, *Mother Teresa: A Simple Path*, this quote was widely attributed to Mother Teresa. However, it was later recognized as an excerpt from "The Paradoxical Commandments" by a then-nineteen-year-old Harvard College sophomore, Kent M. Keith. Although there is some confusion, the version I quote here is most likely the version Mother Teresa used. See www.paradoxicalcommandments.com/mother-teresa-connection.html.

Page 18, *"the Cycle of Sacrifice and Renewal"*: Boyatzis and McKee, *Resonant Leadership*, 61.

Page 19, *"I'd worked just dozens and dozens of jobs…"*: Mike Judge, interview by Terry Gross, *Fresh Air*, NPR, August 25, 2009.

Page 20, great leaders *"deliberately and consciously step…"*: Boyatzis and McKee, *Resonant Leadership*, 7–8.

Chapter Two. Legacy of Power

Page 25, *The request for backup was unprecedented:* John R. Barletta, *Riding with Reagan: From the White House to the Ranch* (New York: Citadel Press, 2005), 3.

Page 26, *"Our chief supervisor at the time rightly said…"*: Ibid., 3.

Page 26, *"When the gunshots echoed through the air…"*: Ibid., 171.

Page 27, *He was so feisty, Barletta reports:* Ibid., 112.

Page 27, *El Alamein was so intense and flighty:* Ibid., 59.

Page 31, *In the 1980s, researchers at the University of Parma:* G. di Pellegrino, L. Fadiga, L. Fogassi, V. Gallese, and G. Rizzolatti, "Understanding Motor Events: A Neurophysiological Study," *Experimental Brain Research* 91, no. 1 (1992): 176–80.

Page 32, *"Mirror neurons have a particular importance…"*: Daniel Goleman and Richard Boyatzis, "Social Intelligence and the Biology of Leadership," *Harvard Business Review* (September 2008): 3 (reprint).

Page 32, *"the delivery was more important than the message…"*: Ibid.

Page 32, *researchers from the Swedish University of Agricultural Sciences:* Linda J. Keeling, Liv Jonare, and Lovisa Lanneborn, "Investigating Horse-Human Interactions: The Effect of a Nervous Human," *Veterinary Journal* 181, no. 1 (July 2009): 70–71.

Page 33, *"This ultrarapid connection of emotions, beliefs, and judgments…"*: Goleman and Boyatzis, "Social Intelligence and the Biology of Leadership," 4.

Page 34, *not only does a person's blood pressure escalate:* Daniel Goleman, *Social Intelligence: The New Science of Human Relationships* (New York: Bantam, 2006), 21.

Page 35, *In 1990, psychologists Peter Salovey and John Mayer:* Daniel Goleman, "Emotional Intelligence: Issues in Paradigm Building," in *The Emotionally Intelligent Workplace: How to Select for, Measure, and Improve Emotional Intelligence in Individuals, Groups, and Organizations*, ed. Cary Cherniss and Daniel Goleman (San Francisco: Jossey-Bass, 2000), 17.

Page 36, *The authors argued that "emotions are contagious"*: Daniel Goleman, Richard Boyatzis, and Annie McKee, *Primal Leadership: Realizing the Power of Emotional Intelligence* (Boston: Harvard Business Press, 2002), summation on front flap.

Page 36, *"Great leaders move us…"*: Ibid., 3, 5.

Page 36, *"The notion that effective leadership is about…"*: Goleman and Boyatzis, "Social Intelligence and the Biology of Leadership," 3.

Page 36, *Goleman and his colleagues continue to search:* Ibid.

Page 37, *anthropologist E. Richard Sorenson's concept:* I first encountered Sorenson's work in an article by Christian de Quincey: "Consciousness: Truth or Wisdom? *IONS (Noetic Sciences Review)*, no. 51 (March–June 2000).

Page 37, *affect contagion, a term I came across:* Elio Frattaroli, *Healing the Soul in the Age of the Brain: Becoming Conscious in an Unconscious World* (New York: Viking, 2001), 44.

Page 39, *"whose only job is to detect other people's smiles..."*: Goleman and Boyatzis, "Social Intelligence and the Biology of Leadership," 3.

Page 40, *"Being in a good mood, other research finds..."*: Ibid.

Page 40, *As Winston Churchill once said:* Richard Langworth, ed., *Churchill by Himself: The Definitive Collection of Quotations* (New York: PublicAffairs, 2011); and Robert Andrews, ed., *Famous Lines: The Columbia Dictionary of Familiar Quotations* (New York: Columbia University Press, 1997).

Page 41, *polo was a game that Churchill himself played:* Wyatt Blassingame, *His Kingdom for a Horse* (New York: Franklin Watts, 1957), 144.

Page 41, *Sword drawn, racing toward the enemy:* Ibid., 154, 156.

Page 41, *As horse and rider careened through:* Ibid.

Page 42, *"without the leadership of Churchill, World War II..."*: Ibid., 157.

Page 43, *Plutarch wrote that "in Uxia, once,..."*: Lawrence Scanlan, *Wild about Horses* (New York: HarperCollins, 1998), 117.

Page 43, *"During the final battle in India..."*: Ibid.

Page 44, *"psychopaths are often witty and articulate..."*: Robert Hare, *Without Conscience: The Disturbing World of the Psychopaths among Us* (New York: Guilford Press, 1999), 34–35, 52.

Page 44, *For most people, Hare explains, "the fear produced..."*: Ibid., 54.

Chapter Three. Hidden Wisdom

Page 46, *the "dinosaurs of the future will be those who keep..."*: Robert K. Cooper, *The Other 90%: How to Unlock Your Vast Untapped Potential for Leadership and Life* (New York: Three Rivers Press, 2001), 12.

Page 47, *"In the 1990s," Cooper reports:* Ibid., 16.

Page 47, *As author and researcher Dr. Candace Pert asserts:* This is the working premise of Candace Pert's engaging audio book *Your Body Is Your Subconscious Mind: New Insights into the Body-Mind Connection* (Louisville, CO: Sounds True, 2004).

Page 52, *"Lord Cornwallis was on the march..."*: Edwin M. Stone, *The Life and Recollections of John Howland, Late President of the Rhode Island Historical Society* (Providence, RI: George H. Whitney, 1857), 74.

Page 52, *"The bridge was narrow..."*: Ibid., 73.

Page 53, *"Horses were screaming on the battlefield":* James Parrish Hodges, interview by author, winter 2009.

Page 53, *"the best horseman of his age..."*: Thomas Jefferson, *The Writings of Thomas Jefferson*, ed. H.A. Washington, vol. 6 (New York: Riker, Thorne, and Co., 1855), 287.

Page 54, *"The weather being fair," Chastellux wrote:* Chastellux's *Travels in North-America: In the years 1780, 81, 82* was translated by Scottish-born traveler and writer Basil Hall and appears to have been first published in English in 1828. A paperback version was published by Applewood Books, Carlisle, Massachusetts, in 2007. The quote is featured on page 69 of that edition.

Page 54, *Joseph J. Ellis describes him riding around the farm:* Joseph J. Ellis, *His Excellency: George Washington* (New York: Vintage, 2005), 241–42.

Page 55, *When he returned to the mansion around two o'clock:* Ibid., 242.

Page 55, *"leading by listening":* Ibid.

Page 55, *"He possessed a nearly preternatural ability to remain silent..."*: Ibid., 193–94.

Page 56, *"When dinner was over, we visited the General's stables..."*: Valley Forge Historical

Society, *The Picket Post: A Record of Patriotism*, vol. 37 (Valley Forge, PA: Valley Forge Historical Society, 1960), 19.

Page 57, *"while calmly sitting astride his horse…"*: Ellis, *His Excellency*, 120.

Page 57, *"Will, the huntsman, better known…"*: George Washington Parke Custis, *Recollections and Private Memoirs of Washington* (New York: Derby and Jackson, 1860), 387.

Page 58, *"Treat them with humanity…"*: While I cannot find the original historic record of these orders, this quote appears in many books, articles, and speeches, including the September 28, 2006, *Congressional Record, Senate*, vol. 152, pt. 15, p. 146.

Page 59, *To encourage them, he "marched the prisoners…"*: James Parrish Hodges, *Beyond the Cherry Tree: The Leadership Wisdom of George Washington* (N.p.: Great Leaders Press, 2008), 45.

Page 59, *"We were fighting for the rights of ordinary people"*: Hodges, interview by author.

Page 59, *"about 40 percent of the Hessians…"*: Ibid.

Page 59, *"In 1778, Colonel Charles Stuart wrote:* David Hackett Fischer, *Washington's Crossing* (New York: Oxford University Press, 2004), 376–77.

Page 59, *"In the end, our founding fathers not only protected…"*: Robert F. Kennedy Jr., "America's Anti-torture Tradition," *Los Angeles Times*, December 17, 2005 (available online at http://articles.latimes.com/2005/dec/17/opinion/oe-kennedy17).

Chapter Four. Revolution and Evolution

Page 61, *"She awed me in the midst of her kindness…"*: George Washington Parke Custis, *Recollections and Private Memoirs of Washington* (New York: Derby and Jackson, 1860), 131.

Page 63, *"The experiment ended with the death…"*: Marion Harland, *The Story of Mary Washington* (Boston: Houghton, Mifflin, 1893), 72.

Page 63, *he admitted the facts "promptly and squarely…"*: Ibid., 73.

Page 65, *"Thou art not yet dead, my father":* Joseph J. Ellis, *His Excellency: George Washington* (New York: Vintage, 2005), 14.

Page 66, *"Seeing the decay of public virtue everywhere…"*: Ron Chernow, *Washington: A Life* (New York: Penguin, 2010), 329.

Page 66, *Chernow finds it "astonishing…"*: Ibid., 326–27.

Page 66, *"projected leadership in nonverbal ways…"*: Ibid., 326.

Page 67, *"I see their situation, know their danger…"*: George Washington, *The Writings of George Washington*, collected and edited by Worthington Chauncey Ford, vol. 1 (New York: G. P. Putnam's Sons, 1889), 249–50.

Page 68, *"He pined for her presence"*: Chernow, *Washington*, 330.

Page 69, *"I never knew him to be so anxious…"*: Ibid.

Page 69, *"Not enough historians have recognized…"*: Thomas Fleming, *Washington's Secret War: The Hidden History of Valley Forge* (New York: Smithsonian Books/HarperCollins, 2005), 184.

Page 69, *"She well deserved to be the companion…"*: Chernow, *Washington*, 330.

Page 70, *"evidence of her business acumen…"*: "Martha Dandridge Custis Washington," undated, National First Ladies' Library, www.firstladies.org.

Page 70, *"With her extremely large inheritance…"*: Ibid.

Page 70, *"I never in my life knew a woman so busy…"*: Chernow, *Washington*, 330, citing a quote reported in Harlow Giles Unger, *The Unexpected George Washington: His Private Life* (Hoboken, NJ: Wiley, 2006), 122.

Page 71, *she was a "modest and respectable person…":* Chernow, *Washington*, 295.

Page 71, *"especially in the early stages of the war…":* Ellis, *His Excellency*, 74.

Page 71, *he "never walled himself off from contrary opinion…":* Chernow, *Washington*, 306.

Page 71, *"the halt, in immobility, contains the energy…":* Sherry Ackerman, *Dressage in the Fourth Dimension* (Novato, CA: New World Library, 2008), 10.

Page 72, *"Impulsion is a power surge…":* Ron Meredith, "Training Mythunderstandings: The Training Tree: Impulsion," undated, Meredith Manor International Equestrian Centre website, www.meredithmanor.edu/features/articles/drm/impulsion.asp.

Page 73, *"Young dominator stallions…":* Kip Mistral, "The Secret Life of Stallions," *Horse Connection* (February 2006): 32.

Page 74, *"We even have foals here…":* Ibid., 33.

Page 76, *This horse is "extremely dependable and confident…":* Mark Rashid, *Horses Never Lie: The Heart of Passive Leadership* (Boulder, CO: Johnson Books, 2000), xiii.

Page 76, *Rashid once watched an alpha horse:* Ibid., 37.

Page 76, *"In almost every case," he writes:* Ibid.

Page 76, *Watching one such mare effortlessly lead:* Ibid., 35.

Page 76, *Most horses, Rashid insists, seek out a leader:* Ibid., xiv.

Page 77, *"survival of the kindest":* Marc Ian Barasch, *Field Notes on the Compassionate Life: A Search for the Soul of Kindness* (Emmaus, PA: Rodale Books, 2005), 35.

Page 78, *"a cultural swing toward pacifism…":* Natalie Angier, "No Time for Bullies: Baboons Retool Their Culture," *New York Times*, April 13, 2004, www.nytimes.com.

Page 78, *"if bonobos instead of chimps had been taken…":* Barasch, *Field Notes on the Compassionate Life*, 34–35.

Page 78, *"Let your heart feel for the affliction…":* William J. Bennett, ed., *Our Sacred Honor: Words of Advice from the Founders in Stories, Letters, Poems, and Speeches* (New York: Simon and Schuster, 1997), 162.

Chapter Five. The Lion and the Horse

Page 82, *"I was a terrible kid…":* Sam Powell, with Lane Carter, *Almost a Whisper: A Holistic Approach to Working with Your Horse* (Loveland, CO: Alpine Publications, 1999), 31.

Page 84, *"the delicacy of touch and feeling of a woman…":* Quoted in Robert M. Miller and Rick Lamb, *The Revolution in Horsemanship and What It Means to Mankind* (Guilford, CT: Lyons Press, 2005), 81.

Page 85, *"If this has been fortuitous for the equine industry…":* Ibid., 80, 81.

Page 85, *"both masculine and feminine traits are needed…":* Ibid., 81.

Page 87, *"Washington's tenure as commander in chief…":* Ron Chernow, *Washington: A Life* (New York: Penguin, 2010), 286–87, emphasis mine.

Page 88, *"There is a hundred times more enthusiasm…":* Joseph J. Ellis, *His Excellency: George Washington* (New York: Vintage, 2005), 101.

Page 88, *"less out of conviction than a realistic recognition…":* Ibid., 100–101.

Page 89, *"Congress was apparently taken aback…":* Ibid., 101.

Page 89, *"guerilla and terrorist strategies of the twentieth century":* Ibid.

Page 90, *"The rich warriors on the gleaming red animals…":* Renate Rolle, *The World of the Scythians*, translated from the German by F. G. Walls (Berkeley: University of California Press, 1989), 109.

Page 91, *"which until then had led an effective and long-standing…"*: Neal Ascherson, *Black Sea* (New York: Hill and Wang, 1995), 81.

Page 93, *"Oliver Cromwell had not surrendered power…"*: Ellis, *His Excellency*, 139.

Chapter Six. The Melancholy Truths

Page 94, *"I learned a lot from horses…"*: "A Look at Rep. Gabrielle Giffords' Career," interview by Guy Raz, National Public Radio, January 8, 2011, www.npr.org/2011/01/08/132769563 /A-Look-At-Rep-Gabrielle-Giffords-Career.

Page 96, *"I know there are still barriers and biases…"*: Anne E. Kornblut, "Clinton's Last Hurrah," *Washington Post*, June 7, 2008, www.washingtonpost.com.

Page 97, *"Our party and our country are stronger…"*: Ibid.

Page 97, *"The higher you go…"*: Marshall Goldsmith, with Mark Reiter, *What Got You Here Won't Get You There: How Successful People Become Even More Successful!* (New York: Hyperion, 2007), 42.

Page 97, *"from needlessly trying to be the alpha…"*: Ibid., 46.

Page 97, *"the need to win at all costs…"*: Ibid., 40.

Page 97, our *"obsession with winning rears its noisome head…"*: Ibid., 46.

Page 102, *"The Enron traders never seemed to step back…"*: *Enron: The Smartest Guys in the Room* (New York: Magnolia Home Entertainment, 2005), DVD.

Page 102, those traders and executives *"who stayed and thrived…"*: Bethany McLean and Peter Elkind, *The Smartest Guys in the Room: The Amazing Rise and Scandalous Fall of Enron* (New York: Portfolio/Penguin, 2003), 121.

Page 102, *"no company can prosper over the long term if…"*: Ibid., 56.

Page 103, *"I failed to find — although I was eagerly looking…"*: Pyotr Alekseyevich Kropotkin, *Mutual Aid: A Factor of Evolution*, 1st ed. (London: William Heinemann, 1902), vii, emphasis the author's.

Page 103, he *"could agree with none of the works…"*: Ibid., ix, x.

Page 104, When *"animals have to struggle against scarcity…"*: Ibid., ix.

Page 104, *"All that natural selection can do…"*: Ibid., 73.

Page 105, *"followed by a third, a fourth,…"*: Ibid., 20.

Page 105, *"In the Russian Steppes, [wolves]…"*: Ibid., 41.

Page 105, *"the first thing which strikes us is…"*: Ibid., 38–40.

Page 106, *"the top-down models of communism's…"*: Geoff Olson, "Kropotkin vs. Darwin: Cooperation as an Evolutionary Force," *Common Ground* (September 2005): 3, www .commonground.ca.

Page 106, *"A particular essay by 'Darwin's bulldog,'…"*: Ibid., 4, emphasis mine.

Page 107, *"It's undeniable,"* Olson concludes: Ibid., 5.

Page 107, *"[If we] ask Nature: 'Who are the fittest…'"*: Kropotkin, *Mutual Aid*, 6.

Page 107, *"enables the feeblest of insects…"*: Ibid., 57.

Chapter Seven. Abel's Genius

Page 110, *"Now Abel kept flocks…"*: Genesis 4:3–7.

Page 111, *"I don't know,"* Cain replies: Genesis 4:9, 10, 12.

Page 111, *"the father of those who live in tents…"*: Genesis 4:20–22.

Page 113, *"Semitic peoples have called wilderness 'God's land,'..."*: Jim Corbett, *Goatwalking: A Quest for the Peaceable Kingdom* (New York: Penguin, 1991), 83.

Page 114, *"Settled people,"* Corbett observes, *"work relentlessly..."*: Ibid., 84, 25.

Page 116, *"not a single domestic animal can be named..."*: Charles Darwin, *The Origin of Species* (1872; reprint, Charleston, SC: Forgotten Books, 2007), 8.

Page 117, *"Several of our domesticated foxes have escaped..."*: Lyudmila Trut, "Early Canid Domestication: The Farm-Fox Experiment," *American Scientist* 87, no. 2 (March–April 1999): 2, www.americanscientist.org.

Page 118, *"the domestic fox is not a domestic dog..."*: Ibid., 4.

Page 118, *as behavior-changing hormones go, oxytocin:* The insight into oxytocin's role in the human-animal bond was first suggested by documentary film producer Meg Daley Olmert, culminating in her 2009 book *Made for Each Other: The Biology of the Human-Animal Bond,* which I quote directly later in this section.

Page 119, *"In pregnancy, nursing, and close contact..."*: Kerstin Uvnäs Moberg, *The Oxytocin Factor: Tapping the Hormone of Calm, Love, and Healing,* trans. Roberta W. Francis (Cambridge, MA: Da Capo Press, 2003), xiii–xiv.

Page 120, *"Uvnäs-Moberg returned to her lab..."*: Meg Daley Olmert, *Made for Each Other: The Biology of the Human-Animal Bond* (Cambridge, MA: Da Capo Press, 2009), 28.

Page 120, *"Many women find breastfeeding to be a deeply absorbing..."*: Susan Kuchinskas, *The Chemistry of Connection: How the Oxytocin Response Can Help You Find Trust, Intimacy, and Love* (Oakland, CA: New Harbinger, 2009), 6.

Page 120, *"When given oxytocin,"* Uvnäs Moberg explains: Uvnäs Moberg, *The Oxytocin Factor,* 66.

Page 121, *"Surprisingly, to a lesser degree,* animals that live in the same cage..."*: Ibid., 114, emphasis in the original.

Page 121, we *"need calm and connection not only to avoid illness..."*: Ibid., 14.

Page 122, *"when eighteen men and women interacted with their dogs..."*: Olmert, *Made for Each Other,* 74.

Page 122, *"instills courage by making the individual feel aggressive..."*: Uvnäs Moberg, *The Oxytocin Factor,* 66–67.

Page 123, *Rather, it reinforced "an egalitarian outlook..."*: Natasha Fijn, *Living with Herds: Human-Animal Coexistence in Mongolia* (New York: Cambridge University Press, 2011), 133.

Page 124, *"Mongolians do not eat animals that are under..."*: Ibid., 227.

Chapter Eight. Herd Power

Page 128, *"a two-species social system,..."*: Dale F. Lott and Benjamin L. Hart, "Applied Ethology in a Nomadic Cattle Culture," *Applied Animal Ethology* 5, no. 4 (October 1979): 312.

Page 128, *deprive "the animal of most of the alternatives..."*: Ibid., 309.

Page 128, *An alternative approach to restraint:* Ibid.

Page 130, *"aren't much interested in debating the finer points..."*: Jeremy Rifkin, *The Third Industrial Revolution: How Lateral Power Is Transforming Energy, the Economy, and the World* (New York: Palgrave Macmillan, 2011), 139.

Page 130, the *"two generations whose sociability..."*: Ibid., 139, 5.

Page 130, *"The collaborative power unleashed by the merging..."*: Ibid., 5.

Page 131, *these expert herdsmen "may be thought of as..."*: Lott and Hart, "Applied Ethology in a Nomadic Cattle Culture," 312.

Page 133, *"observed several occasions when non-Fulani cattle handlers..."*: Dale F. Lott and Benjamin L. Hart, "Aggressive Domination of Cattle by Fulani Herdsmen and Its Relation to Aggression in Fulani Culture and Personality," *Ethos* 5, no. 2 (Summer 1977): 180.

Page 134, *spending "considerable time moving among the cattle..."*: Lott and Hart, "Applied Ethology in a Nomadic Cattle Culture," 316.

Page 134, *"it is not clear how herdsmen become able..."*: Ibid., 315.

Page 135, *"The adaptive value of following a leader..."*: Ibid., 314.

Page 135, *these tribes "apparently began their penetration..."*: Lott and Hart, "Aggressive Domination of Cattle," 177–78.

Page 135, *"both in the sense of lacking fear..."*: Ibid., 181, 182.

Page 138, *"During the sharo ceremony, blows are delivered..."*: Ibid., 183.

Page 140, *Female hormone fluctuations "present a confusing..."*: Shelley E. Taylor, Laura Cousino Klein, Brian P. Lewis, Tara L. Gruenewald, Regan A. Gurung, and John A. Updegraff, "Biobehavioral Responses to Stress in Females: Tend-and-Befriend, Not Fight-or-Flight," *Psychological Review* 107, no. 3 (July 2000): 4–5 (reprint).

Page 140, *What if, they asked, inconsistencies in the female data:* Ibid., 5

Page 143, *"Late autumn over-cast / raindrops..."*: Paul Riesman, "Defying Official Morality: The Example of Man's Quest for Woman among the Fulani," *Cahiers d'études africaines* 11, no. 44 (1971): 607.

Page 143, *"Our relationship with the villagers..."*: Ibid., 612–13.

Page 144, *"Fulani culture offers to its members..."*: Ibid., 613.

Page 144, *"I think that many Westerners feel that our culture..."*: Ibid.

Chapter Nine. The Invisible

Page 152, *an emotion that, Riesman noted, the Fulani didn't have a word for:* Paul Riesman, *Freedom in Fulani Social Life: An Introspective Ethnography*, trans. Martha Fuller (1977; reprint, Chicago, IL: University of Chicago Press, 1998). See page 156 for an intriguing discussion of how emotions like boredom, anxiety, and depression are "quite rare." According to Riesman, "Although there exists a rich vocabulary for naming feelings, the Fulani do not seem to have words for these." The only time he thought he "detected boredom among the people...were times when they were in the city and were deprived of their contacts and their habitual occupations. As for anxiety and depression, I have never observed them in that form of vague and more or less acute malaise which we know in our society."

Page 160, *"Everything has both yin and yang..."*: There are numerous translations of the Tao Te Ching available. In this chapter I'm quoting from the visually engaging, easy-to-understand interpretations in *The Illustrated Tao Te Ching*, a modern translation by Man-Ho Kwok, Martin Palmer, and Jay Ramsay (Rockport, MA: Element, 1993).

Page 165, *an indescribable "one other thing that makes it all work..."*: Linda Boston, "Ray Hunt: A Legend in His Own Time," *Ranch and Country* 3, no. 4 (August–September 1977): 9.

Page 166, *"similar to a person pointing his finger at the moon..."*: *The Shurangama Sutra*, vol. 2 (Burlingame, CA: Buddhist Text Translation Society, 2003), 60. This is an English translation of the 1908 Chinese book *The Shurangama Sutra with Commentary*, by Hsuan Hua.

Page 166, *"Animals reflect our internal states...."*: Ulrike Dietmann, *On the Wings of Horses: A Hero's Journey into the Heart of the Creature* (N.p.: Spiritbooks, 2011), 29.

Chapter Ten. Moon Dance

Page 169, *"[Siddhartha] watched a buffalo straining…"*: Thich Nhat Hanh, *Old Path White Clouds: Walking in the Footsteps of the Buddha* (Berkeley, CA: Parallax Press, 1991), 47–48.

Page 171, *"When he got to the stables he found Channa…"*: Deepak Chopra, *Buddha: A Story of Enlightenment* (New York: HarperOne, 2007), 104–5.

Chapter Eleven. Sticks and Stones

Page 186, *That's what Karen Allen calls a stress test:* I first learned of Karen Allen's experiment with stockbrokers in Meg Daley Olmert's *Made for Each Other: The Biology of the Human-Animal Bond* (Cambridge, MA: Da Capo Press, 2009), 213–14.

Page 187, *"It's clear that the pet dog did not act merely…"*: Karen M. Allen, Jim Blascovich, Joe Tomaka, and Robert M. Kelsey, "Presence of Human Friends and Pet Dogs as Moderators of Autonomic Responses to Stress in Women," *Journal of Personality and Social Psychology* 61, no. 4 (October 1991): 587.

Page 188, *"the stress buffering role of pets may…"*: Ibid., 587, 588.

Page 190, *"In response to the Jay Treaty…"*: Joseph J. Ellis, *His Excellency: George Washington* (New York: Vintage, 2005), 231.

Page 190, *"But in the supercharged atmosphere of the time…"*: Ibid.

Page 191, *"Washington described the Republican campaign against the Jay Treaty…"*: Ibid., 229–30.

Page 191, *"These things, as you have supposed, fill my mind…"*: Ibid., 230.

Page 191, *The Jay Treaty "exposed a major fault line…"*: Ibid.

Page 192, *"in the spot he cared about most passionately…"*: Ibid.

Page 195, *"Dickinson raised his pistol and pulled the trigger…"*: H.W. Brands, *Andrew Jackson: His Life and Times* (New York: Anchor, 2006), 137–38.

Page 195, *"shattered itself against Jackson's breastbone…"*: Ibid., 138.

Page 196, *"In the saga of the Jackson presidency…"*: Jon Meacham, *American Lion: Andrew Jackson in the White House* (New York: Random House, 2009), xix.

Page 198, *"Nothing angered Jackson more than mismanagement of the horses"*: Brands, *Andrew Jackson*, 453.

Chapter Twelve. The Challenge

Page 200, *Jonah Lehrer describes the surprisingly intricate:* Jonah Lehrer, *Imagine: How Creativity Works* (Boston: Houghton Mifflin Harcourt, 2012). This book received extensive critical praise and press coverage, bringing together compelling scientific research and case studies in business and the arts — until the author's quotes by Bob Dylan were discovered to have been fabricated from the implied meaning of previous Dylan quotes. For our purposes here, however, I have decided to include his case study of Procter and Gamble's creation of the Swiffer, which has not been challenged.

Page 200, *"I wanted to forget everything I knew about mops…"*: Ibid., xii.

Page 201, *"You've got this unwieldy pole…"*: Ibid., xii–xiii.

Page 201, *"returned to making house visits, hoping for…"*: Ibid., xiii

Page 201, *"the product scored higher in focus-group sessions…"*: Ibid., xiv.

Page 209, *According to philosopher Martha Nussbaum, objectification occurs when:* An accessible, in-depth discussion of Nussbaum's observations on this topic can be found in Ann J. Cahill, *Overcoming Objectification: A Carnal Ethics* (New York: Routledge, 2011), chap. 1.

Page 213, *I highly recommend reading Debbie Ford's:* Debbie Ford, *The Dark Side of the Light Chasers: Reclaiming Your Power, Creativity, Brilliance, and Dreams* (New York: Riverhead, 1998).

Page 217, *"shame is much more likely to be the source of destructive behaviors…":* Brené Brown, *I Thought It Was Just Me (but It Isn't): Telling the Truth about Perfectionism, Inadequacy and Power* (New York: Gotham Books, 2007), 14.

Page 217, *"Shame is about who we are…":* Ibid., 13–14.

Page 218, *"the fear of setting boundaries…":* Brené Brown, *The Gifts of Imperfection: Let Go of Who You Think You're Supposed to Be and Embrace Who You Are* (Center City, MN: Hazelden, 2010), 16.

Page 218, *The author herself was "stunned" to find that "compassionate people…":* Ibid.

Page 219, *"We live in a blame culture — we want to know whose fault…":* Ibid., 17.

Page 219, *"Shaming and blaming without accountability is toxic…":* Ibid., 18–19.

Chapter Thirteen. Guiding Principle 1. Use Emotions as Information

Page 232, *"a hatred of 'enthusiasm,' for its emotional, wild surges of knowing…":* Jay Griffiths, *Wild: An Elemental Journey* (New York: Tarcher, 2006), 16.

Page 235, *high emotional intelligence is four times more important:* G. J. Geist and F. Barron, "Emotional Intelligence and Academic Excellence in Career and Life Success" (paper presented at the Annual Convention of the American Psychological Society, San Francisco, June 1996). I first read a summary of this study in Bob Wall, *Coaching for Emotional Intelligence: The Secret to Developing the Star Potential in Your Employees* (New York: AMACOM, 2007), 47–48.

Page 237, *If you want more information on how to use emotions to navigate:* Karla McLaren, *The Language of Emotions: What Your Feelings Are Trying to Tell You* (Boulder, CO: Sounds True, 2010).

Page 238, *A bare-bones outline of the chart is featured:* The Emotional Message Chart outline form was originally suggested by Epona instructor and psychologist Nancy Waite-O'Brien, who served as head of clinical services at the Betty Ford Center for many years. She streamlined my original chart with commentary into an abbreviated grid that many clients have found useful over the years.

Page 257, *According to Karla McLaren, this misunderstood emotion:* Karla McLaren, *Becoming an Empath: How to Develop the Power of Your Emotional Intuition* (Boulder, CO: Sounds True, 2005), quotes transcribed from the audio book section on sadness; emphasis mine.

Page 260, *For more information on how to work through grief:* Deborah Morris Coryell, *Good Grief: Healing through the Shadow of Loss* (Rochester, VT: Healing Arts Press, 2007). This tenth-anniversary edition of a book originally published in 1997 by the Shiva Foundation features an audio CD of the author reading select passages from the text.

Page 260, *A RAND Corporation study found that people with depressive symptoms:* The RAND Corporation statistics were reported in K. B. Wells, M. A. Burnam, W. Rogers, R. Hays, and P. Camp, "The Course of Depression in Adult Outpatients: Results from the Medical Outcomes Study," *Archives of General Psychiatry* 49, no. 10 (October 1992): 788–94.

Page 261, *"interpersonal conflicts, work demands, organizational politics,..."*: Quoted in Andrew A. Cox, M. Kathryn Ness, and Robert F. Carlson, "Depression in the Workplace," undated, 2–3, Counseling Outfitters website, counselingoutfitters.com/vistas /vistas08/Cox.htm. The report is based on a program presented at the American Counseling Association's Annual Conference and Exhibition, March 26–30, 2008, Honolulu.

Page 261, *Classic symptoms of clinical depression include:* D. J. Conti and W. N. Burton, "The Economic Impact of Depression in a Workplace," *Journal of Occupational Medicine* 36, no. 9 (September 1994): 987.

Page 261, *"Treatment," she notes, "includes medication, short-term talk therapy,..."*: Sherman's article has been printed in numerous employee-oriented newsletters and websites. One source is page 1 of the *Faculty and Employee Assistance Program Newsletter*, published online by the University of Virginia Health System.

Page 263, *"In a world where we're taught to ignore our emotions..."*: Karla McLaren, *Becoming an Empath: How to Develop the Power of Your Emotional Intuition* (Boulder, CO: Sounds True, 2005), audiobook.

Page 266, *Depression takes over when "what we were doing..."*: Ibid.

Page 267, *The suicidal urge, McLaren says, often "emerges..."*: Ibid.

Page 268, *"If you ask these questions prayerfully and ceremonially..."*: Ibid.

Chapter Fourteen. Guiding Principle 2. Listen to Your Horse

Page 275, *"the body posture won out when the subjects..."*: Frans de Waal, *The Age of Empathy: Nature's Lessons for a Kinder Society* (New York: Harmony Books, 2009), 81.

Page 275, *the Body First Theory, which holds that:* Ibid., 82.

Page 276, *"our mood can be improved by simply lifting..."*: Ibid.

Page 276, *there "are times when matching the other's emotions..."*: Ibid.

Page 276, *"driving emotions in the right direction..."*: Daniel Goleman, Richard Boyatzis, and Annie McKee, *Primal Leadership: Realizing the Power of Emotional Intelligence* (Boston: Harvard Business Press, 2002), summation on front flap.

Page 282, *"The primacy of the body is sometimes summarized..."*: De Waal, *The Age of Empathy*, 82.

Page 284, *brain injury patients who've lost contact with key emotional centers:* See the intriguing case study of "Elliot" in Antonio R. Damasio, *Descartes' Error: Emotion, Reason, and the Human Brain* (New York: Avon Books, 1995), chap. 3.

Page 284, *people must learn to "feel their thinking"*: Christian de Quincey, *Radical Knowing: Understanding Consciousness through Relationship* (Rochester, VT: Park Street Press, 2005), 33.

Chapter Fifteen. Guiding Principle 3. Manage Contagious Emotions

Page 298, *leaders learn to drive others' emotions "in the right direction..."*: Daniel Goleman, Richard Boyatzis, and Annie McKee, *Primal Leadership: Realizing the Power of Emotional Intelligence* (Boston: Harvard Business Press, 2002), summation on front flap.

Chapter Sixteen. Guiding Principle 4.
Master Boundaries and Assertiveness

Page 310, *"Incorporating what I've learned from my Eponaquest experiences…"*: Lauren Loos, email interview by author, May 2012.

Chapter Seventeen. Guiding Principle 5.
Develop a High Tolerance for Vulnerability

Page 343, *"weaknesses, skill deficiencies, interpersonal shortcomings,…"*: Patrick Lencioni, *The Five Dysfunctions of a Team: A Leadership Fable* (San Francisco: Jossey-Bass, 2002), 196.

Page 343, *"the higher you go, the more your problems…"*: Ibid., 195; Marshall Goldsmith, with Mark Reiter, *What Got You Here Won't Get You There: How Successful People Become Even More Successful!* (New York: Hyperion, 2007), 42.

Page 343, *"in the context of building a team, trust is the confidence…"*: Lencioni, *The Five Dysfunctions of a Team*, 195, 196.

Chapter Eighteen. Guiding Principle 6.
Choose the Programs; *Be* the Programmer

Page 355, *"something that never was, but is always happening.…"*: Jean Houston, *Myths for the Future* (Boulder, CO: Sounds True Audio, 1995). The Houston quotes in this paragraph and elsewhere in the chapter were transcribed from this audio presentation.

Page 358, *"this doubleness, this strange duplicity of life.…"*: James Hillman, *The Soul's Code: In Search of Character and Calling* (New York: Random House, 1996), 180.

Page 358, the *"twin nature of light as waves and particles…"*: Though the paper that originally introduced me to Teich's work has disappeared into the ether since I came across it during an Internet search in 2003, I highly recommend reading his article "The Twin Heroes: Campbell's Solar/Lunar Vision of the Masculine," which can be viewed on Teich's website, www.solarlunar.com. As *The Power of the Herd* was going to press, Teich also referred me to his 2012 book, *Solar Light, Lunar Light: Perspectives in Human Consciousness*, which I'm looking forward to reading.

Chapter Nineteen. Guiding Principle 7.
Conserve Energy for True Emergencies

Page 361, *As a radio announcer on Florida's Gulf Coast:* I originally presented the "radio station in a hurricane" analogy in *Way of the Horse: Equine Archetypes for Self-Discovery* (Novato, CA: New World Library, 2007), a guidebook accompanied by a deck of horse-wisdom cards with images created by Kim McElroy.

Chapter Twenty-One. Guiding Principle 9.
Prepare for Difficult Conversations

Page 374, *Bob's "structured format for coaching"*: Bob Wall, *Coaching for Emotional Intelligence: The Secret to Developing the Star Potential in Your Employees* (New York: AMACOM, 2007), 111–18.

Chapter Twenty-Two. Guiding Principle 10.
Engage in Consensual Leadership

Page 384, *In this trio, the dominance hierarchy varied:* I first presented observations of this herd's behavior in relation to the notion of "consensual leadership" in the book portion of *Way of the Horse: Equine Archetypes for Self-Discovery* (Novato, CA: New World Library, 2007).

Page 385, "*Researchers have often assumed* a priori that...": Larissa Conradt and Timothy J. Roper, "Consensus Decision Making in Animals," *TRENDS in Ecology and Evolution* 20, no. 8 (August 2005): 454.

Chapter Twenty-Three. Guiding Principle 11.
Cultivate Emotional Heroism

Page 388, "*When another person makes you suffer...*": Thich Nhat Hanh, *The Heart of Buddha's Teaching: Transforming Suffering into Peace, Joy, and Liberation* (New York: Broadway Books, 1999), 196.

Chapter Twenty-Four. Guiding Principle 12. Enjoy the Ride

Page 401, "*Chauvet Cave had art that was not simply...*": David S. Whitley, *Cave Paintings and the Human Spirit: The Origin of Creativity and Belief* (Amherst, NY: Prometheus Books, 2009), 53–54.

Page 401, "*This first art consists of true aesthetic masterpieces...*": Ibid., 255.

Page 401, "*many archeologists believe the ancient art we see...*": Meg Daley Olmert and I exchanged several emails discussing her work, as well as her opinion on the cave art. This quote comes from comments she sent me on August 13, 2012.

Page 403, *the cave artists "knew these animals...*": Meg Daley Olmert, *Made for Each Other: The Biology of the Human-Animal Bond* (Cambridge, MA: Da Capo Press, 2009), 35.

Page 403, *They "approach you, slowly, oblivious...*": Whitely, *Cave Paintings and the Human Spirit*, 75.

Page 404, "*Our ceaseless need to assess the strengths...*": Olmert, *Made for Each Other*, 5.

Page 404, "*Oxytocin may have stoked the warmer social climate...*": Ibid., xvi.

Page 405, "*Animal bones excavated from living areas...*": Whitley, *Cave Paintings and the Human Spirit*, 31.

Page 405, "*In the middle of the Ice Age, the human heart was melting...*": Olmert, *Made for Each Other*, 65.

Page 407, *the belief "that a kind of collective consciousness...*": Larry Dossey, *Recovering the Soul: A Scientific and Spiritual Search* (New York: Bantam, 1989), 101–2.

Page 407, "*in the nonlocal, collective consciousness...*": Ibid., 105.

Page 407, "*I cannot help but wonder about the centrality of the horse...*": Whitley, *Cave Paintings and the Human Spirit*, 77.

Page 408, "*It is well known that emotions acutely affect heart rate...*": Ann Linda Baldwin created this summation of heart-rate variability as an informal handout for my students in 2012.

Page 409, "*The results show unequivocally that horses make us feel great...*": This and the following quotes from Baldwin were created for a currently unpublished article on the study results that I helped write.

INDEX

ABOUT THE AUTHOR

*L*inda Kohanov is an internationally recognized author, speaker, riding instructor, and horse trainer. In 1997, she founded Epona Equestrian Services, an Arizona-based collective of horse professionals, educators, coaches, and counselors exploring the potential of the horse-human bond. Due to increasing international interest, the business expanded, becoming Eponaquest Worldwide as she and her colleagues trained instructors who now practice on five continents.

Linda is the author of the bestseller *The Tao of Equus*, *Riding between the Worlds*, and *The Way of the Horse* (with artist Kim McElroy). Linda's books have been translated into French, German, and Dutch, and are used as texts at universities throughout the United States.

Linda lectures and conducts workshops at conferences and retreat centers throughout the world, and since 2002, she and her colleagues have trained thousands of people. Seminars at her home base in Amado, Arizona, attract business leaders, entrepreneurs, educators, scientists, mental health professionals, artists, and coaches from around the world. Linda has developed innovative, highly effective approaches to leadership training and team building that have been embraced by executive coaches, sales managers, and major players in the aerospace industry. Starting in 2003, Linda and her colleagues began training instructors capable of leading their own seminars in the Eponaquest approach to equine-facilitated learning. By 2012, close to two hundred Eponaquest Instructors from the United States, Canada, Europe, England, Ireland,

Australia, and South Africa had graduated from an apprenticeship program covering the most beneficial practices for enhancing the physical, mental, emotional, and spiritual well-being of their clients.

Linda's main website is www.eponaquest.com. A web symposium with in-depth conversations on the material and practical skills presented in *The Power of the Herd* is available at www.poweroftheherd.com.

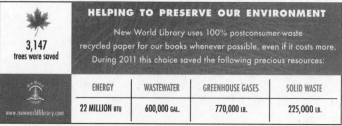

HELPING TO PRESERVE OUR ENVIRONMENT

3,147 trees were saved

New World Library uses 100% postconsumer-waste recycled paper for our books whenever possible, even if it costs more. During 2011 this choice saved the following precious resources:

ENERGY	WASTEWATER	GREENHOUSE GASES	SOLID WASTE
22 MILLION BTU	600,000 GAL.	770,000 LB.	225,000 LB.

www.newworldlibrary.com

Environmental impact estimates were made using the Environmental Defense Fund Paper Calculator @ www.papercalculator.org.